PRAISE FOR
HELLA NATION

"Some top-drawer writing . . . reflects a literary rebel who wants to break convention." —*Publishers Weekly*

"Hugely entertaining . . . funny, mesmerizing, frightening and mind-boggling (sometimes all in the same essay)." —*Booklist*

"Unforgettable . . . the arrival of a major chronicler of those who live on or beyond the margins of the American mainstream." —*Kirkus Reviews*

GENERATION KILL

"A pungently written combat narrative and a close-range study of a bunch of twentysomething warriors trying to get a handle on who they are."
—*Time*

"A stellar reporting achievement . . . think *Black Hawk Down* or Michael Herr's *Dispatches*."
—*Ottawa Citizen* (Named one of the Top 10 Must-Reads of Summer)

"One of the best books to come out of the Iraq war . . . an adrenaline rush of intelligent prose." —*Financial Times*

"Nuanced and grounded in details often overlooked in daily journalistic accounts . . . a complex portrait of able young men raised on video games and trained as killers." —*The New York Times*

"A provocative, personality-driven portrait . . . shockingly honest, carefully balanced . . . A." —*Entertainment Weekly*

continued . . .

"Harrowing . . . important."   —*The Sunday Oregonian*

"Sidesteps Greatest Generation clichés to find the unexpected—a self-described 'Marine Corps Killer' who listens to Barry Manilow, a corporal who compares a gunfight to Grand Theft Auto: Vice City."

—*The Washington Post*

"Wright wrote about [his] experience in a three-part series in *Rolling Stone* that was hailed for its evocative, accurate war reporting. This book, a greatly expanded version of that series, matches its accomplishment. Wright is a perceptive reporter . . . a personality-driven, readable and insightful look at the Iraq war's first month from the Marine grunt's point of view . . . compelling portraits . . . a vivid, well-drawn picture."   —*Publishers Weekly*

"Wright's account of the 2003 Iraq invasion is often more thrilling than a Jerry Bruckheimer picture—and not just because the bullets are real."

—UPI

"Visceral, sometimes shocking . . . a brutally honest account of America's latest generation to experience the stark, horrifying realities of warfare."

—*Boston Herald*

"Its timeliness notwithstanding, this chronicle of an American reconnaissance platoon's mission to spearhead the invasion of Iraq is not one of those hastily thrown together 'instant books' . . . perceptive, often troubling."

—*Booklist*

"The language is blue, the blood red and the action explosive. This may be *the* book of the Iraqi engagement."   —*Richmond Times-Dispatch*

ALSO BY EVAN WRIGHT

Generation Kill

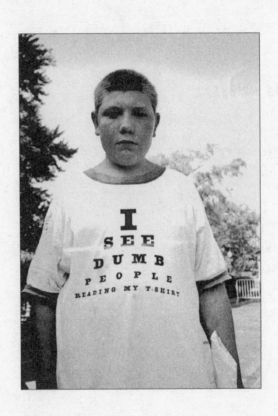

HELLA NATION

Looking for Happy Meals in Kandahar, Rocking the Side Pipe,

Wingnut's War Against the Gap, and Other Adventures with

the Totally Lost Tribes of America

EVAN WRIGHT

BERKLEY BOOKS, NEW YORK

A BERKLEY BOOK
Published by the Penguin Group
Penguin Group (USA) Inc.
375 Hudson Street, New York, New York 10014, USA
Penguin Group (Canada), 90 Eglinton Avenue East, Suite 700, Toronto, Ontario M4P 2Y3, Canada
(a division of Pearson Penguin Canada Inc.)
Penguin Books Ltd., 80 Strand, London WC2R 0RL, England
Penguin Group Ireland, 25 St. Stephen's Green, Dublin 2, Ireland (a division of Penguin Books Ltd.)
Penguin Group (Australia), 250 Camberwell Road, Camberwell, Victoria 3124, Australia
(a division of Pearson Australia Group Pty. Ltd.)
Penguin Books India Pvt. Ltd., 11 Community Centre, Panchsheel Park, New Delhi—110 017, India
Penguin Group (NZ), 67 Apollo Drive, Rosedale, North Shore 0632, New Zealand
(a division of Pearson New Zealand Ltd.)
Penguin Books (South Africa) (Pty.) Ltd., 24 Sturdee Avenue, Rosebank, Johannesburg 2196,
South Africa

Penguin Books Ltd., Registered Offices: 80 Strand, London WC2R 0RL, England

While the author has made every effort to provide accurate telephone numbers and Internet addresses at the time of publication, neither the publisher nor the author assumes any responsibility for errors, or for changes that occur after publication. Further, the publisher does not have any control over and does not assume any responsibility for author or third-party websites or their content.

PRINTING HISTORY
G. P. Putnam's Sons hardcover edition / April 2009
Berkley trade paperback edition / March 2010

Berkley trade paperback ISBN: 978-0-425-23237-8

The Library of Congress has cataloged the G. P. Putnam's Sons hardcover edition as follows:

Wright, Evan.
Hella nation : looking for happy meals in Kandahar, rocking the side pipe, Wingnut's war against the Gap, and other adventures with the totally lost tribes of America / Evan Wright.
p.   cm.
ISBN 978-0-399-15574-1
I. Title.
PN4874.W75A25   2009   2009002291
814'.6—dc22

PRINTED IN THE UNITED STATES OF AMERICA

10 9 8 7 6 5 4 3 2 1

To the great American humorist,
cynic and realist Alan D. Wright, Esquire

CONTENTS

There is almost no circumstance under which an American doesn't like to be interviewed.

—*A. J. Liebling*

After the publication of my book *Generation Kill*, some critics called my work "gonzo," because reporting from the midst of combat as I did struck them as an act of gonzo journalism. For *Generation Kill* and now *Hella Nation*, use of the term is a misnomer insofar as "gonzo" speaks of writing that is more about the reporter than the subject. With few exceptions, my intent has always been to focus on my subjects in all of their imperfect glory. Gonzo journalism was born and died with Hunter S. Thompson, and lives on only in his writing. But not even Thompson himself was entirely gonzo. One of the most astute political observers of his time and a grand American humorist in the tradition of Mark Twain, Thompson was also a prodigious reporter. His *Hell's Angels* stands as a classic of immersion journalism—in which Thompson's adventures in gathering his material never diverted focus from his outlaw subjects—and was an early inspiration for my own reporting from inside American subcultures.

Portions of *Hella Nation* appeared in different form in *Rolling Stone* at a time when I served as the magazine's "unofficial Ambassador to the Underbelly"—a title jokingly bestowed on me in an editorial published by *Rolling Stone*'s managing editor, Will Dana, in 2002. My primary subjects at *Rolling Stone* (and later at *Vanity Fair*) were people I found roaming the great American underworld, from runaway teens trying to make it as eco-terrorists, to Internet scamsters, to human growth hormone hustlers in Phoenix, to celebrity street skateboarders. The young combat troops I reported on in the Middle East represented a new kind of subculture, one that was often as misunderstood by civilians at home as it was by military leaders.

When my father read of the unofficial ambassadorship bestowed on me by *Rolling Stone*, he phoned to congratulate me on the promotion. "Underbelly is one step up from ambassador to the crotch," he explained, referring to my previous job as an editor at *Hustler* magazine. I had started at *Hustler* in the mid-nineties as a triple-X-film reviewer and reporter assigned to cover the adult film industry. Like other hopeful college graduates in America, I had never had a strong ambition to wind up working in the porn industry. But when I found myself in it, assigned to interview porn starlets and write about the sketchy characters running the adult industry (such as my boss Larry Flynt), I drew on the work of *New Yorker* writer A. J. Liebling as inspiration.

While I did not delude myself that *Hustler* was equivalent to Liebling's *New Yorker,* I liked to think that Liebling, who reveled in the Depression-era world of boxers, small-time swindlers, exotic dancers—"people getting by," as he affectionately called them—would have appreciated the rich diversity of characters in Southern California's Porn Valley. Liebling's appreciation for the vernacular spoken by his streetwise subjects and his instinct for humor in even the grimmest of situations offered insight for how I might handle my subject matter. Describing his approach to writing, Liebling said, "The humor, as during a blitz, was rueful and concerned with the imminence of individual disaster."

My career at *Hustler* began with an overdose of Xanax. I had been work-ing a string of temp jobs in Los Angeles when a friend told me about an opening to be a copy editor at the magazine. I sent in a résumé, and a few days later I was called in for an interview. At the time I suffered from an imaginary form of social anxiety disorder. I had a fear of going into social situations that might induce a panic attack. This had never happened to me, but I had read about it happening to other people and developed a fear it might happen to me—a phobia of a phobia, as it were—which I medicated by popping copious amounts of Xanaxes before a stressful social interaction, such as a job interview. Without the crutch of a massive dose of tranquil-izers, I feared that in the middle of an interview I might lose my mind and begin to sweat uncontrollably, speak in tongues and walk in aimless circles through the office of my prospective employer. On the afternoon of my job interview, I overshot the mark. I'd eaten a big lunch that day, and to com-pensate, I popped several extra pills before getting on the bus that would take me to *Hustler*'s offices in the Flynt Building on Wilshire Boulevard. Somewhere in Beverly Hills the bus broke down. I had to jog several blocks to make the interview. The exertion must have released a powerful wave of tranquilizer into my bloodstream. By the time a receptionist showed me into the executive editor's office, I couldn't feel my face.

Allan MacDonell, the executive editor, sat at a broad, uncluttered desk behind which panoramic windows offered a sweeping view of nothing—low, putty-colored apartment buildings and parking lots. In his late thirties, MacDonell wore thick black-framed glasses that gave him a passing resem-blance to Elvis Costello. He had a raspy voice and mumbled like a character in *Mean Streets*. My difficulty in understanding him was compounded by the fact that the numbness from the tranquilizers was radiating from my spine in warm, liquid golden waves of heat. It was so intoxicatingly pleasant I had to concentrate not to slump face forward. Between MacDonell's mum-bling and the extreme effort it took to remain upright, I could only pick up snippets of what he was saying.

I pieced together that my résumé contained a typo, which disqualified me for the position of copy editor. I remember only disjointed pieces of the afternoon from that point on—shaking hands, walking across a floor that felt bouncy like a trampoline, trying to hold on to a No. 2 pencil as I filled out some papers. I came to the next morning in my apartment, wondering what had happened. I phoned *Hustler*'s offices and was put through to Mac-Donell. It was a confusing conversation—I'm sure for both of us—because MacDonell had offered me a job the day before, and I had accepted, and now I was on the phone with him trying to pretend like I knew that already.

It was only on the following Tuesday when I showed up for work and was led to a spacious private office—with a large TV and VHS player across from my desk and stacks of adult videotapes on the shelves—that I discovered I had been hired as *Hustler*'s entertainment editor, responsible for covering the adult industry. Later I would find out that my hiring had come about after the hasty departure of my predecessor, whose heroin problem had gotten so bad MacDonell had been forced to fire him. I was told that my predecessor's heroin problem hadn't been grounds for his termination. It was his other behavior, such as never leaving his office. One of my new coworkers explained, "The guy who had the job before you would come in every morning with a two-liter bottle of Pepsi, drink it all by lunch and spend the rest of the day peeing in the empty bottle, so he could hide in his office." My colleague offered a tip: "Just make sure, no matter what you do in your office, you step out and walk around sometimes so MacDonell can see you. He gets freaked out if employees don't seem to be able to walk around."

If you could meet the minimum standards, the porn industry was a welcoming place to individuals like me who had grave personal problems. Though the business is a legal one, like the manufacture of assault weapons or the marketing of fortified malt liquor in poor neighborhoods, its existence is barely tolerated by the public. Given the social opprobrium under which the business functions, it's tantamount to a black market enterprise. Like any black market, the adult industry is a place of rogues, borderline criminals, people with little to lose. If you are a screwup, an alcoholic, drug addict, nymphomaniac (of course) or freak, failure or deviant of just about any kind, it is a remarkably tolerant place.

My own decline had begun in high school. I had peaked around my junior year as a total nerd. A member of the debate team, I left school early whenever possible to attend lectures at the Council on Foreign Relations on the Strategic Arms Limitations Talks with the Soviet Union. In my free time I read Kissinger's *Nuclear Weapons and Foreign Policy* and Freud's *Civilization and Its Discontents*. I wavered between dreams of attending Annapolis to become a military aviator and my volunteer work with Amnesty International writing letters to urge the release of "prisoners of conscience" held by foreign despots. I was torn by the traditional beliefs I had been raised with in the efficacy of militarism to promote Truth, Justice and the American Way and a growing personal conviction that the only proper course of action in a world of cruelty and horrors was absolute pacifism.

My crack-up began in earnest during a senior seminar on nineteenth-century European political thought when we came to the Russian nihilists, whose motto was "Smash everything that can be smashed." According to my teacher, Bruce Carr, the slogan urged conceptual—not literal—action, to eradicate old, unworthy ideas by subjecting them to hammer blows of withering criticism and retaining only those that survive. The concept set the gears turning in my teenage brain. I resolved to live by subjecting every thought I held dear to extreme criticism, the more destructive the better.

In my career as a high school history student, the more I learned of the world and man's inhumanity to man, the more I was afflicted by intense bouts of sadness, no matter how remote humankind's injustices were in space and time, from the Soviet invasion of Afghanistan to the Defenestration of Prague. It was an intellectual-spiritual malady one of my teachers would identify as "weltschmerz"—a German expression for "world pain." I would attempt to treat it for the next decade or so with puerile nihilism—as in "Nothing matters, nothing means anything anyway"—and bouts of intense drinking. In retrospect I am not sure whether the earliest condition I suffered from was weltschmerz or simple alcoholism.

On the Vassar College campus of the Reagan 1980s, where I did my undergraduate studies, Derrida, deconstructionism, political correctness and identity politics—of gender and sexual orientation since there were few students belonging to racial or ethnic minorities—were the rage. In most of the humanities departments, theory, as opposed to direct study of arts and letters, was paramount. Or perhaps this was my warped, incipient-alcoholic perception of things. In any case, the popular postmodern currents in the humanities departments did not withstand my nihilistic scrutiny. I dismissed the most important trends of my generation as bullshit.

I found refuge in a medieval and Renaissance studies program run by the history department. Students in the program—all three of us—were required to study ancient languages, in my case Latin and Old English. Languages appealed to me because acquiring them was based on the most elemental form of learning: memorization. And once you learned them, voices from the past seemed to speak directly, without being filtered by a professor quoting Kierkegaard and Foucault and Chuck D.

Historical inquiries within the medieval and Renaissance studies program were rooted in observable details—maps, architectural remnants, weapons and tools—and in testimony by witnesses as found in civic records, journals and other sorts of contemporaneous histories. Theory did have its place in the program. Several professors in the history department were under the sway of a theory of methodology referred to as the "*Annales* School,*" named for the French journal *Annales d'histoire économique et sociale,* in which it had been developed in the 1930s. *Annales* historians rejected blind acceptance of traditional histories based on the words and deeds of great men, as well as Marxist theories of economic determinism, and advocated reexamining the past through detailed examination of data previously ignored by traditionalists—tax records, diaries, archaeological digs (especially of trash heaps, to see what people ate, the tools they used, the clothes they wore) and maps. Marc Bloch, a founding *Annales* historian, spent years hiking across France to better understand how the terrain influenced the evolution of agricultural technologies and in turn the social structure of villages. In a sense, *Annales* historians examined history the way police study a crime scene. Like police, they often arrived at conflicting, mutually contradictory narratives. But unlike deconstructionists or economic determinists, *Annales* historians were supremely uninterested in arriving at a unified theory of anything. They were perfectly at home in a *Rashomon* universe of diametrically opposed testimony and facts. "What matters," a professor whom I admired used to say, "is the investigation, not the outcome."

The *Annales* school also had a tragic element that appealed to my melodramatic sense of weltschmerz. Marc Bloch never completed his seminal historical work, *The Historian's Craft*. Before finishing the last chapter he was executed by the Nazis for his role in the French resistance. Drinking heavily and rereading the unfinished final page of Bloch's great book—something I did often during my senior year of college—seemed to confirm the utter futility of existence. By the time I graduated, I had no ambition to succeed at anything. To be a failure was a sort of philosophy to live by.

I would spend the better part of a decade failing to do much of anything except read, watch movies, travel a bit, smoke dope, drink, and of course work as little as possible. By the early nineties, when slackers were becoming celebrated in popular culture, I was, for once, in sync with the times. Slackers I saw on screen—in indie films like Richard Linklater's *Slacker* and Kevin Smith's *Clerks*—were amusing and harmless. My own slackitude seemed ugly and doomed. Most of all it was the drink, the blackouts, the getting beat up in bars, the walking down streets randomly punching windows, the running from cops, the stealing of cars to take them on pointless, drunken joyrides, the waking up in vacant lots or hospital emergency rooms not knowing how I had gotten there, or sometimes what my name was. The increasingly rare sober moments were times of unfocused, clammy terror, hence the massive consumption of tranquilizers.

The job at *Hustler* offered a steady paycheck, health benefits and a structured, nine-to-five existence that I hoped would tamp down my proclivity for increasingly reckless sprees. It seemed the logical end point for my nihilistic beliefs. Being confronted every day with segments of humanity locked in joyless, dead-eyed coupling in front of cameras was proof of the total lack of meaning of things, confirmation of my essential belief in the bankruptcy of the human experience, which was of course highly comforting. The job at *Hustler* was also the first time anyone had ever paid me to write. And getting paid to write, as most people know, is the ultimate and most coveted slacker profession. I lived in fear of losing my job.

In early 1996, *Hustler* assigned me to cover the Adult Video News Awards ceremony—the "Academy Awards of porn"—in Las Vegas. The ceremony took place in conjunction with a nearly week-long convention in which thousands of pornographers descended on the city, schmoozed, partied and sometimes brawled—all while filming impromptu adult movies in hotel suites. I could picture an almost infinite variety of disastrous scenarios I might find myself in if I embarked on a bender in the midst of the porn convention.

I traveled to Las Vegas with a colleague who wrote for another adult magazine. He was a committed heroin, diazepam, crack and meth addict who somehow had struck a chemical balance that enabled him to function. Years earlier he had been an aspiring playwright, doctoral candidate and instructor at a prestigious university. His career had ended after a week-long meth binge in which he'd pulled a loaded gun on a fellow member of his English department with whom he'd been arguing about Faulkner. He was someone I felt comfortable with because he was well-read and at least partially insane enough for me to tell him anything.

When we checked into our rooms at the Frontier Hotel, I pulled him aside and told him that if we ended up at a social gathering where cocktails were being served, he was to make sure I drank no more than six. I confessed to him that any number greater than that might lead to catastrophe. "No matter what I say, no matter what I do," I told him, "get me out of whatever bar or party I am in. If you have to," I told him, "punch me in the face."

He agreed to help but could barely conceal his contempt for my lack of self-control. He'd been slamming heroin, smoking crack and meth for years, and except for his three-week stay in a mental hospital after the Faulkner episode, he had never missed a day of work. Staring at me through his dark black sunglasses—worn at all times of day or night to hide his pinpoint pupils—he asked, "You ever think you might have a problem?"

I managed to stay out of trouble in Vegas. But fearing some other incident that might lead to the abrupt termination of my job, I began trying to clean up. When my own efforts failed, I started to attend a 12-step program. Though the program was based—it seemed to me—on a magical faith in a make-believe "Higher Power," after I had strung together a few weeks of uninterrupted sobriety through my participation in it, the empiricist in me had to concede that it worked.

Waking up clearheaded every morning was like washing up after a shipwreck, nude, badly scraped up, on a foreign shore. Driving to work each day in my fourteen-year-old Mazda GLC—paint peeling, missing its front bumper, and its rear window smashed by thieves who'd broken in to steal a stack of *Hustler* "Beaver Hunt" amateur photo submissions I'd carelessly left in the backseat—I began to wonder if there were greater challenges beyond the horizons of the adult industry.

My career as a mainstream journalist owes its start to the 1973 *Miller v. California* obscenity case, in which the Supreme Court ruled that a work, such as a magazine, might be considered obscene only if "taken as a whole" it "lacks serious literary, artistic, political, or scientific value." The result of this ruling was that porn magazines like *Hustler* had a policy of publishing one article each month that aspired to be of serious value. My first non–adult industry article would be published by Larry Flynt as a form of anti-obscenity case conviction insurance.

I had fewer than sixty days sober in the summer of 1996 when I arrived in Coeur d'Alene, Idaho, to write a feature about the Aryan Nations white supremacist group based in a walled compound outside the town. Weeks earlier I had met photographer Nathaniel Welch on the set of Jasmin St. Claire's *World's Biggest Gang Bang II*, which he was covering as a sort of freak show for the now defunct alternative weekly *Los Angeles Reader*. Welch was interested in photographing American underworld subjects and had proposed that we collaborate on an Aryan Nations story that I would write for *Hustler*. Larry Flynt had a personal interest in publishing an exposé of white supremacists, since he believed the 1978 shooting that left him paralyzed had been carried out by a white supremacist enraged by an interracial photo spread published in *Hustler*. The day before I left to meet the Aryan Nations members, Flynt had called me into his office, bizarrely decorated with Tiffany lamps, Ertés and what looked to be knock-off Baroque oil paintings. Seated across from me in his gold wheelchair, flanked by his personal bodyguard rumored to be armed at all times with a MAC-10 submachine gun, Flynt gazed at me with his head cocked to the side. "When you meet the top man there," he said, "make sure you ask him why they shot me."

When Welch and I drove our rental car up to the security booth outside the Aryan Nations headquarters, manned by guards in SS uniforms, we had no plan in place to gain access. We had agreed that we would not pretend to sympathize with the supremacists or use any other ruses to gain their trust, with the exception that we would tell them we were freelancers (and not that we were on assignment for *Hustler*). In our first approach the guards told us to leave the property. But over the next few days, low-key persistence paid off. We met one member of the group in town who was eager to talk, which led to contacts with more of them, and then an invitation to spend time inside their compound. It was a pattern that would repeat itself, with almost mathematical predictability, with just about every subculture I would later cover.

The fact that Welch and I had told our neo-Nazi subjects that we didn't sympathize or agree with them worked to the story's advantage. It seemed to make them all the more eager to explain themselves. Much as I found their half-baked ideologies repugnant, I was fascinated by their extreme alienation. In my own jangly state of raw-nerved sobriety, their alienation was something I could connect with. I used that connection—a genuine though extremely limited form of empathy I was able to feel for my subjects—to elicit unexpected revelations from them about the intense fears underpinning their hatred and lunatic beliefs. Or maybe it was simpler than that. As A. J. Liebling pointed out, Americans—"pleased by attention, covetous of being singled out"—will always talk to a reporter.

What didn't make sense during the time that I spent among the neo-Nazis was the absence of the many phobias that had long plagued me, and which I had feared might rear their heads in the threatening environment of the Aryan Nations compound. It seemed that investigation—the part of historical studies that had been so absorbing to me as an undergraduate—was even more gratifying when undertaken with contemporary subjects, so much so it seemed to erase all the ambient anxieties of routine existence. Even better, you could interview contemporary subjects without having to translate from a dead language.

I also learned during that time with the neo-Nazis that the closer I came to things that from afar had frightened or disturbed me, the less power they held. Later, I would hear *New York Times* reporter Sharon Waxman refer to reporting from tense situations as the thrill of "mainlining history."

I had given up powerful intoxicants about the time I embarked on a reporting career, and it became obvious that harrowing circumstances in the field helped fill a void created by the absence of personal dramas brought on by drink. (I was the sort of drinker for whom calamity was almost as desirable and stimulating as intoxication itself.) When I arrived in Afghanistan in 2002 on assignment for *Rolling Stone* (accompanied again by photographer Nathaniel Welch), the first morning I woke up in a combat zone felt easier, more carefree than the start of a typical day in Los Angeles after a night—or several—of hard, blackout drinking.

When I sat down to write the neo-Nazi feature for *Hustler* magazine I avoided making overt moral commentary on my subjects, the same as I would in a history paper about a subculture in the remote past. I would let events and sources speak for themselves, which I believed would be the most powerful means of indicting the movement. But when I'd finished writing the piece I worried it was too unfiltered. Perhaps I should have stated the reporter's opinion somewhere that neo-Nazis are bad? I submitted the unpublished manuscript to the Anti-Defamation League (ADL) for its view on the piece. Erin Zelle, an ADL researcher who specialized in white supremacist groups, recommended the story be published without any changes. Zelle believed the piece effectively skewered the Aryan Nations through its members' own words. She warned me of the possibility of reprisals.

The only attack came from *The New York Times,* when Max Frankel, the paper's former executive editor and a Pulitzer Prize–winning journalist, published an opinion piece on Larry Flynt. In it he reviewed *Hustler* magazine, singling out my article on the Aryan Nations, "Heil Hitler, America!" as the "vilest prose masquerading as reportage." He called it a "palpable fiction . . . slyly designed to stimulate skinhead brutalities."

On a certain level Frankel's criticism of the magazine as a source of some of the vilest prose in America was not totally off base. The porn industry, tolerant as it was of personal eccentricities like drug addiction and certain types of criminality, was also cruel and exploitative to the core. The meanness of the industry was reflected in *Hustler.* In the pages of the magazine readers were referred to as "jack-offs," adult performers as "sluts" and "bitches." The rating system for films was based on a scale whose highest honor was a "Fully Erect" and whose lowest was a "Totally Limp." Gallows humor prevailed among the staff. During my stay with the Aryan Nations I fell out of contact with my boss, MacDonell, for several days. He feared the worst. But when I showed up alive and in one piece, he expressed disappointment. He would be unable to print the headline for my obituary that he had planned, based on the film-rating scale: "Evan Wright: Totally Dead."

Mainstream publications had scant interest in assigning work to a *Hustler* editor, but after more than a year of my pressing Glenn Kenny at *Premiere,* he agreed to hire me to write an article on the 1998 Adult Video News Awards in Las Vegas. Shortly before I was supposed to leave for the show, Kenny called to inform me that the article had been reassigned to David Foster Wallace.

Kenny was certain I would understand and even expressed the hope that I would share his excitement given Wallace's staggering contributions to American letters, for which he'd recently been awarded a MacArthur "Genius" Grant. I had no idea who Kenny was talking about. Having been drunk through the first half of the nineties, I'd missed key cultural events. In the past eighteen months the situation had scarcely improved. I had no time for books, movies or TV. The only cultural input I absorbed came from watching the dozens of porn films I reviewed each week, or from listening to people's testimonials—referred to as "drunkalogues"—at the 12-step meetings I attended in my free hours. It was the cultural equivalent of living in a sensory deprivation tank, suspended in a saline broth of pornography and self-help affirmations.

Kenny arranged for me to meet with Wallace in Las Vegas and serve as his guide. When Wallace published his feature, "Neither Adult, nor Entertainment," in *Premiere* ("Big Red Son" in the essay collection *Consider the Lobster*), I appeared in it under the pseudonym he bestowed, "Harold Hecuba." I spent several days trying unsuccessfully to decipher the meaning of his reference to Hecuba, torturing myself over my inability to decode the meaning of the great author's reference. Finally I called Wallace. He was stunned that I didn't get who Harold Hecuba was. "He's, you know, the Phil Silvers character who guest stars on *Gilligan's Island*," Wallace explained. "I thought you would get it. You don't feel bad about it?"

"Why should I?"

"You shouldn't," Wallace said. "Hecuba's not stuck on the island like everybody else. He gets off of it. Makes it back to the mainland, I think, that is, if I have my *Gilligan's Island* references right."

I would make it off of porn island within a year. On my last day at *Hustler*, MacDonell entered my office and closed the door. He regarded me from behind his thick black-framed Elvis Costello glasses. For the briefest instant his face seemed to quiver with emotion. "I just wanted to say, by leaving here today you have completely failed me," he said. "I believe you will fail every employer you have in the future." It was the standard, warm *Hustler* farewell.

Though I left the island, I'm not sure I ever made it to the mainland.

The sense of disconnectedness I carried as a result of both my personal pathologies and my years of employment in an outcast industry seemed to be an asset in my reporting for *Rolling Stone* and *Vanity Fair*. Whether my subjects were the tree-dwelling anarchists of "Wingnut's Last Day on Earth," the San Francisco attorneys who threw away their ties to their community by forming a bizarre family with a prison inmate in "Mad Dogs & Lawyers," or the Hollywood über-agent who fled his lucrative career to make pro-war films in Iraq in "Pat Dollard's War on Hollywood," most shared a similar sense of being exiles from the mainstream of American culture. Even the young troops I profiled in "Not Much War, but Plenty of Hell" had a profound awareness of their separateness—of values, of culture—from their peers at home.

The editors whom I worked with often described my subjects not just as outsiders, but as people who were "disenfranchised." The assumption seemed to be that most of my subjects would have chosen to participate in the mainstream if they hadn't been somehow shut out of it. While I did write about some, such as young Russian immigrant Konstantin Simberg in "The Bad American," who were desperate to reach the mainland of the American dream, most of the people I encountered in writing the essays in *Hella Nation* were rejectionists. They gravitated to subcultures because they didn't want to participate in the dominant culture. Many of the troops I would meet serving in the front lines of America's wars in the Middle East disagreed with the common stereotype that they had joined the military because they had been forced to by socioeconomic circumstances. They insisted they had joined as much for opportunity as to escape the inanities, or as some put it, the "self-centeredness" of civilian life.

Americans are repeatedly told that aside from simplistic red state–blue state political divisions, we are a nation of conformists, cynically shaped and manipulated by advertisers and marketing specialists. In the early nineties the idea briefly took hold that from amid the burgeoning new worlds of Internet message boards, grunge music, indie films, independent coffee shops and independent bookshops—then at their zenith—an alternate culture was arising. A defining moment of the era occurred in 1992 when Nirvana posed on the cover of *Rolling Stone* with Kurt Cobain flaunting his shirt printed with the phrase "Corporate Rock Magazines Still Suck." The next defining moment occurred in 1993 when Nirvana self-censored the artwork and lyrics on its album cover to ensure distribution by Wal-Mart.

The power of America's corporate marketeers to co-opt cultural dissent was driven home to me after the publication of "Wingnut's Last Day on Earth"—which was based on my travels with anarchists as they waged war on the Gap by defacing its stores. The article featured an iconic photograph—shot by Mark Seliger, who also photographed the Kurt Cobain anti–corporate rock cover of *Rolling Stone*—of Wingnut, an anarchist in a black hoodie jacket. The black hoodie had become an anarchist symbol— much in the news then—and a banner of anticorporate sentiment. Within months of the photo's publication, the storefronts of Gaps across America prominently displayed the corporation's new line of black hoodies.

If there was a single strain of thought uniting my diverse subjects it was suspicion of the *Matrix*-like powers of a hostile monolith—the mainstream media, or corporations, or the government—to control people's minds by shaping reality. Yet among the groups and individuals profiled in *Hella Nation,* none would ever agree on what defines the nation, or the forces they believe control it. For Pat Dollard, the nation was a place held captive by the liberal media, for the anarchists it was the corporate capitalist oppressors, for the white supremacists it was "ZOG," the Zionist Occupation Government. Internet huckster Seth Warshavsky, whom I profiled in "Portrait of a Con Artist," had a relentlessly optimistic view of America as a vast happy-land of potential suckers. For many of the troops I encountered, America remained a beacon of democracy, for which they were proud to serve, sometimes despite grave questions about the wars they were fighting. One of the teenage anarchists I traveled with down the West Coast defined the nation this way each time we stopped at a highway rest station: "Wow, it's so hella America."

"What does that mean?" I asked.

"Oh, God," she explained. "Like hella real. Hella harsh."

To the soldiers of the Fifth Platoon Delta Company living at Kandahar Airfield, deep in the former Taliban stronghold of southeastern Afghanistan, dawn breaks each morning with a horrible stench. Their tent is located at the southernmost end of the airfield, not far from the "shit lagoon"—the canal where all the excrement from the camp's five thousand–plus inhabitants is dumped every day. Temperatures in Kandahar soar to more than 125 degrees, and the first hot winds of the morning bear an overwhelming smell of raw sewage, spiced with the odor of disinfectant from the latrines outside the tent, not to mention occasional gusts of diesel fuel blowing off the line of helicopters on the nearby runway. Sitting on the edge of his cot, twenty-year-old Private Joshua Farrar, a former surfer from South Florida, shakes a Newport out of a dust-covered pack, surveys his fellow soldiers getting up to face another day in Afghanistan and concludes, "This all sucks."

The Fifth Platoon Delta are air-assault infantry attached to the 3-187th Battalion, America's main combat force in southeastern Afghanistan. Their job is to fly into battle on helicopters, rappel down and blow the crap out of tanks, fortifications and the enemy. But in Afghanistan the soldiers have been thrust into an ill-defined role. They mount round-the-clock combat recon patrols through former Taliban villages in the Kandahar desert. But the shooting has stopped for the most part, and now the soldiers are called on to enforce a shaky peace while serving as America's ambassadors of goodwill in what remains a lethal land.

As they prepare for their patrol, Farrar and a couple of the other gunners stand on top of two Humvees to mount machine guns in the turrets. Lieutenant Donate D'Angelo, Jr., a twenty-six-year-old from Ramsey, New Jersey, leans on some sandbags outside, studying a plastic-encased patrol map.

The first thing you notice about D'Angelo, the platoon leader of Five Delta, is his physical power. He is about five-feet-eleven and weighs 195 pounds, with much of that weight carried in his shoulders and massive biceps. A week ago, he set a regimental record in Kandahar for his weight class by bench-pressing 325 pounds. D'Angelo played soccer at West Point, boxed for three years and completed Army Ranger school, during which he survived a lightning strike that killed the man next to him.

"Today," he says, "we will drive through some minefields and drink tea with village elders." He looks up with a sort of grin or snarl. It's tough to tell. D'Angelo is the son of Italian immigrants. "I'm like the black sheep of the family for being in the Army," he says. "My brother's twenty-three. He's a bond trader in Manhattan, making a hundred and twenty thousand a year, and I'm making thirty-five thousand living in a tent in Afghanistan with fourteen other guys."

"Step aside, sir!" a soldier shouts. "Dust devil coming." From across the parking lot, a brown cyclone whips up from behind a row of porta-johns; D'Angelo steps back five paces while the funnel slips by. "You get used to the dust here after a while," he says. Most afternoons, forty-mile-an-hour winds kick up dust storms that blow into the airfield like a thick fog, reducing visibility to a few yards.

"Do people at home still care about the job we're doing over here?" D'Angelo asks. He speaks softly, but emphasizes every syllable, as if laboring to make himself absolutely clear, just in case you happen to be a dumb fuck. "Are they still patriotic and all that, or have they forgotten about us?"

D'Angelo spits a thick stream of brown juice and adds, "You know, I took it kind of personally when the Towers fell. That was my backyard. To say I wanted to put my life on the line for America is too abstract. I came to Afghanistan to protect my mother, my sister and my little brother."

THERE ARE ABOUT FOUR THOUSAND SOLDIERS based at Kandahar Airfield, as well as an additional one thousand coalition soldiers, most of them Canadian. The three-square-mile encampment at the base, seized from Taliban control last year, is the one piece of land in southeastern Afghanistan the United States controls absolutely. The barbed-wire perimeter is heavily fortified with machine-gun nests, bunkers and guard towers. Of all the personnel stationed here, less than a thousand are actual infantry soldiers. The rest serve various support roles—truck drivers, computer technicians, inventory accountants—and this is the only Afghan soil they will ever set foot on.

In the six months since the Americans took over, Kandahar Airfield has gone from a mine-strewn ruin to a makeshift thriving city. Life inside the wire has its own peculiar rhythms. Americans at the camp inhabit their own time zone—the Pentagon's worldwide standard, known as Zulu Time, which here is four and a half hours behind local time, meaning that dawn breaks at about 0030, or just past midnight.

At this hour, the bombs usually start going off as part of the work done by the ordnance-removal teams, and you begin to see early-morning fitness nuts jogging, toting grenade launchers and pistols—everyone is required to carry their weapons at all times. By 0400 Zulu, the local Afghan workers show up, including a team of former mercenaries supplied by the local warlord, who tend the old rose garden outside the terminal while armed guards keep a watchful eye, lest one decides to hide a bomb in the bushes. All day long, huge C-130 and C-17 transport planes disgorge steel shipping containers and mountains of supplies. (It takes two daily C-130 flights alone to keep the PX stocked with items like chips and salsa, Eminem CDs and thousands of cans of warm soda.) At two in the afternoon, when the sun starts to set in Zulu Time, officers hack golf balls at a primitive driving range built on the threshold of an old minefield. At about 1500 Zulu, soldiers begin to crowd the "morale, welfare, recreation" (MWR) tents to phone home and watch the shows *The West Wing* and *Fear Factor* on big-screen TVs. Then, at about 1800 Zulu, they hit their tents, where they are rocked to sleep by the thunder of mortar barrages from night maneuvers on the nearby practice range.

Despite efforts to offer the comforts of home, life at the camp is mighty unpleasant. The food is awful—a combination of premanufactured T-rations and MREs (meals ready to eat). Temperatures inside the tents hit 130 degrees in the day, the porta-johns are foul and beastly hot, dust sifts into clothes and sleeping bags, and showers are available for only limited use. Add to that constant bouts of dysentery and the ever-present threat of rocket attacks—none successful so far—and you can understand why the soldiers have bitterly nicknamed the post "Ass-Crack-istan."

Among the stringencies the soldiers complain about most is General Order Number 1, which bans possession or consumption of alcoholic beverages by U.S. soldiers in Afghanistan. "There's a way around everything," says one enlisted soldier. "Some of the guys like to huff," he says, referring to the tried-and-true brain-frying high of sniffing inhalants. "I was against it at first, but we got a good high from Glade."

Sexual relations are banned on the base, but stories of forbidden conduct abound. In April, an Apache attack-helicopter crew, monitoring the camp through night-vision equipment, picked up a couple having sex in a vehicle. And several women have been flown home after it was discovered they were pregnant. Assignations are not unknown at a place dubbed "Terrorist Terrace"—a blown-up bunker at the south end of the airfield. "I hooked up with an enlisted girl at the MWR tent," says a young officer. "We borrowed a Humvee and drove out to Terrorist Terrace. We'd never met before. We talked for a few minutes, and I said, 'Listen, do you want to fuck?' And she said, 'Um, OK.' When I came back and laid down in my tent with her gunk all over my dick, I knew I had done a bad thing. Then I thought, I can't believe it. I just got laid in Afghanistan."

THE FIFTH PLATOON go by a roguish call sign. Over the radio they are the Hell Hounds of the Tank Killer Company Wolf Pack, or Wolf Pack Five for short. But gathering in their tent in the final hour before their patrol, they look more like a small-town baseball team than combat soldiers. The youngest is nineteen, and most of the rest are in their early twenties. The oldest, Platoon Sergeant Patrick Keough, is a thirty-six-year-old father of two. Despite the mad tattoos many display on their backs and arms, the bunch still give the impression of hometown innocence—one that is re-inforced by frequent proclamations of how much they all care about one another. "All of us are brothers," says Private First Class Andrew Wiser, a twenty-year-old from Conneaut, Ohio. "I'd die for any of these guys." Their intense feeling for one another results in an almost naive faith. "Nothing bad is going to happen to any of us in Afghanistan," Wiser says. "We'll do anything it takes to look out for each other."

Wolf Pack Five showed up in Kandahar last March, ready for battle. "I expected to start shooting as soon as we stepped off the plane," says platoon section leader Sergeant Paul Quast, a beefy thirty-four-year-old with a shaved head and hard, deep-set blue eyes. Some of the soldiers, like PFC William Ballard, have been disappointed by the lack of action. A slender, soft-spoken, squinty nineteen-year-old, Ballard says, "I thought there'd be more war in Afghanistan, more like Vietnam." When he came to Afghani-stan, Ballard brought along a custom sniper scope for his M-203 weapon— a combination grenade launcher and assault rifle—telling Keough he needed it to "shoot Afghans." Keough made him send it home to his father in Reno, Nevada.

The Fifth Platoon's only glimpse into the horrors of war occurred early

on the morning of April 18, when they pulled guard on the gunnery range—
"Osama House"—after four Canadian soldiers, serving as part of the U.S.-
led coalition, were killed in a friendly-fire accident. It happened at about
midnight when an overzealous American F-16 pilot dropped a five-hundred-
pound bomb on the Canadians, mistaking their gunnery practice for hostile
fire. "I saw a torso," says Farrar, who spent a whole day with the platoon
guarding the accident site. "That was enough."

Farrar, fair-haired and a lanky six-feet-one, moves with a slowness that's
both lazy and deliberate, and says he joined the Army to get money for college. "I never thought there was going to be a war," he says. "There were guys
at Fort Campbell who squirmed out before we deployed—like a kid who
developed 'dizzy spells.' I thought of doing that, but fuck it." Farrar holds an
unusual position in the platoon. His superiors consider him one of the platoon's best soldiers, but he is also the lowest-ranked. About a week after he
arrived, he was busted down two ranks to buck private when an infraction
he'd committed back at Fort Campbell, Kentucky, caught up with him. Farrar is sketchy about the details but allows it had something to do with a urine
test. (Bad luck seems to dog Farrar. On a recent mail call, while his buddies
opened letters and boxes of cookies from home, Farrar received a parking
ticket. "This girl didn't write me for three weeks," he says. "I told her to pack
her shit and get the fuck out of my house. Now she's got my car.")

AT ABOUT 0600, the platoon strap on about sixty pounds of protective gear
and equipment apiece and climb into three Humvees. They drive out the
front gate of the American camp and go less than a mile, to a former Taliban
command post surrounded by fourteen-foot-high mud-brick walls, which
belongs to America's ally in Kandahar, an army known as the Anti-Taliban
Forces (ATF).

The Fifth Platoon stay here for days at a time while running patrols,
sleeping in heat-up Marine Corps pup tents in a dusty field opposite the
ATF command post. After pulling into the fort, the men scramble out of the
Humvees and make for the tents, each racing to find the one with the fewest

rips and, ideally, zippers that work. You would think staying in the fort would be a hardship duty, but spirits are high. Specialist Armando Ramos, a twenty-year-old from Bakersfield, California, who has a three-year-old daughter back home, says, "Dude, this is the only place where we have the privacy to jack off."

Farrar groans, "I am so sick of beating off." Ramos adds, "I see a stick figure of a naked chick someone drew in the latrines, and I'm ready to go."

Before the first patrol, D'Angelo assembles the men for a briefing held beneath a parachute strung up in a corner of the walled fortress for shade. Once they sit down, D'Angelo turns to the new guy, Private Jason Swinehart, a nineteen-year-old former high school football player from Ohio who arrived in Afghanistan only five days ago, his bag packed with George Strait and Kenny Chesney CDs.

"Private Swinehart, where are we?"

Swinehart looks around, grins, turns red. "I don't know, sir."

"We are outside the wire," D'Angelo says in his most patient, speaking-to-a-dumb-fuck voice. The Kandahar desert is basically one vast, unmarked minefield. Three ATF soldiers were killed several weeks earlier when their Toyota pickup hit a mine less than a mile from the ATF fort. Two more died in a mine blast just beyond the perimeter of the air base. The American and coalition soldiers have been luckier. In April, a Canadian patrol hit a mine, but they were in an armored vehicle and no one was hurt. D'Angelo turns to Swinehart again. "What do the occupants of the lead vehicle do if they hit a mine?"

Swinehart sweats it a moment, squeezing his eyes shut in deep thought, then answers: "Everyone exits through the hatch, sir?"

"Very good, Swinehart," D'Angelo says. Swinehart's ability to quickly adapt to conditions in Afghanistan proves one of D'Angelo's pet theories about young soldiers: It's easier to train the ones who don't have a lot of education. "See," D'Angelo explains as the men start getting into the trucks, "if you took a nineteen-year-old philosophy major in college and gave him Swinehart's job, that guy wouldn't know what to do. We put Swinehart on top of the truck with a machine gun in his hands and drive him into a village where people have their own personal weapons—shotguns, AKs—and they start waving them around." D'Angelo spits a long stream of black Copenhagen juice into the dust. "What do you do if you're Swinehart? We have very simple rules: You don't shoot unless he aims a weapon at you. I trust a guy like Swinehart to follow the rules. If you put that machine gun in the hands of a nineteen-year-old philosophy major, he might think too much. We don't want that. In the Army, everything is decided for you. Just follow the rules."

SERGEANT QUAST, the thirty-four-year-old platoon staff sergeant, leads the initial patrol of the day from the first Humvee. A second Humvee follows about seventy-five yards behind. The basic crew of each consists of the driver, the turret gunner and the TC (truck commander), who also operates the radio. The patrols also include an ATF translator and a medic. For several days the soldiers have been excited about the prospect of driving new "up-armored" Humvees recently shipped in from the States. Until now, patrols were conducted in conventional thin-skin vehicles providing little protection against land mines. The new Humvees are fitted with 3,500 pounds of armor protection. But it's not the safety features that have the men talking; it's the fact that these new vehicles are rumored to have air-conditioning. All morning, Ramos has been repeating, "Dude, we're gonna be cruising in the up-armors with the AC on full, windows all up and shit."

The AC unit blasts with the noise and ferocity of a leaf blower, but hot air and dust pour in as usual through the open roof hatch where the gunner stands. The added armor interferes with the global-positioning-navigation unit, called a Plugger. The TCs now have to hold the Plugger about two feet out the window for it to operate.

There are other problems. The secure radios mounted in the Humvees cease to work once they get a few miles into the desert. So in order to communicate with one another, the soldiers ask friends and relatives to send seventy-dollar Motorola walkie-talkies you can buy at any Wal-Mart in the

States. "The Army issues us its own walkabouts," says Quast. "But they don't work worth shit."

One of the ATF translators has told the soldiers that there is a McDonald's in downtown Kandahar. It's nothing but a cruel joke, but since no one in the Fifth Platoon has ever seen Kandahar—a war-torn city of medieval bazaars and dirt roads clogged with donkeys and chickens—they have no reason to disbelieve the report. "What we ought to do," says Quast, straining to see the trail ahead through the vehicle's two-inch-thick armor windows, "is send one of the ATF guys into Kandahar and do a run on the McDonald's."

He shouts up to the turret. "You hear that, Swinehart?"

Swinehart leans down, hands still on the machine gun. "Yeah!" he shouts. "Get me Supersize everything!"

The desert is littered with the silver hulls of Russian fighter planes, wrecked tanks and missile trucks. Mosques, old Soviet barracks and schools lie in ruins everywhere. You can tell who blew up what by the style of destruction. Russian and warring Afghans flatten structures and whole villages through massive artillery and aerial bombardment. Buildings hit by the U.S. Air Force tend to have one neat blast down the center, leaving the four corners standing.

The destination for Quast's patrol is the village of Mowmand, about seven miles up a dry riverbed. Homes in Kandahar villages are made of mud brick and stucco, shaped like beehives and nestled between a maze of walls the color of the dust that blows in the wind. The land strikes the Americans as so alien that some have nicknamed it Tatooine, after the planet of mud-hut villages in the Star Wars movies. The soldiers call Afghans "Hajis," some say because "Haji" is the honorific term for any Muslim who has made the voyage to Mecca, the Haj. Others say the term comes from *Johnny Quest*, the old cartoon that featured an Arab sidekick character named Haji. Most think it's simply a funny term in keeping with how they goof on Pashto, imitating it with the sound "abadabadaba."

The soldiers' attitudes toward the people are more complex, and it would seem more decent, than their prankish humor indicates. American soldiers are more willing than other coalition forces in Kandahar to mix with the locals. Canadian recon units, which conduct their patrols in tanklike armored vehicles, seldom stop unless by prearranged plan. Steve Marty, a master corporal in a Canadian patrol unit, says, "We know what they did to the Russians. They'd invite them in and give them food laced with hepatitis. The Afghans in the villages still have all their weapons. If we got into a fight, it would be six of us against a whole village. We don't stop unless we have to."

The soldiers in the Fifth, many of whom share dog-eared histories of the Russian defeat in Afghanistan, are as aware as anyone else of the dangers posed by the villages they patrol, but their wariness is tempered by the particularly American faith, bordering on naivete, that most people can be brought around if, as Quast says, "you treat them with respect and dignity."

"First time we came to one village, the Canadians had been patrolling before us," says Quast. "A man hopped out on one leg, giving us the finger. Kids came out with rocks. Our gunner locked and loaded the fifty-cal on a little kid who was aiming to hit him with a rock from a slingshot." The soldiers defused the tense situation by taking a direct approach. "We had our translator ask what they were so mad about. Turns out the patrols had been speeding through the village, kicking up dust, waking everyone up." The Fifth Platoon promised to drive more slowly through the village.

The Humvees stop about seventy-five yards from Mowmand's outermost wall. While Farrar and Swinehart remain in the gun turrets of each Humvee, Quast steps out of the lead vehicle. Following procedure, he will stay here and send in a couple of soldiers to make contact with a village elder. Sergeant Jeremy Ludweg, twenty-four, from Louisville, Kentucky, will go on, along with the ATF translator and a soft-spoken twenty-four-year-old art-school dropout from Detroit, Specialist Sean "Doc" Murphy, the platoon medic.

Murphy normally doesn't tell villagers he is a medic. "I don't have enough supplies for villagers," he says. But during a previous patrol, a man who lives outside the village invited Murphy into his house, telling him his children were sick. At first, Murphy kept quiet, but then the man's daughters came into the room. Their hair had fallen out, and their scalps were bleeding. "They just needed some iodine," Murphy says. "So I decided to bring some."

Even though more than a thousand people live in Mowmand, a spooky silence radiates from the village walls, broken only by the braying of donkeys. Ludweg has never been inside Mowmand before and doesn't trust locals as much as some of the other men do. A wiry redhead who wears small gold-frame glasses and speaks with a mild Kentucky drawl, Ludweg is famous in the platoon for nearly calling in a strike on two rabbits running through the perimeter of the Kandahar Airfield, which he mistook in his night-vision scope for Al Qaeda infiltrators. Ludweg is due to ship home in fewer than twenty days, leave the Army, marry his fiancée, finish college and find "a job where I never wear a uniform again." For obvious reasons, he wants to play it safe. "Doc, we're not going in, are we?" Ludweg asks, scanning the village uneasily, holding his M-203 high in front of his chest.

Murphy explains to the translator, Mohammed Abdullah, that they don't want to go into the village. "Of course, sir," Abdullah says, gazing at the village with a serene smile. He is a pudgy man, about twenty-five, with a fidgety gap-toothed smile. He's unfailingly polite and always appears eager to please the Americans. But like other ATF translators, he often seems not to listen to what the Americans are saying. "I will take you into the village, sir."

Murphy and Ludweg reluctantly follow. Weighted down with about sixty pounds of body armor, ammo and weaponry apiece, their boots whoof up knee-high clouds of dust with each step. Beneath the Americans' helmets, sweat pours down their faces. In the extreme heat, fair-haired Americans develop a strange complexion. Their skin burns red in blotches, but underneath it develops a sickly white pallor, especially on Ludweg. He hangs back, fuming. All the color has drained from his face, except for his nose, which is bright red, almost blinking like a clown's.

By now, children are streaming out of spider holes in the buildings and walls. About twenty boys and a couple of girls, with fly-covered smiles, approach the Americans with their hands out, chanting *"Kalam!"* which means "pen," and begging for candy, even cigarettes. Basic items such as pens are novelties in many poverty-stricken Afghan villages.

After a few minutes, two men emerge from the village, followed by a young girl missing most of her hair. She has an oozing, red sore across the bald portion of her scalp. Murphy gives the men about ten dollars' worth of iodine solution and gauze, and explains how to use it. The two villagers shake his hand, then touch their hands to their hearts, a traditional Afghan show of affection.

Up by the Humvees, a small riot has broken out among children who surround it. Swinehart and Farrar stand in their turrets, hands on their machine guns, faces bright red and sweating. Theirs may not look like the most interesting job in the world, but in moments like this, you realize that holding a finger on the trigger of a machine gun in an alien village half a world away is a fairly profound responsibility. The weightiest challenge faced by the average college student their age is usually on the order of figuring out whether he'll get laid more or less if he goes vegan.

Quast orders Swinehart to throw a plastic water bottle to the side of the vehicle to draw the kids away. As soon as he throws it, two boys, each about nine, race over, and both grab it, then start beating the shit out of each other. A man in a black turban, once the Taliban uniform, approaches out of nowhere. He has a scythe slung over his shoulder, with an enormous blade sticking out. Murphy, Abdullah and Ludweg walk up just as the man in the turban comes their way. Ludweg, nose beating red, drops his M-203 on the guy and stands back. The man in black cuts to the side of the Humvee where the boys are fighting and whacks both of them in the side of the head with his open hands.

It is late in the afternoon when the patrol returns to the Wolf Pack compound inside the ATF fort. D'Angelo calls them together for debriefing. Water bottles chill on a giant block of ice in a plastic chest. The ATF guys control an ice machine in Kandahar and trade the U.S. soldiers blocks in exchange for copies of skin magazines.

"Swinehart, what did you learn on your first patrol?" D'Angelo asks.

"I never seen a camel before, sir."

"What else did you learn?"

"Them kids fighting over a bottle of water. I never seen anything like that. I'll never forget that." He shakes his head, grinning. "I saw another kid; he put his fingers over his mouth like he wanted a cigarette. Kid couldn't have been more than six years old. And already smoking cigarettes?"

Farrar cuts in, saying to Swinehart, "Over here, six years is already like a third of a person's life span. It makes sense to start smoking at that age."

THE MEN IN THE PLATOON, like most other American soldiers, are in the almost unreal position of belonging to a seemingly victorious army that for the most part hasn't fired a shot. Battle-hardened ATF soldiers regale the young Americans with hair-raising tales of shooting down Soviet helicopters, slaughtering Al Qaeda fanatics with grenades, carving Russians up with bayonets. During meals at the Wolf Pack compound, the Americans pass around these secondhand tales as reverently as if they were their own.

But something about their ATF brothers-in-arms confuses the Americans. They are not only the most macho fighting force they have known, they are seemingly the gayest. Open affection between men—and even what might be defined as pederasty back home—is fairly common in Pashtun culture. Traditional Kandahar love songs frequently revolve around themes of love and flirtation between a boy and a man. Even when there's no sexual connotation, Afghan men tend to hold hands and touch each other a great deal.

Sometimes the ATF soldiers will try to explain to the Americans that a life with women only is an unfulfilling one. "When I told my counterparts in the ATF that I'm married," Keough says, "some of them have asked me, 'Is it a marriage of love?' They say, 'Women are for having children. Men are for love.'"

The first time Ludweg came to the compound, he thought he had established a rapport with one ATF soldier, talking to him about the relative merits of the AK-47 versus the U.S.-issue M-4, when Ludweg happened to comment on the nice flowers growing in the lawn. The soldier leaned into Ludweg's face and said, "You have pretty eyes."

Some of the American soldiers refer to their ATF counterparts as "the butt-pirate army," but again, as in the relationships with villagers, their feelings about them are more complicated and open-minded than you might expect. In their free time, some of the soldiers in the Fifth Platoon stop by remote ATF checkpoints farther out in the desert, throw down their weapons and sit around for hours in the primitive guard huts playing cards and watching pirated Jean-Claude Van Damme DVDs. "Their culture is different," says Keough, "but they're soldiers, which makes them our brothers."

Still, the contrast between the Americans and the Afghans couldn't be sharper at night in the ATF fort. When the sun goes down, the ATF soldiers gather on a small, meticulously kept lawn in front of their command post and sit under lamps made from old Soviet bomb casings, stuck upright in the lawn and wired with colorful lights.

ATF soldiers, who run their own patrols by putting as many as three men at a time on tiny Honda 125 motorcycles, zoom in and out all night. Others loiter on their small lawn, wrestling for hours, then holding hands, arms draped limply over shoulders and AK-47s, swaying as they listen to songs blasted from a boom box. Occasionally they hire boy singers, usually about thirteen or fourteen, who sing and dance on the lawn. The older soldiers, bearded men with black, craggy smiles, stand around gazing like fans at a Britney Spears concert.

On the American side of the fort, those not on patrol sit around on up-turned crates bullshitting. One of the most striking aspects of infantrymen's life is the intimate relationships they are forced to maintain with shit. The topic is never far from conversation. At the airfield, the smell of sewage is a constant factor, and everyone has to take his turn on the "shit truck" detail, emptying the base-camp porta-johns. But it's on this patrol where the subject of excrement becomes a near-obsession. Every other day or so, shit here is disposed, a truly disgusting procedure that involves mixing excrement with diesel fuel and setting it on fire. The disposal process requires constant stirring and relighting, which all takes about an hour. "The trick to it," says Keough, "is stay out of the wind so you don't get that shit smoke in your clothes."

They debate the best ways to dig slit trenches (the basic communal toilet first used at Kandahar Airfield) and whether the best source of "field-expedient toilet paper" is to cut off one's T-shirt sleeves or use the upper portion of a sock. They laugh about the time that turbulence from a low-flying C-17 blew over the shitter on the perimeter with an unlucky grunt in it. Or the time Keough laughed so hard about Ballard's bad case of the krud—as the local dysentery is known—he shit his own pants. It's a good time at the ATF fort. The Americans talk about shit, then jack off in their pup tents. The ATF soldiers party with boys on the front lawn.

ONE MORNING JUST PAST DAWN, the Fifth Platoon is ordered back to the airfield. The men are told they will be taking part in a helicopter assault on two villages near the Pakistani border. For the next thirty-six hours, the men practice field drills while battalion commanders speak confidently of taking on "a significant concentration of Al Qaeda forces." But Apache Snow II quickly runs into difficulties, and the Fifth Platoon is cut from the assault. (When Apache Snow II is finally launched ten days later, the two hundred U.S. troops who land in an armada of choppers find villages filled only with women and children, a few boxes of rifle ammunition and three rocket-propelled grenades given to them by a village elder. A suspicious facility in one village, which military-intelligence analysts speculated might be a terrorist weapons plant, turns out to be a lumber mill.)

After being cut from the mission, the soldiers in the Fifth feel let down. "We just want the chance to do what we train for," says Ramos. Alone in the tent, D'Angelo seems the most disappointed. "I joined the Army to do extreme things," he says. "In this kind of war, the Air Force comes in, blows the shit out of everything. The Special Forces does their thing. The infantry comes in and we just guard what's already been taken." D'Angelo spits a stream of brown tobacco into an empty Gatorade bottle. "I think about leaving the Army and going into the real world. But sometimes I think the corporate world is cold. You won't measure up, they fire you. In the Army, if you fail at something, they try to rebuild people. Once you're in, they'll always find something for you. The Army is almost addictive. Everything is taken care of for you. My brother was telling me I should become a cop in the New Jersey Highway Patrol. I wouldn't know how to do that. If I saw someone was speeding, I'd just shoot him."

WHEN THE PLATOON GOES BACK on patrol, military intelligence passes down a report to D'Angelo that the route they had used to deliver medicine to Mowmand was mined after they left. According to the intelligence report, a man was spotted planting a mine on the road and told a local villager, "This mine is for the Americans."

Quast volunteers to take a patrol to a village near Mowmand to inquire with the locals if they have heard anything about mines being planted.

Within minutes of reaching Morgan Kechah—the village where they hope to obtain intelligence about the alleged mining incident—Quast and his ATF translator find a villager named Abdul Raheem. "He wants us to come to his house for tea," Quast tells Ludweg, the other TC on the patrol. "We can't turn down an Afghan's hospitality. It's an insult."

Quast insists that all the men come, including Ludweg. They squeeze through the four-foot-high entrance to Raheem's adobe home and are joined by two bearded, turbaned elders. Ludweg flashes a curt smile and hunches lower on his M-203.

Quast peels his armor off as he sits on the floor. Raheem reaches up to a high shelf molded into the adobe wall and takes down a plastic bottle of Khoshgovar, an Iranian brand of cola. A young man, out of breath from a sprint to a neighboring village, brings in ice in a bucket made from an old antifreeze jug. Raheem picks up several glasses. He ceremoniously inspects one glass and observes a spot. He cleans it by delicately clearing his throat and hocking some spit into it. He wipes it on his dirty robe.

Ludweg's eyes bug out. But when the beverage is served, he and the other

American soldiers raise their glasses and drink. After exchanging awkward pleasantries, Quast brings up the topic of land mines. He asks Raheem if he knows about anyone planting mines to kill Americans. Raheem appears shocked by the story. He and the two elders debate for a long time in Pashto. "The story is not true," he says in halting English. "Impossible." Then, through the translator, Raheem says, "We want Americans to stay. We want to protect Americans. If you leave, we will have more war. We want you to keep coming to our village."

When the Americans say good-bye and walk back to their Humvees, Raheem follows. He becomes agitated, eager to say something, but uncertain of how to express himself. He grabs one of the Americans' arms and asks, "How do I show my love?" The Americans look at him, puzzled.

"In my country," Raheem starts, "I show love to my friend by hold his hand or put my hand on his shoulder. How do I show love to Americans?"

Quast takes his hand and shakes it good-bye.

BY THE TIME QUAST'S PATROL arrives back at the Wolf Pack compound, the second squad of the Fifth Platoon is preparing for its own patrol. Farrar grabs his helmet and groans. "The first thing I do when I get out of the Army is, I'm going to get some piece-of-shit job, go in to work the first day with my uniform fucked up, French fries hanging out of my mouth, all blazed, and they'll say, 'You're fired!' And I'll say, 'Fuck you, too,' and walk out of there laughing. You can do that in the civilian world."

One of the men asks Quast about that run to the Kandahar McDonald's they've been talking about for days now. Quast steps up: "I've got some news about the McDonald's in Kandahar." He stares ahead, his deep-set eyes expressionless. "The translator who told us about that . . . turns out, he lied. There is no McDonald's."

The soldiers stare at the sergeant while the news sinks in: There are no Happy Meals in Afghanistan. One naive belief has been shattered, but the others, deeply held among the men in the Fifth Platoon, remain intact— their faith that brotherly love will protect them against the worst evils of war, and that by behaving with characteristically blind but generous American decency, they will triumph in Afghanistan where all others have failed. No one believes in the latter more than D'Angelo, the platoon realist. Though he often complains bitterly about his failure to engage the enemy in combat, he occasionally brings up his father's experience in Italy during World War II. "My father's family hid in a cave when the Americans invaded and fought the Germans. My father was seven, and his face was bleeding from a cut. They could hear the Americans outside, and my grandmother wanted to take him out to get medical attention. My grandfather said no, but they took him anyway. The Americans fixed his face up and gave them food." D'Angelo stretches out his sleeve, showing off the flag and his patches for Ranger and Air Assault school. "Those were American soldiers."

It's nine-thirty in the morning, and Jim Greco, rising star of professional skateboarding but in his own words a "regular, moderate dude," weaves across the white carpet in his new, all-white luxury apartment just off Sunset Boulevard in Hollywood, sucking on a jug of pink Gallo wine. With his black hair pomaded up in an unruly mass of spikes, black jeans and studded leather wristbands, Greco, twenty-three, bears a spooky resemblance to doomed punk rocker Sid Vicious. But when he speaks, the obtuse inflections that come out of his mouth are pure Italian-American—sly, menacing but playful, like De Niro in some street-corner role. Greco has the build of a bantamweight fighter, and his hands are gnarled and swollen from repeated abuse. "I broke my right hand three times over," he says, reeling off a string of bar fights he's gotten into while he was blacked out. "Then I made ghost"—he explains, using one of his own idiosyncratic expressions, "make ghost," meaning "to leave town"—"and went to Phoenix and got into another fight when I had a cast on. My knuckle kind of healed in the middle of my hand. It's baraka." "Baraka" is another of Greco's own terms. It means anything that's fucked up—after the Baraka character with mutant sword-arms in Mortal Kombat.

"I've been getting fucked up a long time," Greco says, taking another swig of Gallo. "My head's kind of baraka, so I'm sticking to wine today, posting with my homeys." The assembled homeys constitute a pantheon of top street skaters in the world—Andrew Reynolds, Erik Ellington, Jeff Lenoce, James Nichols. A few sit around the breakfast table passing a bong. Others lounge on the couch in front of a massive TV, watching skater videos, drinking beer, smoking blunts and futzing with wheel sets on their boards.

The Ramones blast on a boom box. Someone pounds on the front door. Greco finally opens it, and a guy named Shane steps in. "Check out the digs," says Greco, gesturing to the gallery ceilings and the windows with panoramic views of the Hollywood Hills. "It's high jinks," Shane says appreciatively. "Yeah, high jinks," Greco agrees, then adds, "Excuse me while I puke." He beelines to the kitchen. He leans over the sink, and a shiny yellow sock of vomit jets from his mouth. Wiping his lips with the back of his hand, he looks up at the huge room, sunlight pouring in through the windows, and says cheerfully, "Skateboarding paid for this, motherfucker."

AN UP-AND-COMER in the skate world since he signed his first sponsorship deal at age fifteen, Greco's career took off last year with the release of the *Baker 2g* skate video. Before then, he'd just been the guy who dressed punk rock and got in fights. Since then, he has made the cover of the major skateboarding magazines, launched a line of signature boards that sold out shortly after going on sale in January and signed a major endorsement deal with Vans shoes.

The trick, or "hammer," that made Greco a star is called a "backside nose-blunt slide." In simplest terms, this consists of jumping a skateboard onto a handrail at the top of a staircase and sliding down backward, with just the nose of the board touching the rail. Greco pulled off his now legendary move in late August near midnight in a deserted Los Angeles business district on a flight of stairs reputed among skateboarders to be extremely challenging. His friends bribed security guards and set up a power generator, lights and video cameras in the concrete stairwell behind an office building. Greco, shaky from a weeks-long alcohol binge, made numerous approaches to the top of the stairs before he jumped the rail and "laid down a perfect hammer," doing a trick in a way that has been accomplished by only two, maybe three other pro skaters.

The fact is, no one really knows, because there is no governing body of pro skateboarding. It remains an underground activity in which skaters gain fame by going out in small crews and capturing their stunts on video, which are then studied in minute detail by fans who scrutinize and judge everything a pro skater does, down to the way he ties his shoelaces.

Greco's crew is called the Piss Drunx. They are a bunch of guys (and at least one female) who have been skating together for years. Most, but not all, are pros. There are no formalities that go with being a Piss Drunk, other than that some, like Greco, display a Piss Drunx tattoo—a backward P and a forward D. Many live together or crash in one another's apartments in Southern California and Arizona.

Since forming their own company, Baker Skateboards, last year, the Piss Drunx, thanks mostly to the exploits of Jim Greco, have become the new face of pro skateboarding. And yet, for all his visibility, pro skating is, in many ways, just a part-time job for Greco. In a year, he might spend only a few weeks working on his tricks. It's been nearly twelve months since he's performed a trick. Now, with a follow-up to Greco's breakout video in the works, his friends are starting to ask, When is he going to skate again?

"Jim isn't like other skaters," says Knox Godoy, at twelve the youngest member of the Baker team. "We skate every day, working on hammers. That's how I do it, how guys like Andrew Reynolds do it. But Jim sits on his drunk ass for months, then goes out in a few weeks and lays more gnarly hammers than anybody. Laying hammers is like riding a bicycle for him. He can pick it up whenever he needs it."

"I need to cruise and drink for a while," Greco says. "Then the feeling to do hammers comes up on me. I just let it happen."

"There are no rules in pro skateboarding," says Jeremy Fox, the manager of the team for Flip Skateboards. "It's more like the music industry, where popularity is a factor. Skaters are like rock stars. Kids don't want a Phil Collins of the skate world. They want Marilyn Manson."

LUNCHTIME, GRECO HAS CHUGGED all the Gallo and walks aimlessly across the white carpet of his apartment hunched forward with his arms hanging down, like a Cro-Magnon illustration on an evolution chart. His face is slack and his eyes unfocused. Reynolds follows him across the room with a roll of paper towels and a bottle of 409, picking up trash and wiping off surfaces. He keeps a wary eye on Greco, like a parent watching a toddler. Greco crashes over to the CD player and pops in another Ramones disc and turns up the volume, cranking it. "Jim, keep it chill," Reynolds says, cutting across the room to turn the sound back down.

Reynolds, tall, with moppish, fair hair, sleepy eyes and an unflappable demeanor—he is depicted on his signature boards as the Shaggy character from *Scooby-Doo*—is Greco's physical and temperamental opposite. In the scheme of their odd-couple relationship, he is the neat-freak, the worrier, the caretaker. A Tony Hawk protégé, Reynolds has been a pro skater for nearly a decade. He scored his first major shoe deal a couple of years ago and has been featured as a character in the Tony Hawk Pro Skater 2, the number-one-selling Nintendo and PlayStation game last Christmas, for which he recently received a royalty check for nearly $100,000. Still, when it comes to Greco, Reynolds is in awe. "I can't tell if Greco is completely insane or the smartest person I ever met," he says.

Greco sits on the floor across the room from Reynolds. He has put one

Vans sneaker on his foot. He holds the other sneaker in his hand. "Andrew, where's my other shoe?" he asks.

"It's on your foot, Jim."

Half an hour later, Reynolds is behind the wheel of his gold 2000 Cadillac Eldorado driving to an L.A. skateboarding spot near a high school. Greco is in the passenger seat. Before leaving the house, Greco discovered a half-full bottle of Jack Daniel's. He waves both arms, singing along with "Sympathy for the Devil" playing on the stereo, and swigs from the bottle.

Reynolds begins to get impatient. "Put the bottle down, Jim," Reynolds shouts over the music. Driving down a straightaway, he vents his growing anger by tapping the brakes, ever harder. Greco flops back and forth as if he's on a wave ride.

Finally, Reynolds pulls up next to a trash can in a residential neighborhood. He shuts the music off, leans over and shoves Greco's door open. "Jim," Reynolds says firmly, "put the bottle in the trash."

Greco looks up, gazing at Reynolds with bleary-eyed disbelief. "What? You're throwing me out?" Earlier in the year, while speeding down the 405 freeway in fellow Piss Drunk and female pro skater Elissa Steamer's brand-new $40,000 SUV, Greco had attempted to urinate out the window. Steamer had pulled over, punched Greco in the grille and kicked him out of the car. He was later found wandering the eight-lane freeway, attempting to flag down cars, and was arrested for public drunkenness. Greco seems to think today is a repeat. "OK, I'm going, Andrew," he says. He reaches for the passenger-side door handle, but the door is already open. He grabs air and tumbles partway out of the car, into the street.

"Jim, I'm not throwing you out," Reynolds says. "Just the bottle, OK?" Greco slides back into the car. He guzzles the last of the Jack Daniel's and says, "I thought you were kicking me out."

Reynolds pries the empty bottle from Greco's fingers and places it on the curb by the trash. "No, Jim, I'm not throwing you out."

Greco heaves himself onto Reynolds's chest, sloppy and emotional. "Andrew, I'm sorry. I love you. I thought this was it. You scared me."

"It's OK, Jim." Reynolds pushes Greco away. "Get off of me. Just sit in your seat."

JIM GRECO GREW UP in a crumbling Italian neighborhood in West Haven, Connecticut. "There were mom-and-pop stores," Greco says of his hometown, "and old Italian guys playing cards and gambling on tables in front."

His parents divorced when he was young. His mother is a waitress, and his father, Jimmy Senior, is a machine-tool operator. "Jim was definitely a kid who grew up on the corner," says Jimmy Senior. "He was wise to the street, but he wasn't a bad kid. He was a phenomenal shortstop in the Little League. We wanted him to play ball and go to college."

"I liked baseball," says Greco. "But when I was eleven, I started seeing these crazy-looking punker kids skating around, and that looked like fun."

He bought his first skateboard for ten dollars and, he says, his life changed almost immediately. He quit the baseball team and informed his father that he was going to be a professional skateboarder. Jimmy Senior didn't even know what skateboarding was. When his son took him to the park to show him, Jimmy Senior says he couldn't bear to look: "A father can't watch his son do something dangerous like that. I thought he was going to kill himself."

Jimmy says he gave his boy the best possible advice a father can offer. "Son, you're never going to make it. You should give up now."

"From that point on," Greco says, "I lived, slept, dreamt, ate, shit skateboarding." He pored over magazines at a local skateboard shop and fixated on one pro skater in particular. "Randy Colvin fucked shit up," Greco says. "He was one of the first three motherfuckers to skate handrail." He threw himself into learning Colvin's style. "I spent seven hours a day skating a piece-of-shit curb outside my house learning to grind like he did on those rails."

He started to learn his own tricks, and used his father's video camera to make tapes of himself performing them, sending them out to teams as well as shoe and clothing manufacturers. At fourteen, he skated in a demo in upstate New York. A year later, he caught the attention of Tony Hawk, who invited him to spend the summer skating with his famous Birdhouse team at demos around California and the Southwest.

Andrew Reynolds, turning sixteen and already a three-year veteran of Birdhouse, was in the car when they picked Greco up at the airport. "Jim was already doing that thing of making up his own words," says Reynolds, "and we couldn't understand what he was saying half the time."

What struck Reynolds was Greco's total lack of respect for Tony Hawk: "Tony was the boss to all of us." Except for Greco. "We'd go into restaurants, and Jim would sit across from Tony, with his feet up, shooting his mouth off, acting like Joe Pesci in *GoodFellas.*"

But Greco was a good enough skateboarder that Hawk invited him back to California to skate full-time for Birdhouse after he finished high school. "I got my diploma," says Greco. "But as a result of some problems with the school, I had to finish my classes at home." Greco does not elaborate. "If it hadn't been for skateboarding," he says, "I would probably have ended up doing something drug-related: taking drugs or selling drugs. But skateboarding showed me I had a future."

As soon as he turned eighteen, Greco moved to Huntington Beach, California, where Tony Hawk's Birdhouse team is based. An hour south of Los Angeles, Huntington Beach has been a locus for the skateboarding business since it first sprang up as an offshoot of surfing. Where surfing is bound with the utopian vision of California—a pastime for popular boys destined to get the prettiest girls—skateboarding became a refuge for misfits and social rejects escaping dystopian realities.

Skateboarding hit its first blip of popularity in the early 1960s, but it didn't come into its own as a sport until the mid-1970s, when a surfer named Frank Nasworthy revolutionized boards with the introduction of Cadillac brand polyurethane wheels (earlier skateboards skidded along on clay wheels). Then California was hit by a series of massive droughts. Suddenly, kids had thousands of empty pools to roll around in. A few years later, punk rock hit the West Coast. The anarchic-punk ethos appealed mightily to skateboarders, whose sport was based on running from cops, hopping fences and, in the eyes of authorities, destroying property.

All of these influences converged on a scuzzy section of bars, warehouses, drug-shooting galleries and vacant lots inland from Venice Beach and Santa Monica nicknamed Dogtown. Here, a bunch of street kids, heavily into skateboarding, punk, booze and mayhem, pushed the sport to new limits. They called themselves the Z-Boys, and their fuck-all spirit marked the sport. More important, they showed that a bunch of street kids with no future could find glory in neglected patches of urban concrete.

By the time Greco moved to Huntington Beach to take his place on Tony Hawk's Birdhouse team, the Z-Boys' brand of guerrilla skateboarding had given rise to publicly traded, multimillion-dollar companies like Vans, as well as dozens of smaller enterprises whose combined sales of boards, trucks and wheels exceeded $2 billion. The spread of cheap video cameras had made it possible for legions of kids to go out on their own and capture their tricks, usually in illicit locations, then sell clips to companies for use in their promotional videos. The kids got money or product. The companies received the cachet of associating themselves with edgy street skaters.

Greco's first apartment in Huntington Beach, paid for by Birdhouse, was a "shithole in the barrio," says Jay Strickland, then the team manager, who lived there, too, along with Reynolds and a few other skaters. "The kids were paid a few hundred bucks a month," Strickland says. "They lived on crap from 7-Eleven and on alcohol." Greco's core group of friends in Huntington Beach reflected the heterogeneous mix of pro skaters coming up in the late 1990s. "Most skaters come from sketchy backgrounds," says Strickland, who was raised in a "biker-dude family" and claims to have spent part of his childhood living in a car with his mother. There was Elissa Steamer, who spent a good deal of her Florida youth being educated at the dog track by her father. There was Ali Boulala, a fearless eighteen-year-old from Sweden who has left the United States after various scrapes with the law. There was Australian skater Dustin Dollin, also eighteen, nicknamed Spawn, short for Spawn of Satan, because he decorated his skateboard with the words "Fuck the Bible." Later, there would be Knox Godoy, who is almost like a younger brother to Greco. As Godoy explains it, he was born in the barrio "ghetto-style" and named after the front man of his dad's favorite punk band, the

Vibrators. "Knox hasn't really had a mother," says his father, eighties pro skater Steve Godoy. "But his uncle and I have raised him. So it's like he's had two dads and skateboarding to help him grow up."

This crew, which grew to include more than a dozen other pro skaters, was called the Warner Avenue Mob, after the street where Greco and Reynolds's apartment was located. The crew members spent their days and nights in search of spots to try out and tape new tricks.

When they weren't skating or touring the country putting on demos with their teams, they were drinking beer and smoking weed. "We'd put the product we were flowed"—given by sponsors—"sell it all for cash and party," says Steamer. No one was making much, but, she says, "Skating was not about money for us. A true skateboarder can have more fun on a few feet of curb than six normal people all day on all the rides at Disneyland."

After a year in Huntington Beach, Greco became disenchanted with the organized aspects of pro skateboarding, especially the demos his team participated in. "They wanted me to subscribe to rules," he says. "That's fucked up. Skating is supposed to be free."

At about this time, Greco rediscovered what he saw as the authentic spirit of skateboarding in Phoenix, where it was being kept alive by a group of slightly older skaters who called themselves the Piss Drunx.

Phoenix was beyond his wildest dreams. "Phoenix wasn't nothing but skating, getting fucked up and fucking broads," he says. Among the original Piss Drunx was his childhood idol, Randy Colvin. "He was chopping meat in a butcher shop," says Greco. "He didn't give a fuck. He could still skate." Colvin had turned his back on the world of pro skating and was hanging out with two Phoenix characters, Punker Matt and Jimmy "Moron" Moore, both in their mid-twenties. Punker Matt, a dedicated anarchist who has since moved to Oregon, and Jimmy Moron, a sometime water-quality analyst for the city, were both pool skaters.

Pool skating had fallen out of favor more than a decade earlier, condemning its practitioners to obscurity. "Jimmy Moron is one of the best skateboarders in the world," says Reynolds. "But no one will ever know about it."

To Greco, the Piss Drunx were "O.G., Original Gangsta, no-rules skaters." He came back to Huntington Beach with a PD tattoo and began listening to the New York Dolls and the Sex Pistols. He traded in baggy skate fashions for a lean punk style. He hung a life-size Sid Vicious poster on his wall. Later, when he posed in a skate magazine photo layout, he imitated that poster right down to the crooked snarl.

Soon, just about everyone in the Warner Avenue Mob had Piss Drunx tattoos. But no one else took their unspoken credo of being a "no-rules skater" to heart as Greco did. His behavior while touring with the Birdhouse team became increasingly outrageous. "He was a pile, drunk all the time, fighting," says Strickland. But Reynolds marveled at Greco's ability to draw crowds. "You'd go to a demo with the best skaters in the world, but Jim would get the biggest crowds. He'd be off at the edge of the parking lot, and he'd be drunk off of his ass doing ollies over a beer bottle."

Greco's attitude degenerated to the point that Tony Hawk finally fired him from the team. "He was the cause of so much tension," says Hawk. "Jim is chaos." Kicked out of the Birdhouse apartment, Greco couch-surfed Huntington Beach before being picked up by Jamie Thomas's Zero team. It was not the best match. Thomas, a born-again Christian with a "Jesus Saves" tattoo on his chest, tried to help Greco get sober, but Greco was having none of it. "Jamie means well," says Greco, "but that Jesus shit gets old fast."

Reynolds sneaked Greco back into the Birdhouse apartment, and Strickland began filming Greco, Reynolds and their Piss Drunx friends doing tricks. "It was just high jinks," says Greco. "We kept adding to it, and people would come over and be like, 'Put in that sick video.'"

In early 1999, Jay Strickland and Andrew Reynolds decided to quit Birdhouse and form their own company. They would have their own team, and design and sell their own boards, shirts, jeans and accessories like school book bags. Initially, they thought about calling the company Piss Drunx Skateboards, but, says Reynolds, "the Piss Drunx isn't something anybody can own." Besides, says Strickland, "parents probably wouldn't want their kids wearing Piss Drunx clothes to school. We ended up naming the company Baker Skateboards, after our friend Ali Boulala, who used to sit around all day getting baked."

Reynolds put up half the money and became majority owner. Hawk backed it with a distribution deal, and Strickland became the creative director. One of the first things he did was edit the Piss Drunx high-jinks tape into a raw but commercial product. Called *Baker Bootleg*, it was offered over the Internet. While the skating was unremarkable—Greco's portion consisted mostly of crude tapes made during his teenage years in Connecticut—the unapologetic scenes of Piss Drunx's cockeyed revelry caused a buzz, and the tape sold well.

Strickland took control of the day-to-day operations. Among the Piss Drunx, he was known as Suge because of his vision of turning Baker into the Death Row Records of the skateboard industry. He supervised the business strategy—what Greco calls the "dark stuff." "We wanted to make Baker into the biggest swindle in the industry," Strickland says. Their first act was to hire Greco. "People thought we were nuts."

Tony Hawk remains skeptical. "If Andrew wants Greco on his team, that's his choice," he says. "But it's too bad they don't have friend rehab where you can send people to kick bad friendships."

THE MORNING'S WINE AND JACK DANIEL'S have turned to fumes that fill Reynolds's car. Earlier that day, Greco had passed out before Reynolds made it to the skate spot. Before leaving him in the car to go skating by himself, Reynolds had placed a jacket over Greco, the way you cover something valuable to protect it from thieves. Now, arrived back at their new apartment, Reynolds lifts Greco from the car, then props him on his feet and walks him into the elevator. "Christ, Jim. We just move in, and everyone in the building's gonna think we're junkies," Reynolds says. The whole time, Greco's eyes are rolled back. He has strings of goo hanging from his chin. The two look like they're performing a set piece from a comedy in which someone has to walk around with a corpse and pretend it's alive.

When the elevator doors open, Greco falls to his knees and crawls all the way to his bedroom. Reynolds sits in the waning sunlight beneath high gallery windows. "Jim will be all right when he starts skating again," he says, with cracked hope.

A moment later, Greco's voice echoes from his room. He's talking on the phone to a girlfriend he calls Juice, which is short for his pet name for her, "Juicy Ass." Then, after a loud crash, Greco emerges from his room, half dressed, clutching a phone receiver by its torn cord. He beats the receiver against the wall until plastic bits fly off. "Who's holding the cards now?" Greco shouts at the broken phone.

Greco's theory of relationships is that they all boil down to whoever is "holding the cards." If, for example, you tell your girlfriend you love her, she gets all the cards. Sometimes, as Greco demonstrates by smashing the phone, a man needs his cards back. There are occasions when you might give your cards to that special person—if for example you want to hook up with a broad and do what Greco calls "rocking the side pipe" with her. But when that's over you will want your cards back, and to do this there is only one surefire method, "throw the broad's shit out on the front lawn."

Greco's card theory makes for tumultuous relations. Apparently, he is smashing the phone right now in an effort to get his cards back.

Reynolds approaches cautiously. "Just chill, Jim."

Greco drops the mangled phone. "I'm psychotic," he begins to chant, and stumbles back into his room.

"He goes through phases," says Reynolds. "I wish he would just snap out of this one."

A COUPLE OF DAYS LATER, at ten in the morning, Greco sits at his breakfast table sober and clear-eyed. He sips a cup of herbal detox tea that Reynolds has brewed for him. "I'm on a hammer program," he says, referring to the regimen of sobriety and exercise that he undertakes when skating. "I'm off the booze. I've got my appetite back." He points to a half-eaten 7-Eleven Bakery Stix hot dog. "I'm starting my stretching. I'm gonna skate a little.

Take care of my body. I'm gonna do some rips." He fires up a bong and sucks in a lungful.

He exhales. "If you derange your senses for so long with booze," he says, "physically, what it does to your body is baraka. Whenever I neglect skating, my life turns to shit."

Rest has made Greco uncharacteristically introspective. "The most main reason I skateboard," he says, "is the eight-second feeling I get when I ride away from a hammer. It's the most intense high there is. It builds juices up in my brain. That's how I get kicked on a hammer spree. I do one, and they just start popping. Next thing you know, you've got all these hammers and your life is going great. Because hammers is all kinds of things. Hammers is dough. Hammers is a nice place to live."

That afternoon, Greco walks out on the street in front of his building holding his skateboard. This is the first time he's been sober and capable of riding in a couple of weeks. He drops his board—a "Jim Greco" signature model, decorated on the bottom with a cartoon portrait of himself as a sneering punk-rock icon—onto the asphalt and steps on it. He rolls about twenty feet. He steps off the board and suddenly, and with no explanation, stomps it to splinters. "Fuck it," he says, then kicks over the shattered board. His cracked cartoon image on the bottom of the board faces up toward the sun-bleached Hollywood sky.

Earlier that week, a fourteen-year-old fan named Nick White had put his feelings for his hero into a letter he sent to Greco's fan club: "Deep inside us, we all want to be like Jim Greco. A part of all of us wants to live that type of lifestyle. But only one person can live that life: Greco. His style is amazing. Jim Greco lives for the danger. He tests himself and realizes he has no limits."

But even in the world of Jim Greco, there are limits. Like the one he faces now. Greco's at the front door of his building and he doesn't have a key. He studies the building directory a moment, telling me he will dial his apartment on the intercom and have Reynolds buzz him in, but he gives up. "I don't know what apartment I'm in," he says. Greco slumps on the ground and rubs his chin with a hand covered in scars from alcoholic fights and skating injuries. Greco smiles. "It's a nice day. Fuck it."

> The taxi-dance hall can never be entirely satisfactory as a sub-
> stitute for normal social life. . . . In its catering to detached and
> lonely people, in its deliberate fostering of stimulation and ex-
> citement, in its opportunities for pseudo-romantic excitements,
> it may be seen as an epitome of certain phases of urban life.
> —*Paul G. Cressey,* The Taxi-Dance Hall *(1932)*

P riscilla wears a green floral dress that falls to her knees. She looks about twenty-seven. Her hair and eyes are brown, and her lips are painted rose-petal red. She has a wholesome, decidedly 1940s appearance—accentuated by her sturdy high heels, which she refers to as "my Ginger Rogers dance shoes."

"Guys say they like me because I look clean," she says as she leads me to the Club Flamingo dance floor. It is dimmer here, screened off from the rest of the hall by a rickety wooden trellis. A string of plastic palm-tree lights hangs from the ceiling. A Journey song blares. Couples sit on leatherette benches along the walls, talking, lightly stroking each other's limbs, blowing into each other's ears, sometimes kissing, or just holding hands and staring dreamily at nothing.

Out on the floor, a black man in a white fedora, white suit and crimson shirt stands with his arms raised above his shoulders. He is skinny and tall and undulating in a manner that brings to mind a snake that is somehow standing upright. Two blond Latinas, considerably shorter, reach up, clasping his fingers and spinning slowly on either side as they rub his chest with their free hands.

Most couples have gravitated toward the far end of the floor, as if it were tilted in that direction. A squat pillar with a sign reading "No Lewd Behavior" blocks the darkest corner from view, forming the ideal location for attempts at lewd behavior. Here the dancers grind tightly, or cease dancing altogether and simply lock bodies. I glimpse a tall Asian girl in a long silk dress slit up the side. She stands on one leg. Her other leg is wrapped around her partner, a silver fox in a leisure suit. She hangs from his neck as he pumps intently against her.

"We call those 'corner girls,'" Priscilla says. Her own style of dance—draping her arms over my shoulders and swaying in a slow circle—is less vigorously sensual, yet there is an inescapable erotic charge. I find myself noticing that her perfume is pleasant. I enjoy the way her hair occasionally brushes my neck. It's the sort of boy-meets-girl dream a junior-high dance might have offered had I not invariably spent them getting stoned in the parking lot with friends. As her hips slide in my hands, I feel the slip she wears beneath her dress. I shut my eyes and picture her wearing only the slip, and we are someplace else, anyplace but Club Flamingo.

The eroticism of the moment is, of course, highly odd. Not only is Priscilla a complete stranger, but when we finish dancing to a few songs, she clocks me out on a punch card, whispering, "I'm not allowed to ask for a tip, but most customers feel comfortable tipping us at least fifty percent of the bill." The matron behind the counter tallies the minutes. I pay twelve dollars to the house for half an hour and slip Priscilla a five plus one dollar.

She returns to the couch behind the waist-high fence in the viewing area and waits for her next customer. Still feeling the flush of our intimate encounter, I wave to her on my way out. Priscilla scarcely makes eye contact. She engages a swarthy man in a gold shirt in a direct stare. He rises, apparently taken by the sight of a clean-looking girl, and approaches her for a dance.

IN 1932, UNIVERSITY OF CHICAGO sociologist Paul G. Cressey published *The Taxi-Dance Hall: A Sociological Study in Commercialized Recreation and City Life*, the summation of a five-year study of dance halls in Chicago. This form of entertainment had then, as now, a dubious reputation, but Cressey was more concerned with what he saw as the alienation, loneliness and moral ambiguity of urban life. He believed the taxi-dance hall expressed a fundamental truth about modern relations: a mobile, rapidly changing society produces cities inhabited by rootless, detached people who connect with each other primarily on the basis of mutual exploitation.

The postmodern reader, picking up Cressey's volume after a visit to Club Flamingo, or Club Paradise, or Dreamland, is struck by the convergence of his observations and one's own. In a passage that could describe the "corner girls" of the Flamingo, Cressey writes: "At times certain dancers seem to cease all semblance of motion over the floor, and while locked tightly together give themselves up to movements sensual in nature. . . . These couples tend to segregate at one end of the hall, where they mill about in a compressed pack of wriggling, perspiring bodies."

Cressey occasionally seems a little too fascinated by displays of sensuality, but he was no sexual moralist. What interested him was not that the taxi dancer functioned similarly to the prostitute in terms of hiring out her body, but that she also seemed to be selling her affection, emotional intimacy and the illusion of romance. He believed this barter of simulated emotions between the sexes—what he called the "pecuniary nexus displac[ing] personal relations"—was both a cause and a symptom of the psychological disorganization and demoralization that typified the modern urban experience.

Cressey grows increasingly pessimistic as his arguments stretch across three hundred pages. Everyone is alienated by the process. Loneliness increases. It becomes worse and worse, until we arrive in present-day L.A.— sixty-seven years beyond the scope of Cressey's tome—and discover that the phenomenon he despaired of is bigger than ever. Los Angeles has more "hostess clubs," as taxi-dance halls are called today, than at any other time in its history. There are about fourteen such establishments, according to club owners, most of them clustered downtown within half a mile of the convention center. They employ several hundred young women every night, and draw thousands of customers each week.

The clubs seem to bolster L.A.'s claim to being the most alienated city in America. But for a place whose citizenry is as jaded as L.A.'s is supposed to be, why do thousands of men in the city spend as much as several hundred dollars each per night to dance and hold hands, when the same money could buy direct gratification from any number of local massage parlors and out-call hooker services? Is it really possible to buy emotional intimacy, to soothe big-city loneliness by dancing with a stranger?

I AM ON MY SECOND DATE with Priscilla. (It's not realistic to consider a paid encounter a date, but it's impossible to avoid the natural expectations that arise when meeting an attractive woman under curious yet intimate circumstances. Some part of me wants to transform this abnormal experience into what Cressey called the "substitute for normal social life.") We are sitting on a black Naugahyde love seat in the TV room at the Flamingo, a gloomy hall on the second floor of a crumbling warehouse structure at Twelfth and Figueroa downtown. There are a dozen love seats like ours facing a grainy TV screen on which a violent movie is playing. . . . A man is being handcuffed to a car parked on a train track. A speeding locomotive is about to hit the man, now inescapably chained to the door handle of the car. . . . But no one is paying much attention. The couples scattered around us are tangled together, as they were on the benches along the edge of the dance floor. Few seem to be talking or moving much, and I don't look too hard. The dead stillness and rows of shabby, utilitarian couches bring to mind an airport waiting lounge where people have been waiting a long time.

Priscilla and I touch at the knees only. She talks at the rate of forty cents per minute. I have learned these facts about her: She was into punk rock back in the eighties (meaning she's a few years older than she looks to be in the dimness of the club). She moved to L.A. from the South ten years ago. No particular reason brought her here, though she likes the nature—the desert, canyons and coast—which she seldom sees because she drives a beater that barely makes it downtown, let alone out of the city. She takes classes at L.A. City College, and would like to transfer to a four-year university to study a science subject that doesn't entail too much math. She goes alone to Griffith Observatory once a week. She loves the view, the Foucault pendulum—contemplation of which makes her feel profoundly aware of the movement of the Earth—and the display of meteorites that have crashed through people's homes. She finds the latter amusing, and it makes her laugh. Her favorite film is *Once Upon a Time in the West*; she's haunted by the recurring harmonica riff that's revealed at the end to be the song Charles Bronson played as a child when Henry Fonda hanged his older brother. She used to be a drug addict. She adores her father, an accountant, and has not told her parents that she has worked as a hostess dancer for three years.

"I thought I'd walked into *Twin Peaks*," Priscilla says, describing her first impression of Club Flamingo. "But I'm one of those people that when it says, 'Bubbly, energetic waitress wanted for sports bar,' I know that I don't apply for that job. There's a lot of freedom in this job. The hours are flexible. You make minimum wage plus tips, which can go anywhere from fifty to two hundred a night. If I don't like a guy, I clock him out. I don't have to talk to a guy if I don't want to. I used to cocktail at a shithole on Venice—you think a waitress can decide not to serve a table because she doesn't like the customer?"

I remind Priscilla that on or about our fourth dance the night we met, she had begun to run her hand up and down my back. I ask her if such affection is normal with her customers, a question that causes her hand to recoil from my leg, where for several minutes her fingers had been tracing agreeable-feeling patterns above my knee.

"When I'm dancing, I like to feel like I'm at a gathering or a ball," she says, shifting away from me. "I'll touch a guy—I mean like just his back, when we're dancing—because it's kind of a nervous thing with my hands. If somebody is nice, it just seems natural. If somebody's really gross, and I'm afraid they're going to get a hard-on, then I don't touch them. There are things I won't do just to get a tip. I will not go and grind some freak in the corner.

"There are guys that come on real fast on the dance floor—grabbing your hips, centering you, trying to aim, thrusting. You know? I can't handle the pseudo-rape scene. But eighty percent of these girls are supporting some guy or a kid at home. A lot of them are eighteen and very naive. Some of them aren't wound too tight. They totally make out with the guys, full-on French kiss, whatever. Some of these girls sing into the guys' ears on the dance floor. It's really cheesy. Total corn. I'll see the girl in the bathroom, and she'll say, 'This guy gives me a rush.' And I just think, My God.

"But those girls you see in the corner, doing the old whatever, they will consistently make two or three hundred a night in tips, which is more than I do. There are cameras in the club, there are security guards, and the cops come in here. If a girl is caught doing anything wrong, she's fired on the spot. But there are girls that will let guys feel them up. Or they'll put a jacket over the guy's lap and jerk him off. There's not a lot of that here, but it goes on."

Our conversation lasts an hour and a half and costs $36, plus a $20 tip.

CLUB PARADISE, next to the Empire 900 Motel on Olympic Boulevard, strives for a sixties cocktail-lounge ambiance, with dark red walls and swoopy velour lounge chairs, but it nevertheless remains a dump along the lines of the Flamingo. It operates under the same time-clock, punch-card system, but here all the girls are Latino, as are about eighty percent of the men. Tonight many of the girls wear bikini tops and plastic hula skirts, since it's Thursday, which is always "Hawaiian Night." Others wear pretty white dresses suitable for Sunday confirmation, and a few are dressed in filmy, see-through things, such as the young lady in a green-chiffon genie outfit that provides more or less naked views of her white thong panties and brassiere.

The surprise at Club Paradise is not the show of pathetic Hawaiian costumes, nor the displays of flesh put on by some of the girls. The surprise is the dance floor. Club Flamingo–style grinders form a distinct minority. Most of the dancers here skillfully execute formal Latin dance moves. White skirts billow and hula skirts blur as the girls are gracefully flung about by men who seem to know what they're doing. Even the klutzes—young, skinny guys in plaid shirts and jeans who probably spend their days washing dishes or operating leaf blowers—attempt the minimum of a box step, holding their partners stiffly, looking at their feet as they count.

I meet a thirty-year-old white guy, Phil, by the (nonalcoholic) bar. He leans against the wall with his hands buried in his pockets throughout our entire conversation. Despite his boyish blond features, he exudes a shifty vibe, perhaps because he never makes direct eye contact, as he continually looks over my shoulder at the girls wandering the room. He says he's a customer-service representative for an express-mail company and has been coming to hostess clubs for five years.

"Where else can you go and see hot chicks in miniskirts, and you clock 'em in, and two minutes later you've got your hand on her ass?" Phil asks. "You want to feel 'em up, you can. You go to a regular bar and they sock you for drinks. Chicks don't talk to you, anyway."

"What are the rules here?" I ask.

"Money rules, my friend," Phil says. "Here at the Paradise, the girls are nicer. At the Flamingo, there're some nasty girls. Real hotties. But they'll hustle you for everything you've got. Get this, I used to see this chick at the Flamingo. She had real big, big cans. There was a lips tattoo on one of her titties. She disappeared over a year ago. Then, a few months ago, my buddy and me were watching a porno—two dudes doing the same chick. It was her, the chick from the Flamingo. She was in a porno!"

"How many girls have you dated from the clubs?"

"Twelve. I got most in the sack, but not all. The last one was number eight."

"Number eight?" I ask.

"Number eight. It's the number on her dance card, a girl from a club on Spring Street. Her name's Eve. She's hot. A couple of weeks ago I got her to my parents' house—I live with my mom and dad—and got her into my bedroom. I stripped her and ate her out.

"The trick to getting some from a girl is she has to see you around a few times. If there's a girl you dig, clock her in three nights, and you can usually get her phone number and a date.

"Go to Dreamland if you want action. The girls don't hustle as much as the chicks at Flamingo, but do they put out? Heck, yeah. I've seen a girl riding a guy at Dreamland. It was real dark in there. Used to be a big fern there you could hide behind, pretty much do anything you want with a girl."

Phil peels himself off the wall, signaling the end of the conversation. "I think Ruby's here. I've been waiting for her."

"Is she one of your girlfriends?"

"Nah, just a friend," Phil says. "But sometimes she lets me take her into the corner and suck on her titties."

I leave twenty minutes later. Phil still leans against the wall.

THE PARKING-LOT SECURITY GUARD grins when I tell him I'm going to Dreamland.

"Looking for a girl?" he inquires in a conspiratorial whisper.

"What's the best technique for getting one?" I ask.

"The girl wants you to dance, to tip with all your money. Maybe she gives you something, maybe not. It all depends on how much you want to pay for a piece of beef."

The metaphor seems appropriate when I am once again seated in a viewing gallery.

The nucleus of any downtown dance hall is the viewing gallery/selection area, wherein the girls are displayed on couches like market produce. Club Starlight, whose interior resembles a collision between the traditional Chinese opium den and a 1970s disco, deviates from the norm with a totally separate girl chamber. It is a well-lit glassed-in room, stocked with young dancers reading *Cosmo* and *Allure*, doing their nails or gossiping. It's a high-girlie scene, like that of a beauty parlor. Men are not allowed to enter. Instead, they point to the desired girl in the window, and a matron is sent in to retrieve her.

The girls-on-couch system is almost creepier—especially in the clubs where there is no fence marking off the female territory—because it so flagrantly violates social standards. We men sit at tables across from the girls. We stare. It is disconcerting to sit among strange men, all of us visibly sober (since dance halls aren't licensed to serve liquor) and silent. We simply stare. In Dreamland I sit next to an Asian man in dungarees. His hair is long and disheveled. He pulls his chair up close to the couch of girls, to within three feet. He sits for two hours. Occasionally he yawns, holding his gaze like a cat.

Cressey observed the same phenomenon in 1932, noting that "ogling, in fact, seems here to be the chief occupation of the male."

Brazen public ogling that in normal social intercourse would be deemed disrespectful, hostile or predatory seems to be one of the chief perks of the five-dollar admission fee to any of L.A.'s dance halls. (A high proportion of customers never seem to dance.) But it is also a critical element of the selection process. We are customers, and we have the right to inspect what we are paying for. We are, of course, buying beauty, but we are also purchasing friendliness (if we have had a rough day and wish to avoid conflict), sympathy (if we care to talk about our problems), romantic desirability (if we hope to fall in love) or sluttiness (if we are here basically to feel someone up and perhaps obtain a hand job or similar favors).

Indeed, the whole woman-as-meat worldview is one of the illusions being sold in dance halls that quickly falls apart. It holds up reasonably well so long as the girls are just being looked at from across the room. It crumbles the moment contact is established, not merely because many of the girls resist being treated that way, but because even those who encourage anonymous, impersonal groping are making economic calculations based on their own self-interest. They are trying to get a bigger tip by exploiting the weakness of the male fantasy. United on the dance floor, the woman feels for the man's wallet as he feels for her body.

The sign outside the Fenton Building on Spring Street is original, a two-story neon ribbon hanging on the north corner. It flashes "DANCING" in white, then blinks to red letters that spell "GIRLS." The club itself is reached through an interminable ride on a freight elevator. Inside Dreamland, the stage where swing bands once played has been plastered over, as have the cathedral windows, in order to create flat, even walls, uniformly painted matte black except for the holes where people have punched their fists through for reasons now lost to posterity. Unfortunately, the club's famous "Anything Goes" Wednesday-night wet-T-shirt contest has been canceled this evening, apparently due to lack of interest. Most of the clientele mill around the pool tables, furiously smoking cigars and cigarettes beneath the "No Smoking" signs while conducting loud, polyglot conversations on cell phones.

The viewing area is nearly pitch-black. Overweight twentysomething Latinas sprawl on the couches. Excess flesh spills out from halter tops and underwear worn as outer garments. Sitting alone at one end of a couch is a green-eyed blond. Her legs are so long that her knees almost brush her chin.

Entering meat-consumer mode, I make my choice. Katya is twenty-one years old, from Orange County. She wears a stretch miniskirt and bare-midriff top. Her skirt is bunched up on one side, an appealing kind of slop-piness that carries over in her loose, hip-swaying gait. I think to myself that Phil, my romance adviser from Club Paradise, would be proud of my selection. I've found a hottie.

Katya yanks me against her on the dance floor. The embrace is forceful and direct, like someone hugging a refrigerator in order to move it. "You look like my father," she says. "In pictures when he was young, before he got sick."

"Is he OK?"

"He's schizophrenic."

One other couple dances. A stocky man in a gray suit—perhaps forty-five, handsome and blond, a well-fed downtown businessman with a gold wedding band on his finger—and a short, chunky Latina wearing a black negligee as a dress. The woman is older than the other dancers, somewhere between thirty-five and forty-five. Her partner has backed her against a mirrored wall. He pulls her negligee up and watches the reflection of his hands fondling her red satin panties.

Katya glimpses the peep show in the mirror and stiffens, as if with revulsion. "I'm tired," she says. "Can we sit down?"

The Dreamland TV room offers the same airport ambiance as the Flamingo's. Katya presses into the opposite end of the love seat, pointedly avoiding physical contact, which is good, because she gestures frequently with her long arms. I wince several times, fearing she's going to hit me in the eye.

"My problem is focus." Katya bangs her knuckles on her forehead. "Up here, in my mind. I'm diagnosed as ADD, attention deficit disorder?" She stares with dilated pupils. "I grew up on Ritalin, but it wasn't strong enough. I smoked crystal meth in high school. Now I'm clean. My doctor put me on Dexedrine."

The poor girl is whacked out on speed.

"I'm an actress. You know, I'm in a workshop, and I do a performance about working here? This is it." Katya waves her hands as I duck. "We go in front of the class, and we mime to three songs. I start with Madonna, 'Live to Tell,' because of her prostitute image, which is how I feel working here. Then I play 'People Are Strange.' The Doors. Because that's how I feel about the world and people in here.

"I do my whole act like I'm in my bedroom getting dressed for work. I'm holding a teddy bear. It's a symbol for, like, growing up, but I'm still like a child inside. The last song I play is the Police, 'Roxanne.' When they sing, 'You don't have to put on the red light,' I go into a rage. I tear the head off my teddy bear." She flings her wrist. "Then I rip his guts out and kick him across the stage."

Katya's recitation, which also includes dramatic monologues from her favorite film, *Frances*, costs more than $75. We spend two hours and ten minutes together.

My attempt to select a girl merely as a piece of meat is an abysmal failure. Doing my best to find a girl who would "put out" in a Phil-my-romantic-adviser sense, I instead choose a dance partner who hates her job, seems conflicted by displays of sexual promiscuity, has a history of psychopharmacological treatment, clings desperately to unfulfilled dreams, is deeply angry, speaks openly of a father fixation and is just too tired to dance. In short, Katya is exactly the type of woman I invariably select when dating in the real world. No doubt, were I to make visits to Dreamland a habit, I would ask Katya to dance again. I might fall in love.

VERONICA IS THE ONLY DANCER I encounter who leaps from the viewing couch and insists we dance. Coming from any other girl in a hostess club, an aggressive move like hers might feel like a hustle. But Veronica radiates joy.

She holds my hand over her head on the dance floor and spins. Her smile flashes each time her eyes lock onto mine. She is dark-skinned, with delicate features. She tells me she comes from Brazil. Her mother brought her to America when she was eight.

"My mother was difficult." She wraps both her arms around me, then springs away.

"How so?" I catch the dervish in my arms again.

"My mother whipped me. She burned me. She suffocated me. She knocked out two of my teeth. She scarred my back. And there was a little sexual abuse, too."

Veronica reels off this list of horrors in a cheerful singsong. She tells me she hopes to go to school someday to become a psychiatrist, so she can help other girls with backgrounds like her own.

Later, we go to the TV lounge. Veronica raises her skirt and shows me her bare ass, wanting to know if I like it. She admits she's not sure if she wants to go to medical school first or act in porn movies.

Veronica is twenty-one, and her body looks perfect, but she is saving for plastic surgery. She has $2,100 stuffed in a sock hidden somewhere in her apartment that will cover breast implants.

"I will make myself look like a Barbie doll," she says. "I'll be perfect."

SERGEANT ROBERT VELIZ, of LAPD Central Vice Unit, sighs wearily throughout our interview. His beat is to investigate dance halls for lewd conduct and prostitution. I sense he is frustrated, and might have more on-the-job satisfaction if he could arrest more citizens.

The problem with dance halls, as Veliz outlines it, is that some customers do utilize the girls purely for sexual gratification. However, no one can be arrested unless caught committing a lewd act (such as direct hand-to-genital contact), or unless prostitution can be established (i.e., a customer pays a girl to perform a specific sexual act). If a man tips a dancer generously because she allows him to rub himself on her leg, and he climaxes as a byproduct of their dance, no crime can be established. In short, Sergeant Veliz cannot arrest citizens for what occurs in the privacy of their own pants. By all accounts, the used condoms I observe in the restrooms of various clubs are merely leftovers from lawfully obtained frottage.

"Who is most exploited in the clubs?" I ask Sergeant Veliz. "The customers or the hostesses?"

"Indirectly, the girls. Directly, the men," he says. He adds with a final sigh, "Those girls work the guys any which way they can."

Taxi-dance halls sprang up in the 1920s and 1930s in major cities across the United States in response to a social-reform movement that had sought to wipe out prostitution. (The same reformist wave sweeping the land also ushered in Prohibition, the Hays Commission and the federal government's first serious efforts to suppress the leafy scourge, marijuana.) The bordellos and red-light districts that had thrived openly following the post–Civil War industrial boom were shut down by the late teens. In San Francisco, bar owners immediately began hiring unemployed prostitutes to work as hostesses. Their job was to lure customers and ply them with drinks while entertaining them on the dance floor. These establishments became known as "closed" dance halls, meaning they were closed to couples. Men only were invited; women were provided gratis.

At the same time, dance instruction academies in New York and Chicago, teaching the latest fox-trot, Charleston and tango moves, began seeing a rise in patronage. The new breed of customer seemed less interested in footwork than in simply holding a woman. Many of these dance academies employed a uniform payment system in which students purchased tickets good for a single lesson that lasted the duration of one song. The female instructors frequently sat on chairs or couches in a gallery while waiting for students to show up with tickets.

It is believed that a Chicago-based Greek immigrant started the first taxi-dance hall after a trip to San Francisco, where he had been impressed by the success of closed dance halls. Returning to Chicago, he and his brothers borrowed the ticket-a-dance system as well as the girls-on-a-couch setup from the dance academies and opened the first hall dedicated exclusively to renting women as dance partners. (Thus the "taxi" in "taxi dancer.")

The idea spread to Los Angeles, and by the early 1930s there were at least four halls operating downtown. The dancers became known as "dime-a-dance girls" or "nickel hoppers." The halls continued to flourish after Prohibition ended in 1933, and ten years later, at the height of World War II, two Los Angeles brothers, Ed and Ben Fenton, took over a club called Roseland Roof, at 833 South Spring Street. They soon eliminated the ticket-a-dance system and replaced it with the punch clock.

Roseland Roof never really shut its doors. Although taxi dancing died out in most American cities by the 1960s (when it became quaintly obsolete against the onslaught of the sexual revolution), the Fentons continued to run their hall until 1981. By this time, the swing bands they had employed were long since gone, and the dancers no longer wore formal gowns on Friday nights. Despite changing mores, the Fentons found a buyer for Roseland Roof when they retired, and it continues to operate today, as Dreamland, occupying the same ballroom that had served Roseland Roof since it opened in 1933.

Edward Fenton, ninety-one, stands at the window in his second-floor office in the Fenton Building. He shows me the corner on Spring Street where he sold newspapers in the early twenties, and then recalls the night his brother phoned to ask if he wanted to go in with him in purchasing

Roseland Roof. Ben was an attorney who had been representing the club's owner since 1938, and in "nineteen hundred and forty-three" the owner wanted to sell.

"I'd never heard of a place like this," Fenton says. "I didn't have any idea how it was operated. I came here on a Thursday night to check the place out. I see a bunch of women and a bunch of customers, and I say, 'What's this business all about?' So my brother explained it to me, and I said, 'Not a bad idea. How's the supply of girls?' And he said, 'We don't have any problem with that.'"

I ask Fenton to describe the old days, the color, the spirit.

"Well . . ." He pauses, thinking a long time. "The customers wore neckties. They were well-dressed."

"Is there anything else you can think of?"

"The customer was lonely, that's the word. The club brought in lonesome people. They came here to meet with girls and carry on a secret romance."

"You mean they had affairs with the girls?"

"No. I didn't say that." Fenton appears momentarily annoyed with my complete ignorance. "The customer lived in a fantasy."

THE SMELL OF LYSOL mingles with perfume in Club Fantasy, located in a basement on Third Street. It is smaller and cleaner than the other establishments. The walls are freshly painted. It has the feel of a community-center rec room in which most of the lights have blown out. Drinks (soft) are served in styrofoam cups.

"There is a spiritualness about this place," says Ted, the manager, a third-generation Asian-American and former used-car dealer. He stands by the viewing gallery, surveying his club. "There is a whole conglomerate of emotion in here. It is more than it looks like.

"On the surface, behavior is based on a code of law. If the customer makes certain demands on the girl, he will go to jail. But there is also a psychological code. The customer is lonely for a woman. On a date, a girl might make him feel inadequate, like he isn't funny enough or interesting, or he doesn't earn enough money. He comes here to detox from reality.

"One-third of my customers are regulars. They enjoy themselves here every night, even though most are spending two to three times their hourly wages, and for what? So they can dance and talk to my girls."

Ted waives the two-drink minimum at the viewing tables and allows me to sit for free. An Asian man in a white tropical suit slips into the seat next to me. He is powerfully built and moves with athletic grace.

"If two strangers meet more than one time, it is destiny," the man in white says, tipping his styrofoam cup. "I have seen you at Club Flamingo, no? Would you like a Coke or a 7UP?" He signals the waitress—an almost imperceptible flutter of his hand. The gesture is pure class.

"You think this place is a dump, yes?" He reads my expression accurately. "You are not correct. It is never the location. It is the women. If they are beautiful, the club is beautiful."

My new friend's name is Lee. He started coming to hostess clubs five years ago, two years after he arrived in America. He has worked as a bit player in martial-arts films. He continues acting in Asian films shot in L.A., and manages a restaurant in Beverly Hills.

"I first came to these clubs because I had a handicap," he says. "I am a foreigner. My English was very bad. I needed girls to talk to. I was so lonely." Lee's excellent English is a testament to his years of study at various clubs. "In Asia, hostess clubs are very common. I know the idea offends many Americans. I tried going to regular clubs, but the girls in Los Angeles are game players. How can I approach them just to talk? The girl here talks to me. How can she refuse? She is making the money."

"Does the fact that you pay them make them prostitutes?" I ask.

"These girls are not prostitutes." Lee raises his voice, offended. "The problem is the customer." He leans toward me. "The majority of the customer is the geek. They are not attractive men. They are not fun to be with. Some of them try to treat the girl like a prostitute. But she is not.

"One time I had sex with a girl from a club. We danced until she finished work. I walked her to her car, and we had sex. I offered her money, and she threw it at me. I dated her for three months."

"And you never paid her?"

"I did, but for a reason. She had a boyfriend and a kid. If she saw me and didn't go to work at her club, how could she come home with no money? So I did pay her each time she came to my house. But she was not a prostitute. The money was an alibi."

Lee hastens to add, "That happened four years ago. But I keep coming back. Why? If I wanted physical satisfaction, I would go to a prostitute. Here it is mental.

"I am in love with a girl at one of the clubs. I met her two years ago. I see her every week two times, two hours each time."

"And you tip her?"

"Fifty dollars each time, plus fifty for the club. I spend two hundred dollars a week on her."

I add up two years of this courtship: $20,000.

Lee laughs. "And I never touch her. If I touch her, she gets mad."

"Have you ever seen her outside of the club?"

"I went to her house last week and cooked dinner for her."

"This was the first time you saw her at her home?"

"The second time. The first time was three months ago. I rented a truck to help her move into a new apartment."

At ten to eleven, Lee leaves. He has an appointment to meet his "girl-friend" at her club. Once a week he brings her shrimp on dry ice from his restaurant.

Cressey writes: "Many of the romantically inclined patrons crave affection and feminine society to such an extent that they accept willingly the illusion of romance offered in the taxi-dance hall. . . . They usually lead a rather detached life and sometimes give vent to city loneliness by an ardent and sincere wooing of the taxi-dancer. . . . If receiving a good wage, they may even lavish gifts upon their favorite taxi-dancers."

Gift-giving stories abound at hostess clubs. Girls often speak of presents that have been lavished on them in the past. I wonder if these aren't *Pretty*

Woman fantasies dreamed up or exaggerated to make a depressing job more tolerable. But I meet several former hostess dancers—a clothing designer (the wife of a friend), a website designer, an advertising sales rep for a magazine—who corroborate the tales of generosity I have heard.

"I worked at the Flamingo for three months," the advertising sales rep tells me during her lunch break at a mid-Wilshire restaurant. "It was right after I came to L.A. after graduating from college. I couldn't stand sitting on the couch like a cattle call, but I used to ask myself how would it compare to working at a place like Hooters. Hooters is predicated on beer and boobs. The Flamingo is predicated on romance, however twisted that sounds. There were lots of creeps there, but lots of guys go there to fall in love. People don't go to Hooters to fall in love.

"There was a guy who came in one night. I had never met him before. He had hair apnea—meaning it grows from your head in clumps. He asked me to stand next to him while he played pool. After his game, he walked me to the window behind the pool table. We were just looking out the window at the city, and I said, 'Look at the blue sky-light at night.' He said I had reminded him of a poem. He opened up his wallet and handed me ten one-hundred-dollar bills. He never asked for anything from me."

RUMORS OF OBSESSED CUSTOMERS whose fixations have boiled over into violence also circulate freely in the clubs. Several of the girls mention an incident last spring, a fatal stabbing, or shooting. One tells me, definitely, it was a close friend of hers who was strangled in the parking lot, but it wasn't by a customer, it was her jealous boyfriend.

"The attacker's name was Amolak Singh," Detective Russell Long of LAPD Central Homicide states in a telephone interview. "He was East Indian or Pakistani, although the man spoke fluent Spanish.

"The young woman was employed at the Las Palmas Club. At approximately two forty-five A.M. on April 8, Singh shot the young woman outside the Las Palmas Club when she got off work. She was wounded, but she did not die. She has recovered, as far as we know.

"An off-duty police officer was employed by the club as a security guard. He ran out when he heard the shots. He fired his gun and fatally shot the young woman's attacker, Singh." (Indeed, the off-duty officer reportedly shot Singh eight times, the final two rounds going into Singh's body while he lay on the ground.)

Detective Long says Singh had had no contact with the young woman outside the club. But "he was definitely obsessed with the victim."

MY LAST TAXI DANCE is with a girl in plum-colored velour hot pants and a matching tube top. A silver ring on her index finger covers the first two joints; it flexes in the middle and is crafted to look like a miniature leg from a suit of armor. The girl's name is Sarah, and she says she's an artist, but she can't draw, so she color-copies images she likes at Kinko's and makes collages. She says her collages are six by ten feet; I imagine the Kinko's bills must be large.

It is a slow night, and the dance floor is nearly empty. Sarah squeezes next to me in a booth by the dance floor and puts her hand on my leg.

"I've never been to one of these clubs," I tell her. "Is this a sex club?"

Sarah's hand freezes. "No. Gentlemen come here to enjoy themselves. A lot of people say these clubs are sleazy. They're not. These are nice girls."

"Why do people come here?"

"Gentlemen come here to be with attractive young girls. It's not a place to cheat. My customers say coming here is foreplay for going home to their wives. A lot of my customers are friends. We go back years."

"You mean you know all about them?" I ask. "They're 'friends' like you call them up, ask them how their day went, go to the movies, visit them in the hospital if they're sick?"

"No," she says, "I never see them outside the club. They're only friends here, when I'm working."

"You ever date a guy from this place?"

"I would never date a guy from this place." Sarah removes her hand from my leg. "I have a boyfriend."

"Having a boyfriend must be tough."

"My boyfriend says he can't trust me, because I make my living touching people." She adds, "He always brings up my job when he makes a mistake."

"What kind of mistake?"

"Cheats on me."

Sarah looks incredibly sad, and I am sorry to be sitting with her, carrying on a lying conversation in order to elicit something personal from her. I tell her it's time to clock out.

She clamps her hand on me. I look around the half-empty club. There are few prospects for Sarah tonight. I may be her only chance for a good tip.

"My boyfriend says his cheating is a Clinton thing."

"Clinton?"

Her armored finger crosses a boundary. Sarah places her hand in a position that in Sergeant Veliz's book would probably constitute lewd conduct. She looks directly into my eyes.

"A Clinton thing. My boyfriend says some sex isn't cheating. Not even if someone gives you a blow job. What do you think?"

In 1932, Cressey saw the modern city fragmenting into "a mosaic of contradictory moral worlds." He saw a future in which city dwellers, fundamentally detached from one another, move among these contradictory worlds, forming temporary alliances of mutual exploitation according to their needs.

The taxi-dance halls of today, which appear to be little more than seedy anachronisms, may in fact be the realization of that future—not substitutes for normal social life, but what is normal today. Isn't the bartering of money for cheap fantasy what L.A. is all about?

I HAVE MY THIRD DATE with Priscilla. I show up at her bungalow apartment on a Sunday afternoon.

"Oh God," she says, opening the door. "I totally forgot to call you. I have to go in to work in ten minutes. Come in anyway."

There's a computer on the kitchen table. Science textbooks are jumbled beside it. She boils water in a frying pan on the stove and makes me a cup of instant coffee.

"Sorry I don't have any milk." She stands at the mirror. Her hair is pinned up. She removes the pins and combs it out. "I always wear my hair down. I don't make my dance card if I wear it in a bun," she says.

We step outside into the courtyard. Unseen neighbors can be heard shouting through thin walls, a multicultural cacophony. Busted screens flap out of windows. There's a broken lamppost. Someone has placed an empty can of beans where the light used to be.

"I'm the only one that works in this courtyard," Priscilla says. "I'm the only one that doesn't live in a one-bedroom with ten other people.

"My neighbors call me 'the bitch.' The lady who lives next door came up to me the other morning. 'I'll kick your ass, bitch,' she said. 'You bore me,' I said. She was totally confused."

Priscilla stops. She notices I have a new car.

"Is that yours?"

I nod.

"We could drive someplace in your car." She thinks about it for a moment. "I love nature. We could drive someplace far out of the city. I'll call you." Her smile is clean and warm, and I never hear from her again.

WINGNUT'S LAST DAY ON EARTH

It's a couple of Saturdays before Christmas at the Out of the Fog coffee shop in Eugene, Oregon, a place where Santa Claus is just another capitalist oppressor. The Fog, ground zero for Eugene's thriving anarchist population, is located in a warehouse at the edge of town. A young man who calls himself "Wingnut" sits at a rickety wooden table on the loading dock. A week ago Wingnut was living atop an old fir tree west of town to prevent it from being cut down by loggers, but in just the past few days his life has gotten considerably more complicated, and now it looks like he had better get out of Eugene quickly.

Wingnut, twenty-six, is one of about twenty local anarchists who nearly a week earlier crashed the demonstrations at the World Trade Organization (WTO) conference in Seattle. Conference organizers, among them President Clinton, had intended this meeting to cap a decade of efforts to reduce trade barriers and usher in a new era of globalization. Tens of thousands of protesters opposed to the WTO had begun converging on the city days before the conference began. They planned attention-getting but peaceful demonstrations. An advance cadre of anti-WTO organizers had rented warehouses where they built floats and constructed elaborate "street theater protest costumes" that would call attention to species and habitats threatened by globalization. They would take on the forces of transnational capitalism by dressing as endangered sea turtles and owls. So efficient were their preparations, organizers planned a brigade of volunteers whose sole job would be to march alongside the sea turtle and owl people—as well as the steelworkers and other labor union protesters, the socialists, the students and "Free Mumia" people—and pick up their litter. Organizers whom I interviewed days before the protests revealed an obsession for order that likely would have impressed the corporate interests they were taking on. In one meeting I sat in on, they used Microsoft PowerPoint to lay out organizational charts for their nonviolent protests.

But within hours of the peaceful demonstrations beginning on the morning of November 29, Seattle's four hundred riot police deployed on the streets began firing tear gas, pepper spray and rubber bullets into the crowd of nonviolent protesters. Tens of thousands of demonstrators, WTO attendees and downtown office workers were caught up in the melee. Much of downtown Seattle was enveloped in clouds of tear gas and smoke from trash fires (some set by tear gas canisters, which detonate with a small, fiery explosion; others set by protesters). State police, then National Guardsmen armed with military-grade CS tear gas, joined the fray. More than five hundred citizens were arrested. But Wingnut and his anarchist friends from Eugene were not among those arrested. For four days, they eluded the paramilitary crackdown and roamed the city, smashing windows, throwing rocks at police, setting fires and redecorating storefronts with anticorporate slogans. The rampage cost Seattle business owners some $20 million.

Police, the media and many nonviolent protesters have blamed the anarchists for sparking the riots, and anarchists like Wingnut are more than happy to take the credit. "The Battle of Seattle," as the media have since dubbed the four days of rioting, was a high point for American anarchists in terms of their ability to wreak havoc and draw attention to themselves, which are key goals of the movement. Havoc, as they see it, makes the state look incompetent and forces it to expose its true face of repressive brutality, typically in the guise of club-wielding, tear gas–spewing police. Attention, it's believed, attracts more followers to the cause, bringing them closer to their final goal: revolution. As one would expect, overthrow of the state and allied corporate entities remains the traditional goal of most anarchists. But where anarchists used to see themselves as battling to defend the human spirit from the degradations of the state, the goal of the movement, as it has evolved in the past fifteen years or so, is to defend the environment from the degradations of humankind. The state remains the enemy, but not because it destroys the individual's soul. Instead, the state must be dismantled because it allows the clear-cutting of forests, the creation of genetically modified crops and the construction of ski resorts on pristine mountains. As Wingnut inevitably says, when asked by police who his leader is, "I work for Mother Earth, arrest her."

In the Battle of Seattle, Wingnut was at the center of the action, earning a reputation as one of Eugene's most hard-core revolutionaries. He fought cops and National Guardsmen, brawled with security guards, "unarrested" three friends by yanking them from the arms of the police, and almost single-handedly wrecked a Starbucks, a Gap and a McDonald's.

"Wingnut kicked a lot of ass for all of us," says Carlos, one of Wingnut's comrades in the riots.

In the past few days, images of anarchists have been splashed across national television, picked up in shaky news camera shots as they ran through smoke-filled streets, smashing windows with rocks and rebars. Nobody's identifiable in the footage because the anarchists wore some form of dark hooded jacket and mask—initially, the media called them "the Black Clads"—but it did make them easy to locate on the streets of Seattle.

I found Wingnut's group of cohorts on the third night of the riot. They were sitting along the curb of a side street in the Capitol Hill district of

Seattle, resting while a few blocks away riot police were launching tear gas canisters and concussion grenades on Broadway, the main commercial street of the district. There were no civilians out on Broadway at the time. Police were apparently just trying to keep it clear, or perhaps were simply blowing off their less lethal weapons out of frustration. Coming upon Wingnut and the other black-clad kids (some as young as sixteen), I introduced myself as a reporter. They spoke cautiously at first and denied being responsible for any of the vandalism in the city, until Wingnut stepped forward and told me he believed that destroying property was a valid form of protest. He invited me to follow him on a "direct action mission" to find a Starbucks whose windows were still intact and smash them.

I followed Wingnut and a hooded girl (whose face I never saw but who sounded to be in her mid-teens) to a Starbucks near Pioneer Square, about a forty-five-minute walk distant. The girl produced a heavy crescent wrench from a knapsack and handed it to Wingnut as we neared the shop. She remained across the street to serve as lookout. Wingnut asked if I was interested in going with him up to the window. It was a dare.

Since he was about to commit a relatively minor act of vandalism, I didn't experience much moral angst about the deed itself. The more important question was whether my presence as a journalist would be inciting the act, altering my subject's behavior, which would in the strictest sense falsify the reporting. But given the enthusiasm Wingnut expressed for property destruction I concluded that he was probably going to break that window this night whether a reporter was with him or not.

So I followed him to the window. His first blow bounced off the glass. The second made a wrench-size slice in the glass. Wingnut wound up for a harder strike, but the girl across the street shouted a "Hey," indicating that someone was coming. The three of us walked off. For me, it was a disappointing foray into revolution. But my willingness to follow Wingnut seemed to satisfy him that I could be sort of trusted. Wingnut and his friends invited me to follow them to a warehouse loft they were sleeping in across town, and the next day we left for Eugene, driving in an old Chevy Cavalier borrowed from an anarchist sympathizer.

Wingnut is about five-eight and slightly built, but with the large, power-ful hands of someone who is good at physical labor, such as laying bricks, fixing cars or learning to assemble land mines from objects commonly avail-able at the hardware store—all of which are activities Wingnut discusses with ease. (While Wingnut claims to know how to build bombs, he main-tains he has not yet used one. He later admits to helping set fires to burn down an empty ski lodge in Colorado, and when discussing the evils of corporations that sell genetically modified crops he argues that the final solution may be to "blow up the motherfucking buildings.")

Wingnut lives on food scavenged from trash dumpsters or shoplifted from stores. Theft from corporations is an honorable means of survival, according to his anarchist code. It ensures that as little capitalist lucre as possible dirties his hands. He does not own a car, rent an apartment or sleep in a bed, ever. Before his stay in Seattle, Wingnut had spent just about every night of the past eighteen months sleeping in a "tree sit"—a ten-by-twelve-foot pad—perched 170 feet up a fir tree outside Eugene that was slated to be cut down by a local lumber company.

Aside from the practical benefits of Wingnut's black hoodie—it keeps him warm, shades him from the sun and makes him blend in easily with a crowd—Wingnut is proud of the fact that the hoodie gives him a passing resemblance to the famed composite sketch of his hero the Unabomber. Wingnut feels Ted Kaczynski is a misunderstood author. "The corporate-controlled media makes him look like a maniac."

Wingnut's mask, a black bandanna that he wears around his neck but which can be pulled over his face at a moment's notice, is a tribute to another of his heroes, Subcomandante Marcos, leader of the Zapatista rebels in Mex-ico. Wingnut claims his bandanna is identical to one he saw worn by the Subcomandante in a photograph. When not wearing his Zapatista mask, Wingnut's face is obscured by a woolly, Unabomber beard. Dreadlocks spring wildly from his head. Woven into a dreadlock by his left ear is a large wingnut, a fashion statement that also serves as inspiration for his current alias. Wingnut brags that he has not cut or combed his hair in five years. His dreadlocks, he says, are flame-proof, which is a lucky thing because he chain-smokes "rollies"—all-natural, hand-rolled tobacco cigarettes that seldom stay lit and require constant relighting. Wingnut uses a lighter with a torch-like flame he calls his "pocket dragon." When he fires up a rollie with the massive pocket dragon flame, his dreadlocks spark but never catch fire.

Seated with his friends at Out of the Fog, Wingnut shares exploits of the previous days' rioting. Recounting how a riot cop in "full Darth Vaders"—body armor—swung at him with a club, Wingnut says he blocked it with his hands and taunted his attacker, shouting, "Hit me! Hit me!" He laughs. "That probably wasn't the best tactic." Additional riot cops piled on Wingnut, clubbed him and shot his eyes full of pepper spray. Wingnut was saved when several anarchist Samaritans "unarrested him"—pulled him from the cops. Much as he laughs about it, the riots have taken a toll on Wingnut. He has a terrible cough from breathing clouds of tear gas and pepper spray. One of his ribs is cracked from a cop's baton. There are doughnut-size bruises on his back from getting shot with rubber bullets. He has tinnitus in one ear from a concussion grenade that exploded near his head. More alarmingly, on the second night of the riots Wingnut suffered a seizure. He had been drinking tea in a warehouse in Seattle, when he began to sweat. Then he blacked out. His eyes rolled back in their sockets, and his legs began to twitch uncontrollably. Wingnut snapped out of it after a few minutes, and now shrugs it off as probably a normal side effect of being exposed to the military CS gas employed by the National Guard. Wingnut discusses his riot-induced aches and pains with the same cheerfulness with which he speaks of all his endeavors, as if war against the state is one giant Halloween adventure of toilet-papering the neighborhood. "Just 'cause revolution is hard doesn't mean it can't be fun," he says.

Out of the Fog serves only one kind of coffee, a militantly correct brew allegedly made from beans picked by supporters of the Zapatista rebellion in Chiapas, Mexico. Drinking cup after cup of the black brew the morning of their return from Seattle, Wingnut's fellow anarchists are blitzed on triumph. "The inferno is way out of control," says Shade, a local rabble-rouser. In his mid-thirties, with thinning blond hair, Shade is one of the oldest anarchists in Eugene. Before moving to Oregon, he fronted a Seattle punk band called Total Toxic Rebellion. "The Man just wants to tighten his fat fucking white ass on the throne," says Shade. "They can't crush us like in a Raid commercial. If they try, it's going to be North Vietnam all over again, and this country will know what it's like to lose a big one."

It is freezing cold outside the coffee shop, but a half-dozen kids sit outdoors since no smoking is permitted inside. Everyone smokes rollies, and no one has any matches, since they rarely go into a 7-Eleven except to steal.

Seated nearby at a crude, scrap-wood table, a young man in a knitted cap offers to sell me a hunting knife for $6.50 so he can buy strings for his guitar. There is a guy with frizzy hair expounding on the fundamentally good nature of human beings when they are liberated from the oppression of institutions. There are two boys, thirteen and fifteen, kicking a can onto the roof, waiting for it to roll back on the ground, then kicking it up again. The boys, who lived for a while in the woods near the coffee shop, say they were booted from their respective parents' homes months ago. Recently they found an abandoned car to move into. The thirteen-year-old says his parents are Christians and they kicked him out for smoking a cigarette. The fifteen-year-old says his parents kicked him out simply because "my parents are assholes."

"It's beautiful to be free at your age," says the man with frizzy hair.

"It sucks, dude," counters the homeless thirteen-year-old.

Across the street a police cruiser crawls past at walking speed. Wingnut eyes it grimly. He is no stranger to run-ins with the local cops. "Some are rednecks," he says. "Some are ex-LAPD. Most are just boneheads who got the ball taken away from them when they were a kid."

His concerns right now revolve around federal law enforcement. Wingnut believes that because of the publicity surrounding the WTO riots, the FBI has begun watching him and his fellow anarchists from Eugene. He has decided to leave town with two other anarchists, a girl who goes by the name of "Siren" and a young man who calls himself "Panic." All of the anarchists choose *noms de révolution*, in part because they sound cool, but also because it makes it more difficult for authorities to track them. Wingnut says he has gone by a variety of names: "Critter," "Pine Cone," "Swamp," "Scrotum." Not even his friends know his real name. He and Siren and Panic will share a car down to Los Angeles. Wingnut hopes to hook up with some animal rights activists down there and disappear with them into the desert. "After the new year, there will be no more Wingnut," he says. "You can't fight a revolution from jail."

IN SEPTEMBER 1999, the Portland *Oregonian* published a series of articles on ecoterrorism that identified one hundred significant acts of destruction in the West since 1980 that were linked to environmental saboteurs. One-third of these occurred in the past four years, notably the pipe bombing of a Utah fur-breeder-supply company in 1997; the Vail, Colorado, lodge burnings in 1998 tied to the Earth Liberation Front; and the partial destruction of an Orange County, California, animal-testing lab in 1999 by the Animal Liberation Front. While not all activists connected to the radical wing of the eco movement identify themselves as anarchists, their methodologies are comparable, in particular the lack of hierarchy and use of autonomous cells to conduct direct action. "Anarchists have created a leaderless resistance movement," says Bryan Denson, a coauthor of the *Oregonian* series. "It's not a unified movement in the traditional sense. It's a polka-dot thing that's not easily tied together."

"Anarchism among those resisting the dominant paradigms in American society has been on the uptick in the last decade," says University of Oregon sociology professor Michael Dreiling. Anarchism, which was associated with the radical fringe of the American labor movement in the nineteenth century, largely faded by the time of World War II. But according to Dreiling, in the past fifteen years the theory of anarchism—both as a means and an end—has grown in popularity among forest activists in the West, anti-racism movements in the Northeast and Midwest, and in labor movements increasingly disenfranchised by the waning power of unions.

The current movement is loosely organized in a series of co-op houses in a dozen cities in the country. Anarchists are active in antihunger programs like Food Not Bombs. They have lent support to labor strikes. "They avoid traditional employment," says Dreiling. "They avoid using money. It's a movement that's difficult to categorize or quantify. Anarchist tactics are based on direct action—the destruction of property—carried out by small 'affinity' groups of, for example, two to six individuals. Affinity groups are a highly effective tactic for mobilizing wide groups of loosely networked individuals."

Many factors are converging to create today's anarchist movement, Dreiling says: "The 1970s and 1980s were a period of consensus and conciliation between environmentalists and the power elite, but the economic boom of the nineties has benefited primarily the upper reaches of society. The kids identifying themselves as anarchists today are mostly middle-class white kids. They are offered the neon-pleasure-dome vision of society on TV. They are promised life will be an endless Mountain Dew commercial, but they end up with jobs assembling burritos. They have a lot of anger. No one wants to hear their rage. And they can't afford to plant a million-dollar lobbyist in the Beltway to solve their problems."

Eugene, Oregon, has long been a haven for militant anarchists, going back to the labor movement among loggers. But in the past few years the new wave of eco-anarchists has made its presence known. The tree-sitters, dedicated to taking on the lumber companies, arrived in the mid-nineties. In June 1999, they stepped up their anticorporate campaign in the town by smashing storefronts and tagging shops along the main commercial strip. A year before, they trashed the local Niketown. Eugene's mayor calls his city "the anarchist capital of the world."

While most anarchists define their goal as something along the lines of global revolution, many of the most ardent "brick-tossers"—as some like to call themselves—admit they would be satisfied if their efforts changed how existing corporations and states do business. Even Wingnut's friend and fellow anarchist Shade believes his extreme acts like smashing windows and defacing corporate storefronts helps make more traditional environmentalists and their causes seem more reasonable to the public. For Shade, it's okay if smashing the window of a Gap doesn't lead to the abolition of corporate franchise shops, so long as the action brings scrutiny to their business, labor and environmental practices. As Shade puts it, "When the anarchists do their thing . . . the liberals look middle-of-the-ground all of a sudden."

I NEVER WOULD HAVE BEEN ASSIGNED a story on the WTO protests by *Rolling Stone* if the anarchists hadn't smashed up the city. Weeks before the demonstrations in Seattle, I found out about elaborate preparations being undertaken by nonviolent protest organizers and began meeting with them, visiting a warehouse factory where they were assembling agitprop costumes and gearing up to peacefully confront the WTO. They expected a turnout of tens of thousands of demonstrators and predicted—rightly, as it turned out—that this would be one of the largest protests in an American city in at least the past decade. I wrote this up in a pitch to my editor at *Rolling Stone*, and a few days later the magazine rejected the story idea. *Rolling Stone* had no interest in covering the protests, however huge or colorful or significant the cause might be. It wasn't until the second day of the protests, when TV news showed anarchists rioting, that my editor called to assign the story. "You've got to find those black-clad kids," he said.

After I found Wingnut, I initially questioned whether my presence would influence him to perform for me, the media. Later I realized I'd had it backward. It was the anarchists who had succeeded in influencing *Rolling Stone* and other media through their destructive acts.

Riots are made for television, and news broadcasts around the planet lavished viewers with those images of black-clad anarchists smashing windows, of burning trash cans, of police firing tear gas and wielding batons. The images were presented with a simple narrative: that peaceful protests had turned violent when anarchists went on a rampage. Reports from Seattle included wild embellishments. *The New York Times* published (and later retracted) a story that anarchists had attacked police and WTO delegates with firebombs.

Events on the ground didn't exactly correspond to the media narrative. The WTO conference was slated to begin at ten in the morning on November 30 in the Washington State Convention Trade Center, a massive complex spanning a city block between Pike Street and Union Street in downtown Seattle. Some five thousand WTO attendees—delegates from 135 signatory countries, and many times their number in lobbyists, industry representatives, politicians and media personnel—were staying at nearby hotels. WTO planners had expected to begin shuttling the dignitaries to the convention center starting at about nine that morning.

But before sunrise several hundred nonviolent protesters began to take up positions along Pike and Union, near the convention center. Hundreds of police were already on hand—including specially equipped riot police (whose most psychologically imposing weapon was a black, armored personnel carrier, nicknamed the "Peace Keeper" and adorned with an inspirational slogan printed alongside the rear hatch: "Move fast, kick ass"). Though nonviolent, the protesters implemented a highly aggressive form of civil disobedience. As delegates' limousines attempted to drive toward the convention center, protesters formed human barricades on the streets, locking their arms together, with some chaining themselves to fences and lampposts. By nine in the morning, tens of thousands of demonstrators paraded into the area from other locations in the city. These included students and environmentalists in fanciful costumes, as well as thousands of blue-collar, vaguely biker-looking Teamsters and steelworkers. The city center was impassable to vehicle traffic. The police were isolated in small groups, pushed back along the sidewalks by the sea of protesters, or clustered around a handful of black SWAT vans parked in the streets.

Despite my not getting the story assignment from *Rolling Stone*, I showed up anyway. For several blocks in all directions from the convention center, the city had the feel of a Mardi Gras celebration. There were Mother Earth floats, stilt-walkers, puppeteers, jugglers, bands of marching drummers, hippies with flutes and, of course, hundreds of people costumed as sea turtles and endangered owls. Many chanted, "This is what democracy looks like," whenever cops or people in suits or news camera crews stopped to look at them or take pictures. A flock of nude women who called themselves the Avenging Lesbians of Seattle ran about. The most hard-core nonviolent demonstrators, those who used U-shaped bicycle locks to pin their necks to light posts, grinned like freak-show performers. Teamsters interrupted the democracy chants by rolling in trucks that blared reggae and R&B tunes. In one episode I witnessed, several cops handed protesters bags of M&M's. Down the street a WTO delegate from an African country grabbed a bull-horn from a demonstrator and gave an impromptu speech denouncing globalization.

Late in the morning, after the WTO's opening ceremonies had to be scuttled due to the inability of delegates to enter the convention hall, the authorities decided they had had enough. Riot police formed several phalanxes and moved toward the main human blockade at Sixth and Union. They initiated their assault by lobbing explosive tear gas canisters, concussion grenades and pepper spray bombs into the crowd. (Police later gave conflicting accounts about which type of irritant they initially used on the crowd, pepper spray or tear gas.) In any case, their attack coincided with a crescendo of explosions (characteristic of tear gas canisters) and stroboscobic flashes (characteristic of concussion grenades), and a fog of noxious, stinging air rose from the intersection. The most committed protesters dropped to the pavement and linked arms, forming dense human pileups called "lockdowns." Witnesses reported that at about this time several cops standing on the roof of a van opened fire on the lockdowns, spraying the demonstrators with "rubber bullets"—solid polyester projectiles the size of gum balls. (Police later gave contradictory reports as to whether they fired rubber bullets or beanbag projectiles first.) As I pressed through the crowd on Sixth, trying to move closer to the intersection, a tearful woman in her fifties grabbed my arm to tell me a friend of hers had been hit with a rubber bullet. "The police shot him in the mouth," she said. "He lost his teeth." She repeated this detail several times, looking at my pad of paper, insistent that I write it, then ran off. About a hundred yards from the intersection, I was stopped by several cops in riot gear—helmets, clear visors, with respirators over their mouths and black vests that looked like turtle shells.

The police said nothing to me, and I barely seemed to register in their eyes. But the one in the lead was holding a wooden pole, maybe five feet long, which he held in front of him, with both hands, like a weapon from a martial arts film. I hovered back several feet. Through the smoke that hung in the air (which was breathable, though it burned my eyes and nose, indicating it was pepper spray and not tear gas), I could see cops in a line down on the intersection where protesters were locked down—a jumble of people in multicolored raincoats. The cops stood over the human chain. Some swung clubs. One, armed with either a plastic-bullet or a beanbag gun—I couldn't distinguish which—appeared to take a shot at a protester lying just a few feet from the barrel of his weapon. Many cops were armed with what looked like fire extinguishers but were in fact pepper spray canisters. They pressed nozzles into protesters' faces and sprayed in zigzag patterns across protesters' mouths and eyes. They moved at a leisurely pace, meticulously spraying, clubbing and shooting the writhing pile of demonstrators, breaking apart the human chain. In their riot gear the cops resembled futuristic Orkin men, exterminating an infestation of squirming hippies.

I was later told by someone who claimed to have been in the human chain that as the police assaulted them, the protesters began to sing "My Country 'Tis of Thee." From where I stood all I could hear were screams and what sounded like a collective roar of "Ow!" The people moving nearest me formed a kind of riptide pulling in both directions. The problem was, nobody could figure out which way to move, since groups of police began assaulting clumps of citizens at different points within the extremely crowded downtown corridors. Even those who wanted to comply couldn't discern which direction the cops were trying to push the crowd. When riot police managed to clear one section of street, a crowd of people pushed back from another group of cops and would just as quickly fill it. Through several hours of pandemonium I had yet to see a single anarchist throw a rock at a window.

Wingnut later told me how he and about two dozen fellow anarchists came to form the first "black bloc" later in the day. They spent the morning running interference on lines of riot police. When they saw police engaged with locked-down protesters, the anarchists ran between them, butting the cops and trying to knock them over. Outfitted that morning in shoplifted swim goggles intended to protect his eyes from pepper spray, Wingnut had the goggles torn from his face in his final encounter with cops a couple hours into the street fight. "I burled inside my mask," Wingnut says, describing the spray-induced vomiting. "I tried to get away and was slammed in the back by a cop taking a baseball swing with his bat. Two people dragged me out of there. I have no idea who they were."

Sometime after midday, Wingnut and several friends gathered at Westlake Park, a few blocks from the convention center. The night before, anarchists had distributed a flyer among black-clad kids printed with the words "Westlake Park at 11:11 am. Take back the streets." In characteristic anarchist fashion, no one knew who printed it, or what they were supposed to do. Also characteristic of the movement, Wingnut estimates he and his friends—a dozen or so Eugene anarchists—arrived at least an hour late. They found a similar number of other young people in black masks and hoodies already there. Many of them carried backpacks laden with pry bars, spray paint, monkey wrenches and rocks—what Wingnut calls "art supplies."

No one was really sure how exactly they should act on the flyer and "take back the streets." According to Wingnut, the anarchists milled around the park for an hour or so watching the police beat up nonviolent protesters down the street. Wingnut says "a kid in black" finally broke the tedium by slashing the tires on a nearby news van. When a driver leaped from the van and grabbed the kid, several anarchists pulled him from the man's arms. The tiny melee grew as several anarchists smashed open newspaper-vending boxes and threw papers in the air.

Wingnut says a girl of about sixteen, a peaceful protester—or in his words, a "peace Nazi"—ran up to the anarchists, shouting at them to stop throwing newspapers in the air. She attempted to shame the anarchists by picking up the newspapers and stacking them on the sidewalk, telling Wingnut, "I live in this city. It's a beautiful city!"

Wingnut tried to explain to her that he and his fellow anarchists were merely trashing Seattle to help prevent gentrification. Wingnut believes gentrification is bad for the working classes. Therefore, littering in cities is good because it lowers rent. His debate with the "peace Nazi girl" ended abruptly when a fight broke out nearby.

According to "Carlos," a Eugene anarchist also on the scene (whose day job is to make phone calls for a company that does polling for the Republican Party), a security guard from a nearby office building ran over to an anarchist kicking open a newspaper vending box and bashed him in the head with a walkie-talkie. Carlos says a quick-thinking anarchist spray-painted the security guard in the face. When I asked him if assaulting and possibly injuring a security guard with spray paint violated anarchist principles of focusing their efforts on property destruction, Carlos argued, "That's not really being violent. That's like protecting each other and being unified as a movement."

The fracas by the newspaper boxes energized the Black Clads. They formed into a black bloc—perhaps thirty of them, a third of whom were female and several of whom were as young as sixteen—and left the park. Wingnut claims they marched right past groups of riot police. He says police didn't stop them because they were afraid. "They [the police] beat up people who weren't willing to defend themselves. They like weak targets."

This far into the riots, Wingnut had observed that whenever police began to assault groups of nonviolent protesters, surrounding crowds would go haywire, running in all directions. The anarchist black bloc timed its first direct action off an assault by riot police. When police started clubbing and gassing a group of nonviolent protesters, the black bloc took off down an adjacent street. The anarchists ran through a shopping district throwing monkey wrenches, rocks and bricks through the windows of stores such as Gap, McDonald's and Starbucks. Other corporate targets, from bank branches to oil companies to lumber companies, were on their hit list. On several of the streets that they targeted for anticorporate vandalism, Wingnut claims, "There were cops just around every corner, but none came near us."

Wingnut says, "We had more trouble from peace Nazis." When the anarchists attempted to destroy a Niketown shoe store, a half-dozen peaceful demonstrators broke off from a parade on the street and formed a human shield in front of the store's imposing plate-glass windows. They prevented the anarchists from throwing rocks through the windows; however, a group of local toughs sensed a golden opportunity to stock up on their favorite Nike goods. They rushed the peaceful protesters defending the store, punched a few and looted the place. Disappointed that he and his friends hadn't been the ones to smash the windows on Niketown, Wingnut returned later in the day and graffitied the shattered storefront with tags that read "Fuck you, Nike."

The afternoon's black bloc lasted no more than thirty minutes. During that time, Wingnut and his friends trashed storefronts along a six-block swath of the city. Their actions brought out follow-on looters who set trash fires and tried to torch several police cars.

Throughout the rest of the afternoon and into the evening, increasingly frustrated cops began attacking groups of citizens farther from the convention center. Late in the afternoon, spotting a group of protesters in turtle costumes, who were walking in the opposite direction of the convention center, several riot police battered them with clubs, then moved off without arresting any of them. Longshoremen who had marched in the morning reported similar attacks on them as they walked away from the marches. In a residential district far from the convention center, I witnessed a group of riot police hurl several concussion grenades—each of which detonate with enough blast to take out an eye or blow off fingers—near a group of people walking near a supermarket. Police stopped a motorist attempting to videotape police brutality and blasted her with pepper spray. Similar attacks by police continued, though at a diminishing rate, during the next forty-eight hours. Dr. Kirk Murphy, a physician from the UCLA medical school who had come to the protests as an observer, ended up treating dozens of victims for face lacerations, knocked-out teeth, torn gums and broken ribs. He sent one woman in her fifties to the hospital for a detached retina, a result of being shot in the eye with a rubber bullet. "Many of these people weren't trying to block streets," says Murphy. "They were trying to get away."

When I later interviewed Seattle's assistant police chief, Ed Joiner, he defended the police department's widespread use of force on the grounds that even the "supposedly nonviolent" protesters were a "willing crowd that prevented the police from apprehending" the anarchists. Joiner also was insistent that *Rolling Stone* note the sacrifice made by a "selfless Seattle police officer" whose fingers were severely burned when a concussion grenade with a faulty fuse detonated in his hand before he could hurl it at some citizens.

In demonstrations that continued the next day, which were permitted by city authorities on streets far from the convention center, where the WTO conference did eventually commence, anarchists were shunned by other protesters. Teamsters and longshoremen shoved anarchists—or anyone in all black—out of the streets. Wingnut claims a nonviolent protester tried to punch him when he attempted to join a street march.

Wingnut believes that peaceful protesters live in a dreamworld. "People think they have freedom of choice because they can buy six different brands of jeans. If we're so fucking free, why did the police beat the shit out of all those nonviolent protesters exercising their so-called freedom of speech and so-called freedom to assemble? We live in a police state."

After I caught up with Wingnut and began to follow him, I witnessed him debate several marchers committed to the principles of nonviolence. One such protester, beaten by police a few days earlier, admitted to Wingnut he fantasized about someday being able to use "nonviolent weapons" against the police—nontoxic smoke grenades, liquid nitrogen spray that would ice over the streets and cause attacking police to fall over.

Wingnut looked at the young man and shook his head in pity. "I tell you what, I is pissed off now."

FOR NEARLY TWO YEARS before his protest in Seattle, Wingnut had been battling government forces and corporate interests on a daily basis by living in a tree in the Willamette National Forest, a forty-five drive from Eugene, Oregon. The old-growth firs in the Willamette Forest are five hundred to seven hundred years old and can reach a height of 350 feet. Unfortunately, very few of these old-growth trees remain. Much of the forest is covered in young, thirty-foot firs, or worse yet, scrub pines that could hardly qualify as Christmas trees. The giants of the forest have nearly all been chopped down and turned into two-by-fours and toothpicks, an act of destruction that forest activists might liken to Huns smashing apart Roman temples to make rocks for filling in chuckholes.

In 1998, one of the last remaining stands of old-growth trees in the Fall Creek area of the Willamette Forest was sold off to a logging company. As U.S. government policy plays out in many national parks, the logging companies own the trees; the public ends up with the stumps. In April 1998, a ragtag group of tree-climbers took direct action to prevent several of the oldest trees in Fall Creek from being felled. They moved into the trees.

Wingnut arrived in Eugene in the spring of 1998. He had just been paroled from a California jail after serving six months for dealing marijuana. (At one time, he says, he made $200 a day dealing acid and pot in San Diego.)

His activism began in a haphazard manner. Bumming around in the South a few years earlier—dealing a little, taking in the sights, riding the occasional freight train—Wingnut says he came across some church signs that bore antihomosexual messages. He was moved to vandalize them. He claims that on another occasion, he sabotaged a Pepsi bottling plant by dumping several trash bags of burning weeds into the building's air intakes.

Wingnut drifted into Eugene merely to visit a friend. But around the time of his arrival in Eugene, the (incredibly named) Zip-O-Lumber company had begun preparations to clear-cut the last remaining old-growth firs in the Fall Creek area of the Willamette National Forest. A small group of local activists formed a collective to protect the trees. They called their group Red Cloud Thunder (RCT). "We were just a bunch of fuck-ups—gutter punks and anarchists," says "Pacific," a founding member. Wingnut heard about RCT while smoking a bowl on a back porch in Eugene. The next day he caught a ride to Fall Creek and joined a road blockade.

To prevent the company from accessing the stand of trees, activists employed an extreme form of confrontation. They blocked the main logging road with monopods, twenty-foot poles held aloft by ropes and occupied at the top by a lone activist. The premise behind a monopod is that authorities cannot remove its occupant without possibly killing him.

Wingnut spent days at a time atop a monopod. He and other protesters upped the risk of being removed by tying nooses around their necks. In their attempts to flush them out, Forestry Service agents harassed the tree-sitters with low-flying helicopters. At night they saturated the forest with floodlights, and patrolled the woods in order to capture RCT's support-activists bringing food and supplies. During the day they blared country music from loudspeakers. The tactics failed.

"The kids out there stick up for each other," says Terry Bertsch, a federal law enforcement officer with the Forestry Service who has fought the activists at Fall Creek since the beginning. "What they do is insane, but I guess that's part of the anarchist belief."

After several weeks, the Forestry Service brought in cherry pickers, and climbers of their own who wrestled Wingnut down from the monopod. Wingnut has scars on his chin to commemorate the day of his removal. The Forestry Service agents dropped him face-first onto the road before hand-cuffing and arresting him.

Wingnut claims that Forestry Service agents beat him after putting him under arrest, and brags that he provoked it by taunting the agents, whom he refers to as "Freds." He says, "I'd heard one of the Freds who'd arrested me had a daughter who'd run off with a hippie. With my dreads, I figured the guy she'd run off with might have looked like me. I told him, 'You're just pissed because I look like the kind of guy your daughter likes to fuck.'"

When Wingnut got out of jail a few days later, he returned to Fall Creek and moved into a tree sit, where he remained for the next eighteen months, until the Seattle protests.

BEFORE LEAVING EUGENE, I accompany Wingnut on a visit to RCT's protest "village" among the trees in Fall Creek. As I enter the forest, the scent of living pine feels like a stimulant. Douglas firs, soaring three hundred feet, grow from trunks that are only four to five feet wide on the ground. The sky is screened from view by a thin canopy of pine needles that grows along the trees' upper branches. The tree-sitters live in platforms about two-thirds of the way up the trees, between 170 and 210 feet above the ground. The platforms are made from scavenged plywood, with plastic tarps billowing overhead to keep out the rain. According to Wingnut, no nails or screws are used to attach the platforms to the trees. Like the monopods they build on the road, the platforms are jerry-rigged with ropes. Should anyone from the Forestry Service cut a single line, the platform is designed to come crashing down, inevitably killing its occupant.

The platforms are about ten or fifteen feet square, but looking up at them from the ground, they seem to be the size of postage stamps. White plastic buckets—for food, water, excrement—hang from the edges. "Tree villagers" on the ground run supplies up to the sitters using ropes.

Fewer than a dozen trees are being defended at Fall Creek. They have names like "Igdrazzle," "Happy" and "Grandma," and are clustered on a spot of land not much bigger than a baseball field. What I hadn't anticipated before walking into Fall Creek was that the battle was being waged over so few trees, fewer than a dozen according to Wingnut. Outside this small old-growth stand, thousands of acres have already been clear-cut.

Wingnut's purpose in coming here is not just to say good-bye. Several weeks ago he stowed his extra pair of long johns in a plastic bucket that he stashed near the village. While he sets off in search of his long johns, I chat with an activist named "Fin." Fin drove up with us, and after spending a few days' vacation in town, he will be occupying one of the tree sits.

About twenty years old, Fin looks like he crawled out from an alley behind a punk bar. Studded black leather bracelets adorn his wrists. Dyed-blond hair grows up from the top of his head in a six-inch-long pressed wedge that resembles the blade of an ax. Fin says he gets by when he is in the city by living out of dumpsters and stealing money from girlfriends. He tells Wingnut he has been staying with a stripper he met in town. "I'm fucking raw," he says. "We fucked all night, but she was too cute to rip off."

Fin prepares for the climb up to his tree sit by getting stoned. The climb will take forty-five minutes. Fin attaches himself to a climbing harness with a Swiss seat, then to the single rope hanging 170 feet down from the tree. Fin looks up at the tree and mumbles, "Beautiful." Half an hour later, he hangs one hundred feet in the air, motionless, staring at the bark, enjoying the buzz.

Wingnut returns with his long johns, crusty with mud and twigs and pine needles. He shouts up to a tree in response to a female voice calling to him. The canopy above and the bed of pine needles and humus at our feet create a perpetual hush. The voices on the platforms high above are crystal clear. Two girls sharing a platform invite us up to smoke a bowl. Intriguing as their offer is, I have my doubts about the rope-tying skills of stoned activists. I am relieved when Wingnut declines their offer.

Before we leave, Wingnut sits on the ground and takes in the "village." He tells me one of the advantages of living in a tree is the simplification of time. "When I'm in the forest, there are three times of day: dark, purple and light. I wake up at purple and go to bed at dark.

"I can't stand to hear a radio in the forest," Wingnut adds. "I love the sound of the forest. My first audio hallucination was in the forest. I heard every single needle moving on the fir trees, every single pebble in the creek as the water was going through it. It was incredible."

Wingnut admits that living in a tree has its downside. When he stayed up in it for weeks at a stretch during particularly confrontational periods with the Freds, it felt like a jail cell. In the winter, when it rains for days, sometimes weeks on end, he loses all sense of human contact. The tarp over his platform blocks out much of the light. The steady drumming of raindrops is ceaseless. It was under these conditions of extreme isolation that Wingnut first read the Unabomber Manifesto.

"The most important thing about the Manifesto," Wingnut insists, "is that Kaczynski says 'we.' He says 'we' believe, 'we' are revolutionaries. The Manifesto was written for everyone."

Through the medium of his Manifesto, Kaczynski and Wingnut found each other. They shared a certain symmetry. Kaczynski wrote it while living alone in a shack; Wingnut read it while living alone in a tree. When Wingnut mentions Kaczynski's use of the word "we," he sounds a bit like a teenage girl at a concert who believes the singer performed the love song just for her.

IN 1975, EDWARD ABBEY published *The Monkey Wrench Gang*, a novel that fictionalized the real-life exploits of four radical activists who roamed the West in the 1960s sabotaging machinery and property to defend the environment. "Monkey-wrenching" entered the lexicon as a verb meaning basically to sabotage property in defense of the environment. Abbey himself was cited as an inspiration behind the radical environmental group Earth First! when it was founded in 1979 with the motto "No compromise in defense of Mother Earth."

By 1985, Earth First! members pioneered the use of tree sits to protect forests from logging. Many in Earth First! also advocated (and no doubt practiced) monkey-wrenching, including driving spikes into trees, which pose the threat of serious injury or death to loggers. Though spokespeople for Earth First! disavow monkey-wrenching, the *Earth First! Journal* website sells *Ecodefense: A Field Guide to Monkeywrenching*, coedited by one of the group's cofounders, Dave Foreman.

Doug Peacock, the ex–Green Beret medic and a Vietnam vet who was a member of the actual "Monkey Wrench Gang" on which the 1975 book was based, argues that the radical environmentalism, including monkey-wrenching, he practiced in the 1960s and 1970s didn't go far enough. He believes the only hope for saving the environment lies in dismantling the entire system. When I spoke to him shortly after the WTO protests, Peacock said, "I'm right up there with those Eugene kids when it comes to throwing bombs at the system. Out of monkey-wrenching came Earth First! and out of Earth First! came anarchy. Monkey-wrenching was never enough by itself to take on the system. I see new hope in the upswing of the anarchist movement. I thank those kids for doing what they did in Seattle."

Anarchism as a political philosophy was originally more concerned with the deleterious effects of the state on the human condition than the harmfulness of technology. In the nineteenth century, when anarchism became fashionable in England, it was embraced as much as an aesthetic and moral philosophy as it was an actual political movement. If the point of anarchism was to explore the untapped potential of humankind free from the tyrannies of the state, the next logical step would be to imagine the liberated, natural human in harmony with wild nature. Technology, like the state, came to be viewed as a tyrannical force that corrupted humankind and nature alike. Mary Shelley—daughter of seminal anarchist thinker William Godwin and wife of anarchist-inspired poet Percy Bysshe Shelley—would pen the original horror story of technology, *Frankenstein*.

Utopian anarchist thought and the musings of Romantic poets permeated the back-to-nature spirit of 1960s environmentalism. While Earth First! activists adopted, or at least talked about, use of militant, destructive tactics like spiking trees, the idea of anarchism as both means and end of the environmental movement didn't take root until the 1990s.

Wingnut's hero, Ted Kaczynski, advocated waging war against technology, corporations and the political order in order to restore humankind to its proper state of subservience to nature. Where Mary Shelley's fable about Dr. Frankenstein's monster served as warning about the dangerous effects of technology on the human race, Kaczynski's Manifesto, published in *The New York Times* in 1995, was both anti-technology and anti-human, calling for murder, if necessary, to protect nature from humankind's rapaciousness.

Kaczynski's rise as guiding light of radical environmentalists like Wingnut was promoted by Portland, Oregon–based author and thinker John Zerzan, who describes himself as a "leading theorist of the anti-civilization movement"—what he sometimes calls the "primitivist movement." Zerzan came of age as an antiwar protester in San Franciso in the 1960s. Employed as a social worker by the city, he earned a master's degree in history from

San Francisco State University and gradually evolved from being a garden-variety left-wing activist to an anti-technology theorist. In 1988 he published *Elements of Refusal*, a collection of essays in which he began to formulate his argument that all technology developed since about the time of the Paleolithic era has harmed the human race.

After Kaczynski's arrest in 1996 for his seventeen-year Unabomber terror campaign that injured eleven people and killed three—all strangers to him selected because of their roles in fostering technology—Zerzan began meeting with him in prison and sharing ideas. He later dedicated the second edition of *Elements of Refusal* to the Unabomber. Wingnut and other anarchists speak of Zerzan and the Unabomber in the same breath, and Zerzan's books are as widely read as the Unabomber Manifesto.

One of Wingnut's friends puts me in touch with Zerzan and we meet at an upscale pasta and panini shop in a gentrified section of Portland, which Zerzan selected. Zerzan, fifty-six, would not look out of place at a college faculty meeting. He wears dark loafers with cream-colored socks, and a brown leather jacket over a University of Paris sweatshirt. His graying beard is neatly clipped.

Zerzan describes himself as an anarchist opposed to nonviolent protest on the grounds that "civil disobedience is just the agreement that you respect the law. It's a very explicit consecration of the system."

Both of us order salads. As we wait, Zerzan speaks movingly of Kaczynski as a martyr who was "willing to put his life out there. The most humiliating thing for Ted was to be portrayed as crazy. He is not crazy at all."

By the time our salads arrive, Zerzan is explaining the desired end state of the current anarchist-environmental movement as he and Kaczynski see it: to dismantle civilization and turn the clock back to the Paleolithic era, aka the Stone Age.

"You mean so we can live like cavemen?" I ask.

Zerzan laughs and assumes a professorial air as he labors to erase my ignorance. "Think of our ancestors as wonderful primitives, not cavemen," he says. "Before agriculture and animal husbandry," Zerzan states, "when we were a hunter-gatherer society, there was equality between people and between genders. There was no war and no pollution. There was leisure time. Disease was unknown. Cancer did not exist." Zerzan smiles. "How wonderful the Paleolithic era was."

Zerzan refers to the harbingers of this new age—young anarchists like Wingnut—as "future primitives." As I get to know Wingnut better, the influences of Zerzan become clear. "What needs to happen for Earth to survive is for a few billion people on this planet to be killed off," Wingnut tells me. "I'm not saying I want it to happen, or that I would try to make it happen. But people are a disease to the planet. If there's nuclear war, good riddance. Some of us will be out here surviving at the hunter-gathering level, where we belong."

Wingnut, his anarchist friends and mentors like Zerzan and Kaczynski have somehow managed to turn love of "Mother Earth" into a cult of apocalyptic doom.

THE DRIVE FROM EUGENE TO L.A. takes approximately sixteen hours. Wingnut allows me to ride along in his getaway vehicle, the old Chevy Cavalier we have been driving since we left Seattle.

Wingnut spends most of the ride to L.A. dozing in the backseat, waking up occasionally to swig from a bottle of Tabasco sauce. The hacking cough he developed in Seattle has grown louder and more frequent. Wingnut believes Tabasco sauce has medicinal qualities for treating his cough. In addition, since Tabasco is made from capsicum similar to that used in police pepper spray, Wingnut believes that consuming it in large quantities inoculates him from future run-ins with the law.

The two other passengers who have joined us now occupy the backseat: Panic, a wiry, unsmiling revolutionary in his late twenties, and Siren, a young woman about eighteen who assures me she is not a runaway. One of them has a boom box on which they blast their favorite anarchist punk bands, the Subhumans and Crass.

Siren, who does not own shoes, rides with her bare feet draped over the front-seat headrests. Her jeans hang in ragged strips at her ankles. Her dyed-black hair is dirty blond at the roots. She has a pierced nose, and the skin rises around her piercing in a gray-pink bubble that indicates a nasty infection.

Six weeks ago, Siren ran away from her parents' home in Southern California and landed in Eugene, where she lived under a tarp by the river.

Her flight had as much to do with her parents as it did with a young anarchist named Austin. "I left town to get away from Austin. We split up. Austin and I did everything together, every day for two years."

When Siren arrived in Eugene, she dabbled in being a hippie but quickly grew disenchanted. "Hippies call themselves a family full of love and beauty. But I found out hippie men think I'm weak and stupid and lie to me. Because I'm a girl, and I'm on the street."

Siren met up with anarchists in Eugene shortly before their excursion to Seattle. "Anarchists give me hope. When I'm around them I forget there is racism and sexism."

In L.A., she aims to hook up with her ex-boyfriend and make another go of their relationship. Her involvement in vandalizing Seattle during the WTO convention has inspired her to write more songs for the band she had with Austin. Her only fear of coming back is the off chance that she might encounter her parents, though she plans to crash with Austin at an anarchist co-op.

Despite her youth, Siren has the voice of a calm, centered thirty-year-old woman. She punctuates her sentences with laughter that sounds like humming. It catches you off guard when she talks about how much she hates her family in those soothing tones, with her gentle laughter.

The chief cause of her estrangement from her parents, she explains, is the fact that they are Christian fundamentalists. "My mother doesn't even listen to music. She is not human. She only listens to Dr. Laura," she explains. "My father is the ugliest man in the world. I can't stand his smell. I can't eat meals with my family. The sound of my father chewing makes me want to vomit."

Siren describes a violent home life, though laughing lightly she admits she was the cause of most of it. She claims that her father has a permanent quiver in his hand that is a result of her punching him in the back so hard it caused nerve damage. "That's what he claims," she says. "But I don't believe anything he tells me. When we fight, he cries and cries. My mother doesn't even love him."

She chose Siren as her name because, as she explains, "sirens sang the most beautiful song, and it killed men. Isn't that crazy? I want to paint a picture of that in my mind."

Panic, twenty-nine, is shirtless in a pair of black overalls. He is tall and thin, to the point of looking starved. He is going to L.A. to attend a three-day anarchist get-together called Solidarity Fest. Panic says he has been an anarchist since he got into punk at the age of ten.

Panic grew up in Southern California but has lived in anarchist-punk squats in San Francisco, New York and Berlin. It wasn't until he moved to Eugene a few years ago that he became active in the environmental wing of the anarchist movement. He recently enrolled in the University of Oregon in Eugene to study forest ecology. Panic says it has taken him a long time to find himself.

On the outskirts of Fresno, California, Panic makes a confession. "I was a Nazi," he says. "Just a few months in high school. My girlfriend helped me get out of it. She came over to my house one day, and she said, 'This is not you.' She brought out my old records, she got me back into my punk."

Next to having been a Nazi, Panic's second most shameful episode occurred during a dark time when he wore a tie and worked for a bank. "It all started during a really fucking bad acid trip," he says. "I heard my dad's voice telling me I was all wrong, that I was a loser." Shortly after that bad trip, Panic got a job counting money for ATMs. It lasted only a few months. "Yeah, punk brought me back to sanity again," he says.

Riding in the car with Panic and Siren, Wingnut tunes out discussions having to do with identity crisis or searching for a place in life. Wingnut says he has never wondered who he is, questioned his beliefs or worried about his future.

Asked if he could ever imagine giving up his nomadic life and becoming an office clerk in ten years, he answers, "There won't be office clerks in ten years. There won't be offices, there won't be cities."

There are a number of reasons why Wingnut despises cities. One of them is toilets. "A toilet is a fucked-up thing," Wingnut says. "The first rule of living in the forest is, never piss or shit in good drinking water. What's a toilet? You piss and shit in good drinking water, push a button and throw it away."

At a refueling stop outside Bakersfield, Siren wanders barefoot on the asphalt, looking for a ladies' room, while Wingnut and Panic go across the street to a McDonald's. When they return a few minutes later, they are in getaway mode. "Let's go, quick," Wingnut says, jumping into the car. For a moment or two no one says a word; then Wingnut and Panic crack smiles.

"We wrote 'McMurder' on the walls of the men's room," Panic finally says. "The red paint dripped perfectly, like blood."

"Break it! Break it!" Wingnut says in a Beavis voice.

Panic and Wingnut giggle together.

"You guys?" Siren says, frowning. "I'm left out of things because I'm a woman. I wish you guys would include me in everything."

THE L.A. CO-OP is a ramshackle stucco house in a suburban section of Inglewood, under the landing path of jets flying into LAX. A "Free Mumia" banner is draped across the backyard fence. There are car seats on the lawn. Inside, more car seats serve as living room furniture. Posters tacked up in the kitchen depict small, furry animals being tortured in scientific labs. A chunk of uneaten vegan casserole sweats in a pan on the stove. The four full-time residents are all vegans.

A harried-looking twenty-year-old named Kendra is the only co-op member home when the Eugene anarchists show up. Kendra and her three housemates are helping to organize Solidarity Fest, the festival of punk bands and political workshops Panic has come to California to attend. It is scheduled to begin tomorrow at a community center north of downtown Los Angeles.

In the living room of the anarchist co-op, Siren reunites with her ex-boyfriend Austin. The reunion appears to be a shaky one. Austin, a skinny sixteen-year-old, dressed all in black, kneels on the floor plugging wires into a guitar amp.

In happier times, Austin and Siren sang together in his band and carried protest signs that read "You're Eating Kak Burgers" outside a local McDonald's. (Siren explains that "kak" means "vomit," "penis" or "come," depending on the context.) But today their reunion is strained. Siren sits in a chair made from a car seat across from him and smiles. He avoids eye contact with her.

"What are you doing for the holidays?" Siren asks.

"Dose on acid to write songs for my band," Austin mumbles. "Fry some more on Christmas. Go to San Diego on New Year's and fuck shit up."

As the sun sets, a cluster of punks from Phoenix arrive in two beat-up vans. Among them is a fourteen-year-old girl who ran away from her home in Texas. She says her parents had her under virtual house arrest. She escaped by propping the automatic garage door open with a paint can and wiggling out after her parents had gone to sleep. "I'm not really an anarchist," she whispers. "I'm just looking for a place to stay until I find my sugar daddy."

She surveys the scene. "This is just so hella California."

"Hella fucked," Siren adds, walking away from her ex-boyfriend Austin.

I join Wingnut outside when a gangly boy comes up the driveway with a guitar and a backpack slung over his shoulder. His name is "Sorrow," and he is sixteen years old. He rode a freight train into L.A. two days ago. He has walked approximately forty miles across the city looking for the co-op. He did not realize how big a city Los Angeles was.

Sorrow came to L.A. from the Minnehaha Free State, an organized blockade of a highway expansion across sacred Native American grounds in Minnesota. Like Wingnut, he has battled federal law enforcement agents from atop a monopod and lived in a tree. Unlike Wingnut, Sorrow identifies himself as a "nonviolent anarchist."

Sorrow, whose mother passed away when he was very young, was raised on a farm by foster parents. He wandered from home when he was fourteen and has been living the life of a drifter-activist ever since.

Wingnut offers Sorrow a rollie, and the two join a circle of young punks sitting outside the house on the bare dirt (where a lawn used to be). Wingnut begins to tell the young punks about the Unabomber Manifesto and the need to take up armed resistance against the state.

Wingnut's and Sorrow's paths have been crossing a great deal recently. They have both spent time in Eugene together and at the tree sit in the nearby forest. They both smashed windows at the WTO protests in Seattle. Meeting again in L.A., they resume a long-running argument. While Sorrow believes in the right to destroy property for political protest, he calls taking up arms a "horrible thing." He adds, "The Unabomber just killed people. It was wrong."

Wingnut counters, "If you don't riot, you don't have the right to complain."

Sorrow retorts, "The Unabomber didn't riot. He just killed people."

Wingnut asks, "If people broke into your house and were raping your mother, would you fight back by any means necessary? What about Mother Earth?"

"You can't win against the U.S. Army," says Sorrow.

"A single Molotov can take out twenty-five soldiers," says Wingnut.

"They have nuclear bombs," says Sorrow.

"I'd rather die standing than on my knees." Wingnut launches into his favorite parable, about militiamen defeating the much more powerful British army in the American Revolution.

The punk boys seated nearby side with Wingnut. One of them says, "A violent struggle must be fought."

"You're mowing me down," Sorrow says to the group.

"You're talking until I'm blue in the face," Wingnut says, causing the punk boys to laugh. One of them, who looks like a young Johnny Rotten, sneers at Sorrow. It's a schoolyard look of contempt—pacifists are wusses. Sorrow takes his guitar and leaves.

Wingnut pulls out his knife and sharpens it.

THE SOLIDARITY FEST OPENS at the Aztlan Cultural Arts Foundation the next morning. The building is a barely refurbished former county jail not far from Dodger Stadium. There are still bars on the windows and cells upstairs.

A hundred anarchists and punk rockers in black leather, mostly from the Southwest, arrive by noon. Half of them sit on folding chairs arranged in a circle. A lone black man enters the circle and takes a seat. He introduces himself as Bloodhound, a Bloods gang member, and says he represents his chapter in an outreach program aimed at white outlaw groups.

Bloodhound asks the assembled white kids what punk rock means. A few raise hands. The room has the politely strained atmosphere of a 12-step meeting. A guy with his head shaved down to a Mohawk defines punk as "resisting the system."

"That's about the same with us," Bloodhound says. "That we was an outlaw criminal gang was just a smear put on us by the media." Bloodhound then regales his audience with tales of being shot at by rival gang members, being beaten up in alleys by cops who then dropped him into rival gang turf to be killed. He asks whether any punk rockers have similar stories.

The room is silent.

DESPITE WINGNUT'S DETERMINATION TO HIDE his pre-anarchist identity, he lets slip innumerable details. He describes wet snow that fell in the small New England town where he was raised in a close-knit Portuguese family. Growing up, he says, he wrecked several cars even before he got his license, nearly chopped his thumb off with a hatchet, burst the cartilage in his nose and drove a four-inch screw into his ass cheek by wiping out on a skateboard. Wingnut's grandmother gave him the nickname *mosca tonta*, Portuguese for "dizzy bug."

Not surprisingly, his school years were characterized by rebelliousness, which began when teachers asked him to say the Pledge of Allegiance. "I didn't believe in saluting a piece of cloth," Wingnut says. "I may as well salute my pants. Pledge of allegiance to the flag. Why? So I'll run into a burning building and pull it out? Fuck no. I'll be the one lighting the flag on fire to start the building burning."

Wingnut says anarchy sounded like a good idea to him ever since he heard the Sex Pistols sing about it when he was a kid. He also credits Metallica and the death-metal band Sepultura for being major influences on his political development.

Wingnut brags that in high school he failed gym three years in a row. "I don't think a coach would have had much for me unless he showed me how to throw rebar through windshields like a javelin, or showed me how to tackle a cop. I don't see any point in learning competition. I just want to win."

His real education, he says, began after he took twenty-five hits of LSD one afternoon when he was fourteen. "I wouldn't be who I am without acid," he says. "In general, if I take acid, I hallucinate so hard I don't even know I'm a being anymore."

Against his free-spirited nature, Wingnut describes a decidedly working-class upbringing. His father was what Wingnut describes as a "hard-core Reagan Republican." He attended trade school and studied auto-body repair. He apprenticed for three years with a brick mason. His dad, an NRA instructor, taught him marksmanship and respect for firearms.

Eventually he drops enough clues about himself that a twenty-minute Web search yields the phone number of his parents' house. Wingnut's father corroborates Wingnut's description of him as a Reagan Republican and a gun advocate; he adds that he was a combat engineer in Vietnam. But he has no problem with his son's chosen path.

"I wish that more people had more guts to do a little bit of civil disobedience," he says. "He's happy, he's healthy. He's not filthy. The dreadlocks don't look clean, but that's what he's happy with. He's living in a tree—who cares what he looks like?"

Wingnut's mother gets on the line. She emphasizes that her son "from a child has always been very sensitive to living things, animals. We've always had cats and pet fish. He used to go hysterical when a fish died. He'd get upset that we were going to flush it down the toilet."

Wingnut's father says his boy takes after his own older brother. "My brother was a fisherman. He was what they called a pirate, because he would shell-fish at night. He had a code of ethics, but it did not agree with the law. [Wingnut] is in the same mold."

Then Wingnut's father launches into a tirade, accusing the federal government of training Russian troops in Texas to fire on U.S. citizens. He praises the Michigan Militia as an outfit that "keeps the government a little bit honest."

IT IS JUST AFTER SUNSET on Wingnut's last night in L.A.—his final hours as Wingnut. He emerges from a Marina del Rey supermarket, the pockets of his camo pants bulging with tubes of Super Glue he's lifted, along with a box of Top tobacco for making rollies.

The plan tonight is to bring some revolution to L.A., and I am the designated driver.

"Let's hear some fuck-shit-up music," Panic says, sliding a CD by Crass, his favorite anarchist punk band, into the boom box.

Panic missed the WTO protests in Seattle due to exams in his forest ecology class. Tonight will be an opportunity to put the cans of black and red spray paint he has been carrying in his backpack to good purpose.

Siren has decided to come along since she has nothing better to do, now that she and her ex-boyfriend are finished for good. For the night's action she's borrowed a pair of shoes and a sports bra from an anarchist girl in the co-op, so she can run fast if there's trouble with cops.

The three of them form an "affinity group"—a leaderless, autonomous cell formed for revolutionary action. Wingnut distributes the Super Glue.

Along with spray paint and rocks, Super Glue is a favored "direct action tool" of anarchists. The glue will be used to sabotage select retail establishments by squirting it into their door locks after closing time.

Siren tears open the containers of Super Glue. "Look at all this wasteful packaging," she frets.

In the darkened car in the parking lot, the anarchists plot.

Siren favors tagging anticorporate slogans on a local Tower Records store.

"What are their specific offenses?" Panic asks.

"They're a huge corporation," Siren responds.

"Selling crappy corporate rock isn't good enough," Panic says. He adds, "According to Martin Luther King, the first principle of direct action is identifying a specific offense committed by your target."

Wingnut makes a bold proposal. "Let's fill buckets with paint, go into a Gap and heave the shit at racks of clothes."

Siren disagrees with the tactic of destroying clothing. "It's still a waste, even if it is Gap."

Panic and Wingnut recall an action in which the two of them threw a bucket of urine into the kitchen of a McDonald's. "It was classified a toxic hazard," Panic says, laughing. "They had to shut it down for twenty-four hours."

"We could do that in the Gap," Wingnut says.

"Not if we destroy clothes." Siren remains opposed. "Unless we could call the Gap store later and tell them to donate the damaged clothes to charity."

"No one's going to want clothes covered in piss," Wingnut reasons.

"Then we shouldn't do it."

They agree to tag the Gap with slogans but leave the clothing undamaged. They also decide to hit any Starbucks they encounter along the way, though no one can think of a specific offense committed by Starbucks.

"It doesn't matter," Siren reasons. "There are really only six corporations that own everything in the world. It doesn't matter who you hit. It's all the same."

Panic wants to tag a Starbucks with "I came in your coffee."

"That's offensive," Siren counters. "And it doesn't educate people."

Chastened, Panic says, "Maybe we should only do child-labor tags. We can hit dozens of targets across the city. Then call the media and tell them what we've done. We will say . . ." Panic's voice changes into a menacing monotone, like that of a TV terrorist. "We demand you focus on child-labor issues, or we will not stop."

Wingnut scoffs. "The media doesn't care about graffiti unless it's racial shit like swastikas."

AN HOUR LATER, Wingnut enters a Gap in Santa Monica. He pulls his Zapatista bandit mask over his face and walks up to a customer. She is picking through a stack of khakis. "Did you know these clothes are made with slave labor?" His voice is midway between speaking and shouting.

The woman jumps. In the brightly lit Gap, Wingnut is a gnomelike figure in his black mask and hoodie. The woman is blond and in her late twenties. She has probably devoted more time to grooming herself in the past twenty-four hours than Wingnut has in the past five years. She hurriedly exits.

A salesgirl approaches.

Wingnut shouts, "The Gap uses slave labor!" A dreadlock falls from his hoodie and shakes over his mask as he repeats himself.

The salesgirl giggles nervously.

Wingnut turns and walks out as calmly as he entered. Siren and Panic were supposed to have followed Wingnut into the store and shouted slogans with him. Instead, they remained outside and tagged the wall with the anarchy symbol in black and the word "GREED" above it in red. The entire tag is about six feet tall, dominating the white stucco wall that faces Wilshire Boulevard.

Wingnut walks past it, around the corner. He pulls his mask down and yanks his hoodie off, like a superhero changing back into street clothes.

They feel emboldened by their success at the Santa Monica Gap, and I spend the next several hours driving them across L.A. to attack additional outposts of capitalist oppression. Panic assures me he would drive if I weren't in the car with them, but by this point I am enjoying the lawlessness for its own sake. I am coming to suspect that the simple, transgressive thrill of committing vandalism is a major draw for their particular revolution.

They spray-paint "WE WON WTO" on the wall of a Jaguar dealership. They tag a Starbucks with "STARBUCKS RAPES RAIN FORESTS." They hit a McDonald's with "McMURDER." Wingnut Super Glues the locks of a Venice Gap.

By midnight we are in Long Beach searching for additional targets. Wingnut's lingering cough leaves him so breathless he can barely run. He suggests everyone call it a night. But Panic and Siren want to keep going, so they leave Wingnut and me by the curb and head for a nearby Gap.

Panic and Siren stride to the Gap, shaking their spray cans. They have done this so many times in the past couple of hours, they become careless and take too long as they spray-paint the wall with the Gap's alleged crimes— clear-cutting redwood forests, using child labor.

A cop car zooms onto the curb a few feet from the taggers. Panic takes off down an alley. Siren stays behind, and two cops hustle her to the ground.

Wingnut and I watch helplessly from a couple hundred feet away. We see the cops put Siren into a car and drive her off. Panic's fate is unclear. A police helicopter beats overhead, washing rooftops and pavement in white light. Wingnut walks toward the Gap to look for Panic. As he approaches, a cop beams a flashlight in Wingnut's face but lets him pass, probably assuming he is just some homeless guy. None of the cops pay much attention when Wingnut walks away shouting "Panic" into the night.

The next morning at the co-op Kendra learns that Siren and Panic are being held at the Long Beach jail on misdemeanor charges for their acts of graffiti on the Gap. Siren contacts her parents and asks if they will post her $300 bail. They agree to do so only if she renounces anarchy and agrees to pray with them and read the Bible every night for one hour. Siren refuses to renounce the revolution. Both she and Panic opt to do a few days' jail time in lieu of paying fines.

Wingnut ceases to exist the following afternoon when I drop him at a truck stop in the Inland Empire east of Los Angeles. I last see him walking toward a truck, a future primitive going nowhere.

Fewer than six months later the young man named Craig Marshall is arrested for setting fire to several SUVs at a car dealership in Eugene, Oregon. I know him as Wingnut. Prosecutors allege he is a member of Earth Liberation Front and claim he is responsible for causing more than $43 million of property damage during the previous five years. They charge him with several arson counts related to the car dealership fire, and Marshall accepts a plea deal, drawing a five-and-a-half-year sentence. His co-conspirator in the crime, Jeff Luers, a twenty-three-year-old with the revolutionary name "Free," takes his case to trial. He is convicted of multiple counts of arson and sentenced to twenty-one years in prison.

In Pastor Richard Girnt Butler's Church of Jesus Christ Christian Aryan Nations, the cross and the swastika are united, and prayers are said with a Sieg Heil salute. The good news Pastor Butler preaches is that race war is coming to America. Each summer his Christian Identity followers—an assortment of skinheads, Nazis and Klansmen—gather at his Aryan Nations compound in Hayden Lake, Idaho, to celebrate white pride under the warm glow of flaming crosses. This past July at the 1996 Aryan Nations World Congress, we were on hand to observe the festivities.

Pastor Butler calls his religion Christian Identity, and its tenets are simple: White "Aryan" Americans are God's chosen people. There will be a race war. Blacks and all other nonwhite "mud people" will be kicked out of America. The Jews will be exterminated.

In 1983, nearly a dozen of Pastor Butler's followers put the Aryan Nations on the map by forming a secret paramilitary group they called "The Order" to start the prophesied conflagration of the races. The war began in an adult bookstore in Spokane, Washington, where members of the group burst in with guns, sucker-punched the clerk and made off with $379.10. It was not an auspicious beginning. The pipe bomb they set off at a local synagogue failed to kill anyone, and the counterfeit money they had printed on the Aryan Nations printing press—normally used to run off their raving, misspelled hate literature—was spotted as bogus as soon as they tried to pass it.

The Aryan Christian soldiers had better luck murdering a Jew. They ambushed Alan Berg, a Denver talk-radio personality famous for belittling the far right on the air, and shot him dead outside his home with multiple rounds from a MAC-10.

The white supremacists successfully robbed a series of armored cars and filled their coffers with enough loot to buy land for paramilitary training camps, purchase weapons and supplies and donate $40,000 to Pastor Butler's Aryan church. One Aryan Nations member was sentenced to death for boasting about the group's exploits in a local bar. His Christian Identity brothers lured him into the woods, beat him with a sledgehammer, then shot him in the back of the head.

The crime spree—or "race-war operation," as the perpetrators saw it—came to an end when the FBI traced a gun used in a Brinks truck heist to one of the members. Twenty-two race-warriors were hunted down and arrested. One was burned to death in a shoot-out with the FBI.

The government was unable to prove any direct connection between Pastor Butler and the crimes committed by his acolytes. He was charged with sedition, but was acquitted after a lengthy trial—saved by the First Amendment.

Butler's Aryan Nations compound in Idaho thrived, pumping out hate tracts for distribution in prisons and offering sanctuary, paramilitary training and race salvation for homicidal white men from around the nation. Among Butler's most prominent followers were Oklahoma City bomber Timothy McVeigh and his accomplice Terry Nichols.

THE 1996 ARYAN NATIONS WORLD CONGRESS begins on a warm July day in Hayden Lake, an astonishingly beautiful land of crystal lakes, blue mountains, golden fields and world-class golf club resorts, for which it is famous. Down Rimrock Road, an unpaved track marked by shot-up "Do Not Discharge Firearms" signs, FBI agents sit in unmarked vans watching the entrance to the Aryan Nations compound.

Screened off from the road by pine trees, nestled in a woodsy clearing, is the small steepled Church of Jesus Christ Christian Aryan Nations, with attached offices and outlying cabins. An ominous guard tower, hung with a swastika banner, gives the place the feel of a concentration camp—or the set of *Hogan's Heroes*.

A "Whites Only" sign is posted on the guard shack at the entrance to the parking lot. Two teenage sentries stand outside, checking IDs. One of the sentries is a sullen fifteen-year-old boy named Clinton Matthews; his father led the original band of Christian Identity race haters who launched the 1983 murder and crime spree that put Aryan Nations on the map. Matthews's father is the "Aryan martyr" burned to death in the shoot-out with the FBI.

The other sentry is a scarred, tattooed skinhead with a broken-tooth, checkerboard grin. "Welcome to the one place in America you can be free and white," he greets a visitor.

Members of the Aryan Nations security detail, paunchy, middle-aged men in blue storm trooper uniforms, display equal good cheer. "Hey, we're white people," a grinning swastika saluter implores. "We're not rabid, we don't bite."

"Once you see what's going on," drawls a stringy southerner with yellow hair and brown, tobacco-stained teeth, "it's kind of catching."

A wooden platform is set up on the lawn for Pastor Butler's first address of the Congress. Fifty to sixty Aryan Nations followers are assembled on the lawn, dressed in odd costumes—men clad in assorted Nazi regalia, skinheads in Dr. Martens and bomber jackets, and young girls who wear folkloric, eighteenth-century dresses with bonnets and aprons like Amish maidens, but accented with swastika jewelry. As part of his call to purify contemporary America from "modern, Jew corruptions like Hollywood movies, television, homosexuality and pornography," Pastor Butler's religion calls for a return to a pastoral, eighteenth-century lifestyle, though one heavily armed with the latest, high-powered, automatic weapons.

The mood among the crowd is festive. It's as if devotees of a particular fetish or perversion have all found one another and are coming out together at once. Many appear giddy with the excitement of showing off once secret, forbidden Nazi attire for the first time in a public setting. Best of all, no one need feel any shame for who they are. As Pastor Butler taught in a previous sermon, "There is no shame in being white, no shame in being proud, no shame in hating the nigger and the Jew."

Pastor Butler strides to the platform in a somber, brown business suit, looking fit for his age of seventy-four. A hush spreads among the followers, and they turn their rapt attention to the platform. Butler's features are stern as he begins his speech. His eyes gaze majestically into the horizon, as if reading invisible letters printed across the blue sky. He lectures about Jewish conspiracies, ZOG (Zionist Occupation Government) control of America, treasons committed by the UN and race war. "This land shall be cleansed," Butler promises. "There will be a lot of blood running one day. This land shall again become white and Christian."

Audience members nod assent as Butler explains the Aryan Nations' view of world history. The white race lost World War II. No peace treaty was ever signed with Germany, and Hitler's Third Reich still exists—although nobody in the Jew-controlled media will report this.

"Good men are coming forth," Butler assures his listeners, "solid men, men with iron wills, men who are determined that their race is not going to die."

Hearty applause greets the conclusion of his speech. Over the next three days, right-wing leaders from across the land will regale the assembled visitors with nearly two dozen speeches. Outsiders from the press are barred from attending, but individual Aryan Nations members are more than happy to share their stories with reporters, and for a $100 fee, Butler will grant a private interview to just about anyone who dares to listen.

PASTOR BUTLER'S OFFICE IS CLUTTERED with conspiracy books, pamphlets and stacks of correspondence from Aryan Nations followers from around the country. There are portraits of Hitler everywhere—a stern-faced Hitler in his military uniform, a businesslike Hitler in a brown civilian suit (much like Butler's) and a lovable Hitler at play with his dog. The pastor's own dog, Hans, lies at his feet under the desk, growling every time footsteps approach. Pastor Butler leans back in his desk chair, hands clasped behind his head, and delivers his opinions as if they're self-evident truths:

"Nazism and Christianity are two sides of the same coin. The SS was a Christian organization.

"Homosexuals are mostly Jewish. The cure, of course, for homosexuals is death.

"The Oriental knows not to mongrelize with other races. You have your exceptions, like that Connie Chung who married a Jew."

He tells a story about a friend whose son was recently eaten by black cannibals in the Bahamas and talks of black doctors in South Africa routinely performing organ transplants by stealing livers and lungs from living white donors. He elaborates, "They say the screams of the white victims strengthen the organs that the blacks are receiving. Of course, when they eat part of a white man, they believe that they're getting his strength and knowledge too."

RICHARD BUTLER WAS BORN in Colorado and studied aerospace engineering in Los Angeles. After World War II, during which he served in India as an aircraft technician, he settled in Southern California and worked in the aerospace industry, working for Hughes and Lockheed.

Throughout the 1950s and 1960s, Butler was active in the far right causes, participating in dozens of cross burnings and neo-Nazi rallies. During this period, he came into contact with the Christian Identity teachings of Wesley Swift. Swift was an ordained Methodist minister who delivered sermons from the pulpit of his Hollywood, California, church that blended Nazi propaganda with Christian fundamentalism, science fiction and, perversely enough, myths of the Torah. From Swift came the basic tenets of Christian Identity: That the Hebrews were Aryan. That the Jews were spawned by Satan. That nonwhite races, called "muds," belong in the animal kingdom. Only people of Aryan descent can claim to be God's children, his chosen people.

In the Christian Identity telling of world history, the white man is the perpetual victim of a diabolical Jewish race. According to Butler and his flock, it was a Jewish trick claiming that Jesus was a Jew; he was an Aryan. The Israelites were not Jews; they were Aryans. Hebrew is not a Jewish language, it's Aryan.

Butler cites from a considerable body of conspiracy literature—much of it printed by him on the Aryan Nations printing presses—proving that the Jews brought all the slaves to America, the Founding Fathers were anti-Semites and wanted to expel the Jews from America, and the Federal Reserve Bank and the United States Marine Corps are owned by Jews. It's only fitting that the same printing press used to produce counterfeit money during the Church's most overtly violent period in the 1980s also produced so many of these bogus historical documents. Some of these forgeries are spotted just as easily as the funny money was. An anti-Semitic speech attributed to Benjamin Franklin, for instance, uses phrases not found in the English lexicon until the 1930s.

In the coming war prophesied by Pastor Butler, most races—blacks and all the other "mud people"—will be spared from death, so long as they get out of America. The Jews are not so lucky. "If the Aryans win, there won't be any more Jews," Butler says.

A skinhead office boy enters and stands respectfully at attention to ask Butler a question about prison inmate correspondence. As the young skinhead leaves, Butler gives him a paternal smile. "The skinheads who come here, of course, resent. They resent what's been taken from them by the Jew.

But they're not dressed like street bums coming out of a trashy ghetto. What they have on is clean, it's good and everything is in perfect order. And they realize that picking on some little Jap or Chink isn't the answer."

He continues, "In America today, the children talk back, sass to get their own way and take drugs. Anyone who's ever seen *Triumph of the Will* can see the decline of our youth by comparing the youth at a rock concert today to the youth in *Triumph of the Will*. There's a stark difference. Our youth today dress in run-down shoes with their hats on backwards. Whereas the Germans were taught to dress up, to look like somebody."

Pastor Butler lays the blame for the degeneration of social values on the Jewish influence in Hollywood, citing the movie *Independence Day* as an example. "A nigger and a Jew save the whole white race!" Pastor Butler says, outraged at the preposterousness of it.

Even lower than the Jews are traitorous whites, the "wiggers," or "white niggers," who sell out the race by promoting interracial sex. One of the worst "wiggers," according to Pastor Butler, is *Hustler* magazine publisher Larry Flynt, paralyzed by a round fired by white supremacist Joseph Paul Franklin, who later admitted he had been outraged by the "Peaches" pictorial in the May 1978 *Hustler*, which featured a black man screwing a white woman. Butler claims to have helped minister to Paul before his attempted execution of Flynt for being a race traitor, and also to possess inside knowledge of what transpired. He says, "I understand there was a chain-link fence between where Joseph Paul Franklin was shooting and where Larry Flynt was standing. The bullet grazed the chain-link fence and was deflected a little bit so it just paralyzed him. Which is too bad." Butler leans back and guffaws. "But I guess he's going to suffer for the rest of his life."

ON SATURDAY NIGHT, Butler and about a hundred of his followers stage a triple cross burning by the hill outside the compound. Crosses made from thirty-foot-tall trees are wrapped in burlap and soaked in kerosene. In the flickering light and intense heat thrown off by the fires, Pastor Butler performs the marriage ceremony of two young followers from Pennsylvania.

The bride, a petite twenty-one-year-old nursing student with long blond hair, wears a white Victorian dress purchased at a thrift store. The groom, a lanky twenty-two-year-old with a protruding Adam's apple, wears an SS uniform, complete with Sam Browne belt and a swastika armband. Pastor Butler performs traditional vows and pronounces them "Aryan man and Aryan wife."

Kevin, the groom, is an "aquatic technician," or pool cleaner, currently unemployed since losing his job as a result of what he calls "religious persecution."

Rebecca, the bride, elaborates: "His boss told him he was fired because he dropped a radio in a pool, but we know the real reason. They fired him because he talked about his religion, Christian Identity."

Kevin credits his interest in the Nazis to a childhood fascination with World War II, which he thinks occurred sometime in the 1950s. He never graduated from high school because, he claims, he was expelled by a "Jew principal."

"I got tired of my teachers always trying to make me look dumb in front of the other students," Kevin says with a weary sigh. The chance discovery of an Aryan Nations pamphlet prompted Kevin to make a Forrest Gumpian journey of walking across America. When he arrived at the Aryan Nations compound, he was dismayed to learn that there was only a handful of followers living on the premises. Someone had told him there would be a community of thousands. He nevertheless stayed on for a year, putting his education in the hands of Pastor Butler and working as a "grounds supervisor." Upon his return to Pennsylvania, Kevin met his bride-to-be.

At that time, Rebecca was going through a troubled period. Describing herself back then as "a spoiled Catholic school girl, with multicultural parents," Rebecca was floundering in her sophomore year of nursing school. "I was lost."

Rebecca hesitates before revealing a painful secret. "I was hanging out with an older man named Mouthy."

"He was black," states Kevin, as if discussing a detail from a crime.

"It's not like I was a wigger myself," Rebecca says. "I was only with him for a month before I came to my senses."

A chance meeting with Kevin turned her life around. Romance blossomed. Kevin moved into Rebecca's parents' house with her and converted her to Christian Identity.

Since Rebecca's parents are currently paying for her college education and are opposed to both her beliefs and the idea of her getting married, Rebecca and Kevin plan to keep the wedding a secret.

"My family has a lot of problems," Rebecca explains. "They're very multicultural."

"Her brother goes out with a Jew," Kevin, the new son-in-law, says with thinly veiled contempt.

"She's a Russian communist Jew, and she's ugly." Rebecca scrunches her face with distaste. "She goes against her people all the time. She never goes to synagogue and she practices Christmas."

"Doesn't that sound like a Jew," Kevin adds. "They want the best of both worlds."

"She just preys on my brother like a parasite," Rebecca says.

"See, it's a basic, scientific fact," Kevin lectures, showing off some of the learning he acquired from Pastor Butler during his year of study. "The Jewish bloodline cannot exist without an Aryan host. After three generations of Jew breeding with Jew, they produce defects, blood disorders, Tay-Sachs—they come out all messed up. It's a proven fact they need to breed with us, Aryans, in order to live. You can't imagine what a Jew would look like mixed up with an Oriental, or an Asian or a Negro. It would be hideous."

HANNAH, a stout twenty-year-old Aryan mother of two, with a pudgy face and a pug nose, stands in the bright sunlight outside the Aryan Church hall, testifying about the miracle of her conversion to Christian Identity. "When I was sixteen, I was trying to kill myself. I overdosed on Prozac. I should have died, but Yahweh [the Christian Identity name for God, taken from the

Hebrew] gave me a miracle. He gave me a child. I started studying Identity when he was in my belly." She adds, "My little one came out saluting Yahweh just like this when he was born." She demonstrates by giving a Hitler salute.

Hannah is married to Bill, a wiry twenty-six-year-old who wears his hair in a small ponytail that makes his odd SS uniform even odder. In the Pennsylvania town where Bill and Hannah live, Bill is a leading Christian Identity "teacher of Yahweh." He learned about Christian Identity from a friend in prison.

"We're persecuted for our beliefs," Bill explains. "I used to get hate mail stuffed in the mailbox. One of the worst was a drawing of a white man on his knees praying while a nigger urinated on his face. The cops wouldn't do anything, so finally, my buddy and I made a KKK snowman in the front yard. We did it right around Martin Luther King's birthday, so it got a lot of newspaper coverage. People have left us alone after that."

A sense of oppression—fear of the world and of nonwhite people—weighs heavily on Bill. "We're in bondage until Yahweh's hand comes across the land. People say I'm paranoid, and I am. I have a lot of anxiety. If I go to the store, man, and I get around two big, black boys, my heart friggin' thumps. It's Yahweh telling me, Get the fuck out!"

"I feel very spiritual because of Yahweh," Hannah cuts in, as her four-year-old wanders past. "Yahweh protects me from every bad thing that can happen, because I am of Aryan race. I—not the Jews—am God's chosen. My whole life, I knew that I was special inside. Finding Yahweh explained to me why I'd felt that way."

Hannah picks up her son and kisses him on his cheek, gooey with a banana he's eaten. "I've taught my son to shout 'shibbia' whenever he sees a nigger on TV. In Hebrew, our language, 'shibbia' is the term for a biped beast. I was at the supermarket and the lady doing the checkout was black, and he pointed at her, freaking out, going, 'Mommy, Mommy, beastie, shibbia, beastie!'"

"But the worst threat to our race," Bill says, "is not the nigger and the muds. It's the wiggers, white traitors, who betray their own people."

Hannah adds, "A white guy once told me that I'm going to hell for hating the Jews. Sometimes, all I can do is laugh at how confused white people are in our own homeland."

Before leaving, Hannah demonstrates an innovation she claims to have contributed to the Aryan Nations. She lowers herself into a curtsy, then looks up smiling as she gives the Nazi salute. "This is my Nazi curtsy for you." She smiles. "I invented this."

DURING HIS CAREER as a soldier in the United States Army, James A. Dillavou washed out of helicopter pilot school because of color blindness, was kicked out of MP training because of a prior criminal record and flunked airborne assault school because of bad knees. In four years in the Army, he never achieved a rank higher than private. In the Aryan Nations, he is Major James A. Dillavou, commander of the North Central Territory.

Like others interviewed at the Congress, Dillavou, twenty-five, comes from a broken home and a hardscrabble childhood.

"You know the banana seat on a Schwinn?" Dillavou asks, squinting nearsightedly beneath the visor of his black Aryan Nations cap. "My grandfather invented that, and Schwinn stole it from him. My family lost all its money."

Dillavou grew up in Southern California's San Gabriel Valley. His mother—dispossessed heiress to the banana seat fortune—went through a succession of marriages and supported the family by working as a waitress.

At the age of fifteen Dillavou discovered white power, and he spent the next five years listening to Nazi rock-and-roll punk, drinking 40s with his buddies and "fighting muds every other day." He and his friends dressed in the skinhead uniform of braces, Dr. Martens and Dickies—the work pants sold at Kmart. They traded tales of Odin—Norse warrior myths gleaned through comic books—and carried around copies of *Mein Kampf* when they visited high schools to recruit members for their organization, Western Hammer.

"I went back to L.A. after getting discharged from the Army," he says.

"But I was just ready to blow up like that guy in *Falling Down*." It was around this time that Dillavou was arrested for his role in an attack on a black man. "We were driving around doing the usual stuff you do when you see niggers on the street—you know, shouting 'Nigger' out the window at them and whatnot.

"I had this idiot in the car, trying to show off and be Mr. White Power. We seen this nigger on the street in a three-piece suit. He smiled and waved at us when we drove by shouting at him. So this guy in the car with me jumped out and hit him in the face—nothing too hard, just slapped him a little bit.

"It was stupid, because there was no way we wouldn't get caught. I drove an orange Pinto, and everyone knew it was like the white-power car around town.

"After I got arrested, we kicked the idiot who did it out of the organization. There were rumors he might have been a homosexual. And we found out he was dating a Mexican broad."

Released after serving seventy-seven days in the county jail, Dillavou found sanctuary in Iowa and converted to Christian Identity.

At the 1996 World Congress, Dillavou announces that he has registered to run for political office in Iowa. He plans to campaign as an independent in the race for state representative for the 34th District of Iowa. "It's not like I can run on segregation," he says of his candidacy, "but I might be able to do something like bring the Bible back into our schools, which is at least a start."

ON A LAZY SUNDAY AFTERNOON down on the banks of Hayden Lake, several miles from the closing ceremonies of Aryan World Congress, two scruffy nineteen-year-olds sit with fishing rods. One of them holds an out-of-tune guitar, playing Nirvana and Deep Purple riffs over and over as he tokes on a cigarette.

"The Aryans are a bunch of assholes," says the one with a flat, stoner's laugh. "Unless you want to get drunk. They'll get you drunker than hell.

"After high school, my friend Eric became an Aryan. Bald, stocky, two hundred and eighty pounds, he was a big boy. So they gave him the name Ogre and tattooed it on his hand.

"Mostly, they'd just sit around Eric—I mean Ogre's—house drinking beer, talking about how they wanted to go to L.A. and 'take people out' like Jean-Claude Van Damme in that movie *Hard Target*. It was pretty stupid," he says, flicking his cigarette into an empty, wide-mouth beer bottle.

THE FINAL ACT of the 1996 Aryan World Congress is the Soldier's Ransom. After prayers are offered to Yahweh, Nazi colors are raised and solemn tribute is given to the martyrs of the Aryan Nations war—the brave men and women who have sacrificed their lives setting off bombs in synagogues, burning crosses in people's yards and assaulting strangers in the street.

When it is over, Pastor Butler pulls a reporter aside and offers these final words: "The press seeks to convince the people that we're losers, we have no agenda, and we're haters, bigots, discriminators. Well, the press isn't the people. I'd rather let the people decide for themselves what we are."

1. THE KILLING

KONSTANTIN SIMBERG HAD LIVED in America for about a year and a half when, according to police, three of his friends led him into the Yavapai woods north of Phoenix on December 15, 2001, and prepared to kill him. Simberg was twenty-one. Two of the alleged killers were Soviet-bloc immigrants like Simberg. The third was a rich kid, an eighteen-year-old freshman at Arizona State named Chris Andrews, a private-school kid whose dad worked at IBM. The four of them knew one another from the Phoenix rave scene. Though Andrews had recently been kicked out of his dorm for alleged cocaine possession, none of the accused killers had criminal records. Mikhail Drachev, also eighteen, was still in high school; classmates described him as "weird" and nicknamed him Mikhail Jack-Off. The other accused killer, twenty-year-old Dennis Tsoukanov, who had immigrated to Phoenix from Estonia nearly ten years earlier, seemed the least likely to be caught up in murder. He lived at home with his father, a successful builder, worked as a supermarket checkout boy and studied graphic design at a community college. Even though he is slightly cross-eyed, Tsoukanov dreamed of modeling for Abercrombie & Fitch.

According to police, the three young men had lured Simberg the day before his murder to an apartment shared by Andrews and Drachev. There they beat him, bound him in duct tape and held him prisoner in a closet for nearly twenty-four hours. Once in the Yavapai woods, they offered him one last smoke. Simberg, wrists still duct-taped, accepted the cigarette they pressed to his lips, took in the desert forest of scrub bush and pines and said, "Hey, this isn't Mexico."

During the hundred-mile drive up to the Yavapai woods from Phoenix, the alleged killers had told Simberg they were going to take him to Mexico and drop him off below the border. But instead, one of the young men pulled out a handgun, a TEC-9, bought the night before, and tried to shoot Simberg in the head. The pistol jammed. So they attempted to slit Simberg's throat with a large hunting knife, but he struggled and they managed only to hack a piece of flesh off his chin. Finally, one of the attackers drove the knife into his back, puncturing a lung. As he fell to the ground, they could hear air gurgling from the hole in his back. His friends then doused him in gasoline and threw rocks over his body. They set him on fire and ran to their car as their friend screamed and writhed in the makeshift grave.

The flames that consumed Simberg also melted the duct tape that bound his wrists, as well as the flesh on his arms and hands. Somehow he managed to pull himself up on the bony claws that remained of his two scorched hands, tear off his burning trousers and run about three hundred feet to the banks of Fossil Creek, where, finally, he collapsed in the shade, next to a rock. Hunters discovered his corpse the next day.

Like other immigrants, Simberg had come to the New World in search of the American dream. In his own way, he came remarkably close to achieving it—his idea of it, at least: a B-movie, gangsta-video version that revolved around fast cars, flashy babes, get-rich-quick schemes, high-tolling con men and, in Simberg's case, a strange, semi-legal drug catering to the nation's fixation with eternal youth.

2. THE WONDER DRUG

GROWTH HORMONE SUPPLEMENTS have been used since the 1950s to treat patients whose pituitary glands could not produce enough on their own. Typically, these were infants who suffered from congenital pituitary disorders or children whose gland functions were damaged by illness or head trauma. Failure to produce sufficient growth hormone inhibits development and leads to dwarfism. Growth hormone therapy was a major breakthrough in treating dwarfism, but until the 1980s it could only be obtained in limited quantities by harvesting it from corpses. That changed in 1981 when researchers at the biology research firm Genentech succeeded in synthesizing it from genetically engineered bacteria, a process that promised unlimited quantities at greatly reduced cost. By then growth hormone was increasingly being used to treat the wasting symptoms—the shriveling of muscles and organs—caused by HIV/AIDS. In 1985 major pharmaceutical manufacturers began selling synthetic growth hormone. In a classic bit of marketing double-speak, vendors touted this new product as "human growth hormone," or HGH, even though they were in fact selling a synthetic version of it.

In 1990 *The New England Journal of Medicine* published the findings of a study that suggested HGH supplements slowed or even reversed some symptoms of aging in adults, the most dramatic of which was the increase of muscle mass and corresponding reductions of body fat. Other studies quickly followed. Preliminary results suggested that in addition to increasing lean muscle mass and burning fat, HGH might promote the growth of damaged organs, increase lung capacity and strengthen the heart. Though the studies offered only the most preliminary of findings, they were seized upon by a market primed for any kind of new miracle drug. That market, driven by legitimate doctors and unlicensed quacks alike, had been born in the fitness and health boom of the 1970s and was always on the lookout for the latest performance, health and diet enhancers, from herbal remedies to GHB—used as much by bodybuilders as ravers—to steroids. Starting in the early nineties, HGH became the ultimate wonder drug, touted as an elixir that builds mass like steroids but cuts fat like ephedra. Despite a paucity of evidence, many users believe that HGH removes wrinkles, cures baldness and, among men, has a Viagra-like effect on penile function.

The dangers of excessive HGH consumption are well known to researchers and are not a matter of dispute. As with steroids, too much HGH can cause a condition known as acromegaly, in which victims suffer acute joint pain, organ swelling, excessive hair growth all over their bodies and unnatural bone growth that results in enlarged brows for a Cro-Magnon-like appearance. Worse yet, chronic abuse of HGH can shut down the body's natural production of it in the pituitary gland, hooking abusers for life. If that isn't bad enough, HGH is also suspected of accelerating the growth of cancer cells and inducing diabetes.

Despite all the risks, by the late 1990s HGH had become a multibillion-dollar business. Leading pharmaceutical companies, among them Eli Lilly, Novo Nordisk, Pfizer and Serono, all manufactured synthetic hormone and pumped it into the market via an ethically shady but FDA-approved complex of secondary wholesalers.

One of the biggest of these was a Phoenix-based company called Peak Physique. At the time of his murder, Konstantin Simberg was a government witness in a million-dollar HGH-theft case being pursued against the founder of Peak Physique, Troy Langdon.

Langdon launched Peak Physique in 1994, when he was a twenty-three-year-old drugstore clerk. Langdon, who did not even possess a pharmacist's license, managed to build his drug-distribution company by exploiting FDA loopholes. Within a couple of years Langdon's Peak Physique became one of Serono's biggest customers for HGH it sold under the brand name Saizen.

Through Langdon's pioneering use of the Internet, his firm became a leading national seller, providing the drug to physicians and clinics as well as individual professional athletes, fitness freaks and a handful of aging A-list celebrities.

Records show Peak Physique achieved a cash flow of $25 million a month, but the phenomenal growth of the business, like that of HGH, proved to be highly problematic. Despite the cash churned by the company and the high-rolling lifestyle Langdon achieved, by 2001 his firm was on the ropes. Langdon and his partner were implicated in a robbery of Langdon's own business and an insurance fraud scheme, but before police could bring them to trial, Konstantin Simberg, the chief witness against them, was burned alive in the Yavapai woods.

3. THE WONDER BOYS

LANGDON DESCRIBES HIS OWN BACKGROUND as "being from dirt." His father was a twenty-year enlisted Navy man who later worked as a roofer. Langdon brags he "never spent a day in college." His greatest career move was to marry his high school sweetheart, Jennifer Shaffer, whose parents owned Cactus Pharmacy in North Phoenix. Shortly after his marriage, at age twenty-one, Langdon became a clerk at his in-laws' pharmacy.

Never a particularly good athlete himself, Langdon had always been a sports fan. He'd hung out with jocks in high school, and later, even after his marriage, used to hang out at a Phoenix strip club called Christie's Cabaret in the hope of meeting players from the Arizona Diamondbacks, among whom the place was popular. Police believe that Christie's was sometimes used, without the knowledge or consent of its owners, as a location for buyers seeking the purchase of illegal steroids to meet with sellers. Langdon denies being involved in the illegal sale of steroids, but at the same time he admits that from the start of his career at his in-laws' pharmacy, "I had a lot of dealings with athletes who used anabolic steroids."

Langdon says it was through his contacts with professional athletes that he first became aware of the demand for HGH. Like other drugs in the United States, HGH falls into a regulatory gray area. Since the FDA has only approved HGH for use in children suffering from dwarfism and for HIV/AIDS patients suffering from wasting, manufacturers are only allowed to market the drug to treat those conditions. When Genentech attempted to market its synthetic HGH as a panacea for aging adults and athletes seeking to enhance performance, it was sued by the FDA, and in 1994 the company was forced to pay a $50 million fine.

But even as the FDA restricts how drug manufacturers are permitted to market medicines, doctors are allowed by law to prescribe drugs for any malady or condition they see fit. So as long as a doctor wrote a prescription, there were no restrictions on how HGH could be used. Langdon recognized the void between FDA regulations and the potential for demand in the marketplace and stepped into it. As he explains it, "The HGH manufacturers had a monster sitting there, but they couldn't go out there and advertise their product. They couldn't put their logo on the back of a NASCAR car and say, 'Growth Hormone: Good for Your Future.' But they could provide it in bulk to a guy like me who would go out there and sell it far and wide."

Langdon calculated—correctly, as it turned out—that as long as he didn't place high-profile ads for HGH and worked beneath the radar by calling doctors directly to inform them of the benefits of HGH, then he could conduct the marketing that pharmaceutical companies themselves were barred from carrying out. Though Langdon didn't have a pharmacist's license of his own, he was able to buy and sell drugs by piggybacking his company, Peak Physique, onto the pharmacy owned by his in-laws. Armed with lists of doctors from their records, as well as with his contacts in the world of athletes, Langdon set about touting the wonders of HGH, which he billed as a "glory drug." To prove his point, he began taking it. Though he stands over six feet tall, he had always been, in his own words, "a fat kid." Six months of being on HGH, as well as working out at the gym, gave him a strikingly lean, chiseled physique. Langdon told customers that they need only look as far as his own six-pack to see the awesome fat-burning powers of HGH. While proclaiming the health benefits of the "glory drug," he continued his two-pack-a-day Marlboro habit.

Langdon founded Life Medical Research Clinics with several local doctors and was granted a license from the FDA to engage in medical "research" with HGH. Life Medical Research Clinics could not directly market HGH to potential customers, but could promote the opportunity for people to become research subjects in antiaging and performance-enhancement studies, for which they would have to purchase their own HGH—as much as $20,000 worth—from Langdon. He franchised Life Medical Research Clinics to more than 160 physicians before the FDA revoked his research license in early 2002.

Langdon extended his operations as a middleman to online retailers. Internet sales, especially unregulated and difficult to track in the mid-1990s, skirted the law by allowing customers to purchase HGH (and other drugs) after filling out electronic questionnaires that served as "consultations" with physicians, who then wrote prescriptions. In practice many such sites employed doctors whose sole job was to rubber-stamp prescriptions for each order that came in, without performing even the most cursory review of a customer's records. While the practice was against the law in the state of Arizona, Langdon supplied online retailers in nearby states where more relaxed regulatory climates allowed such businesses to thrive. While major drug manufacturers generally shunned doing business with shady, online enterprises, their responsibility for the HGH ended once it was sold to a trusted wholesaler like Langdon's Peak Physique.

As the business grew, Langdon and his wife purchased a $700,000 home in Carefree, Arizona. They were soon awash in all the bling needed for the late-twentieth-century American Dream, from Rolexes to powerboats and Jet Skis to Mercedes AMGs, customized BMWs and Porsches. For Langdon, exotic cars gave him additional entrée into the world of pro athletes. In his first contact with police, Langdon would brag that the 2002 Porsche Turbo Carrera he was driving was one he had just bought from a friend, Arizona Diamondbacks pitcher Juan Cruz.

While Langdon was a gifted salesman, his business skills were wanting. When the HGH market changed, Langdon failed to adapt. The problem was the very success of HGH. The drug had become so sought after, pharmaceutical manufacturers no longer needed entrepreneurs like Langdon to market the product. In addition, the number of middlemen trying to get in on the action had skyrocketed. To deal with the competition, Langdon cut prices so low he began losing money on every sale he made. "What Langdon got into was a downward spiral," says Dr. John Musil, who runs Valley Services, a Scottsdale pharmaceutical wholesaler. "He became one of the biggest, but he was no longer making any money."

In early 2000, Langdon lost a lucrative supply contract with an Internet HGH seller. According to a Phoenix doctor I spoke to, Langdon invited him out to lunch about this time. As the doctor recalls, "Troy said, 'Gee, I just bought this new Acura NSX sports car last week, and suddenly my relationship with this online HGH company has ended.'" The doctor says that Langdon sounded him out on the possibility of writing illegal HGH prescriptions for thousands of customers Langdon hoped to sell to directly, but he declined. Later, Langdon's brother-in-law, who worked for his parents' Cactus Pharmacy, would admit to police that he forged HGH prescriptions at Langdon's direction. When I visited the pharmacy and asked him about this, he would neither confirm nor deny it.

At the time of Langdon's business disintegration, he fell into the thrall of an oddly charismatic ne'er-do-well named Sean Southland, two years his senior. When the two met in late 1999 in a VIP room at Christie's strip club, Southland carried with him a sheaf of slick brochures advertising a company he had recently founded, Sea Castle Ventures. The idea behind Sea Castle was a sound one, to make the world of luxury yachting—previously available only to the superrich—affordable to the merely affluent through the sale of time-shares. (George Hernandez, a Los Angeles yacht broker whom Southland subsequently retained, told me that the idea was actually kind of brilliant, saying, "Sean's idea could have made him the Bill Gates of time-shares.") His prospectus for Sea Castle outlined a bold plan: to launch twelve mega-yachts, anchor them in prime harbors from Cancún to Nassau and ultimately to earn a projected $300 million annually for investors wise enough to get in on the scheme early. Though the business was just getting under way at the time Southland met Langdon, he flashed ads he'd recently taken out in yacht magazines, advertising Sea Castle with the slogan "Your Ship Just Came In."

Langdon says that as soon as he met Southland he felt they were "two peas in a pod." That Langdon felt a keen sense of familiarity with Southland, as well as what he would later term "profound admiration," is no surprise. Both were natural hucksters, but where Langdon functioned within a realm where real products were exchanged for money, Southland functioned almost at the level of pure con artistry. From the moment they met, almost everything about Southland was a lie, or some kind of trick.

When they first met, Southland was living in a small apartment in a building managed by his mother. It was his mother who provided the initial investment of $10,000 into Sea Castle that enabled him to print up brochures and take out ads in yachting magazines. Since the early nineties Southland had embarked on a variety of careers—police officer, U.S. Army soldier, gun-sight salesman, tow-truck operator—which had all ended either in his dismissal or his leaving under abrupt, unexplained circumstances. By 1999 he was surviving on handouts from his mother and wages his wife earned working as an airline hostess and stripper.

Though Southland and his wife were raising two young children together, he had recently begun dating a Russian immigrant whom he had persuaded to take a job as a stripper at Christie's Cabaret. The Russian stripper girlfriend would later admit she had helped engineer his encounter with Langdon in the belief—which later proved not quite accurate—that he had a lot of money and would be able to finance Sea Castle.

As Southland later explained, "Troy knew he was in a diminishing business. He looked to Sea Castle as the future."

For Langdon the future that Southland offered would prove extremely costly. Shortly after their first encounter, Langdon put Southland on salary and gave him the title of director of marketing at Peak Physique. He also made out a check to Sea Castle for one million dollars. Southland was wise enough not to cash the check (given Langdon's increasingly precarious cash flow), but he would use it as a sales tool, flashing it to other investors as proof of the venture's worthiness.

The two became inseparable. Southland started taking HGH with Langdon. They worked out together every morning at Langdon's home gym, admiring the muscles on each other's bodies as they grew. They spent evenings together at Christie's Cabaret and weekends at Lake Powell partying on boats and Jet Skis. Langdon's wife became best friends with Southland's girlfriend. In a photograph commemorating an outing at the lake, the two women stand flashing their breasts at passing boaters. Langdon and Southland stand by their sides laughing. "Not a day went by that we didn't see each other for over a year," says Southland of his relationship with Langdon.

Even today, as they face felony charges and possibly even murder charges stemming from their partnership, Langdon speaks of Southland in inspirational terms, saying, "There are few people I've ever met who have the qualities Sean has, who wants what I want for myself, for my family. Sean has what I aspire to become."

Through 2001 and 2002, Southland sold individual shares of Sea Castle for as much as $50,000 each. He focused on strippers and hairdressers he met through his girlfriend. A few borrowed money from their parents in order to meet the $50,000 minimum. Flashing his brochures and the million-dollar check from Langdon, and warning potential investors that he had just one share remaining to sell, Southland often closed the deal with people of little means by arguing that their relative poverty was precisely why they needed to get in on the ground floor. "It's easy for rich people to invest in something like this," he would say. "But I'd rather make a poor person rich than a rich person richer."

The statement was true, as long as the poor person in question was Southland himself. As the money rolled in, he went on a spending spree. While he shared Langdon's love of exotic cars, boats and Jet Skis, Southland's tastes also ran to Prada suits, French wines, marble statues from Italy, and a white grand piano for his girlfriend (before she became a stripper she was a classically trained pianist). Initially, the luxury goods piled up in the cramped apartment Southland still occupied with his two children and wife. Langdon solved this problem by helping Southland purchase a $700,000 home in a gated community on the sixteenth hole of the Wildfire Golf Course.

By the middle of 2001, Southland had burned through nearly a million dollars of Sea Castle investment funds and payments made to him by Langdon through Peak Physique (as well as cash he took from his girlfriend, who continued to strip at the club). Not all the money was frittered away on his lifestyle upgrades. In July 2001, Southland gave $150,000 to a yacht broker as deposit on two boats, a forty-eight-foot yacht under construction in Taiwan and a slightly used seventy-three-foot Empress Cruiser being sold by a businessman in Bahrain.

According to the contracts he signed, Sea Castle Ventures was required to pay the broker nearly a million dollars in early October 2001, or risk forfeiture of the deposits. Police believe that the deadline for this payment drove Southland and Langdon to attempt a million-dollar theft and insurance scam targeting Langdon's own firm, Peak Physique. To that end, police allege, Southland recruited Konstantin Simberg, as well as a gang of high school kids, to serve as their muscle in the crime.

4. THE RECRUIT

FEW IMMIGRANTS ARRIVE in the United States as primed for American life as Konstantin Simberg. Born in the Russian industrial city of Rostov-on-Don, he grew up as the Soviet empire was collapsing and American movies and television were flooding his hometown. By his early teens, Simberg dressed in baggy hip-hop pants and T-shirts with obscure skateboard logos. He kept a baseball cap planted sideways on his head and squinted at the world through yellow-tinted glasses like those worn by hipsters on MTV.

People in the conservative town used to come up to his mother, Anna, on the street and tell her, "Your boy belongs in America."

After graduating from high school, Simberg attended a local university. He studied law but told friends he hoped to become a journalist or a poet. His parents, desperate to provide a future for their only child, decided to move to Phoenix, where they had relatives. They emigrated in the spring of 2000, believing that, as Anna Simberg says, "everything was going to be good."

From the start, Simberg had trouble. He found it nearly impossible to learn English. "Konstantin didn't really know how to fit in here because of the language," says a neighbor of the Simbergs. "But he seemed to me like a basic twenty-year-old kid. He thought about three things: fast cars, getting laid and making a lot of money."

A few weeks after arriving, Simberg realized his first ambition when his dad helped him purchase an old Camaro. In early June 2000, barely a month later, Simberg fulfilled his second ambition when some Russians he met at a nightclub invited him to a friend's birthday party. There he met another recent Russian immigrant, Ksenya Vybornova, who was celebrating her twentieth birthday. Simberg was immediately smitten by the petite young woman with frosty green eyes and dyed-platinum bangs.

Ksenya soon fell for Simberg. "He brought me into his world," she says. "And turned me around and around until all I could see was him."

Ksenya's brief trajectory through American life had already been fraught with drama. She arrived in Phoenix in the fall of 1999 at the urging of her sister, Olga, who had immigrated a few years earlier and was now convinced the world was about to end because of Y2K. Ksenya says Olga, four years older, pleaded with her to leave Moscow immediately, saying, "This is your last chance to see me."

When Ksenya arrived she found her sister's life had fallen apart. The American husband she had married a couple years earlier had recently left her, and Olga had been fired from the bank she had been working in as a teller. Not all was lost; recently Olga had started dating a new guy, Sean

Southland. When Ksenya met him she approved. Southland had a muscular, athletic build, drove a customized BMW and seemed to her like a "successful American businessman."

As the sisters, both unemployed, ran low on funds, Southland advised them that big money could be made dancing at local strip clubs. Olga and Ksenya took the plunge, stripping side-by-side in a stage act, for which they became known as "the two titty-dancing sisters from Russia." After their earnings started to kick in—on good nights they made more than $1,000 combined—Southland invited them to move in with him on the condition that they turn over their wages to him. "We have to be together like a family," he told the sisters. "And I am the man of the family."

Ksenya initially consented. Turning her money over to Southland wasn't all bad. He reassured her that he had invested $35,000 of her money by purchasing a share of Sea Castle.

But after meeting Simberg, Ksenya began to question the arrangement. Sensing the threat Simberg posed to his "family," Southland urged Ksenya to dump him. When Simberg drove over to pick her up, Southland wouldn't allow him in their apartment.

Eventually, Ksenya left the "family" and moved into an apartment with Simberg, which she paid for. Though Simberg was unable to hold down a job, he had a whimsical side that Ksenya found irresistible. She says, "Sometimes in the morning he would wake me up and put a blindfold on my eyes and drive me out of the city to look at a mountain." He wrote her poems and notes incessantly.

In the summer of 2001, about the time Southland and Langdon placed their deposit on the two yachts for Sea Castle, Ksenya noticed a change in Southland. He began to warm up to Simberg. Ksenya discovered in late August that Simberg and Southland were spending time together alone. After returning from one of his meetings with Southland, Simberg told Ksenya he was on the verge of making between $25,000 and $50,000.

5. THE FIRST HEIST

TROY LANGDON OPERATED PEAK PHYSIQUE out of a no-frills office suite in an anonymous-looking North Phoenix business park, adjacent to the almost equally nondescript Cactus Pharmacy, the company owned by his wife's parents.

On the morning of September 24, 2001, a FedEx truck pulled into the Peak Physique parking lot carrying eighteen boxes—each about the size of a milk crate—packed with Saizen-brand HGH shipped by Serono. The cost of the order was $1 million, but the resale value was more than three times that. As the FedEx driver stopped his truck in front of Peak Physique, a group of young men emerged from the parking lot and surrounded it. One, later identified as Simberg, approached the driver's window.

"I've got business for you," Simberg said in an accent so thick the driver had difficulty understanding him. Simberg continued, repeating himself a couple of times to make himself clear. "We'll give you twenty thousand cash. You open your truck, and we empty it." The FedEx driver refused.

"Tell the police a black man robbed you," Simberg told him.

When the driver continued to reject his advances, Simberg's resolve folded. He walked off, and the other young men who had been standing several feet away from the truck followed him. The FedEx driver watched them disappear behind some parked cars and drive off. He made his delivery to Peak Physique, then quietly phoned the police.

Because of the 9/11 attacks less than two weeks earlier, the nation was at the highest state of vigilance and fear since at least the Cuban Missile Crisis, if not Pearl Harbor. Even in normal times, the FedEx driver would have reported the menacing approach of the young man and the suspicious offer he made, and police would have begun an investigation. But in the post-9/11 hysteria that focused on foreigners and the possibility of biological weapons attacks, the driver's report of a heavily accented young man who tried to illegally obtain a million-dollar shipment of pharmaceuticals sent alarms to the highest level.

6. THE COP

THE DAY AFTER THE 9/11 ATTACKS, Detective Tom Britt, forty-one, who had been working on an organized crime unit, was told to focus on counterterrorism. Nobody in the police department knew exactly what "counterterrorism" work might mean, but Britt was a good candidate for the job. Raised in Southern California, he attended California State University, Northridge, on a baseball scholarship. In 1984 he enlisted in the Navy. Displaying a facility for language and a near-photographic memory, he was sent to the elite Defense Language Institute in Monterey, California. Jokingly referred to as the "American spy school," the institute has long provided language instruction for all branches of the military, as well as other federal agencies, including the CIA. As part of its language course, students are immersed in the culture of their particular area of study. Britt, who entered during the peak of the Reagan defense buildup, was put into the Russian program and spent nearly a year living in a simulated Russian home, where the meals, the clothing he wore, even the matchbooks he used, were replicated from life in the Soviet Union. When he graduated, Britt was placed into a secretive branch of the Navy that involved monitoring Soviet communications. In his final years of service, he spent several months living at a Soviet missile base, where he served as a nuclear weapons monitor under provisions of the Strategic Arms Reduction Treaty.

Britt joined the Phoenix Police Department after leaving active-duty military service in 1994. An avid golfer, he jokes that he was drawn to Phoenix because "I wanted to be close to some of the best golf courses in the country." In the nineties, the city had become a popular destination for former Mafia members relocating from the East Coast in the Witness Protection Program. Among them, Sammy "the Bull" Gravano used the federal program as cover to launch an Ecstasy-smuggling ring in alliance with a local white supremacist gang. The Phoenix Police Department's organized crime unit launched a major operation against the burgeoning crime wave. Britt was assigned to the unit, but his superiors had special plans for him.

Phoenix was undergoing an influx of tens of thousands of Russian immigrants, drawn by the seemingly boundless opportunities offered by the city, as well as the limitless sunshine. He was given the task of thwarting Russian mob influence among the city's émigré community. While much of his job with the organized crime unit would entail hard police work, it also included, as Britt describes it, "the stuff I like, going to people's homes and businesses, eating pickles and talking."

Britt affects a relaxed bearing, favoring a work uniform of jeans and golf shirts. Compactly built, athletic, with an easy smile, he is the master of the soft approach. But when focused on a case, he speaks in a clipped, rapid-fire manner that reveals his almost unsettling ability to recall details. If you were a criminal, Britt would be the worst kind of cop—stealthy in his nerdy golf clothes, likable, extremely intelligent and armed with his freakish, near-photographic memory.

Britt started investigating the failed robbery at Peak Physique two days after the FedEx driver reported the incident to the police. His involvement was prompted by a phone call from a North Phoenix homemaker, Tina Swindle, who contacted the police department to report that her son Dusty had been recruited by a high school classmate to help rob the FedEx truck outside Peak Physique. Britt was assigned the interview with Swindle because she had indicated that Russians had been involved.

7. THE INFORMATION

BRITT DROVE TO THE SWINDLE HOME within hours of Tina's call. Located on a quiet, suburban street of comfortable, two-story homes in North Phoenix, the Swindles' house was distinguished by several beat-up vintage muscle cars in various states of disrepair in the front yard, some on jacks. Dusty, an eighteen-year-old senior at North Phoenix High, was a total gearhead, heavily into classic V-8 rides. He told Britt he had been working at a local tire shop on Saturday, September 22, when a friend, Sergei Guk, stopped by with a proposition.

Guk was a seventeen-year-old junior at North Phoenix High. Despite his deeply Russian-sounding name, Guk had lived in Phoenix for more than ten years with his family and was thoroughly assimilated. That day at the tire shop, Guk told Swindle he had an older Russian friend, Konstantin Simberg, who needed five or six strong guys to help him with a job. Guk told Swindle that Simberg was offering them $700 each to help unload some boxes from a FedEx truck.

According to Swindle, Guk reassured him that the FedEx driver had been paid off. He would look the other way when the high school kids unloaded his truck. The whole job would take a minute or two.

Swindle told Britt he initially reasoned that the job didn't exactly seem like a robbery since everyone, including the driver, was in on it. He told Guk, "For seven hundred dollars, count me in."

The next day, Guk came by Dusty's house and told him they needed to meet Simberg and another guy whom Guk referred to as the "Big Boss." They drove to an apartment across town where Simberg lived. Simberg's car was parked in front, a black Camaro that was easily identifiable because it was missing a hood and the windshield was cracked. Inside the apartment, Swindle met Simberg—tall, gangly, dark-haired, with a stubbly beard, wearing baggy hip-hop clothes and a sideways baseball cap. When Simberg spoke, his accent was so heavy Swindle could barely understand a word he said.

Simberg informed Swindle and Guk that they would follow him in his car to go pick up another kid involved in the plot. Simberg led them to a motel-style courtyard apartment across town. It was built around a pool, which had been drained and was now filled with old shopping carts and trash. Simberg walked Swindle and Guk up to an apartment occupied by an eighteen-year-old named Tom Southerland. He had dropped out of North Phoenix High the previous year, and lived in a one-bedroom apartment with his mother and two infant siblings. Southerland's job would be to drive the U-Haul truck that they would load with the boxes taken from the FedEx truck.

After they picked up Southerland, Simberg led the small gang he'd assembled to a cul-de-sac where they were to be inspected by the "Big Boss." Along the way, two other North Phoenix High students met them in their cars. Simberg told everyone to wait inside their vehicles until he told them to get out.

Dusty Swindle saw a black BMW 750 with smoked-out windows stop about a hundred yards from the cul-de-sac. Guk told Swindle the BMW belonged to the "Big Boss." Simberg stepped out of his car holding a cell phone to his ear, from which he was apparently receiving instructions from the "Big Boss." He told each kid to step out of his car, one at a time, turn around and get back in. When the last kid had done so, the BMW with tinted windows drove off.

The next morning, September 24, Swindle told Britt he cut school and met up with Simberg and the gang of kids at a nearby Wendy's. There were a total of six guys spread between two cars and the U-Haul. Dodging police, who they feared would stop them for ditching school, Swindle says they converged at the parking lot by Peak Physique at about ten. Simberg handed out latex medical gloves, then wandered off shouting in Russian on his cell phone.

Simberg returned a few minutes later, highly nervous. Speaking in a combination of broken English and Russian that Guk translated, he told the gang there was a change in plan. The FedEx driver who was supposed to show up that day and allow the robbery to take place had called in sick. Simberg told the kids in the gang he needed volunteers to step forward and help him "take the truck by force." He offered $10,000 to anyone who would join him.

Recounting this to Britt, Swindle said the gang was unfazed by the change of plan. He and his friends reasoned "there was a bunch of us and one dorky driver. We could beat him up and throw him through the little door in the back."

As the FedEx truck pulled into the parking lot, the six boys followed Simberg across the asphalt toward it. Swindle noticed a man, about thirty, with "a very powerful build" sitting in a silver Infiniti parked a hundred feet away. Swindle assumed he was the "Big Boss," especially after he began waving frantically to Simberg, urging him forward.

But when the boys neared the FedEx truck, Simberg told them to stop. He had apparently lost his stomach for physically overpowering the driver. Instead, he approached the driver's door alone and made his offer of a bribe. When the driver refused, Simberg and the rest of the gang fled in their two cars and rented U-Hauler.

After hearing this story, Britt asked Swindle to drive him to the apartment complex where he'd first met with Simberg. Swindle was never told Simberg's name. But when he led Britt to Simberg's apartment, his black Camaro with the missing hood and smashed windshield was parked in front. Britt traced the license plates and immediately obtained the name of the registered owner, Konstantin Simberg.

When Britt did a search on Simberg's criminal record he found nothing. But four months earlier Simberg had filed a police report after he lost his wallet at the Biltmore Fashion Park mall, a popular hangout for teenagers in Phoenix. Britt read the report Simberg filed for his missing wallet and discovered that he had written his cell phone number on it.

Britt obtained a subpoena to examine the call record of Simberg's cell phone. It revealed that on the morning of September 24, the time of the failed FedEx truck robbery, Simberg had placed eighteen calls to a cell phone belonging to Sean O. Southland. Britt discovered that a day earlier, around the time Swindle described being inspected by the "Big Boss," Simberg had also made numerous calls to his number.

Britt concluded that Southland was the "Big Boss." But at this point he was the Big Boss of nothing, since he was head of a gang that had bungled its first crime so badly they hadn't yet managed to break a single law.

8. THE BIG SCORE

EARLY ON THE MORNING OF OCTOBER 1, a burglar alarm went off in the offices shared by Peak Physique and Cactus Pharmacy. When patrolmen arrived at around one A.M., they found a window facing the street had been smashed and a storeroom appeared to have been emptied.

Peak Physique was already flagged within the Phoenix Police Department as a place of interest because of the attempted robbery of the FedEx truck less than a week earlier. Britt was called at his home, where he was asleep with his wife beside him. He managed to dress and reach the pharmacy in under half an hour.

Within minutes of Britt's arrival, Troy Langdon rolled into the parking lot driving the Porsche he'd recently purchased from Diamondbacks pitcher Juan Cruz. Langdon emerged wearing shorts, flip-flops and a $35,000 Rolex.

Britt walked over to him and asked, "Who are you?"

"I'm the owner," Langdon said. Initially, Langdon gave Britt the impression of relaxed confidence. But when Britt asked him to follow him to the burgled storeroom, Langdon appeared to grow nervous. Britt noticed he was chain-smoking Marlboros. He asked Langdon what had been stolen.

Langdon told him it was eighteen boxes of HGH, sold under the name Saizen, which had been delivered on September 24. Britt failed to mention that he was already far into the investigation of the failed robbery of the FedEx truck on the twenty-fourth. Nor did he reveal that someone at Serono had explained to him what Saizen was. He wanted to hear what it was from Langdon, so he asked him, "What's Saizen?"

"It's amazing," Langdon said. "It's human growth hormone, a glory drug. You can eat sixteen hamburgers and not get fat."

"Did you place the order for it?" Britt asked.

"I did," Langdon told him.

Britt shook hands with Langdon, promising to do his best to find the thieves responsible for the break-in, and left at about two-thirty A.M. After he left, Britt ordered undercover cops to tail Langdon.

Langdon lingered in the Peak Physique offices until six in the morning. The cops followed Langdon behind the wheel of his Porsche to a diner, where he met with Sean Southland, who arrived in a Yukon Denali. An undercover cop took a table across the room. He was not near enough to hear the conversation. He noted that Langdon chain-smoked, and the other man—whose name he did not know yet—had powerfully built arms.

Both men departed the diner. One officer tailed Langdon to his home in Carefree. Another officer followed Southland to his home on the sixteenth hole of the Wildfire Golf Course. Southland opened his garage door, allowing the cop surveilling him to look inside. The three-car garage held a 2002 Porsche Turbo Carrera (like Langdon's) and a pair of BMW 750s, one with tinted windows. Southland exchanged his Denali for the BMW with tinted windows and drove across town to a bank parking lot. It was still early. The bank wasn't open yet. The lot was empty. Southland waited several minutes until Simberg arrived in his black Camaro, with the missing hood and cracked windshield.

When Britt read the surveillance report the next day, the location of Southland's home caught his interest. Britt knew it well. He often played at Wildfire and had a clear mental image of the home on the sixteenth hole. It was among the grandest along the course. Situated on a nearly two-acre lot, the yard featured a private putting green, a half-size basketball court, a pool and Jacuzzi, and was partially screened from public view by a stand of giant, candelabra-shaped saguaro cacti.

From his earlier investigations, Britt already knew about Southland's relationship with Simberg and his role as the "Big Boss" in the failed FedEx heist of September 24. Britt now looked into Southland's relationship with Langdon through Peak Physique and Sea Castle Ventures. He reexamined his interviews with people at Serono and noticed that not only had Langdon placed the order for Saizen, he had added the unusual request that all of it be shipped at once, so it would arrive on one truck.

Britt interviewed the FedEx driver who normally delivered to Peak Physique and Cactus Pharmacy. He had called in sick the day of the attempted heist, and Britt was curious about this. Dusty Swindle, the high school student Britt interviewed, had told him the driver was supposed to be in on the job. The driver, David Ludwig, denied any involvement.

But when Britt subpoenaed Langdon's phone records he discovered Langdon had placed several calls to Ludwig's personal phone in the weeks leading up to the attempted heist. When presented with this evidence, Ludwig admitted that he had agreed to allow his truck to be robbed in return for $100,000. Ludwig told Britt that Langdon enticed him with cash. "Troy came out to my truck and fanned several thousand dollars under my nose. He told me that plus a lot more could be mine if I walked away from my truck at the right time."

But Ludwig got cold feet, and phoned in sick hours before he was supposed to begin his rounds. When the driver who replaced him failed to accept Simberg's offer to "make business" and delivered the Saizen, Langdon immediately owed Serono a million dollars for that order, as well as an additional quarter million he hadn't paid the firm for a previous order. Britt discovered that a day after taking the delivery, Langdon phoned his insurance company and upped his theft coverage at Peak Physique from a quarter million to a million dollars.

Britt learned from employees at Cactus Pharmacy that the storeroom allegedly burgled on October 1 had been emptied of its eighteen boxes of Saizen a few days earlier. Then he received an interesting report on the forensic examination of the storeroom itself. Police examiners discovered that whoever smashed the window on the storeroom had apparently entered and hit the burglar-alarm motion detector with a blunt object. The motion detector was left hanging by its wires, but it continued to transmit data to the main hard drive of the building's alarm system. Data from the motion detector indicated that after the window was smashed, burglars had spent fewer than sixty seconds inside. Britt deemed it highly unlikely that all eighteen boxes could have been removed from the room in under a minute.

The final pieces of Britt's case fell into place when he learned that a few days before the "robbery," Langdon had sold the entire lot of Saizen HGH to a pharmacy wholesaler across town for under a million dollars. The eighteen boxes of Saizen had been delivered on a flatbed truck registered to Payless Towing—a company Southland had purchased in 1998 with promissory notes that he failed to repay (resulting in his forfeiture of the firm in early 2002).

Langdon, Southland and Simberg were arrested fewer than seventy-two hours after the staged break-in. Langdon refused to speak. Simberg, who had been in bed with his girlfriend, Ksenya, when the police arrested him, fell apart in his first interview with Britt. "He broke down crying like a baby," Britt says. "This kid was not cut out to be a career criminal." Simberg spilled every detail of the crime, from his first contact with Southland through Ksenya, to Southland's recruitment of him the previous summer, to the recent staged burglary. Simberg told Britt that on that night outside Peak Physique, Southland used a crowbar to smash the window of the already empty storeroom. Simberg climbed through the shattered window and ran around the room to leave footprints, intended to give the appearance of the place having been robbed by a gang.

As Britt saw it, the crime was garden-variety insurance fraud, which had been horribly executed from the start. With the mountain of evidence he'd gathered and Simberg's incriminating testimony, bringing an indictment of multiple fraud and conspiracy counts against Langdon and Southland would be a slam dunk.

In his first interview of Southland, Britt had no need of his cooperation given the strength of the case. But given Britt's own background with the Russian community, he was curious as to why Southland seemed so adept at manipulating Russians. When Britt sat across from Southland in an interview room, Southland appeared calm and expressed an interest in being helpful. But he explained to Britt that he could not divulge certain secrets surrounding his dealings with Langdon and the Russian community. Southland retrieved an official-looking but outdated military ID from his wallet, showed it to Britt, then lowered his voice and spoke a few words of Russian. South-land informed Britt that he was a former CIA employee now working as a "secret agent" in a capacity that he could not disclose under penalty of law.

"Oh, really?" Britt replied.

9. THE CIA AGENT

SOUTHLAND AND LANGDON POSTED BAIL and left jail within days of their arrests. Simberg was held until November, when his parents paid his bond. Britt had advised Simberg to remain in jail. He hadn't offered the young Russian any kind of deal because he didn't want him to have the appearance of cooperating with police, as he was doing. The longer Simberg stayed in jail, the safer he would be. Britt's worst fears were borne out when Simberg was murdered on December 15. Britt was certain that the murder had been ordered by Southland and Langdon, that a ho-hum white-collar crime had ended with the shooting and immolation of Simberg in the Yavapai woods. It was among the cruelest murders he had ever investigated. And it eliminated his key witness in the insurance fraud case. But as of early spring 2002, Britt remained unable to link Simberg's killers to Southland or Langdon.

When I visit Southland's house by the Wildfire Golf Course in March 2002, he greets me at the door with a friendly smile. I had phoned Southland a few days earlier and he had invited me over to "chat." On bail for the robbery and fraud charges and with a cloud of murder hanging over his head, Southland exudes an easy calm as he shakes my hand in the white marble foyer. He is about five-ten, with chestnut-brown hair and curiously soulful eyes. He has broad shoulders, with disproportionately huge arms, like Popeye's, which are a tribute to the power of working out, HGH and probably steroids, too. (DEA representatives informed Britt around the time of Southland's arrest that in an unrelated investigation, their undercover agents had made illegal buys of steroids from Southland at Christie's Cabaret, and he was believed to be a major player in the steroids scene.) The only signs of stress I detect in Southland's features are puffy bags under his eyes the color of mud.

Southland leads me across the two-story great room of his home, apologizing profusely for its diminished appearance. Cavernous rooms that once contained the billiard table, the Italian statues, the white grand piano and a plethora of wide-screen TVs have been stripped bare by police asset seizures. Under the 1984 Crime Control Act, law enforcement officials may in special circumstances obtain warrants to seize assets that they argue are derived from criminal enterprise, even before any suspects have gone to trial. Britt has pursued such asset seizures against Southland and Langdon with a vengeance. He has personally scoured every receipt, bill and transaction involving Southland, Langdon, their businesses and families. From Southland alone, he has seized assets and drained bank accounts totaling more than $400,000.

We sit across from each other at one of the few pieces of furniture remaining in the house, a round black-marble breakfast table in the kitchen. I ask Southland about the death of Konstantin Simberg. He shakes his head sadly. "You mean his 'murder,'" he says, making little quotation marks with his fingers. "To me, he was a kid that had a lot of different angles going on."

Southland dips out of the room to answer a phone. His girlfriend, Olga, enters wearing white open-toe sandals and a tight jumpsuit made of something that looks like rattlesnake skin. She is taut and slim, with perfectly erect posture and comically large breasts—when she first got serious with Southland two years ago, he outfitted her with implants. Her brittle yet overanimated style contrasts with eyes as dull and lifeless as the button eyes on a rag doll.

She asks if I would like a drink. I request coffee. She shouts, "I do not know how to make coffee!" and storms out of the room.

Southland enters, still talking on his phone, and brews me a fresh pot of coffee. When he hangs up he shakes his head and apologizes for Olga. You get the idea that their domestic arrangement is a precarious one. Southland knows that a few months ago, Olga made a voluntary statement to Britt, backing up everything Simberg had said before his death. She later recanted her statement and refused to cooperate. Britt has found no way to compel her to talk. Southland's hopes for staying out of prison rest primarily on her continued silence. He smiles at me and says, "I hate Olga." Then, after a long pause, he adds, "I love Olga, too. But she's a twenty-four-year-old ditz. Unfortunately, with Russians, they get into your life and then they're kind of like a tick. They get under your skin."

He sits across from me again and returns to the topic of Simberg, claiming he befriended the young Russian with the purest of intentions. "I was thinking this kid needed some guidance," he says. "I was going to help him out."

Southland explains that Simberg was a master criminal who fooled him. He refers to Simberg as "Mr. Al Capone." Southland asserts that Simberg orchestrated the failed truck heist and then the robbery of Peak Physique in such a way that he framed both himself and Langdon. "Simberg dated my girlfriend's sister," Southland says, referring to Ksenya. "He pumped me for information about my business affairs. Ksenya was naive and she trusted him. I forgive the girl. She didn't understand he planned to use it all against me." Southland says that Simberg's "master plan" was to rob Peak Physique and blackmail him and Langdon with the threat that he would pin the crime on them.

Southland advances the theory that Simberg was killed by professional hit men sent from New York or San Francisco by the "Yugoslavian mafia." "This had nothing to do with the deal at the pharmacy," he explains. "Konstantin was into a lot of things." Southland says that as soon as he clears his own name, he vows to launch his own investigation.

One of Southland's impressive qualities is his ability to expound on any topic, no matter how outrageous or absurd, without modulating his tone of pleasant, almost smarmy cheer. He admits that he encouraged his now ex-wife, Kimber, his current girlfriend, Olga, and her sister Ksenya to become strippers, then took as much of their money as he could. Somehow, he makes his pimping sound like a good deed.

"I told Olga," Southland says, "'This is my deal. This is what I got going on. If you want to come in and dance and help me out, then I'll take care of you.'" According to Southland, when he started Olga dancing, she made $10,000 to $15,000 a month. "At one point, I had, like, seventy or eighty thousand dollars of hers in my safe." Southland looks up and smiles expectantly, as if waiting for a pat on the back for saving so much of Olga's cash. "So I took Olga's money and bought the Porsche, because it's an asset."

I ask Southland about the $35,000 Ksenya gave him as an "investment" in Sea Castle. Britt has told me that when Simberg got out of jail in November, he took it upon himself to demand the return of Ksenya's money.

"That was his blackmail," Southland says. "He tells me, 'You give me, like, fifty thousand or I tell the police you stole the HGH.' That's exactly, you know, what he told me." For the first time, Southland's cheery façade cracks. With obvious anger he says, "This kid's a twenty-one-year-old. I mean, I could have killed him." Southland, the suspected murderer, pauses to reconsider his choice of words. "Not 'kill' him, you know. But for this kid to, like, threaten me, it was a joke to me. This kid is nothing, he is nothing to me."

Southland invites me to join him while he picks up his kids, Brandon, ten, and Britney, fourteen, at a local racquet club where they take lessons. Getting into his car, a $40,000 Acura SUV, he apologizes for the downscale ride. Joking about Britt's zeal in pursuing asset seizures, he says, "If I was going to kill anybody, it would be that cop, Britt."

Negotiating afternoon traffic in Scottsdale, Southland challenges the accuracy of reports made by the cops who surveilled him. He notes that in one report they misidentified the type of car he was driving. "They thought I had an Acura, when I didn't have it, because I switched cars on them."

"Why were you switching cars on the cops if you weren't doing anything wrong?" I ask.

Southland ignores the question. "Mind if we stop by the fish store?" He turns into a mini-mall. Southland is an exotic-fish enthusiast. He managed to hold on to a few aquariums through Britt's asset seizures, though he lacks funds to keep them stocked.

Inside the shop he spends about ten minutes talking to a salesgirl about proper salinity levels for his custom tank. Though he lacks money, Southland makes a big show of telling the salesgirl about all the fish he plans to buy. "Put that clown on hold for me," he says, pointing to an eighty-five-dollar fish. "I'll be back for him tomorrow. Is he gonna be okay with my fox-face fish?"

We pick up Southland's kids at about four o'clock outside the Camelback Racquet Club. Brandon and Britney climb in the car chattering excitedly about their lessons. Brandon wears Coke-bottle-lens glasses that give him a resemblance to Harry Potter. Britney, confident and manipulative, treats her dad like a lovable dork.

"Dad, can't you take me to my horse today?" she whines. "I want to go riding."

"No, baby," Southland says. "It's going to rain."

"But the sky is blue," Britney says.

Southland hasn't told her yet that her horse was seized as an asset gained through criminal enterprise, through Britt's efforts. He switches subjects, gently scolding Britney for being late.

We drive to a mall. In greater Phoenix, with its brutal heat, air-conditioned malls are the town square, the center of social life as nowhere else in the country. Southland parks far from the entrance. "In the good old days, before the government took all my money, we used to valet," he says. "Isn't that right, Brandon?"

"Yeah," Brandon says uncertainly. "Are you going to write how they took my dad's money?" he asks me.

We get food at a Panda Express and sit at communal tables in the food court.

Southland pats Britney's head and says that the government case against him has ruined her acting career. He explains to me that his ex-wife—the kids' mother—used to fly Britney to Los Angeles once a month to audition for parts in commercials. But he can no longer afford it. "This really sucks for the kids' sake," he says. "Does the government realize what they're doing to my children?"

Britney mulls her father's comment. She points out that she hasn't auditioned for a commercial since she was very little. It's been at least six years—

long before the current difficulties. "Dad, you spoiled my acting when we moved to Germany," Britney says, referring to a period in the mid-1990s when Southland joined the Army and was posted in Europe.

"You were a fireman or something," Brandon says.

"No, you were a cop," says Britney.

"No, baby," says Southland. "I was working for the government."

"You've had so many jobs," his son says. He makes it sound like an accusation.

Southland casts a worried glance at my tape recorder, then warns his kids, "You guys have got to be quiet, because you don't know what you're talking about."

After our meal I ask Southland about the statement he made to Britt that he worked for the CIA. Southland sighs and shakes his head. "Wow," he says. "He's not supposed to say things like that. He should know better." Southland levels his gaze at me. "It's against the law for me to tell you what I did for the government."

You can't blame Southland's kids for being confused about their father's past. His autobiography is a mixture of bald lies shaded with subtle deceptions and rounded out by a few essential truths.

Southland was born in Portland, Oregon, in 1969. By his own account, his "father was a millionaire. He owned a ball bearing factory."

Southland's parents divorced after he was born, and his mother married a man named Harold Short. I interview Harold to fact-check Southland's version of his father's career. For instance, did he own a ball bearing factory?

Short laughs. "His father was a bookie. He was a salesman for a ball bearing company." But, Short claims, Southland's father quit his sales job to work full-time as a bookie. "In his apartment he had, like, numerous TVs and telephones and he would take bets on all kinds of sporting stuff."

Southland tells me, "I wanted to be a cop since I was fifteen. I had Britney and did the whole marriage thing when I was nineteen, then went to college to become a cop. The chief of the L.A. Harbor police was my mentor."

Expecting this to be another of Southland's tall tales, I track down Los Angeles Harbor police chief Noel Cunningham. He confirms that in 1990 Southland was enrolled in a community college in Walnut Valley, California, earning an associate's degree in criminology. Cunningham was his instructor in a seminar on criminal justice. He says, "Sean was probably one of my best students. He had charisma, beautiful children, and an attractive wife. My wife and I socialized with his family often."

In 1991, Southland became a police officer in Azusa, a middle-class bedroom community near Los Angeles. His tenure lasted eighteen months. Southland says he was fired after arresting the son of the mayor, or the son of the governor of California. His account varies. No record of that arrest exists, and an Azusa Police Department official only confirms that Southland worked there as a police officer and was "terminated."

Cunningham says, "Sean became kind of a strange guy after he left the Azusa police force. He joined the Army and went into some kind of high-powered elite military unit. He spoke Russian and worked for a clandestine group."

When Britt looked into Southland's past he discovered that he had in fact successfully completed advanced Russian training and cultural immersion at the Defense Language Institute in Monterey. Britt had completed the same course.

After his training at Monterey, Southland was stationed in Augsburg, Germany. In the mid-1990s, when Southland was stationed there, the U.S. military base in Augsburg was a primary intelligence center for debriefing Russian government and military personnel fleeing the collapsing Soviet empire. For reasons that remain unknown, Southland's deployment to Augsburg and his service in the Army were cut short. He was dismissed from the military three years into what was to have been a five-year commitment. When Britt examined papers seized from Southland's home, he found his military DD-214 discharge papers. But a critical portion of them had been torn off, making it impossible to determine the conditions under which he left the military. Britt queried the military about Southland's discharge, but his sources could not provide him with any records to indicate why Southland failed to complete his five-year term of service.

Because of Southland's training at Monterey and his service in Augsburg, his claims of having been a CIA agent have a kernel of plausibility. More likely, Southland underwent training at Monterey to prepare for more prosaic Russian-language intelligence-gathering duties such as those performed by Britt. However, if the CIA's intent had been to create a deep-cover identity for Southland as a total screwup, the effort would have been deemed a success.

Southland claims that after his discharge from the military, he moved to Portland, Oregon, and "helped launch Crimson Trace," a manufacturer of laser gun sights. Adam Wilder, a spokesman for Crimson Trace, says, "Sean Southland worked for us as a salesman. He was very effective for the short time he worked for us. He did a damn good job." But he adds, "I can tell you that he took opportunities to exaggerate things many times. He was let go from the company."

After being fired from Crimson Trace, Southland and his wife and two children moved back to the Phoenix area, where his mother and stepfather lived in semi-retirement. They advanced him money to obtain an apartment, helped him finance his tow-truck company and provided the seed investment for Sea Castle Ventures. Southland's mother even introduced him to Olga, his future girlfriend, when Olga was still working as a bank teller in the hope that she could introduce her son to rich investors.

His former instructor Los Angeles Harbor police chief Cunningham kept in touch with Southland. He says, "It seemed like Sean just couldn't get it together. His wife became the provider for the family."

Southland's wife, Kimber, had begun working as an air hostess when he was in the Army. After they moved to Phoenix, she began to work as a stripper; she currently dances full-time at a club called Babes. Despite their divorce, Kimber lives in an apartment next door to Southland's mother and stepfather.

I visit Southland's mother and stepfather in a tiny but well-kept ground-floor apartment on a busy thoroughfare in Scottsdale. Jane, a fiery, petite woman with the same soulful eyes as her son, also shares his easygoing hospitality. Harold, a retired construction engineer in his late fifties, wears a short-sleeved shirt that shows off his impressive build and ornately inked skin. When I ask them about the veracity of certain aspects of Southland's story, Harold is happy to point out inconsistencies, such as correcting the notion that Southland's biological father was a millionaire. But at the same time, both profess a belief in his innocence. They have poured their life savings into his legal defense, and Harold has recently come out of retirement in order to help support Southland.

I point out the irony that they live in a small apartment with burglar bars while supporting a son who lives in a mansion inside a gated community.

"We are an extremely close family," Jane says.

In a way, you couldn't imagine cooler parents. They provide a cheerful rationalization for everything. Late in the afternoon, Kimber traipses into the kitchen, looking for a snack before heading into her shift at Babes. Jane rushes into the kitchen and fusses over her, making sure she finds some leftovers in the fridge. Kimber pokes her head into the living room and says good night to Harold before leaving the apartment.

"You know she works at a strip club," I say to Harold and Jane.

"Goodness." Jane laughs. "In Scottsdale, half the girls dance."

"Doctors, lawyers, judges all go there," Harold says. "Kimber's even seen Charlie Sheen in there."

When I leave they walk me to the door. Harold shakes my hand. Jane hugs me. Both make me promise I will write the truth about their son.

10. BLACKMAIL

I MEET WITH SIMBERG's former girlfriend, Ksenya, twenty-two, outside a coffee shop at the Camelback Mall. She is not much over five and a half feet tall, with platinum bangs hanging over her face in a way that exaggerates brilliant green eyes and wide, Slavic cheekbones. She wears a slick black coat and jeans. Though she is perilously thin, her jeans are so tight they appear on the verge of splitting every time she shifts her legs to light a cigarette. She seems to snarl every time she puffs on her cigarette. But when the subject of Simberg is raised, she rolls her eyes and laughs, her entire body shaking. "Kostya," she says, using the diminutive of his first name. "He was so stupid." Ksenya recalls an especially funny memory. "He drove his stupid car, with the cover in front gone"—she's referring to the missing hood on Simberg's Camaro—"and I would laugh."

Ksenya says that when Simberg was released from jail in November, he did not tell her that he had provided key evidence against Southland. If he had, Ksenya would have scolded him. She and her sister had come to believe that Southland was a CIA agent possessed of extraordinary powers.

Simberg became obsessed with retrieving the $35,000 Southland had taken from Ksenya (telling her he was investing it in Sea Castle). "He did not want me to work at the club," Ksenya says of Simberg. "He would say, 'This is a disgusting job. You should not be doing it.' But he had no money."

Ksenya is certain Simberg originally agreed to work for Southland to obtain money to impress her. After his release from jail in November, she says, the two of them planned to move to New York. Simberg planned to use her Sea Castle investment as their stake for getting out of town.

He confessed to Ksenya that he was cooperating with Britt against Southland. Soon, Ksenya suspected Simberg threatened Southland and Langdon that he would testify against them unless they paid Ksenya her $35,000. He began confronting Southland and Langdon at Christie's Cabaret and calling their homes, telling them if they simply handed over Ksenya's money, he would skip town.

Ksenya believes she is responsible for Simberg's death. "He met Sean through me. He worked for him because of me. He tried to get my money back and he was killed." She tells me this sitting in a rental car late one night outside her apartment. She dreads going inside. Since Simberg's death, she says, she gets through nights by turning on every light in her apartment and drinking vodka until she passes out.

She gestures toward Phoenix—empty streets, blinking traffic lights, mini-malls. "There is nothing here," she says. "People my age, all they do here is smoke pot and listen to techno."

Ksenya pauses a moment before portraying to me the fantasy she had for her future in New York. "I told Kostya I would be a businesswoman when we went to New York. I would be in my Mercedes convertible, with my hair up, wearing a suit, doing something like real estate."

Ksenya recalls the last time she saw Simberg alive, December 14. That morning Simberg woke up uncharacteristically early and prepared to leave. Ksenya asked what he was doing. He said, "Don't worry, it's a good thing."

Later that afternoon, Simberg met up with the three young men now accused of killing him—Chris Andrews, Dennis Tsoukanov and Mikhail Drachev. Of the three, he was closest with Tsoukanov. Simberg often hung out at Tsoukanov's house and went to clubs with him.

Simberg met his alleged killers that day in order to borrow $400. Simberg needed the money to pay off some parking tickets, which would enable him to take out a $2,000 title loan on his Camaro. All four of them went to the bank together to get the $400 and then headed to the apartment Andrews and Drachev shared. By then it was about six P.M. Soon after arriving at the apartment, Simberg called Britt. Since Britt arrested Simberg, they had formed an odd bond. Because of Britt's fluency in Russian he was the only American Simberg knew, aside from Southland, with whom he could communicate freely in his own language. Simberg called Britt merely to say hello—Simberg was the type of guy who, if he was friends with you, would call five or ten times a day for no particular reason—and Britt put him on hold when he received another call.

While Simberg waited, one of the young men in the apartment, most likely Drachev, put on a pair of brass knuckles and slammed Simberg in the back of the head.

When Britt clicked back to Simberg's line, all he heard was screaming.

11. THE KILLERS

THE THREE YOUNG MEN who murdered Simberg are believed to have met through the local rave scene. Dennis Tsoukanov, the eldest at twenty, had immigrated to Phoenix with his family from Estonia fifteen years earlier. He grew up speaking fluent, unaccented English. His sister, Katie, two years younger, says that in high school Tsoukanov "was afraid of people, very shy."

After graduating from high school, he worked as a clerk at a supermarket and studied graphic design at a community college. Tsoukanov's sister says that then her brother changed: "He was like, 'I've been missing out on the fun for all these years. I need to get out there and do fun stuff.'" She adds, "Everything changed. He started listening to techno and dressing in Abercrombie. He told me he wanted to be a model for Abercrombie."

Tsoukanov began hanging out at the Buddha Lounge, a popular club frequented by Simberg as well as Chris Andrews and Mikhail Drachev. Chris Andrews was an eighteen-year-old freshman at Arizona State University in Tempe. Just five-five, and with barely any facial hair, he was sometimes mistaken for a fourteen-year-old. He had arrived at ASU in the fall of 2001 to study engineering. He was the son of a wealthy Maryland family. His father was an executive at IBM, his mother a teacher at a Montessori school. An ASU student who met him during freshman year says that Andrews bragged to him, "My parents are rich and buy me anything I want."

A few months into his first year, Andrews was kicked out of student housing on suspicion of dealing coke. Shortly after that incident, the student who had reported him had his bicycle destroyed in a peculiar act of vandalism. It was doused in gasoline and set on fire. The student believed that the act was carried out by Andrews as retribution for snitching on him.

But true to Andrews's boast, his parents bailed him out. His mother purchased him a new, $12,000 Kawasaki Ninja he had long coveted and rented an apartment for him in town. By then Andrews was hanging out with Mikhail Drachev. Eighteen years old, Drachev was still technically a student at North Phoenix High, but his parents had recently kicked him out of their house, and he moved in with Andrews. The two of them worked together as small-time drug dealers. Their apartment was filled with trays for growing hallucinogenic mushrooms and chemicals for manufacturing meth when police searched it after the death of Simberg.

Tsoukanov's sister found her brother's friendship with Drachev particularly disturbing. Unkempt and unsmiling, Drachev spit in her face, then laughed when she was introduced to him at a party. Tsoukanov's sister says, "He was scary. I don't know why my brother looked up to him, but he did."

When police searched Drachev and Andrews's apartment after the disappearance of Simberg on December 14, the walls were covered in bloodstains. Tsoukanov, who ended up confessing, confirmed that Simberg had indeed been struck from behind when speaking on the phone. According to Tsoukanov—whose account may be as self-serving as any co-conspirator's in kidnapping and murder—Drachev and Andrews tied Simberg up and took turns beating him through the night. At one point, the killers left to purchase a handgun—the TEC-9—from some local white supremacist gun dealers Drachev knew. Early the next morning, they drove Simberg, bound and severely beaten but still conscious, a hundred miles to the Yavapai woods in Andrews's Jeep Cherokee. Along the way, they stopped at a gas station, where a security camera recorded Andrews filling milk containers with the gasoline they would use to set Simberg on fire.

Britt had been out of town in Salt Lake City on business when he received his last call from Simberg. After Simberg screamed and the line went dead, Britt initially wondered whether Simberg was fooling around. Simberg had phoned from a blocked number and Britt was unable to return the call. Growing concerned, Britt had the police department search Phoenix hospitals for any John Does fitting Simberg's description. Early the next morning—just hours before Simberg's murder—Britt issued a missing-person report.

When hunters found Simberg's body on the sixteenth, Britt subpoenaed his own phone records in order to determine the identity of the blocked call from which Simberg had phoned on the fourteenth. Britt discovered that the telephone Simberg used had been purchased by Chris Andrews a couple of weeks earlier. On the purchase order Andrews had written the address of his apartment. Andrews's phone records also yielded numerous calls Britt traced to Drachev and Tsoukanov. Andrews's bank records indicated he'd made a $400 withdrawal twenty minutes before Simberg had used his phone to call Britt. Bank security camera footage yielded images of Simberg, Drachev, Andrews and Tsoukanov together at the time of the $400 transaction.

Drachev and Andrews made plans to flee town within hours of the murder. They traded the TEC-9 pistol they'd used on Simberg, the motorcycle Andrews's mother had bought him a few weeks earlier, and a Sony PlayStation 2 for an old Mercedes they drove to the East Coast, where they separated.

Tsoukanov returned to his parents' house in Phoenix. Police arrested him for the murder of Simberg a few days before Christmas. Shortly after New Year's Eve he confessed. In his initial meeting with Britt, Tsoukanov provided detailed descriptions—corroborated by forensic evidence—of how he and his two friends murdered Simberg. He said they had "tricked" Simberg into meeting them by offering to loan him money. Tsoukanov explained that the crime was a "murder for hire." He promised to tell Britt soon who had hired the murderers.

Britt was absolutely certain Southland was responsible for Simberg's murder. When Britt reviewed the statements made by Dusty Swindle about the day before the first heist, when the gang of high school kids drove to a cul-de-sac to be inspected by Southland in the guise of the "Big Boss," Britt discovered that the inspection had taken place in front of Tsoukanov's home. When I visit the Tsoukanov residence in the spring of 2002, a member of his family tells me that Southland had visited the home on a few occasions prior to the murder of Simberg. Days later the same Tsoukanov family member calls me at home to say her recollection was faulty. Southland was never there.

In subsequent interviews with the police, Tsoukanov retracted his statement that Simberg had been killed as a murder for hire. Tsoukanov denied ever having met Southland. He couldn't recall why he and his friends had committed the murder. Richard Bolinski, a friend of Tsoukanov's who has visited him in jail, says, "I think Dennis is scared to death of somebody. He's afraid for what could happen to his family if he talks."

When I meet with Tsoukanov in the spring of 2002 at the Maricopa County Jail in Phoenix, he tells me that he hopes that after he speaks with me and is written about in *Rolling Stone*, "girls will write me letters." It turns out he doesn't have a lot to say. The food at Maricopa is "retarded." He shows me drawings he's made of a hill in Estonia where he used to sled. He wants to know if his sister showed me the amateur modeling photos a local photographer took of him for his bid to become an Abercrombie & Fitch model. I look into Tsoukanov's unnervingly cross-eyed gaze and tell him I saw the photos and they are good, especially the ones where he is in profile.

12. JUSTICE FALLS

BRITT HAS BEEN UNABLE to link Southland or Langdon to the murder of Simberg. The problem is no phone calls exist between Southland and Tsoukanov, or either of the other killers. Absent testimony from Tsoukanov, Britt is unable to pursue a murder case against Southland.

Troy Langdon and Sean Southland never stand trial for robbery, conspiracy or insurance fraud. With the death of Simberg, the main witness against them, their attorneys negotiate lenient deals in which they plead to lesser fraud charges and are sentenced to time served—the few days each served in jail after their arrests in October.

While awaiting final disposition of his case, Langdon continues to live in Carefree with his wife, who just gave birth to their second baby. He still works at his in-laws' pharmacy, though he has dissolved Peak Physique and quit the HGH business. "People in my neighborhood look at the HGH business almost like it's sleazy," he says.

Langdon attributes the "bogus case" Britt and others in the Phoenix Police Department pursued against him to "jealous cops working their pissant jobs, and they can't figure out how a kid like me is making this much money. They conclude with their pea-size brains that I'm doing something illegal."

Langdon and Southland aren't as close as they used to be. But Langdon still calls Southland a "good friend" and Sea Castle "a damn good idea."

For his part, Southland expresses his sincerest remorse at all the events of the past year, even Simberg's murder. He stands in the half-light by his private basketball court watching his son and daughter shoot hoops. "It's really sad," he says. He's alone with the kids tonight, as he is most nights, since Olga spends every free hour working to pay for their home and his legal defense. And, he laments, he has become something of a pariah. "Parents don't let their kids come over," he says.

13. "THE TWO TITTY-DANCING SISTERS"

CHRISTIE'S CABARET, the club where Ksenya and Olga still perform their act, is one of the largest in Phoenix, with a vast interior that somehow manages to be dark and glittering at once. Most nights you can see the sisters working their act up onstage before they begin to solicit lap dances from customers. They are a bit of an odd couple. Olga, tall and angular, holds her head high like an Olympic figure skater gliding past the judges. Ksenya, shorter and rounder, projects a sort of defiant barroom sloppiness. She drinks on the job, chain-smokes and greets the looks from her customers with a churlish snarl.

Though Olga and Ksenya work together on physically intimate terms, they hate and fear each other intensely. Ksenya believes that Southland is responsible for Simberg's death; Olga fears that Ksenya's testimony might send Southland or even her to prison. Even though their breasts will some-times touch in the course of a lap dance, they seldom talk to each other, except to exchange the briefest, most impersonal information. Explaining how they manage to work together, Ksenya says, "I don't think about my sister or the customer or anything. I only think about the money."

When she gets off work, at about two A.M., Ksenya invariably thinks about Simberg. She often remembers the day the police showed up at her door and asked Ksenya to sketch one of Simberg's four tattoos. She drew a sunburst that had been high on his arm. When a policeman looked at Ksenya's sketch and nodded, she knew it meant her Konstantin was dead.

Later, Ksenya drove up to the Yavapai County morgue to identify her boyfriend's body. "What they did to him was disgusting," she says. "His face was swelled like a ball, and his skin was burned off the top of his head." She prefers to remember the last time she saw him alive. He had big plans then. He said, "I'm getting money. Tomorrow we are going to Vegas, and we are going to have so much fun."

14. AFTERMATH

CHRIS ANDREWS TURNED HIMSELF IN to police in January 2002, and in 2003 he was tried and convicted of murdering Simberg. He was sentenced to life in prison without parole. Dennis Tsoukanov was tried as an accom-plice to murder and convicted. He will be eligible for parole in fifteen years. Mikhail Drachev was tried in absentia for murder, convicted and sentenced to life without parole. In April 2007, Drachev, who had been living in To-ronto under a false name, was turned in to Canadian police by his girlfriend, who recognized him on *America's Most Wanted*. He was extradited to Ari-zona to begin serving his sentence. Drachev, Andrews and Tsoukanov have not implicated Southland in the crime.

On July 1, 2004, Sean Southland was arrested in Canada across Alexandria Bay, New York, trying to smuggle six kilos of cocaine into the United States on a boat, with the help of a Canadian girlfriend.

After his arrest by Canadian authorities, he informed them that he was an undercover DEA agent working on a sting operation. He produced a business card belonging to Phoenix police detective Tom Britt and told his questioners that Britt would vouch for him. When called, Britt did not.

Southland was transferred to U.S. custody. Convicted of drug trafficking, he was sentenced to ten years in prison. In court documents it emerged that Southland had promised his girlfriend they would use the money from drug smuggling to invest in a company called Sea Castle.

When Britt calls me with the news of Southland's arrest for coke smuggling, he turns back to Simberg, as he frequently does. Aside from Simberg's parents and his girlfriend, Britt appears to be the only person in America who mourns his death. "Kostya was not a bad kid," Britt says, using Simberg's diminutive nickname. "He just had the wrong influences. He became involved with a very bad American, Sean Southland."

It was about four o'clock on a Friday afternoon, January 26, 2001, when Esther Birkmaier, a single retiree in her seventies, heard screams outside her front door. Birkmaier lives on the sixth floor of an Art Deco apartment building in the Pacific Heights area of San Francisco, one of the city's prime neighborhoods, known for its panoramic views of the Golden Gate Bridge. As Birkmaier pressed her eye against the peephole, a woman in the hallway outside yelled, "Help me!" Birkmaier couldn't see much from her limited fish-eye perspective, but what she did see shocked her. There was a blond woman on the floor. A huge dog was attacking her.

Birkmaier phoned 911 and reported "dogs running wild" in her hallway. When she hung up, something began pounding on her door. She panicked, phoned 911 again and this time just screamed into the phone. A man heard the screams and also phoned 911 to report what he thought was a rape. Alec Cardenas, a SWAT-team medic and one of the first cops on the scene, arrived about seven minutes later to find the victim lying facedown on the hall carpet in front of her apartment. She was naked, covered in blood, her upper back punctured with dog bites. Blood was splashed on the walls for about twenty feet down the hall. As Cardenas approached, the woman attempted to push herself up and crawl into her home.

About this time, a middle-aged woman who identified herself as Marjorie Knoller stepped out of apartment 604. She too was covered in blood. But aside from a cut on her hand and a few scratches on her arms, she was not injured. She told the police she had been walking her dog Bane down the hall when he lunged at the victim, who was entering her apartment carrying a bag of groceries. "I told her to stay still," Knoller said. "If she had, this would have never happened." Knoller told police she had managed to lock Bane and his mate, Hera, in her apartment. She was afraid to go back inside.

Animal-control officers found Bane in Knoller's bathroom. The officers inched open the bathroom door and peeked inside. Bane was a massive creature. He weighed 120 pounds and was just under three feet tall, with a brindle coat of black and tan tiger stripes. Most of his weight was centered in his powerful chest, bulging legs and squat head, his most imposing feature. Bane had defecated all over the bathroom. He was soaked in blood. Even his teeth were red.

The animal-control officers carried a tranquilizer gun that shoots darts potent enough to knock out a large dog. They fired three into Bane and waited fifteen minutes, but he remained standing. Two of the officers ended up hooking Bane with "catch" poles and walked him down to their van, where they euthanized him with 25cc of sodium pentobarbitol a short time later.

Five hours later, the victim, Diane Whipple, a popular thirty-three-year-old lacrosse coach at nearby St. Mary's College, died at San Francisco General Hospital. Her larynx had been crushed and her throat punctured. But the cause of death was cardiac arrest; she had lost nearly all of her blood.

Whipple had been an all-American lacrosse player at Penn State, then an Olympic track-and-field hopeful—an aspiration she was forced to give up in her mid-twenties to battle cancer. Less than a week before the attack, she had run a marathon.

One police officer initially called her death a "tragic accident," but a morally neutral judgment failed to satisfy the public, whose outrage soon turned on Bane's owners, Marjorie Knoller and her husband, Robert Noel. Outwardly, they seemed exemplary San Franciscans. They were do-gooder attorneys honored by the Bar Association of San Francisco for their work helping the homeless and mentally disabled. They were opera patrons who hobnobbed with some of the city's wealthiest citizens. Both on their third marriage, they had wed twelve years earlier and were seen by friends such as their colleague Herman Franck as being "deeply in love, devoted to each other."

But an investigation into their private lives soon yielded secrets that defied explanation. The couple—she is forty-six, he's sixty—had recently adopted an inmate at California's Pelican Bay State Prison, a thirty-nine-year-old man serving a life term for armored-car robbery and attempted murder. Their "son," Paul "Cornfed" Schneider, is one of the most feared leaders of the Aryan Brotherhood prison gang and is currently facing federal trial on an indictment for racketeering and a series of murders he allegedly orchestrated from behind bars.

Schneider, who lived in an eleven-by-seven-and-a-half-foot concrete cell, had somehow managed to set up a dog-breeding operation—he called it Dog o' War Kennels—outside the prison walls. Schneider's associates raised Presa Canarios, an unusual breed of attack dog from Spain introduced to the United States a decade or so earlier. Bane, the dog that killed Whipple, was Schneider's prize stud dog—Presa puppies sell for as much as $2,200. Prison investigators suspected that the dogs were being raised to protect Aryan Brotherhood criminal enterprises such as meth labs.

The fact that Bane and his mate, Hera, wound up living in Knoller and Noel's Pacific Heights apartment was odd enough. Even stranger was the relationship among Knoller, Noel and their adopted son. It included pornographic letters that the couple exchanged with Schneider and, it was rumored, photographs of Marjorie Knoller having sex with the dogs. It did not help Knoller's cause that days after the city filed a warrant to search for photos that depicted "sexual acts . . . that involved dogs" in Schneider's cell, she admitted that her nickname for one of the dogs had been "my certified lick therapist."

Nothing in the portrait of the couple that was emerging made sense. Nor did the bizarre statements they made in public. They suggested Whipple might have egged on the attack by wearing a pheromone-laced perfume or by menstruating. When Knoller appeared before a grand jury, she wove an almost moving tale of how she risked her life trying to save Whipple's, then blew whatever sympathy she was gaining by saying that Bane had sniffed Whipple's crotch "like she was a bitch in heat."

Since late January, Knoller has been on trial for second-degree murder, and her husband for manslaughter. Because the case has received such extensive coverage in their hometown, the trial is being held in Los Angeles. "Bob and Marjorie were so hated in San Francisco," says Herman Franck. "You half expected to see an angry mob with pitchforks and torches show up outside the courthouse."

If Knoller and Noel were simply on trial for acting like jerks, this would be an open-and-shut case. But proving that this strange couple had a murderous intent will be difficult for prosecutors. Nor will the trial answer all questions about this case; the story of how the once-prominent San Francisco attorneys wound up adopting an Aryan Brotherhood gang leader and his killer dog reveals as much about individual human folly as it does about the peculiar, corrupting hell of the American penal system. Perhaps it should come as no surprise that their journey into this hell was paved with good intentions.

ORIGINALLY LOCKED UP IN 1985 for an armored-car robbery, Paul Schneider has been incarcerated since the early 1990s in the Security Housing Unit of Pelican Bay State Prison, where he is locked in his cell twenty-two and a half hours per day, never allowed outdoors, and permitted contact with the outside world only through letters and strictly monitored visits. Keith Whitley, a former guard who first encountered Schneider in 1987, calls him "the most dangerous man in California." Schneider is deemed such a security risk that when he was moved last fall out of Pelican Bay in preparation for his federal trial, U.S. marshals and the California Highway Patrol blocked traffic on the Oakland Bay Bridge in order to transport him across it in a heavily defended motorcade.

When I first meet Schneider, he appears across the reinforced-glass visitation window at his temporary home in the Sacramento County jail looking amazingly fit despite his chalky complexion. Throughout the interview, a steady clanking sound emanates from deep within the jail—chains sliding, locks tumbling, doors slamming, which together sound like the rumbling of the empty stomach of a mechanical beast. Schneider has thick blond hair combed straight back, a direct, blue-eyed gaze, stands about six-feet-two and weighs 220 pounds. Muscles, traced with blue veins, bulge beneath his pale skin. His right hand is tattooed with an A and a B, spare advertisements for his affiliation with the notorious Aryan Brotherhood gang.

Schneider, born in 1962, grew up in Cerritos, California, with two younger sisters, his mother and his stepfather, a retired Air Force officer who ran an industrial-cleaning service. He portrays his childhood as a happy one. "My stepdad used to take me flying in Cessnas," he says. "I worked on pit crews for drag-racing boats."

Schneider's sister Tammy offers a much darker view of her brother's childhood than the idyllic picture he paints. Tammy, thirty-eight and married to a firefighter, lives in a rural community about an hour from where she and Paul grew up. She is an attractive woman with an almost doll-like presence, an impression created by her limited ability to move her hands or arms as a result of the brain cancer she has battled for twelve years. According to Tammy, the house where she and her brother grew up was run on a regimen that blended military discipline and sadism. "Our house was a prison, and our stepdad was the warden," she says. He would wake the children up in the middle of the night to make them scrub pots or scour the bathroom floor with toothbrushes. Tammy's first beating occurred when she was eight. A couple of years later, her stepfather began to sexually abuse her. "Paul was very protective of me," she remembers. "He stood up to our stepdad. That man used to beat the shit out of Paul."

Early in his childhood, Schneider says, he fell in love with dogs. When he was about sixteen, Schneider found a summer job with a Los Angeles company called Continental K-9, which specialized in lending junkyard-protection dogs to small businesses in the city's crime-ridden industrial zone. He would drop off the dogs at night and pick them up early in the morning. Most of the animals were semi-wild, vicious mutts. "Thieves would cut tendons in the dogs' legs," he says. "That was when I learned how loyal dogs are. They would still try to do their job even when their legs were sliced."

In 1979, after graduating from high school early, Schneider joined the Air Force and was assigned to a special Strategic Air Command unit in eastern Washington. He worked as a crewman aboard KC-130 aerial refueling tankers, large planes that accompanied heavy bombers to the edge of Soviet airspace. He lived a week at a time in an underground bunker called a "mole hole," and he participated in round-the-clock drills in which crews were told nuclear attack was imminent and were given five minutes to scramble their jets. They were never told whether these drills were actual or make-believe Armageddon until their missions were over. The isolation and intense psychological pressure of his military duty would later prove excellent preparation for withstanding torturous conditions within the corrections system.

Schneider did not last long in the authoritarian world of the military. According to Tammy, he and his wife split up two years after he enlisted, and he was kicked out of the Air Force for writing bad checks. He moved back to Cerritos and became the manager of a local pizza parlor. On one of his nights off, he put on a mask, armed himself with a handgun and robbed the restaurant. A short while later, he began to notice the big sacks of money carried by armored cars at the Alpha Beta supermarket where Tammy worked as a checkout girl. He developed an irrational personal hatred of the guards. "I couldn't believe how arrogant the guards were," Schneider says. "They'd come into the store, with their little revolvers pointing to the ground, and they'd bump into people without even apologizing. I wanted to show them that they weren't so tough."

Schneider robbed the guards and got away with nearly $100,000. Several weeks later, according to his sister, he showed up at his stepfather's house flaunting a new motorcycle. His stepfather, suspecting that Schneider was behind the robbery, tipped off the cops, who began to build a case against Schneider. In 1985, at the age of twenty-three, he was arrested and eventually sent to New Folsom State Prison, in California. By July 1987, he had earned his way into the Aryan Brotherhood by stabbing a guard in the neck.

Schneider thrived in the brutal prison environment, pitting his will against the authorities' every chance he had. In 1990, when he was brought into a courthouse under heavy guard to testify in a case involving another inmate, Schneider pulled a knife he had fashioned from a prison soup ladle and stabbed a defense attorney several times. Like a magician guarding the secret behind a trick, Schneider has never revealed how he smuggled the weapon into the courtroom, though his victim's wounds contained unmistakable clues: They were infected with fecal matter.

After the incident, Schneider penned a declaration explaining why he'd attacked the attorney. The assault stemmed from his desire to humiliate a warden at New Folsom State Prison. "I took [associate warden] Campbell's boasting of his new vaunted security procedures as a challenge," he wrote. As for why he chose his victim, he wrote, "I didn't like his attitude, his smart-aleck remarks, nor his demeanor. So I stabbed him. In retrospect, it was a bad idea."

Schneider picked up a life sentence. Displaying an uncanny ability to harass the system even in defeat, he successfully sued the prison administration for excessively X-raying him every time he was transported before and after the soup-ladle knife episode and collected $11,666.66.

In the meantime, Schneider was transferred to Pelican Bay State Prison shortly after it opened in 1989. The prison was intended to be the crown jewel of the California Department of Corrections (CDC), which operates one of the largest penal systems in the world, a gulag with ninety-eight facilities, more than three hundred thousand inmates under its jurisdiction and nearly fifty thousand employees.

Pelican Bay rises unexpectedly out of redwood forest a few miles off Highway 101, on the desolate Northern California coast, 360 miles north of San Francisco. Its antiseptic corridors resemble passageways in a large, slumbering spaceship. "When you first go inside Pelican Bay," says Russell Clanton, an attorney who represents several inmates there, "it feels like being inside an enormous sensory-deprivation tank." The 3,200 inmates are stored like factory-raised poultry in small concrete cells.

Within a few years of the prison's opening, reports began to leak out suggesting that Pelican Bay's neat façade served mainly to conceal its interior horrors from the outside world. In two early incidents, guards were caught using medical facilities to torture inmates—strapping one man to a gurney and beating him, submerging another in scalding water and flaying him with wire brushes. Eventually, several brutality cases filed on behalf of inmates were rolled into a class-action suit. After a two-year trial that ended in 1995, U.S. District Court Judge Thelton Henderson ruled that prisoners at Pelican Bay had been subjected to cruel and unusual punishment. His lengthy opinion detailed "assaults, beatings and naked cagings in inclement weather," and concluded that "the misuse of force at Pelican Bay is not merely aberrational but inevitable." (Since the ruling, prison authorities say conditions have improved.)

In 1997, Schneider was taking a shower in Pelican Bay when, he claims, a guard popped open an electronic door and allowed a sworn enemy from a rival African-American gang called the Black Guerrilla Army to enter the shower area and ambush him. Schneider overpowered his assailant. The guard intervened with a weapon misleadingly named a "gas gun." The firearm actually uses a gunpowder charge similar to a twelve-gauge shotgun to fire plastic projectiles the size of Ping-Pong balls. Schneider took multiple shots to the head and was taken to the infirmary with a concussion and lacerations. Afterward, Schneider, a jailhouse lawyer of some renown, sued the prison over the incident. His case, however, was thrown out of court.

Upon his release from the infirmary, he was sent into Pelican Bay's Security Housing Unit. Schneider speaks of living in the extreme confinement of the SHU with a sort of twisted pride. "They put us in the SHU to keep us away from the rape-os and chesters," he says, referring to rapists and child molesters. "I'm proud of that. I don't want to be associated with them."

The role of the Aryan Brotherhood, like other race-based gangs, is a complex one within the hostile prison universe. On the one hand, these gangs enforce segregation. But the gangs are also likely to do business with each other: smuggling drugs, manufacturing weapons, running numbers and brewing alcohol. The gangs also share (along with many guards) a more or less openly homicidal contempt for sex offenders. Under Schneider's leadership, the Aryan Brotherhood is alleged to have recruited at least three guards in its efforts to identify and attack sex-offender inmates. In its case against Schneider, the federal government charges him with masterminding the murder or attempted murder of twenty-four people, including the killing of a cop.

In person, Schneider maintains an unnervingly pleasant, almost bland smile, whether he's discussing killing rapists or reading one of his favorite authors, J. R. R. Tolkien. He says his entire mental and physical effort in the SHU "is structured around not going insane." The last stop for those who lose this battle in the SHU is the prison psychiatric unit. Here, the most critical mental cases can be put on heavy doses of psychotropic drugs, then given "group therapy." In these sessions, individual prisoners are locked in telephone-booth-size boxes with plexiglass-and-barred fronts that prisoners call "man cages," and these are propped upright, arrayed in groups of four or six around a therapist.

"You definitely don't want to lose your marbles in the SHU," Schneider says. "But you can find things that cheer you up—getting a cup of instant coffee, news or a box of saltines. It's important to keep your day full." He stays in shape by banding together law books he keeps in his cell and using them as weights. Sometimes he lays his cell mate, a murderer named Dale Bretches, across his arms and bench-presses him like a barbell.

Several years ago, Schneider and Bretches began producing artwork. Since they were forbidden art supplies by prison authorities, they collected scrap paper and soaked it in toilet water until the ink came off. They made pigments by scraping the colors off ads in magazines. "If you want a lot of red," Schneider says, "you look for a Marlboro ad."

His intricate creations look like a cross between tattoo art and the airbrushed murals that adorned vans in the 1970s. The paintings are frequently chock-full of runes—cryptic symbols found in the works of Tolkien. Schneider often depicts himself in his paintings as a bare-chested Norse god riding on the prows of ships surrounded by noble animals.

Devan Hawkes, a special intelligence officer for the CDC, has spent years investigating Schneider. He believes the runes found in Schneider's work contain "secret codes" that convey instructions to Aryan Brotherhood associates outside prison.

Looking for subjects to draw, Schneider began to pester his sister for pictures of the "white Siegfried and Roy tigers" and for copies of *Field & Stream*, which he claims was banned by the prison because it contained photos of guns. Then Schneider came across a magazine that would change his life: *Dog Fancy*. "Looking at dogs made me forget I was in prison," says Schneider. Soon, they inspired him to become a dog owner once more.

AFTER THEY WERE ARRESTED for the dog-mauling case, Knoller and Noel were so broke they were unable to make bail. They have spent nearly a year living separate but parallel lives in different wings of the San Francisco city jail. When he enters the jail visitation room in his orange jumpsuit, Robert Noel slides into a chair and smiles warmly. Noel is an imposing six-footfour. His golden-boy features have aged comfortably beneath his shaggy blond hair and walrus mustache. Though he faces up to three years in prison, he projects confidence and freewheeling good cheer.

After chatting amiably about his once high-powered social life, Noel produces a copy of a painting that Schneider made. It depicts Noel, Knoller and Schneider at a medieval feast presided over by their "royal dog," Bane. Noel traces his finger across the paper and says dreamily, "There's our family," then points to the big dog in the foreground and says affectionately, "That's the Banester."

Noel's first wife, Karen, whom he divorced in 1986 after nearly twenty-three years of marriage, says, "Robert is mentally ill." She furnishes no proof of her opinion but adds that his three children ceased having contact with him several years ago. Noel's only biological son, his namesake, Robert Jr., who is thirty-one, said of his father, "He's a jackass. I don't like my dad, and I never have."

Noel grew up in a working-class home in Baltimore. His father was a pipe fitter and his mother a beautician. His only brother works in the electrical trades. Robert, the family overachiever, entered the University of Maryland on a Marine Corps scholarship. He married his high school sweetheart, Karen, the day after John F. Kennedy was shot. A year later, he entered law school. In 1969, when he was twenty-seven, Noel took a job in the Justice Department. When he was thirty-four, in 1980, he moved west to become an assistant U.S. attorney in the Southern District Court of San Diego.

Working for the government began to disillusion him. "Being inside the system gave me a unique perspective on its power to crush the individual," he says. He quit the U.S. attorney's office after a year and joined a prestigious corporate-law firm in San Diego. By 1987, he had divorced, moved to San Francisco, briefly married and then divorced a legal secretary, then met and fallen in love with Marjorie Knoller—all in the space of about a year. "I would trust my life in Marjorie's hands," he says.

THE IMPRESSION MARJORIE KNOLLER makes upon entering the visitation room is one of meekness. Her faded, silver-threaded brown hair is pulled back in a ponytail, and her brown, dark-ringed eyes have a worried softness. On March 27, when the police entered the home of friends in Northern

California, where she and her husband were eating dinner, and told Marjorie she was under arrest for second-degree murder, she collapsed and had to be carried out on a stretcher. During subsequent court appearances, her physical and mental states deteriorated. Rolled into the courtroom in a wheelchair, she seemed almost cuckoo, babbling to herself and cursing the prosecutors. By the end of the summer, bruises began to appear on her thighs and lower back. Then, where there had been bruises, hardened nodules of subcutaneous fat, shaped like fingernails, burst from the surface of her skin. Doctors diagnosed it as a nervous-vascular disorder and put her on medication, alleviating her symptoms enough for her to sit comfortably and walk unassisted.

Growing up in Brooklyn, Knoller was a straight arrow who dreamed of becoming an FBI agent. "Marjorie didn't go with the crowd," says her mother, Harriet. "She skipped her high school graduation. She told me, 'Mom, I'm not going. All the kids in my class are on drugs.'"

She met Robert Noel when she was thirty-two, a divorced law school graduate just starting her career at the firm where Noel was already a big shot. They made a lunch date one day and moved in together a week later. By May 1988, they had both resigned their jobs and hung out their own shingle. They moved away from the commercial-contract and tax law that had been Noel's area of expertise and took on more pro bono work. Then, in 1994, their life was to change drastically when they were referred to what seemed like an interesting case.

The client was a man named John Cox, a guard at Pelican Bay State Prison who had recently broken ranks with fellow corrections officers by testifying on behalf of inmates who'd been brutalized in the prison. Now Cox was being harassed on the job and wanted to sue the California Department of Corrections. Knoller and Noel leaped at the chance to represent him. Within a few months they abandoned what remained of their commercial-law practice to concentrate on representing prison guards in grievances against the CDC.

"The good Lord blessed our family by bringing Bob and Marjorie into our lives," says Monica Bermender, who was represented by Noel and Knoller in a First Amendment federal court case. "They believed in me and in our family when nobody else would."

Despite their devotion to their cause, Knoller and Noel racked up an uneven, some say abysmal, record. They lost the harassment case for their first client, Cox, and he subsequently hanged himself. Susan Beck, who analyzed their cases against the CDC in an article in *The Recorder*, a Bay Area legal newspaper, concluded that Knoller and Noel often made basic procedural mistakes and developed legal strategies based on unsupported conspiracy theories. "Noel comes across as someone who is competent, but it appears to me there have been serious problems with his conduct on some cases," says Neal Sanders, an expert in prison law.

The fact was that neither Knoller nor Noel had much experience trying criminal cases. Entering the miasma of the prison universe, they were clearly in over their heads. "Prison is like its own ecosystem, with its own rules," says attorney Russell Clanton. "Life inside the wire is unlike anything most people outside of it can even conceive."

The low point of their legal career came in 1997, when they defended a Pelican Bay guard accused of colluding with the Aryan Brotherhood to set up child molesters for beatings and murder. Their defense failed, and not only was the guard found guilty but one of the inmates they called as a witness was subsequently murdered.

"It was devastating for us," says Knoller. "I was in shock."

Schneider was among the witnesses they called in that case and was presumably marked for death like the other inmate. "We sent a letter to the CDC informing them of our concerns for Paul's safety," says Knoller.

IT WAS ABOUT THIS TIME that Schneider's dreams of once again owning dogs began to take root. Ads in the back pages of *Dog Fancy* and *Dog World* featuring an unusually fierce breed of dog captured his interest. Called Presa Canarios, they were often touted as "guardian dogs," as "man stoppers," tough enough to "take out pit bulls." Presas are "holding" or "gripping" dogs that were bred by Spanish cattlemen on the Canary Islands in the sixteenth century to pin down bulls for slaughter. They are what breeders call "lip and ear" dogs: They immobilize much larger animals such as bulls by clamping their jaws over their most vulnerable features—their lips or their ears. American-bred Presas look like pit bulls but are about twice as big, sometimes weighing as much as 160 pounds.

Dog behaviorist and breeder Saul Saltars calls many of the Presa lines sold in America "junk dogs"—Presas mixed with pit bulls, Great Danes, English mastiffs. "Some breeders take liberties with what they call Presas," he says. "You might not know what you're getting, how stable the dog will be."

Schneider began dreaming of ways to purchase his own Presas in 1998. He had $23,000 to invest, given to him by a fellow inmate who had won a medical malpractice suit. Schneider's plan was to use surrogates outside prison to breed Presas. He purchased more than $1,000 worth of dog-breeding manuals. He sent letters to breeders and trainers. Most refused to have anything to do with a prison inmate. Nevertheless, he located a breeder in the Midwest who seemed like a good prospect. According to the CDC investigation, his name was James Harris, and he operated a Presa business, Stygian Kennels. Schneider would arrange to buy Bane from Harris.

According to Tracy Hennings, a Presa breeder familiar with Stygian Kennels (now defunct) and its brood of pups, "Bane was not a pure Presa. He was a questionable mix of at least four different breeds."

But Schneider, conducting his business from inside his eleven-by-seven-and-a-half-foot concrete box, was unable to do the sort of on-the-spot research other buyers might have undertaken. He had a source for dogs. All he needed was a place to raise them.

Initially, he wrote to his sister Tammy asking whether she and her husband, Greg Keefer, would raise dogs for him. Tammy recalls her reaction when she received this letter from her brother. "What the hell is an inmate doing with dogs? No way."

"One time Paul got us into some deal where he sent us money from one of his legal settlements to buy TV sets for his buddies in prison," Greg Keefer says. "Next thing, FBI agents came to our door and said we were on someone's hit list because we didn't get him a TV."

"I love Paul," says Tammy. "But the guy's in prison for a reason."

Rebuffed by his family, Schneider found the assistance he needed from another quarter. His cell mate, Dale Bretches, the murderer, was receiving regular visits from a woman in a Christian outreach program who came from a small agricultural town about 190 miles from Pelican Bay, called Hayfork. Bretches asked her whether she knew any other good Christians in Hayfork who could visit his cellie, Schneider, and help him out with a problem.

Janet Coumbs is a Mormon woman in her late forties who lived on a four-acre sheep farm in Hayfork, California, with her eighteen-year-old daughter, Daisy. She is a somewhat heavyset woman who scraped by on disability checks and by selling "little baby sheep" to local families for slaughter. A friend of hers stopped by her ramshackle house one day and told her about the mission work she did at Pelican Bay, trying to bring Jesus into the life of a murderer named Dale Bretches. "[She] told me I wasn't doing my Christian duty by not going with her to the prison to help other inmates," said Coumbs.

Coumbs made her first visit to Schneider in January 1998. Within a couple of months, Schneider had persuaded Coumbs to lend her farm to his Dog o' War kennel. Every two weeks, she was supposed to send Schneider pictures of the dogs and letters describing their life on the farm. One photo showed Bane cuddling with a cat. This enraged Schneider. "You're making a wuss out of Bane," he wrote. "These are royal dogs, and they need to look majestic."

Several months later, Schneider and Coumbs had a falling-out. According to Schneider, the root of their conflict was romantic. He says, "She kept dropping hints about how she wanted me to convert to Mormon and marry her." After he spurned Coumbs's romantic overtures, Schneider says, she stopped sending letters and visiting him altogether. Coumbs has told investigators that Schneider threatened her. "Things can happen to you and your home," he allegedly told her. (Reportedly, Coumbs is now in the federal Witness Protection Program.)

IN LATE 1999, SCHNEIDER TURNED to Knoller and Noel to help him retrieve his dogs from Coumbs. Perhaps because of their dismal performance
as attorneys, Schneider had resorted to Knoller and Noel only after another
Bay Area attorney had turned him down.

True to form, the lawyers threw themselves into this new ill-fated cause.
They threatened to sue Coumbs if she didn't turn the dogs over, and then
they spent their own money to hire an animal-transport service and showed
up in person at Coumbs's farm on March 31, 2000. There were now eight
Presas on the farm, four of them pups sired by Bane.

For the previous year, Bane had been chained to an iron stake. Noel
beams when he recalls seeing the dog for the first time. "Bane was confident,
proud, handsome," he says, adding, "Bane had an eye for ladies. He sees
Marjorie, rolls over on his back, and bam, that big red arrow popped out.
He had a hard-on that big." Noel gestures with his hands, indicating Bane's
penis length, then grins. "Boy, was that dog hung."

Noel and Knoller transported seven of the dogs to homes in Southern
California belonging to relatives of Schneider's prison buddies. They kept
Hera, a female that developed a heart condition, and, after spending $3,000
on her veterinary bills, moved her into their Pacific Heights apartment. In
early September, they brought Bane to live there as well. Greg Keefer says
that before Knoller and Noel rescued Bane, the dog had been neglected.
"Flies had chewed Bane's ears down to their nubs," Keefer says.

By now, they were writing letters and sending dog pictures to Schneider
several times a week. Their odd relationship with him was reaching full
bloom. Knoller says she first floated the idea of adopting Schneider, explaining this unusual arrangement in practical legal terms. "By adopting Paul,"
says Knoller, "we now have a say in his medical treatment. If something bad
happens to him in the prison, we can sue. We adopted him to give him
protection."

Her analysis is legally true—and adult adoption has long been a method employed by gay couples to form family units with legal standing—but it fails to explain the couple's interest in a violent inmate. Knoller suggests that she and Schneider had a lot in common, such as mutual interests in *The Hobbit* and in runes. "Paul has an inner life he shares with us," Knoller says. "He's special. He's our kid, and we love him."

She seems almost convincing, like a doting mom, but if that's true, what about the rumors of bestial photos and kinky fantasies traded with Schneider? Knoller allows that "threesomes are a pretty standard erotic fantasy." She says, "It's a tradition to write erotic letters to inmates. It helps them." Then she tries a different tack. "Paul was writing a novel, an erotic medieval fantasy. We wrote chapters back and forth. We were all characters in it."

Knoller says that, along the way, "I flashed my breasts in some pictures. Bob might have sent one of these to Paul. There was nothing with dogs."

Noel describes their unusual family unit in noble terms: "We were a part of keeping something in Paul alive. Bane punched a hole through that cement box Paul lives in and gave him a window on the world. We wanted to help keep that window open."

A COUPLE OF WEEKS before Knoller and Noel went up to Janet Coumbs's farm to pick up the dogs, they had hired a local veterinarian named Dr. Donald Martin to examine them. Though he gave the dogs shots and went home, something about Bane troubled the veterinarian. A few days later, he sent Knoller a letter to inform her of his fears about the dog. "I would be professionally remiss if I did not mention the following so you can be prepared," he wrote. "These animals would be a liability in any household."

Knoller says she didn't read the letter until long after receiving it. She and Noel nicknamed the dogs "the Muttleys" and "the kids." They structured their lives around the animals, never leaving them alone for more than an hour. Several mornings a week, Knoller woke up early and cooked bacon, pork and hamburger for the dogs, which she fed to them along with their dog food.

Keith Whitley, the former guard who used to socialize with Knoller and Noel, noticed the change in them. "I'd get on the phone with Bob to ask him about a case," he says, "and all he did was talk about how big Bane's balls were." Whitley visited their apartment about a week before the fatal attack: "They used to have this charming flat. The dogs turned it into a piss pot. Bob had to bring the dogs out one at a time when he introduced them to me because he couldn't control them."

Awful things started happening almost immediately after they brought Bane home. Bane got into a fight with a dog at a beach four days after he arrived in San Francisco and nearly snapped Noel's finger clean off. Bane and Hera scared the hell out of people in the building and neighborhood. Henry Putek, an unassuming parakeet owner who also lives on the sixth floor, was pinned against a wall one evening when Bane slipped out of Knoller and Noel's partially open door and charged him. "He stared at me silently," said Putek. "With drool hanging down, stinking and smelly."

Neighborhood residents claimed that Bane and Hera attacked at least three local dogs, nearly killing one of them, a German shepherd. People who lived in the area describe their encounters with the dogs in almost supernatural terms. One neighbor recalls that birds started flying crazily when Bane and Hera walked by. Another resident, Alex de Laszlo, remembered encountering the dogs outside a local coffee shop. "I put my hand on Bane's head," he said. "It held a sensation very distinct from any dog I had ever petted before. There was incredible tension. There was something strong and dark about this animal."

From the vantage point of his concrete box at Pelican Bay, Schneider had an entirely different perspective: "Everything was going perfect. I was getting photos of Bane. Bob and Marjorie told me everything he was doing." Schneider says Bane was growing up right. "I never wanted to see Bane go looking for fights," he says. "But if he was forced into it, I would want him to represent himself well, and not run away crying."

At this point, Schneider was on the verge of realizing an impossible dream. One of his associates on the outside had secured space in *Dog World* to place an ad for Schneider's Dog o' War kennel. "Life was so good, I felt like I did when I was on the streets," says Schneider. "In some ways, I felt better." He sent a picture of Bane to his sister with the caption "El Supremo Bane. Born to raise hell."

ON JANUARY 11, 2001, Robert Noel wrote Schneider one of his almost daily letters recounting everything that had transpired that day with "the kids." Nearing the end of the letter, Noel described an encounter between the dogs and a neighbor. "As soon as the [elevator] door opens at six, one of our newer female neighbors, a timorous little mousy blond who weighs less than Hera, is met by the dynamic duo exiting and almost has a coronary."

The "mousy blond" he referred to was Diane Whipple, the St. Mary's College lacrosse coach who died exactly fifteen days later in that same hallway. Whipple had had run-ins with the dogs and had made her feelings about her neighbors clear. She told her girlfriend, Sharon Smith, that one of them had snapped at her two weeks earlier. She told her friend Sarah Miller that Noel "was an asshole. He better do something about those dogs."

On the afternoon of January 26, Whipple arrived home carrying a bag of groceries with some ingredients to make tacos for dinner with Smith. Around twenty minutes earlier, at about three-forty, Knoller says, she had been working on legal research alone in her apartment (Noel was out of the city on business) when Bane started to whimper. She put him on a leash, walked him on the roof of the building and came inside to put a bag of his poop in the garbage chute when she noticed Whipple standing about thirty feet away, by her door.

"She was staring at Bane," says Knoller. Then, for no obvious reason, Knoller says, Bane dragged her toward Whipple. "I battled him the whole way," Knoller insists. While Knoller struggled for several minutes with Bane and Hera, who was also in the hall, Whipple, she says, simply stood silently in front of her apartment. Her front door was open, but according to Knoller she didn't bother to go inside, even after Bane jumped up on the wall and stuck his head in her crotch. All Whipple said, according to Knoller, was, "Your dog jumped on me."

Knoller says that she finally tried to push Whipple into her apartment for her own good, but Whipple resisted, at which point Bane bit her throat and proceeded to rip her clothes apart. Knoller claims the entire attack lasted a good twenty minutes, during which time, she says, "I put my life on the line. It's only dumb luck he didn't kill me."

Knoller denies that Hera took part in the attack, though Hera was also found with blood on her coat by animal-control officers. Later, after Hera was taken into custody by animal control, an employee at the city kennel where she was being kept observed fibers that appeared to be multicolored fabric coming out in the dog's stools, though no one at the time thought—or volunteered—to collect this as evidence. Dog behaviorist Saul Saltars points to the shredding of Whipple's clothing as evidence that one or both of the dogs had been taught to be hostile. "Someone trained that dog to bite rags," says Saltars. "It's a technique to build aggression." While Knoller and Noel claim the dogs weren't trained to be aggressive, police recovered a book from their apartment titled *Manstopper!*, a training manual that teaches owners techniques, such as "ragging out," to nurture viciousness in dogs.

Though the grand jury largely rejected Knoller's account of the attack (they found it hard to believe that Whipple would stand motionless for such a long time while Bane rampaged through the hall), until now there has been no concrete suggestion that Knoller fabricated her story. But according to Schneider's sister Tammy, Knoller called her that evening and offered an account of the attack that diverges significantly from what Knoller told the police and the grand jury. "Marjorie said she and her neighbor 'got into it,'" says Tammy. "They had an argument before anything happened with those dogs. Marjorie asked her to shut her door so she could take her dogs out in the hall, and that lady was like, 'No, I'm not shutting my door now. Fuck you!'"

Knoller denies this ever occurred, but if this is true, Knoller's defense—that the attack happened spontaneously—is suspect. From the standpoint of the law, a powerful attack dog might be viewed as a weapon not much different from a gun. In other words, if you were holding a gun, and your neighbor was found shot to death, it's a lot harder to prove the whole thing was accidental if people found out you and your dead neighbor were having an argument right before your gun shot her.

There is one element of Knoller's account of events that afternoon in the hallway that no one disputes:

What was the last thing Diane Whipple said to you?

"'Help me,'" Knoller whispers. Then she pauses. Knoller says, "My husband still talks about Bane like we used to, how much he loves him. I can't think of that dog the same way. All I see is the horror, the horror."

Knoller's adopted son expresses his feelings about the attack differently. Schneider's blue eyes peer out impassively from behind the security glass at the visitation booth, and he says, "For once, I try to do something good, and look what happens. Ain't that buzzard luck."

T ito Ortiz shadowboxes in his dressing room at the Las Vegas Mandalay
Bay Arena while a capacity crowd of more than nine thousand fans chants
his name, making it feel as though the massive concrete walls in the backstage area are vibrating with their enthusiasm. They have come to see a type
of fighting that until recently was against the law in most parts of America.
Tonight, Tito Ortiz will defend his light heavyweight title in the Ultimate
Fighting Championship, the anything-goes, no-holds-barred league in
which combatants fight using any means possible—punching, kicking,
grappling—until one surrenders or is knocked out.

Back in the mid-1990s, Senator John McCain deemed this style of
combat "human cockfighting." Cable TV operators refused to carry the
fights. The taboo contests went underground. The sport was barely kept

alive by a loyal cadre of fans and amateur fighters who gathered for events held in backwater arenas in the Deep South, at Indian reservations and at obscure storefront fighting schools in Southern California.

But now with its first-ever Las Vegas fight, the Ultimate Fighting Championship (UFC) is staging a comeback. New owners are betting that revamped safety rules and a star fighter, Tito Ortiz, billed as the "most charismatic man in Ultimate Fighting," will make the UFC as acceptable to ordinary Americans as apple pie, the WWF and the use of cluster bombs by our military. Tonight's fight is called "UFC 33: Victory in Vegas."

Turnout for the event is astonishing. Las Vegas has been a ghost town in the weeks following the 9/11 attacks. Yesterday at Mandalay Bay several hundred bikini-clad hopefuls in the Hawaiian Tropics beauty contest had lined up in a cold, nearly empty auditorium with only their goose bumps for company. But now, less than twenty-four hours later, the Mandalay Arena is mobbed with screaming fans. Arena cameras pick out celebrities in the crowd and splash their faces across jumbo video screens. Chuck Norris is in the house. No surprise there. So are a handful of barely recognizable subcelebrities like Robin Leach. But then video monitors fill with the authentic, full-fledged A-list crowd—Nicolas Cage, Justin Timberlake, Mike Tyson. People swivel their heads, trying to spot where the heavy hitters are sitting, as if their flesh-and-blood presence somehow sanctifies the event.

"It's about time America wakes up and recognizes the one true fighting sport," says a tall, taut-jawed fan in his late twenties who looks like a drill instructor and wears a T-shirt bearing the legend "Marine Corps Underwater Combat School." He punches the shoulder of a buddy seated nearby and says, "The UFC has landed in Las Vegas, the fighting capital of the world."

WHEN THE UFC WAS STARTED IN 1993, the idea was for two guys to meet in an octagon-shaped ring surrounded by a chain-link fence and beat the crap out of each other until only one was left standing. There weren't many rules back then, except fighters weren't supposed to bite or poke anyone's eyes out. They were sort of allowed to kick each other in the balls, though this was frowned upon. Choking was definitely okay. So was stomping a guy in the head when he was down. It looked like pro wrestling, only the blood and the occasional broken bones were real.

Americans loved it, at least a certain group of people did—one that George Will called the "basest element of society" in a column railing against the UFC that he wrote in 1997. At this time during the UFC's initial burst of popularity, nearly three hundred thousand of the basest element were tuning in to each fight on pay-per-view television. Public outcry against the UFC, led by George Will and Senator McCain, resulted in its banishment from cable TV, the main source of its revenues, and by the year 2000 the UFC was nearly out of business.

Today's rebirth of the UFC has been brought about by two wealthy brothers, Lorenzo and Frank Fertitta. They are Las Vegas insiders who run a publicly traded gaming company, founded by their father, with sales last year of just under a billion dollars. Lorenzo and Frank, thirty-two and forty respectively, are the kinds of guys who travel in private jets—they have a pair of Gulfstreams—drink beer brewed in their own microbrewery, Gordon Biersch, and about a year ago they decided when they hung out with their buddy Donald Trump it would be to watch fights in a championship they owned.

Last January the Fertittas bought the UFC. They reformed it, added safety rules and equipment like ultralight gloves, persuaded cable operators to again carry UFC events and won the all-important sanctioning from the Nevada State Athletic Commission, on which, incidentally, Lorenzo had served for three years as a commissioner. So far, the Fertittas are estimated to have poured $30 to $50 million of their own money into the UFC. They are betting it all on their reigning champ, Tito Ortiz, whom Lorenzo calls the "front and center of our productions."

Lorenzo Fertitta, the younger of the two brothers, is the more visible presence in the creation of the new UFC, controlling every aspect from negotiations with the cable companies to how much smoke will pour out of the smoke machines when Tito enters the arena. Lorenzo is slightly built and from afar looks like a sort of Las Vegas version of a hipster—with blondish hair, a goatee and shiny suits, all accented with a perfect suntan. Despite his status as pretty much the boss of everything, he has a low-key, approachable manner. Lorenzo enjoys sharing his family's rags-to-riches fairy tale, how his father started as a bellhop in 1960, worked hard, put his life savings into a seedy bar—far from the Las Vegas Strip—and transformed this into a no-frills but thriving "locals market" casino, which his two sons took over and expanded into the nearly billion-a-year company it is today.

Lorenzo has a similar strategy for the UFC, taking what he sees as a neglected, undervalued asset—with the UFC being the equivalent of the seedy off-Strip bar his father purchased—and building it into a profitable franchise. "Our job is to educate the public that the UFC is not this brutal animalistic exhibition," he says. "We put on fights in which world-class athletes compete to see who is better."

At the same time, Lorenzo takes pride in the UFC's new over-the-top pyrotechnics show that rivals that of a vintage KISS concert or a space shuttle explosion. Three thousand seats have been blocked in the Mandalay Arena—reducing capacity from twelve thousand to nine thousand—in order to make way for a three-story wall of fire that will herald Tito's entrance atop an elevator rising from the stage. Lorenzo talks of the need to create "superstars." He imagines a day when UFC fights are on television in American homes every week, becoming a "hybrid between boxing and the WWF."

In the six months since Lorenzo pushed through state athletic commission sanctioning of the UFC, rivals have emerged—King of the Cage and Gladiator Challenge in California, and Full Contact Fighter, carried by the Fox Sports network in New York. But Lorenzo is confident that the UFC will prevail, thanks in part to Tito Ortiz, whom he speaks of like a secret weapon. "Tito was our greatest asset when we took over the UFC. It is going to be huge when Tito breaks. He's a great fighter, and he has a powerful aura of destructiveness."

IN HIS CRAMPED DRESSING ROOM, Tito Ortiz is an outlandish, almost cartoonish presence. He is twenty-six years old, stands six-foot-two and weighs 204 pounds. His hair is dyed fluorescent blond. His chest and legs are smoothly shaved. He wears black trunks with orange flames on them. Overdeveloped rhomboids give him a classic case of jock neck—it seems wider than his head. His face looks like a combination of granite and baby fat. In the ring it projects a menacing, apish ferocity. Out of the ring, Tito often displays a boyish, disarmingly goofy grin. There are three hours of undercard fights before Tito's main event at nine. During this time Tito alternates between talkative exuberance and stony silence, pacing, stretching, shadowboxing, conferring with his trainers. One moment he is confidently planning his future as the undisputed UFC champion. "I want to do a Gatorade commercial," he says excitedly. "Can you imagine orange Gatorade against the orange flames on my trunks and my hair dyed bright? It would be awesome."

A moment later, he drops on the dressing room couch and stares moodily at his hands. They are large and covered in thick skin from months of training. If you shake Tito's hand it feels like a brick wrapped in fine-grain sandpaper. Tonight, they tremble with inner tension. "It's not fear," he says. "I'm anxious to go into the ring and fight."

About a dozen of his entourage surround him at all moments. The entourage includes his wife, Kristin—petite, blond, pretty and a former high school sweetheart, now pregnant—his two assistants, three martial trainers and a ragtag crew of fellow fighters who train with Tito under the name Team Punishment. Most are in their early twenties, with shaved heads and arms sleeved with tattoos. They are the kind of guys who work out so much, even their faces have big muscles. There seems to be a competition among them to grow the bushiest and most unusually shaped sideburns and chin beards. Most wear a sort of uniform of black shirts and toques with orange flames on them, matching those on Tito's shorts. One of them carries Tito's

UFC championship belt slung over his shoulder at all times, a hefty black leather truss with a dinner plate–size gold medallion encrusted with bogus gems that fail to catch the light.

This is Tito's thirteenth UFC fight. He entered the UFC in 1997 just as it was sliding into decline. Tito lost two early fights, but showed a willingness to learn new techniques, becoming what even an opponent's coach calls "one of the most well-rounded fighters out there."

By the time Tito won his first UFC belt in 1999, at a match held in virtual exile in Tokyo, he had honed a technique called "ground and pound." It consists of throwing his opponents to the mat, pinning them and striking their heads in an explosion of fists and elbows. By the time the Fertittas took over the UFC, Tito's ground-and-pound tactics had given him the mystique of invincibility. At a fight held in the Meadowlands last June, Tito grounded his opponent, an Australian martial arts champion, and pounded his face into a pretty fair approximation of hamburger meat, winning in under four minutes. In his bout prior to that, Tito scored a knockout in twenty-nine seconds by picking up his 210-pound opponent and dropping him on his head. "I don't make friends with the guys Tito fights anymore," his wife, Kristin, says. "I don't like seeing what Tito does to them."

Tito says that fighting for him is "strictly business." He explains, "The other guy in the ring is trying to take away meal money from me, my wife and my kid that's on the way. I'm ready to fight for it."

Before the Fertittas took over the UFC, fighters weren't earning much more than meal money, sometimes as little as a few hundred dollars for undercard fights and about $15,000 for championships. Under the new regime, champion prizes have zoomed to more than $150,000. Other benefits of its newfound legitimacy have followed. For the first time ever, Las Vegas Sports books are putting up numbers on UFC fights. Tito will be a featured character in UFC games being released for PlayStation 2 and Xbox. Jax Toys, a Mattel spin-off, is tooling up to make Tito Ortiz action figures for kids.

One of the last people to stop by Tito's dressing room and wish him well before the Victory in Vegas fight is Mike Tyson. He enters wearing a dark sport coat, grinning broadly; he is backed by his own well-dressed mini-entourage. Through some unspoken rule of entourage etiquette, Tyson's entourage and Tito's do not mingle or exchange eye contact, while their respective entourage leaders engage in a friendly summit. Tyson smiles. He tells Tito he's a big fan of his, then he balls his fist and taps Tito's fist. "You're gonna kill that guy," Tyson says, encouraging him the way an older brother would. "You're a bad motherfucker."

The main impediment to Tito's ambitions is a 205-pound Byelorussian named Vladimir "Vlady" Matyushenko sitting in a much smaller dressing room a few doors down from Tito. Matyushenko is a taciturn, thirty-year-old former world champion wrestler, fair-haired with Slavic features—a solid build and an almost squarish head, which, his trainer Rico Chiapparelli boasts, "is so hard you can hit him in the head with a sledgehammer and he'll keep coming."

Matyushenko's toughness—Tito calls him the "most powerful wrestler" he's ever confronted—was trained into him from a young age. He grew up inside the old Soviet sports system. He was raised in a state-run wrestling academy from the age of fifteen and went on to become a Russian national wrestling champion and a European Cup winner, ranked sixth in the world. He earned a spot on the Russian team for the 1994 Olympics, which he gave up in order to move to America, where he worked variously as a college wrestling coach and as a ditchdigger, before taking up Ultimate Fighting in 1999.

Matyushenko doesn't have much of an entourage—just Rico and Louie Chiapparelli, brothers and former wrestling champions who run the Los Angeles gym where Matyushenko trains, and two American friends who flew in from Nebraska. Matyushenko displays none of Tito's flights of mood. He is calm to the point of seeming boredom as he sits in his rumpled sweat suit, watching undercard bouts on the closed-circuit TV.

"Aren't you nervous, Vlady?" asks Steve Chapman, one of his friends from Nebraska, a guy who works as an air-conditioning repairman back home.

"No," Matyushenko says. "Why should I? Do you get nervous before you go into work in the morning?"

A relative unknown to Las Vegas bookmakers, Matyushenko was given odds starting at more than four to one that he would lose. The more gamblers and bookmakers learned about him, the more the odds evened out, until by the time the fight draws near, the sports book at the Mandalay pegs Matyushenko as the underdog by a margin of less than two to one.

"Tito's never faced a real athlete like Vlady," says Rico. "The Fertittas are in love with Tito because he dyes his hair and looks like a pro wrestler. They've thrown him easy fighters, built him up, loaded him with belts, and for the first time ever, he's going to face someone who's more powerful and more experienced. This is a fight of style versus substance, a guy with a hairdo against a world champion."

TITO DID HIS MOST INTENSE TRAINING at a camp in Big Bear Lake, California, where he stayed for four weeks before the Victory in Vegas fight. A ruggedly isolated mountain village at an elevation of more than eight thousand feet, Big Bear Lake has long been a popular training spot for boxers. But unlike boxers, whose training often revolves around an intense, almost secretive bond with an individual coach, Ultimate Fighters train in a loose, collegial atmosphere.

Tito's "camp" at Big Bear consisted of a couple of rented vacation cottages, with his Team Punishment crew sleeping on floors, couches and bunk beds. Team Punishment included individual coaches for jujitsu, boxing and kickboxing and an assortment of fighters who served as Tito's sparring partners. Some of these were narrow specialists like the 310-pound kickboxing champ from Tonga and the contingent of wiry jujitsu black belts from Brazil. There were established Ultimate Fighters like Quentin "Rampage" Jackson. There were up-and-comers like the twenty-year-old featherweight from Mississippi named Bobby "Wolverine" Terrel.

Typical of the sort of dedication fueling amateurs in this still obscure sport, Terrel had hopped a Greyhound bus out of his hometown in Mississippi and showed up at Tito's front door several weeks earlier, asking if he could train with him. Tito put him up on his couch. "There's a thousand people in Bobby's town," Tito boasts. "And Bobby's whipped nine hundred of them."

Tito and Team Punishment spent eight or ten hours a day together lifting weights, running, sparring, kickboxing and wrestling. They lived on a diet of protein shakes, fresh fruit, Lucky Charms and lean grilled meat Tito cooked at night on his George Foreman grill. Their only recreation besides fighting one another all day was an ongoing PlayStation 2 Gran Turismo 3 racing tournament held on the big-screen TV in Tito's house. In keeping with the old fighter's belief that feminine company saps male vigor, no women were allowed during the week. On Sundays, wives and girlfriends could visit.

At eight every night Team Punishment assembled in the wrestling gym at a local high school for four hours of peak training. With the 310-pound Tongan kicking and whirling through the air like an elephant ballerina, Brazilian jujitsu fighters bouncing off the walls, guys boxing, guys throwing one another through the air, a skinny blond kid from Georgia who did warm-ups by spinning across the mats in high-speed cartwheels, the mildewy basement gym looked like the setting for a low-rent remake of a grand fight scene in a Bruce Lee movie.

The climax of the training occurred when each fighter took his turn doing his best to beat Tito. They piled on him in a sort of pugilistic tag team. A fresh fighter confronted Tito every ten minutes. If Tito was on the ground with a guy, and it was going slowly, his boxing coach would circle with a punch stick—a boxing glove stuck on the end of a six-foot-long PVC pipe—and repeatedly whack Tito in the head or stomach. Sometimes two guys at once would simultaneously pin and punch Tito. Most nights they fought like this until midnight, finishing with sweat soaking their clothes, blood trickling from noses and mouths, drool foaming from their chins as they spit out mouth guards. They resembled a pack of wild dogs after a fight. "We might look barbaric," said Kyle Johnson, a fighter from Georgia with a thick southern accent and a pale, blood-smeared chest at the conclusion of the night's training. "But we're not barbarians. We're a restorationary movement, bringing back the greatest sport of ancient times."

THE ANCIENT GREEKS WERE FANS of their own Ultimate Fighting sport called pankration. It combined boxing, kickboxing and wrestling, and it became one of the most popular Olympic sports after it was introduced in 648 B.C. A similar sport became wildly popular in America after the Civil War. Called "catch-as-catch-can," it was a fighting style that came out of the prairie states and combined punching, kicking, takedowns, choke holds and submissions—joint locks that force an opponent to surrender or suffer broken bones. In short, it wasn't much different from the UFC's no-holds-barred style of fighting.

At its peak, catch-as-catch-can vied with baseball as America's number-one spectator sport. In 1911, thirty-five thousand spectators filled Chicago's Comiskey Park to watch an American named Frank Gotch take on a European wrestling champion, George Hackenschmidt. It pitted Gotch's free-wheeling American style of fighting against the European's more formal techniques. Gotch trounced the European early in the second round. Teddy Roosevelt signed an order making catch-as-catch-can part of the curriculum at West Point, and universities across America instituted wrestling programs based on a watered-down version of the sport. But the triumph of catch-as-catch-can as a spectator event was short-lived. Crooked promoters discredited the sport by "working," or fixing, fights, and by the time of the Depression it had evolved into the phony professional wrestling now presented by the WWF.

Pure no-holds-barred fighting was reintroduced to America in the late 1980s by two immigrant brothers from Brazil, Royce and Horian Gracie. For several decades, ever since their grandfather had learned jujitsu in the 1930s, members of the Gracie family had been fighting in "Gracie Challenge" tournaments, in which they took on and usually beat all comers in any style of fighting. Royce and Horian opened a gym in Los Angeles to promote their family's jujitsu technique, good against any form of hand-to-hand combat.

A couple years after the Gracies' gym opened, a Los Angeles advertising executive and former Marine named Art Davie and Hollywood screenwriter John Milius, best known for writing *Apocalypse Now* and *Conan the Barbarian,* witnessed a Gracie-style tournament at the gym. They were so impressed, they soon formed a partnership with the Gracies to stage televised no-holds-barred contests under the name Ultimate Fighting Championship.

Milius saw the formation of the UFC as a rebellion against prevailing values. "It was the height of political correctness," says Milius. "Men had lost their manhood in America. We wanted to create real martial arts to celebrate the manly virtues—courage, combat." Milius pushed the UFC in the direction of staging its fights as spectacles. "We put the fighters in an octagon because Conan fought in an octagon pit," says Milius. "We wanted it to be savage. We wanted people to see this and say, 'My God! They're doing gladiatorial combat on TV!'"

While the original UFC founders succeeded in creating public outrage even beyond their expectations—even though no fighters ever suffered permanent injuries or death—those paying attention to the actual fighting witnessed an interesting trend. As expected, early fights were invariably won by Gracie-trained fighters, but within a couple of years American collegiate and Olympic wrestlers, who revived old catch-as-catch-can submissions and choke holds and cross-trained in jujitsu, boxing and kickboxing, soon dominated the sport.

Even after the UFC was driven from mainstream venues, the thriving underground of UFC-inspired, no-holds-barred fighting had taken root in America. According to Todd Hester, editor of a magazine called *Grappling,* which is dedicated to the no-holds-barred fighting underground and which claims, believe it or not, a monthly circulation of about seventy-five thousand, "There's a simple reason UFC-style fighting caught on. There is no professional sport for collegiate wrestlers. Suddenly, the UFC came along, and they had a place to go after college."

———

TITO ORTIZ IS CERTAIN THAT if it hadn't been for high school wrestling he would have gone to prison like many of his friends. He was born Jacob Ortiz in Huntington Beach, south of Los Angeles, to parents of mixed Hispanic and Anglo ancestry. His parents, who according to Tito both became hard-core drug addicts, raised him in affluent Southern California's poor underbelly. "We lived from motel to motel," says Tito. "Sometimes we slept in a car, or in a camper in someone's backyard."

Pro wrestling was his first interest in life. So deeply did he escape into its fantasy world, by the age of nine he started calling himself "Tito" after Tito Santana, the pro wrestler. "I just wanted to be tough," says Tito.

By the time he reached his early teens, Tito had been in and out of various schools and street gangs. "Tito didn't ever want nothing but to be a damn junkyard dog," says his mother, Jacqueline.

It was during his sophomore year at Huntington Beach High School that Tito was recruited onto the wrestling team by a new assistant wrestling coach named Paul Herrera, then twenty-three years old. Herrera says when he arrived in his new coaching job he asked who the toughest kid was in the school. Everyone told him it was Tito Ortiz. Herrera says, "So I went looking for him."

Tito was scrawny, underdeveloped for his age. At fifteen, he was five-seven and weighed 130 pounds. But, Herrera says, "that kid was an animal."

Herrera pressed Tito onto the team, claiming he "chain-locked the doors to the wrestling room to keep the bad influences away." Before tournaments, Herrera forced Tito to pray. "I don't care what people say about prayer in school," he says. "I told Tito, 'You have to choose between God and the Devil. To be a wrestler, you need to be of sound body and of sound soul.'"

After high school Tito placed in state tournaments and wound up in the legendary wrestling program at CSU Bakersfield. But here, according to assistant coach Tom Caspieri, "Tito was not successful." He left without receiving a degree.

The truth was Tito was drifting, working odd jobs, sometimes partying, sometimes excelling, but not quite reaching his full potential as an athlete or as a student. It wasn't until Tito was introduced to the UFC that he found a focus, or what he refers to as his "calling." This happened when he met a colorful Huntington Beach native named Dave "Tank" Abbot while working out at a community college gym.

Abbot was a 275-pound former college wrestler who had become a star in the UFC. Screenwriter John Milius describes Abbot, who could bench-press 625 pounds, as "truly a monster of a man." Abbot had one real passion. "I loved beating the shit out of people," he says. Before entering the UFC, Abbot served six months for assault with a "deadly weapon"—the sidewalk he used to beat his victim's head against. In the UFC Abbot became one of the most popular fighters, despite the fact that he was often beaten by smaller, more skillful opponents.

Tito joined Abbot's "Team Tank," becoming his training partner much the same way aspiring young fighters now work with him on Team Punishment. Even though Tito lost his first UFC fight, he was hooked. A chance encounter with a local Bakersfield nightclub promoter named Sal Garcia was to drastically change Tito's approach to becoming a star in the UFC.

They met while attending a wet T-shirt contest at a popular Bakersfield nightspot called the Rockin' Rodeo. Garcia, a huge fan of the UFC, recognized Tito from across the room. Even though Garcia had seen Tito's one losing fight, he signed a contract to become Tito's manager. For Garcia, who had organized the wet T-shirt contest, the chance to manage a losing fighter in a dead-end sport was probably a step up. "I saw his potential," says Garcia. "But it was different than he saw it. I told Tito, 'So what if you can fight? What matters is bleaching your hair, wearing crazy shorts, adding stuff that will make people remember you.'"

When Tito wasn't training at the storefront no-holds-barred fighting gyms that had sprouted up in Southern California, he and his new manager Garcia spent long afternoons devising routines for Tito's UFC show. Garcia videotaped Tito practicing flamboyant, WWF-style victory dances. They worked on Tito's costume, coming up with the perfect blend of black shorts, orange flames and blond hair. "I hammered it home to Tito," says Garcia. "Having a strong image is more important than winning or losing."

THE AUDIENCE at the Mandalay Bay Arena is predominantly young, male and white. Some have the telltale ramrod posture and severe bowl-cut hairstyles of active military personnel—cross-pollination between the military and no-holds-barred fighting is common, with fighters like Erik Paulson moonlighting as civilian trainers for the Navy SEALs and Marines. Many in the crowd have the shaved heads, tattoos and chin beards common among Tito's entourage. Quite a few have Mohawks. Unlike the stiff, brushlike Mohawks favored in the punk community, here they are grown out and relaxed with greasy pomade, so they look almost like pieces of roadkill draped over their wearers' heads. Eccentricities of style in this group seem less a matter of whimsical self-expression than tokens of defiance they dare you to look at. The profusion of guys with flattened, Z-shaped noses and holes where their front teeth should be is proof how much this crowd likes a good fight.

Their happiest moment before Tito's arrival comes during a middle-weight bout between Dave Menne and Gil Castillo, whose fight turns to a bloodbath in a dramatic third round. It is textbook no-holds-barred fighting. Castillo and Menne start the round boxing. Menne batters Castillo's face, opening wounds. Castillo throws Menne onto the mat. Now Castillo is on top, beating Menne's face. Meanwhile, Menne executes a sneaky jujitsu move and traps Castillo in a choke hold called a "guillotine." Castillo struggles helplessly, blood from eye wounds streaming down his face. With each gasp Castillo's eyeballs roll farther back in bloody eye sockets. His arms flop helplessly. He looks like a rat being strangled by a snake. According to ringside doctor Margaret Goodman, guillotine choke holds are relatively safe, merely a means of "gently putting the brain to sleep by inhibiting the flow of blood." But with images of Castillo slipping into unconsciousness splashed across the jumbo screens, the sadism of the guillotine seems to be on an entirely different level from even the harshest blows in boxing, which deliver knockouts with merciful speed. Overall, there is a plodding deliberateness about the infliction of pain and bodily injury in UFC-sanctioned moves that seems to be missing in boxing.

But what a crowd pleaser the choke hold is. Men jump to their feet and chant, "Guillotine! Guillotine!" Castillo is saved at the last second by a foul and comes back so strongly in the fourth round, the audience is again on its feet, this time giving both fighters a standing ovation. The fight, ultimately given to Menne after the fifth round, exemplifies the finest and the scariest in UFC fighting.

TITO'S FINAL ACT before entering the arena is to vomit into a red bucket handed to him by an assistant. He says this always happens right before a fight. The adrenaline makes him choke. Tito says he enters a sort of dreamworld right before going into a fight. He gets tunnel vision. The butterflies in his stomach go away. He feels numb all over.

A show producer pokes his head in the door and says, "You're on!" Someone hands Tito an American flag, mounted on a pole with a chipped gold eagle on the top. "Let's move out, men!" one of Tito's assistants shouts.

Tito walks into the backstage hallway carrying the flag. Team Punishment rallies behind him. As they march through the cavernous area behind the arena, their ranks grow to nearly two dozen young men, all with jaws set, muscular arms swinging, displaying their flame-decorated Team Punishment uniforms. They escort Tito to the edge of a dark tunnel leading to the stage elevator. "Tito!" they shout, waving their fists in the air. "Get some!"

Tito grips the flagpole in his black ultralight boxing gloves. His cheek muscles twitch spasmodically. He stares dead ahead and steps into the darkened elevator. Tears stream from his eyes—a cold, unemotional crying jag that he later explains always hits him before he takes the stage.

The audience goes berserk when Tito rises into the arena. Behind him the stage set erupts into flames. Twelve-foot-tall letters spelling his name ignite. Cannons go off. Tito jumps up and down, jabbing the American flag in the air. Tito marches down an eighty-foot runway traversing the arena and enters the ring.

Inside, Tito breaks into a run, taking a sort of victory lap in advance. He circles, ripping his shirt off and spinning it on one finger like a stripper. Then he throws it into the whooping audience.

The whole time Matyushenko has been standing on one side of the octagon ring, as unprepossessing as a man waiting for a bus. Matyushenko is two inches shorter than Tito. His body is more heavily layered than Tito's in thick, knotty muscles. But his pallid complexion—he looks likes he's seen about as much sunshine as an onion sitting in the bottom drawer of the refrigerator—makes him look almost sickly. While Tito takes yet another lap around the ring, Matyushenko dips and touches his toes.

The referee brings them together to touch gloves, then shouts the UFC war cry, "Let's get it on!"

The two fighters trade a few punches, then lock up, each trying to throw the other to the mat. In the past, Tito has easily tossed opponents as heavy as Matyushenko, but now he's stuck. Matyushenko pushes him into the fence. The two powerful bodies sag against the fence, seized up together in a near dead heat.

By the second round Tito begins to dominate Matyushenko, throwing him to the ground. But they stick to the mat like flypaper. Each time Tito rears up to execute his ground–and-pound strategy, Matyushenko clinches him.

A few people in the rear seats boo.

"Vlady's eye is opening up," shouts a big fat guy in the lower front seating area. He's a little bit older than the others, in a huge canary-yellow blazer that's impossible to miss. He turns around, trying to inject a note of optimism into those seated behind him. "There's some blood on Vlady's eye," he insists, adding, "Vlady's eye swelled up so bad in Montreal it looked like a little baby's butt."

The few women in the crowd strike the observer as disproportionately young, cute and attentive. They look the way really attractive girls in high school looked, like that one totally hot yet nice girl who sticks in everyone's memory, who was shy and kind but was also a cheerleader and dated the most sadistic goon on the football team. They are like that but slightly grown up. The more their men boo and cast almost babyishly hurt looks at the octagon ring for not giving them what it had promised, the more their women reassuringly pat their legs, snuggle closer and smile optimistically.

By the end of the fifth and final round, Tito has achieved total dominance over Matyushenko, bashing his eye open so that it indeed swells up and resembles the promised "baby's butt," throwing him repeatedly to the mat and hands-down outwrestling the world champion. Matyushenko is so badly beaten he struggles to pull himself up when the round finishes. Tito is boundless energy and goofy grins. It has been perhaps the toughest fight of his career—the triumph of a mediocre junior-college wrestler over a world champion—but this seems lost on the audience, which greets his victory with tepid applause.

Tito starts to perform his standard crowd-pleasing routine. He mimes being a grave digger scooping out a trench for a vanquished foe. Matyushenko stands at the edge of the ring staring at his feet while Tito tosses imaginary dirt on him. The crowd finally cheers, happy to see the Tito they love, the showy winner. Tito suddenly abandons his routine. He walks over to Matyushenko, grabs Matyushenko's arm and raises it with his own. It's a gracious act, Tito's best move of the night. The crowd boos. They came for blood.

By the time he was twenty-three, Seth Warshavsky was regularly being hailed as a visionary. In May 1997, his portrait appeared on the front page of *The Wall Street Journal*, and reporters began flocking to Seattle to cover the extraordinary rise of a new Net prince. Warshavsky was the founder of Internet Entertainment Group, an online porn company that, according to the *Journal*, used "savvy tactics" and "innovative technology that others are too timid to embrace" to "rake in millions."

A Seattle native, Warshavsky was likened by *Newsweek* to the city's most famous son, Bill Gates, and hometown papers dubbed him "the Bill Gates of porn." *Time* compared him to both P. T. Barnum and Larry Flynt. But Warshavsky told reporters his fledgling porn empire was just a stepping-stone. With an apparent technical lead—he claimed that his websites offered the most advanced streaming technology anywhere on the Web—his goal was to transform IEG into a mainstream entertainment giant, a "Viacom for the new media."

Later that year, Warshavsky's renown increased exponentially when he released Pam Anderson and Tommy Lee's X-rated honeymoon video on the Internet. Each time he spoke to a reporter, Warshavsky talked up an array of new ventures he was starting: an online bank; websites for gambling, extreme sports, golf-equipment sales, attorneys' services, psychics and surgeons; a broadband deal to premiere Hollywood movies on the Web; and possible partnerships with RealNetworks and Excite@Home. He was profiled on *48 Hours* and interviewed by Barbara Walters, and he even testified before the Senate, proposing legislation to protect children from Internet porn.

In 1999, *Time* placed him fortieth in its Digital 50—a list of the most influential people in high tech—ranking Warshavsky among the visionaries who had helped make the digital world "a practical, cool and fascinating place." *Time* also noted that the company's "highly respected infrastructure includes a fraud-control database." That same year, IEG was reported to have earned $35 million on revenues of $100 million. Warshavsky planned a public stock offering that had Wall Street analysts predicting a market value for IEG that might reach hundreds of millions of dollars. He carried up to three cell phones and was so obsessed with dealmaking that he was once banned from a Seattle tanning salon for disturbing customers by conducting loud negotiations on his phone while sealed inside his private sunning bed.

But Warshavsky's rise to national prominence as an Internet whiz kid was far more remarkable than reporters had imagined. He liked to tell them that he had been a precocious computer nerd who grew up on Seattle's idyllic East Side, not far from Microsoft's campus headquarters; he liked to say that he had made his first fortune while still in high school, when he started a phone-sex company more or less as a lark, and that one thing had led to another and here he was, poised to become one of the top players on the Internet.

Not long after his ascent to the Digital 50, federal investigators began looking into allegations of wire fraud, money laundering and tax evasion going back to ventures that Warshavsky had started during his teenage years. A new image of the entrepreneur emerged. In this version, Warshavsky had taken advantage of the dot-com fever of the late nineties to sweet-talk the nation's leading news organizations and financial analysts into believing he was the prince of a rising digital empire, and not, as evidence now suggests, a swindler at the helm of a vast subterfuge.

Though Warshavsky will probably never make *Time*'s Digital 50 list again, he may rank as the first and greatest con artist of the digital era. My assessment of his greatness is biased: I worked for him for nearly a year. After I quit and he unsuccessfully sued me in October 1999, I helped expose allegations of his criminal activities made by nearly a dozen of his employees.

I FIRST MET WARSHAVSKY in January 1998 at an adult-industry convention in Las Vegas. At the time, I worked for one of the industry's most flamboyant figures, Larry Flynt, as an editor at *Hustler* magazine. Warshavsky emerged from the pandemonium somber and businesslike in a charcoal overcoat, a white scarf around his neck. Against the raucous backdrop of the porn convention, Warshavsky, flanked by a pair of black-suited attorneys, displayed an almost preposterous air of dignity. He extended his hand and introduced himself. "I'm Seth Warshavsky, president of Internet Entertainment Group," he said. "I'm a huge fan of *Hustler*, and I want you to work for me." He vanished into the crowd, leaving behind the aura of a young man rushing toward his destiny. Much later on, after I had begun working for him, I found out that Warshavsky always hurried through trade shows because he was afraid that somebody he owed money to was going to kick his ass.

I started my job at IEG in November 1998, as a Web editor in charge of all sites, adult and non-adult. Company headquarters were located on the tenth floor of a glass-and-steel office tower on First Avenue in Seattle. White walls, black leather couches and splashes of abstract art provided a fitting atmosphere for the high-tech powerhouse lionized by the media.

Around the office, Warshavsky dressed in casual, hip attire: pressed jeans, a gold Rolex, a V-neck sweater worn without a shirt beneath, to show off his deeply tanned chest. Though *The Wall Street Journal* had described him as an "apple-cheeked" young man, the impression he gave sitting at his desk was that of a thirteen-year-old about to turn forty-five. He had prematurely graying hair and at times conveyed the weary, exasperated air of a man who was stranded on a planet of intellectual inferiors. Only when he laughed—his eyes squeezed shut as he giggled maniacally—did he become the irrepressible boy tycoon portrayed in the media.

Warshavsky's most striking feature was a nervous tic. Every few moments, he would toss his head back and snort. "It's like a trumpet call or something," says Brian Cartmell, a childhood friend of Warshavsky's who served briefly as IEG's president. "It's not one of those 'Follow me' kind of noises. If you hear it, you should go away."

A physician to whom I described Warshavsky's behavior suggested his snorting sounded like a classic manifestation of Tourette's syndrome—though Warshavsky never said he had it. At times the snort came on like an explosive nasal seizure, causing his entire body to shake. Yet in a strange way, the snort was a source of Warshavsky's charisma. It made it impossible to ignore him. He would radiate boundless confidence and enthusiasm, then become utterly helpless in the throes of a snorting fit. As I got to know him better, the snort seemed to hint at powerful forces working beneath the surface, functioning like a relief valve blowing off some kind of ambient soul sickness.

Warshavsky arrived in the office each morning just before ten in a whirlwind of ringing cell phones, snorts, barked commands to his secretary. Some mornings he toured the "design pit," a cramped warren of back rooms where IEG's innumerable sites were being built by nearly a dozen programmers and designers. He interrogated the employees like a general inspecting the troops. "Do it now!" was his signature command. Once, when a designer balked at some seemingly impossible order, Warshavsky pushed him away from the computer. After typing a few lines of code, Warshavsky triumphantly pointed to the screen, making sure everyone knew that he had bested one of his top designers.

"He's a formidable presence," recalls Patrick May, a reporter with the *San Jose Mercury News* who spent two days following Warshavsky. "It exhausted me being around him. He's in overdrive all the time."

Warshavsky often went off on tirades that were aimed at certain employees for no apparent reason. Epithets like "you fucking moron" regularly flew from his mouth. One employee, a middle-aged Chinese man, became, in Warshavsky's lexicon, a "fucking slant-eyed baboon." (Warshavsky denies ever saying this.)

"Power is the only thing Seth thinks about, from the time he wakes up in the morning until he goes to bed at night," says Derek Newman, who served as IEG's general counsel for nearly three years. You could see this need to dominate even in Warshavsky's ostensibly lighthearted moments, when a zany but somewhat cruel clownlike side would emerge. After a box of crab legs on dry ice arrived—a gift to somebody in the office—Seth commandeered it, put on a plastic bib, grabbed the wooden mallet that was in the package and started smashing open crab legs atop his secretary's desk. With shards of crab shell and gobs of cocktail sauce flying around the office, he handed out pieces of crab flesh to his employees, waving the mallet like an overgrown infant with a rattle.

When Warshavsky had trouble sleeping at night he'd call people—friends or employees—at any hour. One night he phoned me at midnight and asked me to drive out of the city with him to look at a house he was thinking of buying. He picked me up in his Porsche 911 moments later, and we drove for forty-five minutes on a winding highway through the Cascade foothills. Warshavsky told me about a girl he'd met on an airplane the previous day. He was intrigued because she was an office worker with no connection to the adult industry. "She's kind of cute," he said.

Then he dialed her on his cell phone. "Hi, this is Seth Warshavsky. What's goin' on?" He spoke in a coy, flirtatious tone, almost a purr. "Yeah, I'm just driving around. . . . What do I do?" He turned to me, and his face lit up mischievously. "I'm in real estate," he answered.

Still talking to the girl, Warshavsky veered toward the exit while going at least sixty-five. I reflexively pushed against my seat as the Porsche wandered across the lanes, then shuddered against the guardrail. The car made snapping sounds as plastic, metal and paint were stripped away.

"Hold on. I'll call you right back." Warshavsky spoke casually into the phone, then flipped it shut and wrestled with the steering wheel. The car slammed into the curb and screeched to a stop.

We stepped out to survey the damage. Not too bad. Rubber guards were scraped off the exterior of the wheel well. The rear fender was dented. "It's gonna cost a lot to fix that," Warshavsky said. He laughed. "That girl's already costing me. Is pussy worth it?" It was a strange question from someone whose fortune had been made from people's eagerness to spend their dollars watching fuzzy, postage-stamp-size images of naked women beckoning on their computer screens.

AT ITS PEAK, IEG had approximately one hundred employees in its headquarters and at a crosstown facility known as the Arcade, which housed the sets for live performers as well as the customer-service and tech-support departments. Fairly or unfairly, a handful of employees were known as Warshavsky's "paid friends." Aaron Seravo was director of advertising. He worked in an isolated office on the eleventh floor, where he had been moved after a coworker complained of harassment. His sole companion there was his assistant, Cole Peterson, a buddy from a rock band who appeared to do little but play computer chess all day; Peterson became known as "the paid friend to the paid friend."

Soon after I started at IEG, Warshavsky's drive for power began to apply to his own body. He developed an obsessive weight-training regimen and supplemented his hours in the gym with a rigid diet of high-protein foods; muscle-mass enhancers, such as a legal form of GHB that he got at a natural-foods store; and a precursor to human growth hormone. For a several-week stretch, liter-sized bottles of pale green fluid began to appear on the floor behind Warshavsky's desk. He said they contained "a really intense but mellow form of GHB." He drank from the bottles throughout the day. When visitors entered his office he recommended they try some, saying it would make them feel "sleepy and horny." The bottles abruptly disappeared one morning. I casually asked him what happened to his bottles of special GHB. "I forbid you to ever mention that again," he said. "Do you understand?" (I was later told that Warshavsky had dosed an employee, who had a bad reaction.)

Warshavsky was assisted in his quest by a three-woman secretarial team. Their job was to procure protein and yogurt dishes specially prepared by chefs from various Seattle restaurants. The team delivered these meals every two hours, whether Warshavsky was in the office or meeting his attorneys across town or at home. They also found nurses to do in-office blood tests to monitor his hormone levels, pick up refills for his tooth-whitening system, arrange for massages, schedule the tanning sessions and book his last-minute trips to Las Vegas, Los Angeles and Cabo San Lucas, Mexico. When needed, they also flew in a hormone specialist from California, a physician who would arrive at the office dramatically attired in surgical togs, as if he'd just stepped out of the operating room. The physician's job was to inject Warshavsky with human growth hormone (HGH), which he began taking in order to build more perfect chest muscles.

Perhaps the oddest denizen of the IEG offices was a character named Cort St. George, who was one of Warshavsky's most valued paid friends, since he seemed to do pretty much whatever Warshavsky wanted him to. A former golf instructor and man-about-town in circles that he described as "Hollywood's sleazy underground," St. George had the blond good looks of a soap opera star. He dressed in a California preppy style—loafers, khakis, polo shirts worn with a white sweater tied over his shoulders—and would sometimes interrupt a business conversation to ask things like, "Dude, does my hair look all right?"

St. George, who left IEG in 1999 to start a celebrity-scandal website, now expresses a mixture of awe and regret regarding his former employer. "When

I first met Seth, I immediately saw his charisma," St. George says. "But I equate working with him as mental hell. I felt like I was Seth's hostage."

WARSHAVSKY SEEMED to thrive on chaos. He relished confrontations, rising to these occasions and showing off his greatest talent, a gift that perhaps bordered on genius: an ability to make people believe just about anything. I saw this most vividly when a man showed up at the office offering to sell what he claimed were videotapes of a former heavyweight boxing champion having sex with a string of prostitutes. The seller, a heavyset black man in a threadbare gold suit and diamond earrings, carried a half-dozen tapes in a tattered gym bag. He called himself Earl and spoke in a strained whisper, as if a block of ice were stuck in his throat.

Warshavsky called me into his office to witness his negotiations with Earl. (Warshavsky later told me he was seized by an irrational paranoia that the prizefighter might send a gunman into our building to retrieve the suspiciously acquired tapes; he wanted another body in the office to distract the imaginary gunman he feared entering.)

Warshavsky asked Earl how he obtained the tapes.

Earl's story—told in his raspy, asthmatic voice—was that he happened to be out jogging one morning in Las Vegas when he discovered the tapes in a trash pile outside a casino. "One man's trash is another man's treasure," he had said, smiling at the conclusion of his improbable tale.

"I like that," Warshavsky said. He dialed Alan Isaacman, the First Amendment attorney best known for defending Larry Flynt. Warshavsky put Isaacman on speakerphone and asked Isaacman if he thought he could circumvent invasion-of-privacy issues associated with showing private tapes online by billing them as being part of a "news story."

Warshavsky giggled, warming to his own idea. "We'll do a story and call it—what'd you say, Earl?—'One Man's Trash Is Another Man's Treasure.' It'll be the life and times of a Las Vegas trash picker. And here's what he finds, some rotten vegetables, maybe some tampons, and look at this, a videotape with a famous prizefighter banging a bunch of whores. See, Alan, it's editorial. We're not exploiting the product for commercial use. It's part of a news story, and we're protected under the First Amendment, right?"

Isaacman's breath sounded like clicks in the speakerphone. He spoke, "That's an interesting legal analysis, Seth, but before we go on, we've got to talk about the thirty thousand dollars you still owe us."

Warshavsky ended the call with a promise that he would send the check immediately.

Earl sat on the couch expressionlessly watching this performance.

"How much do you want for the tapes, Earl?" Warshavsky asked.

Earl wanted a million dollars.

Warshavsky offered him five thousand.

Earl stood up, as if to leave.

Over the next twenty-four hours, Warshavsky bargained him down to $20,000.

The following morning Earl sat on the couch in Warshavsky's office waiting to be paid cash. Warshavsky kept him sitting there for hours, while he paced in and out, shouting into his cell phone and snorting. When Warshavsky darted out to use the bathroom, Earl summoned me into the room and spoke in his icy whisper. "I feel like he's holding me hostage. I am not a violent man." He drilled his finger into my chest. "But I sometimes lose control. I don't know what I might do to him."

Earl stood when Warshavsky came back, still talking on a cell phone. Earl breathed heavily, emitting a thick odor—bad breath mingled with fruity wine, cheap cologne. "When the fuck you gonna pay me, Seth?"

"Calm down, Earl," Warshavsky said. "You're being taken care of."

"Taken care of?" Earl shouted. "You put me up in a fucking fleabag hotel."

"It was not a fleabag hotel, Earl," Warshavsky said, his voice firm. "It was a premium, four-star establishment."

Warshavsky sat at his desk, as if to assert his mastery of the situation. "We're bringing you a check now." Warshavsky shouted to his secretary, "Virginia! Bring the check for Earl."

"I ain't taking no check. You said cash."

"Earl, listen to me."

"You listen," Earl said. "It's not about what Seth wants anymore. It's about what Earl wants."

"Earl, we can't pay you cash."

"No cash?" Earl dropped onto the couch, an air of defeat in his voice. "All we've been talking about is cash. No cash. No deal."

Warshavsky sighed. "Earl, you can't fly out of here with twenty thousand dollars on you. Where are you gonna carry it?"

"Right here." Earl opened up the gym bag in which he'd brought the alleged prizefighter sex tapes. "Put the money in here."

Warshavsky shook his head, as if explaining the obvious. "Earl, it's a federal crime to carry more than ten thousand dollars in an airport. It's against the law."

Earl stared at Warshavsky, thinking hard. "What do you mean, against the law?"

"Earl, there are signs all over the airport." Seth was in his milieu, improvising a string of bald-faced lies. "They arrest you, Earl. You pay penalties, extra taxes. If you really want cash, I'm not going to be responsible."

"Okay," Earl said. "But how they gonna know I got twenty thousand in my bag?"

Warshavsky stood. His snorting disorder completely vanished, as it did in moments that demanded a great performance. He strode over to his black leather overcoat hanging across from his bronzed *Wall Street Journal* article. He pulled out his wallet and produced a twenty-dollar bill, one of the new designs just released that spring.

"Earl, have you seen the new money?"

"Yeah."

Warshavsky held the twenty-dollar bill up to the light and tore at the fringes. "See. There's metal threads in it. You see them?"

There were no metal threads in the money, since Warshavsky was making the whole thing up. But Earl nodded, as if seeing them.

Warshavsky looked into Earl's eyes. He flashed his boyish grin, like a trusted friend. "If I give you cash, you'll set off the metal detectors at the airport."

"Yeah." Earl nodded.

"You see what I'm saying, Earl? I'm writing you a check for your protection."

Earl agreed to take a check.

Around that time, Warshavsky flew to New York to appear on *The View*, the chat show cohosted by Barbara Walters. Walters began the show on the offensive, but Seth was ready. He won the audience over with a rousing speech about protecting children from pornography on the Internet. Despite Warshavsky's claims about the elaborate measures that IEG had taken to protect children, his company was host to a site called HardcoreCarnival .com. Its free splash page, accessible to people of all ages, presented a photo of a woman with a fist inserted in her anus.

DESPITE THE CIRCUS ATMOSPHERE, IEG managed to attract employees with impressive credentials. Warshavsky hired designers away from organizations like Microsoft and Intel, and retained prestigious headhunting firms like the Dallas-based Snelling Personnel to recruit executives. (In a typical postscript, IEG refused to pay the company for its services and was in turn sued by Snelling's Seattle office. That suit was settled, but Snelling pursued additional claims against Warshavsky for misrepresentation and fraud.)

Nothing ever seemed to get done. During my ten months at IEG, the company lost two general counsels, three chief financial officers, a vice president of development, two network administrators, its entire marketing department, a chief technology officer and three of its four staff accountants, as well as half of the design department and a dozen tech-support staffers. Some mornings there was no telephone service. Employee paychecks bounced. The company was engaged in more than a dozen lawsuits with creditors seeking to collect unpaid debts. One day a photographer came in demanding $1,100 and claiming that Warshavsky had called him a "cocksucker" on the phone. He chased Warshavsky down the hall, shouting, "Give me my money, you little prick!"

IEG relied on its infamy as a purveyor of celebrity-scandal materials like the Pam and Tommy video to attract headlines and customers. But most of what it offered on its flagship website, Clublove.com, consisted of put-ons like "a dramatic re-enactment" of an alleged Kelsey Grammer sex video, using a model dressed as the TV star. The adult-content areas of the site included nude-picture galleries, the "101 Fuck Videos"—clips from XXX tapes—and supposedly "live" feeds of nude performers (these were often taped). Few of the picture galleries were ever updated, since vendors wouldn't supply new content. The video streams were often down, because IEG's infrastructure was falling apart. Disgruntled employees sabotaged vital software and sometimes made up for outstanding back pay by walking off with whatever computer gear they could grab.

Warshavsky's non-adult ventures fared poorly. The online bank went bust. The gambling sites ran into regulatory opposition. One site, Online-Surgery.com, which was Cort St. George's brainchild, sold real-time streams of medical procedures. One early webcast showed St. George's mother getting a face-lift. From there it moved on to gory live streams showing brain surgeries and breast augmentations.

Warshavsky would storm around the office berating employees for failing to complete projects for which there were no resources. An online store run by Clublove.com regularly took orders for items like dildos and rubber vaginas, charging credit cards but seldom shipping anything. As it turned out, IEG often didn't have any products to ship. Typically, all the company had was a Web page to take the orders.

WITH PRINT REPORTERS AND TV CREWS showing up nearly every week, IEG's facilities became a backdrop for the surrealist productions that Warshavsky put on for visitors. He would lead them through the First Street headquarters before trooping across town to the Arcade, where performers stripped and masturbated in front of video cameras that sent live streams onto IEG's websites. Warshavsky claimed that 1,400 adult-entertainment webmasters purchased IEG's streams for their sites. The actual number, according to a sworn declaration by one of IEG's staff accountants, was no more than sixty. On most days, the live-performance booths at the Arcade were empty. A supervisor simply replayed old videotapes, making it appear that they were live by typing banter from the supposed performer for the customers in the chat rooms. The system worked well. On some adult sites, IEG charged more than a dollar a minute for these "live" performances.

Before the media arrived, Warshavsky would phone ahead to the Arcade supervisor. She would call performers and have them rush in to fill the booths so that Warshavsky could then show off what appeared to be a dynamo of pornographic activities.

Warshavsky titillated the reporters and investors he led on tours with fabricated visions of growth, profits, new frontiers to be conquered. *Worth* magazine told its readers that IEG's websites had seven hundred thousand paying members, and *Time* spoke of revenue of $100 million and profits of $35 million for 1999. That same *Time* article quoted investment analyst Gail Bronson: "So far as whether [IEG's IPO] would be successful, you betcha. We're talking real revenue, real earnings, real product."

The reporters and analysts, at this point, had no way of knowing that reality distortion was a key element of Warshavsky's business strategy. Not only were checks to vendors and employees bouncing during this period, but in sworn declarations two of the company's four senior staff accountants would say they saw normal daily-revenue figures of about $30,000 (about $11 million per year) and "falling memberships." The declarations indicate monthly memberships of thirty thousand, not the seven hundred thousand that Warshavsky claimed.

Warshavsky once tasked me with the job of leading three young male financial analysts on a tour of the Arcade. They represented a Chicago firm that would be underwriting IEG's planned initial public stock offering. As we approached the Arcade entrance the analysts, in their dark suits, maintained a scrupulous formality. Their job was to scrutinize IEG's assets and operations to assess the company's actual value in advance of their firm underwriting the stock offering—at a potential cost to their company of $50 million.

The absurdity of escorting high-paid analysts—one who told me he had an MBA from Harvard—on a tour of a warehouse where women sprawled on dirty cushions masturbating in front of cameras was lost on me at that time. I felt the burden of my duty to show Warshavsky's company in the best possible light.

When we entered the warehouse I was dismayed to find all but one of the booths were unoccupied. IEG's dirty secret of running loops of old videotape on its website in lieu of actual live performance would be revealed to the analysts. Surely they would rescind their firm's offer to underwrite IEG's stock offering.

But I had forgotten the power of a nude woman. The empty warehouse filled with the sound of hard-leather wingtip shoes scuffling on concrete as the analysts scurried across the room to the one occupied booth. The analysts peered into the booth, decorated to look like a typical suburban teen's bedroom—assuming the typical teen furnished her room with a single mattress on the floor scorched with cigarette burns and surrounded by an assortment of dildos and butt plugs. One of IEG's "Arcade girls" leaned up on the mattress, her back supported by a pillow, silently masturbating in front of the video camera, her eyes glazed with boredom. The financial analysts stared speechlessly at first, then began to whisper excitedly among themselves, still keeping their eyes on the girl.

I stepped outside to call the Arcade supervisor in the hope of scaring up some performers. As I dialed, an Arcade girl pulled up in her junker car and stepped out sucking on a menthol cigarette. She was fairly typical of IEG's live talent—a single mother with little education and a wan complexion indicative of a serious drug or alcohol problem. Standing in front of me, sucking on her menthol, she told me she had come in late because of a toothache.

I asked why she didn't go to the dentist.

"Can't pay for it," she said.

"Don't you have a dental plan?" I asked. A while back I'd read a profile of Warshavsky in which he'd boasted that IEG offered a full health-benefit plan for its live Arcade performers. Despite knowing what I'd already come to know about him, it hadn't occurred to me that Warshavsky would lie about providing health benefits for some of his employees, or that a magazine would totally fail to fact-check the claim.

The Arcade girl laughed in my face, flashing stained, crooked teeth. "We don't have no health plan."

As she entered the building, the financial analysts emerged. The three of them had become animated as they spoke among themselves. The one with the MBA from Harvard suggested I had better insist on receiving stock options from my boss—Warshavsky—ahead of the initial public offering. He shot me a jocular smile.

The analysts hadn't picked up on the empty booths, the video cameras with dangling, disconnected wires, the overall seedy, fraudulent vibe of the place. I drove them back to IEG's offices downtown in my car. Once they were squeezed in, I asked if they really thought the company looked good. The guys in the backseat nodded in unison. The one in the front passenger seat spoke enthusiastically of the company's potential for revenue growth. Each of them had such clean-cut features, crisp suits, fresh-looking haircuts. The whole drive back I kept sneaking looks at them in the mirror, wondering if they were all in on a corporate stock scam together, or if they were simply that stupid.

Perhaps the greatest irony of Warshavsky's success in the media and among outside businesspeople was the fact that he was a pornographer whom other pornographers considered too dirty to do business with. Partnerships and traffic deals, even between rivals, are essential to the success of online adult companies, but IEG was unable to participate. "Seth burned a lot of people in the adult business," explains the president of a competitor. "He can't buy traffic. He can't buy ads. So he goes direct and advertises in the media. They say the name of his website every time he gets in the news."

FOR THE TEN MONTHS that I worked at IEG, rumors of serious fraud circulated around the office. These concerns were even voiced out loud during a department-head meeting in early 1999, when top employees openly speculated that customer credit cards were being suspiciously overbilled.

I quit in September, and a week later I got a call from the company's new general counsel, Eric Blank, who told me that Warshavsky had asked him to sue me on the company's behalf for violating a non-compete clause in my employment agreement and for tortious interference—inducing employees to leave. (I was in negotiations for a job at a start-up Internet company, and I had hastened the departures of several IEG employees by helping them to find other jobs. Adding to Warshavsky's fury, I had directed the employees who reported to me to file complaints with Washington state's Department of Labor & Industries when their paychecks bounced.)

Soon after letting me know of Warshavsky's intention to sue, Blank also abandoned IEG. According to Blank, Warshavsky had told him to file the lawsuit in order to get me to sign a sweeping confidentiality agreement. But Blank refused, telling Warshavsky to "fuck off." "I started feeling like I was helping a scam artist," he later told me. Blank, thirty-one, had taken the general-counsel position at IEG two months earlier. He came from one of Seattle's largest law firms, Graham and James, with the purpose of helping to position IEG for its stock offering. At six-four and 230 pounds, he was physically imposing, and for three years, between Georgetown and the University of Michigan's law school, he had worked as a cop in Washington, D.C. Shortly after Blank quit, Warshavsky hired another lawyer to sue me.

He also named Blank in the suit. Warshavsky had vowed to spend "a million dollars," Blank says, to have him disbarred for his disloyalty. Blank seemed elated by the prospect of a battle with Warshavsky. And given the kinds of battles he'd fought as a cop, Warshavsky hardly seemed an intimidating target. One night six years earlier, Blank was approaching a car on foot when the driver shot him in the chest. A Kevlar vest saved his life, but the bullet pulverized his ribs. Knocked to the ground, he fired his Glock 17 at the car and killed the driver. "Nothing improves your aim like getting shot in the chest," he says. "Your hand is steady because you can't breathe, and your motivation is pretty high because someone just tried to kill you."

Blank set about gathering from our former colleagues compelling evidence of Warshavsky's rumored scheme to bilk credit cards. In nearly four years of operation, IEG had collected hundreds of thousands of credit-card numbers in its database. The system was run by a network administrator who reported directly to Warshavsky, and in the previous six months two of them had quit suddenly. One, Ron Chao, agreed to speak to Blank. Chao explained in detail how Warshavsky had ordered him to "reactivate" accounts belonging to customers who had canceled and to charge current accounts multiple times for the same transaction in order to raise extra cash. Chao provided a sworn declaration: "Seth demanded that I cause the billing system to generate between $400,000 and $2 million on various occasions. Just to be clear, the revenues Seth was demanding that I generate were not to come from corrections of system or database error but from re-billing of credit-card customers for purchases (usually monthly memberships) for which they had already been charged."

John Zicari, a customer-service rep at IEG, volunteered a statement that read, in part: "I and others in customer service have noticed thousands of accounts that have been reactivated and billed. In July 1999, almost every account I came across in Clublove.com was billed two or three times, and some were billed as many as a dozen times."

Zicari's and Chao's statements regarding fraudulent billing were supported by eight others. Two former senior staff accountants also detailed an incident in which Warshavsky had faked accounting records. Somebody else provided an internal IEG e-mail containing a list of more than five thousand credit cards that had been intentionally overbilled. A tape recording of IEG employees discussing double billing also surfaced.

Sharon Waxman, a correspondent for *The Washington Post*, caught wind of the lawsuits and came to Seattle to cover the legal action. When Warshavsky found out, he furiously tried to quash the story. If I and one of my codefendants would fax the *Post* a letter asking it to hold the story until he could provide documents that would contradict our evidence of overbilling, Warshavsky said, he would drop all claims against us and pay our legal fees of $20,000. I agreed. My lawyer provided a note to the *Post* requesting that the editors delay publication of the story.

The *Post* gave Warshavsky several hours to send exculpatory information, but he failed to offer any. The story ran with our allegations of deliberate overbilling unchanged.

Several days later, Warshavsky sent my attorney a check to cover the settlement. It bounced.

THE MOST SURPRISING THING about Warshavsky, I realized at the conclusion of the lawsuit, was how little I knew about him and how much I had to learn about the twisted, unlikely and in many ways sad story of his life. When his parents, Harold and Joyce, moved to Seattle, it was not to an elegant East Side suburb but to Ballard, a tough, grimy, working-class neighborhood twenty minutes north of downtown. Harold was a cable-TV installer; Joyce answered phones at an insurance company. They lived in a single-story clapboard home with their brilliant but troubled son, a chubby, hyperactive, attention-starved kid who, recalls Eric Ensign, a sixth-grade classmate, "used to taunt kids to get attention. He had a snort. It always started when he laughed."

Warshavsky got his first computer in 1985, when he was twelve. In the days before the Web, young Warshavsky set up a bulletin board—a primitive chat room—and started exploring the new world of cyberspace. Hackers he met on bulletin boards traded secrets about how to break into phone systems and get free long-distance services. Armed with this knowledge, Warshavsky blossomed into a tireless phone phreaker—a telephone hacker—and mastered the intricate and laborious processes needed to override switches in the telecommunications grid. According to childhood friend Brian Cartmell, Warshavsky would construct "telephone bridges"—elaborate, illegal teleconferences in which he might bring together as many as sixty people from around the world. Warshavsky admits to certain "instances" when he "used a teleconferencing service and didn't pay for it." Warshavsky also says that by his early teens he left home because his parents realized that "they didn't want the financial burden of raising a teenager."

What actually happened was that Warshavsky's parents sent him to a psychiatric facility after the phone company warned them that their son was committing fraud over the phone lines from their home. According to Toni Ames, a former U.S. West investigator who helped build the case against the young Warshavsky, his indiscretions were wide-ranging, sophisticated and serious. Yet Ames, like many people who have known Warshavsky, still has a conflicting view of him. Despite the fact that she helped to bust him, she felt that his parents had "dumped" him and once thought of adopting him herself. "Seth was being set up by older kids, eighteen and nineteen," Ames says. She recalls visiting Warshavsky in a psychiatric facility. "He was this emaciated little kid who looked like he was ten," she says. "If you talked to him about his parents, he was in a shell. If you talked about computers, it was like he grew to six feet tall."

Warshavsky never returned to live at his parents' house after the age of fourteen. "Seth's parents never wanted a kid like Seth," says Cartmell. "I don't think anyone can imagine how annoying he was back then, with his attention-deficit disorder, his hyperactivity. But you don't just kick him out of the house and send him to a mental hospital." Warshavsky's parents, who still live in Ballard, will only say that these accounts of Seth's childhood are "inaccurate." "I always knew Seth would do great things," says Harold Warshavsky. "I've always been proud of him." When Ames visited Warshavsky in a psychiatric facility for kids with drug and alcohol problems, she told the director that Warshavsky needed to be treated for "phone addiction." She says, "The director looked at me like I was crazy." But, she adds, "he was kicked out a few days later for breaking into the facility's phone system and doing his phreaker stuff."

It is hard to follow what happened to Warshavsky during the next three years. He does not dispute that he spent time in the mental-health system or that he moved in and out of foster homes and, for a while, lived on the streets. But he also does not offer many details. Reflecting on this period in Warshavsky's life, Cartmell says, "I'm amazed Seth is alive."

At seventeen, Warshavsky was on his way to becoming a hard-core loser. He was a high school dropout, he rented a room in an apartment in a crack ghetto, he drove a government-surplus postal jeep, and he sold fish outside a touristy restaurant called the Crab Pot on Seattle's pier. The one bright spot in his life was his friendship with Aaron Seravo, a waiter at the restaurant. "Aaron was cool," says Jimmy Kim, a mutual friend. "He was kind of scary, but people liked to hang around him. He liked to torment people. He once fed a friend of ours a shit sandwich. He made it from dog shit.

"Aaron taught Seth how to talk to girls," says Kim. Sometimes they'd cruise First Avenue, and if they saw a car full of pretty girls, Seravo would get Warshavsky to yell something obnoxious out the window, like "Suck my dick!" If the two had money, they'd go into the Lusty Lady, First Avenue's premier live-girl peep-show theater, where Warshavsky would amuse himself by tormenting the dancers—usually until he got kicked out of the club. "Seth became demented around Aaron," says Kim.

In 1990, Warshavsky took his first stab at running a business when he launched a custom T-shirt venture, Urban Apparel, that by all accounts was wildly successful—he scored contracts to supply local boutiques as well as the Nordstrom department store. But even as he was making money legitimately, Warshavsky got involved in a white-collar scheme, the records of which are sealed in the King County, Washington, courthouse. According to sources, Warshavsky and an accomplice were arrested trying to cross the border into Canada to sell computer equipment they had purchased with bad checks. His accomplice drew a felony conviction and served time in prison. Warshavsky, still seventeen, got off with probation.

IN THE EARLY NINETIES, just before he turned eighteen, Warshavsky entered the phone-sex business. As with porn videos, the boom was closely tied to advances in technology. Thanks to a combination of digital telephone switches and cheap computers, phone-sex operators were able to efficiently handle large volumes of specialized calls. Audiotext, as it is known within the industry, is a business that also combined all of Warshavsky's obsessions: his love of phone phreaking, his bent for shady dealings and the delight he took in his peep-show adventures with Aaron Seravo.

All it took to get started was a credit-card link—a little box like the ones used in restaurants and bars—along with a couple of girls willing to talk nasty from their apartments, a cell phone and a toll-free number, which was 800-GETSOME. He advertised on flyers that he posted on pay phones and in booths at the Lusty Lady. Customers who called rang directly into his cell phone. He took their credit-card information and routed them to the girls. "I was getting fifty calls a day and charging $34.95 per fifteen-minute call," Warshavsky claims today.

Within a year of starting 800-GETSOME, Warshavsky traded in his jeep for an Acura, moved into a studio apartment on First Avenue and began hanging out at Casa-U-Betcha, an upscale Mexican-themed nightspot on First Avenue owned by two local businessmen, Peter and Jeff Steichen. "Seth was kind of a local character," says Peter Steichen. "He walked around with a cell phone in his ear, wearing an Armani suit. And he has that snort thing. But he was endearing. He had this incredible enthusiasm and was very bright."

Demand for phone sex had far outstripped Warshavsky's capacity to provide it. He dreamed of opening a central call center where dozens of operators could handle the volume in shifts, and he talked the Steichen brothers into putting up $100,000 as participating lenders for a facility in Southern California. Their partnership, Telecom Development Group, ran into trouble after a few months and ended badly when the Steichens realized that they were being taken. "Seth is a thief," Peter now says. "He cooks the books. We never saw a dime. A twenty-year-old kid comes along and runs circles around two pretty experienced, pretty savvy and pretty cynical businessmen. We're still laughing at what that asshole did to us."

After the Steichens quickly ended their partnership with Warshavsky, he became the sole owner of the phone-sex company. Warshavsky denies any wrongdoing. "They got all their money back," he says. "They made fifty percent in eight months." Meanwhile, he rented space for another of his audiotext entities in the IBM building in downtown Seattle and opened a call center in California that employed more than thirty operators. He was still just twenty years old.

Soon afterward, Warshavsky became close friends with Ian Eisenberg, a phone-sex player whom Seth would later characterize as his mentor. Three years older than Warshavsky, Eisenberg was set to one day inherit the massive audiotext fortune amassed by his father, Joel, a man known as the George Washington of phone sex.

Eisenberg and Warshavsky began their business relationship as collaborators. Together, they designed a software program to streamline the billing process. But they soon became embroiled in a lawsuit over who owned the software. *International Audiotext v. Seth Warshavsky* was Warshavsky's first major civil suit. After the preliminary hearing, Judge Nancy Holman issued an oral opinion that offered an illuminating portrait of Warshavsky, then twenty-one. "And with all [his] talent and impressiveness, I am concerned about just how irrepressible, and maybe irresponsible, Mr. Warshavsky can be."

Eisenberg and Warshavsky reached a settlement, but the experience seemed to awaken an addiction in Warshavsky that would rival his dependency on phones. Warshavsky became a litigation junkie. He once sued a local Internet-porn rival for spitting in his face and calling him a "little pussy" on a website. More recently, Warshavsky sued a young woman for allegedly stalking him and throwing eggs at his BMW. Though he did not pursue the case to trial, it perhaps brought him special satisfaction. The alleged egg thrower was an eighteen-year-old girl whom, he says, he'd "hung out with occasionally." She was Julie Eisenberg, the kid sister of his erstwhile mentor Ian.

Warshavsky's dealings with Eisenberg exposed him to a relatively sophisticated world of business, where vast sums were being made from intricate technological and financial setups. Which makes it all the more remarkable that during this period he hooked up with a young guy named Sean Sullivan, who was burglarizing computers from area businesses.

Shortly after Sullivan's burglaries began, Warshavsky took out an ad in a local paper to sell a laptop computer that had been stolen by Sullivan. The cops busted him, and he pleaded guilty to two counts of possession of stolen property—but later changed that plea to not guilty. Sullivan went to prison. When I recently asked Warshavsky about this, he said, "I was a kid. I didn't know what I was doing."

That seems an odd excuse given the fact that only a few months after his arrest, when he was twenty-one, Warshavsky and two partners invested $1 million to form their own long-distance phone company, WKP. The company was born out of Warshavsky's desire to bill consumers directly for audiotext purchases. The way the business worked then, when you called a phone-sex line, you had to punch in a credit-card number. But once Warshavsky had created his own long-distance company, phone-sex charges showed up directly on his customers' phone bills.

Warshavsky and his partners signed agreements with the Baby Bell phone companies to operate their national long-distance service and began billing several million dollars a month. Most of their revenue came from selling phone sex, but they also ran a regular long-distance phone company called Starlink Communications. Just eight years earlier, Warshavsky had been confined in a mental hospital after stealing services from U.S. West. Now he was the president of his own phone company, and it was grossing $60 million a year. It was a situation that so alarmed the government, the FCC issued an opinion saying it was illegal for audiotext companies to enter the long-distance market. WKP chose to liquidate.

Despite the government crackdown, Warshavsky bounced back with a slew of ever more sophisticated schemes. He established ties with the small South Pacific island of Vanuatu and evaded FCC regulations by routing phone-sex calls through there. He opened a company in Aruba and even started an aboveboard company to transmit voice data to Hong Kong.

WITH THE NEW REGULATIONS making the phone-sex business less profitable, Warshavsky turned his attention to the Internet in the mid-1990s. At the time, companies like GE, Time Warner and Microsoft were beginning to sink millions into money-losing websites. But Warshavsky was confident he could turn a quick profit in the new medium by using the Net to distribute pornography. He launched his first site in 1996, naming it Candyland after the children's game sold by Hasbro. The toymaker sued. Warshavsky was forced to rename his adult site Clublove—but only after receiving valuable free publicity.

A year later, Clublove became infamous for releasing the Pam and Tommy video, and Warshavsky emerged as a star. "After that," says Cort St. George, "Seth could tell people anything. Everyone said, 'This is the guy who knows how to make money on the Web.' He took advantage of people's ignorance."

The posting of this video became the most celebrated event in the early history of the Internet. Pamela Anderson Lee's name became among the most searched items on the Web. According to *The Wall Street Journal*, notoriety from the sex video turned Lee's name into a brand to "rival Coke or Pepsi."

"Money was rolling in," says a programmer who worked at IEG in the early days. "But the double billing started then. Seth has always liked to do things a little underhanded."

In March 2000, assistant U.S. attorney Mark Bartlett subpoenaed the sealed records of the lawsuit that Warshavsky had filed against me and two other defendants in October 1999. Agents from the FBI, the IRS and the Treasury Department interviewed Eric Blank about a criminal investigation into Warshavsky, and soon afterward, I met with Bartlett and an FBI agent in the U.S. attorney's office in Seattle. Bartlett informed me that Warshavsky was suspected of wire fraud related to allegations of overbilling customers on IEG-operated websites and also of laundering money through foreign trusts in order to evade federal income taxes. Bartlett's questions appeared to be based on many of the allegations I had helped to raise during the lawsuit, as well as on information provided by others who had worked with Warshavsky in business ventures going back to the early 1990s. Warshavsky downplays the significance of the investigation. He claims that he runs a clean operation that is completely aboveboard. "Allegations of wrongdoing were made to *The Washington Post*," he says. "Of course the feds are going to investigate."

Despite all the hits that Warshavsky has taken, he pushes on, putting the best face on his business—even though IEG has recently flirted with bankruptcy. He sold off its crown-jewel assets, domain names like Pussy.com and Blowjobs.com, to raise cash to stay afloat; he also brought in new designers and management. IEG successfully launched a redesigned adult site and announced a partnership with Heidi Fleiss, the former Hollywood madam and a convicted felon. One new senior employee resigned, describing the atmosphere at the company as "hopeless" and Warshavsky as "impossible to work with." As for the Fleiss deal, that also seems doomed. "All our dealings with him have been bad," says Jesse Fleiss, Heidi's brother and business manager. "We haven't given him any content, not a single photo. His first check to us bounced."

Jimmy Kim once told me that Warshavsky knew how to push everyone's buttons. "But he's got a button, too," Kim had said. "Alienation. That's why he's always on the phone, surrounded by people. Seth never cuts people off. They cut him off. But not Seth. He can't stand alienation." Which, perhaps, is why Warshavsky asked to meet with me several months after his trouncing in our civil suit. (The court had ordered his claims against me to be "withdrawn with prejudice"—a stern dismissal of his suit.) He said he wanted to show me the results of a "five-hundred-thousand-dollar audit" he had commissioned to prove that "there was no intentional double billing" at IEG.

When he pulled up in his Porsche, squeezing it into a rubble-strewn construction zone to avoid the five-dollar parking fee in a nearby public lot, he waved and smiled as if greeting an old friend—not an ex-employee he'd accused of theft and whose fraud allegations had brought on a federal investigation.

His physical transformation was astonishing. When he stepped out of the car, he looked as though his head had been grafted onto the body of a short, powerfully built, barrel-chested man—testament to the massive amounts of HGH and steroids he had been injecting. We went into a Thai restaurant—he recommended the shrimp, fielded a couple of phone calls and made some wheedling small talk. There was a strange disconnect, as if Warshavsky were unwilling to acknowledge the enmity between us. I attempted to bring up the issue of credit-card fraud. "You did a terrible thing to me," Warshavsky said. "The whole situation with the lawsuit was crazy." I mentioned the federal investigation. "It's probably just a fishing expedition," he said. "Don't you think?" Warshavsky looked weary. His eyes were bloodshot. His complexion, normally a tanned golden brown, was gray. Even the familiar snort sounded tired, almost like a sigh.

I asked him whether he'd brought along the audit that he had promised would absolve the company of any wrongdoing. But now he said he couldn't show it to me. He went into a familiar mode, inventing a string of excuses. I asked him who had prepared the alleged audit. "I won't tell you who did the audit," he said. "It was a major, major consulting firm." He started to go on, but I interrupted him and told him he had to be the biggest, most amazing bullshitter I had ever met.

Warshavsky considered what I'd said for a moment and smiled. "I think I'm just an optimist. Like if I say the check is in the mail. It's because I look at the bright side, and I really believe I intend to send it." He became silent for a moment, then added, "I never think about why I am the way I am. Something just directs me from inside."

In 1995, I was hired as entertainment editor of *Hustler* magazine at Larry Flynt Publications. I was thirty, divorced and at the end of a screenwriting career that had been flatlining for several years. Not only had I failed as a writer, but I had functioned only marginally in a variety of menial, no-brainer day jobs. On my first day as an assistant location manager in charge of finding an office building for a commercial shoot, I had become lost. As a telemarketer of computer-printer supplies, I earned $61 the first week my employers put me on straight commission. I failed at other jobs simply because I didn't get out of bed. Before working at LFP, I had found a niche at a Beverly Hills law firm, where I temped in the word-processing department, correcting typographical and format errors in legal documents. It was a dull job, but its focus on minutiae dovetailed nicely with my habit of smoking several bowls throughout the day in the parking garage. Sitting for hours in a white cubicle hunting through densely written two-hundred-page legal contracts for missing periods and double commas was a pleasant way to ride out a solid buzz. I held that job for nearly three months, a record length of time in my employment history.

I lasted at LFP for more than three years. Destiny may have played a part in this. My first pornographic experience was with a copy of *Hustler* that I discovered in a drainage ditch when I was eleven. The magazine, still in its flat brown paper bag but soaked through, had appeared like a gift from the gods of puberty. I painstakingly removed the binding staples and dried out the pages in the garage of a neighbor who was away on vacation. After careful and repeated examination of each of the pages in the privacy of my bedroom, I sold them to my friends at school for their lunch money. Telling this X-rated Horatio Alger story in an interview for a copyediting job at LFP helped get me hired. (Though not as a copy editor. There were too many typos on my résumé.) By the time I left, I had achieved rank on the list of the Top 50 most influential people in the adult industry. Granted, I had written that list myself, and it was published in *Hustler*, but deception and lies are the essence of pornography. It's no different from any other branch of the entertainment industry. In porn, for example, we had the same thing that they call "magic" in Hollywood—except we called it "bullshit." This is the power to create seductive illusions that move and entertain a mass audience, and perhaps give them that ineffable gift, hope.

But porn is a crude business. Even the fantasies it sells have the feel of cheap disillusionment. What seduced me was the reality.

LARRY FLYNT USED TO DEFEND *Hustler* by calling the nude photo layouts "art." I would come to joke that the porn video is indigenous Southern California folk art. The cheesy aesthetic—shag-carpet backdrops, tanning-salon chic, bad music, worse hairdos—and the everyman approach to exhibitionism are honest expressions of life in the land of mini-malls, vanity plates and instant stardom.

In 1996, an unknown named Jasmin St. Claire set out to have sex with three hundred men in a triple-X video titled *The World's Biggest Gang Bang II*, thereby breaking an alleged record of 251 men set a year earlier by Annabel Chong. By the mid-nineties, gang-bang films had become a hot product in the industry. They not only created overnight stars but added a new dimension to celebrity worship. Where once an autograph served as a hallowed connection with a famous person, now fans, invited to participate in these spectacles, could actually fuck a star.

Late one Sunday morning on the second floor of a decrepit Hollywood sound stage, Jasmin held a press conference before the shoot. Reporters and photographers from such esteemed publications as *Club*, *Screw* and, of course, *Hustler* packed the room. Champagne was served. Jasmin, twenty-three, entered in skintight red latex. She moved imperiously, with her head held high and her surgically augmented D-cups thrust forward. Jasmin's ethnic origins were a mystery. Her skin was coppery brown, like a glass of tea in sunlight. She told people her dark complexion came from Sicilian blood, and there were rumors that she was the granddaughter of a New York mobster. She denied those, and claimed to have been raised by an international-financier father, to have been educated in continental boarding schools and to have an undergraduate degree from Columbia. (Years later, Jasmin's first manager, Charlie Frey, told me he'd discovered her doing lap dances in an outer-borough New York strip club. "I don't know about her dad," Frey said. "Jasmin's mom is a dot-head Indian.") At the press conference, Jasmin responded in French, German and Spanish to questions from European porn-magazine stringers. As cameras flashed and the room filled with the staccato sound of twenty reporters calling her name, the scene took on the air of an old-fashioned Hollywood movie premiere. I asked Jasmin why she was having sex with three hundred men, and she answered, "To achieve my dreams."

The event began on a set decorated with paper palm trees and tiki lamps. Perhaps a hundred men showed up. They were authentic amateurs, a cross section of humanity that might have been culled from an unemployment line: old, young, fat, bald, skinny. They wore tennis shoes and work boots, but no pants or underwear, as they were herded into groups of five along lines taped onto the concrete floor. A half-dozen fluffers knelt by the taped lines and prepared the men for their encounter with Jasmin. She lay on a low stage and could barely be glimpsed through the clutches of hairy asses flexing around her. Jasmin's hands grasped at erections as the men circled her, copulating with her mouth, vagina and ass. The teams of gangbangers were given five or ten minutes with Jasmin. They wore condoms when they penetrated her. They removed their condoms to ejaculate on her stomach, thighs, breasts, face, or in her thick, wavy brown hair. When the men finished, they sat in bleachers at the edge of the sound stage or milled around and lamely jacked off, trying to nurse fresh hard-ons for another go.

I experienced a sense of numbness on Jasmin's set—as I would on many others—that I can compare only to combat. It was the sense of being in a group of people deliberately and methodically engaged in acts of insanity. In contrast to combat, I was not numbed out by the horror of it, but by the grand-scale stupidity, which crystallized that day as I stood by the craft-services cart. Boiled hot dogs on cold white buns were being dispensed. A man next to me politely passed the mustard. The bottle was sticky with K-Y jelly. I never attempted to eat on a porn shoot again.

It was during Jasmin's bid for the title of world's biggest gangbang queen that she acquired her reputation as a bitch. One of the men I spoke to, forty-ish, with the tan and physique of a lifelong desk worker, summed up his experience as a star-fucker. "Jasmin is cold," he said, then compared her with Annabel Chong, whom he'd met a year earlier when he'd participated in her *World's Biggest Gang Bang*. "She's not friendly like Annabel was."

I asked him what constituted "cold" or "friendly" in a five-minute encounter with a woman, shared with a half-dozen other men, all circling to pleasure themselves on tiny pieces of her body. His voice had a childlike plaintiveness when he answered. "Annabel said, 'Hi.' She looked at me in the eyes. Jasmin just said, 'Don't come in my hair.' She wasn't nice at all."

HUSTLER'S BARELY LEGAL was a magazine I associate-edited under the name "Serena Dallwether." It was subtitled *A Celebration of Sexual Debutantes*, and the premise was that all the girls in the photographs were between the ages of eighteen and twenty, and that all their stories were true. In reality, the girls were porn models, and I supplied them with names and brief biographies, or "girl copy." Though *Barely Legal* was sold almost exclusively in XXX shops and liquor stores, its monthly U.S. circulation pushed 250,000. The English-language edition also sold well internationally. On a trip through Italy, I saw it prominently displayed at a news kiosk near the Vatican beside photos of Pope John Paul II.

A reasonable person might assume that porn magazines serve but one lowly purpose: to provide "readers" with what we called, in the trade, jack-off fodder. But readers of *Barely Legal* were moved to send in dozens of letters each week. Predictably, many contained simple requests: "Please print photos of young girls having fun at the doctor's office, spread out on an examination table." At least half bore return addresses of corrections facilities. The most surprising were those that contained outpourings of emotion from lonely men seeking to connect with our nudie models. By the time I left LFP, I had collected nearly two thousand of the most desperate letters from lonely hearts.

Readers sent Christmas cards to the models. Photographs arrived: John, from NYC, sent a glamour shot of himself, replete with halo lighting effects on his puffy eighties metal-rocker hairdo. Kelly, a scruffy middle-aged man, grinned beside a pumpkin he'd evidently just carved. A man claiming to be "*vraiment* a poet from the 'Sixties" sent a letter in French and English, typed and handwritten in beautiful calligraphy, to a model named "Vivienne: Sex Student." In the bio I'd written for her, she described herself as a Philosophy of Film major who was turned on by Kierkegaard and anal sex. Her fan included a bio of his own in which he purported to have been published in *The Paris Review* and to have taught at Stanford. Expressing the most delicate feelings for Vivienne and shamelessly begging her to write to him, the lovelorn poet closed his letter with a stern lecture about Kierkegaard and Heidegger, stating, "I repudiate Heidegger's fascistic early politics."

"Problem," a young man from a suburb of Philadelphia, wrote to Girl Talk, the advice column I wrote: "I am a 21 year old male who has never had a girlfriend in his life and is quite sadden by this fact. I do have Tourette's syndrome, and when you are considered as a 'f**king retard' in high school, you don't get real far."

That so many readers believed models in a porn magazine offered the prospect of authentic human warmth and understanding was all the more bizarre given the crude, over-the-top nature of the girl copy that accompanied their images. I wrote to alleviate the boredom of producing thousands of words of hack copy every week and strove to make my bios as disturbing as my editor would allow. Fortunately, LFP provided a safe, nurturing environment for disturbed individuals exorcising their personal demons through pornography writing. So long as I stated that the models were at least eighteen (a law stringently followed at LFP) and had consented to engage in the acts described, I was free to develop stories with incestuous overtones and strong hints of violence, stalking, mental illness, self-hatred and death.

A typical bio, one for "Dee: Dementia 19," opened by saying that Dee was "now free of the psychiatrist's drugs that once made her a complete zombie with no will of her own, nor any control over what she did with her body." "Natanya: Nice and Nasty" began: "Natanya's a nice girl most of the time—except when she's nasty. The nice girl plays with Mr. Pookie, the stuffed animal Daddy sent last Christmas before they fried him on Death Row. The nasty girl fingers herself and dreams of a bad man coming to get her. Nice and nasty. Cops are like that too. First they give you a candy bar, then they take Daddy away."

Not all of them presented sexuality with unrelenting gloom. The bio for "Heather: Holy Sister of Fellatio" was an attempt at the transcendent. Heather, a girl with a beatific smile, was described as a student at a junior college run by nuns. She concluded her treatise on oral sex: "The sisters in school tell us that all art is God-inspired. My artistry is a means of bringing man closer to the divine. Picture my face with your dick in it and know how it feels to come in the mouth of God."

The most peculiar aspect of the fan letters was not that the men believed the ludicrous sagas of the models, but that they responded to the graphic imagery by seeking intimacy with them. If pornography indeed objectifies women—and it's hard to argue that a magazine with an amateur photo section called "Beaver Scouts" didn't—many readers sought to flesh out the objectified women in their imaginations. Their sexual fixations blurred into romantic dreams.

The most lyrical note, a mixture of hackneyed erotic clichés and poignant expressions of longing, came from a man whose return address was the cryptic "Lock Bag R." A prison address, a bizarre P.O. box or a location in his head? He wrote to "Dottie: Dirty, Flirty, Delicious," a girl in a baby tee with the word "Flirt" written across the front.

> Dear Dottie:
> Here is one for you, can we be writing pals? . . .
> I wonder where you are from, only because you seem like to my words, A Hip Hop Hollywood Hootchie . . . Those clothes you had on were very nice. You could get right into my world at a breeze on your perfume or maybe on the regular scent of your body . . .
> I can picture you and I kissing. I would just melt the minute your arms [begin] to wisp about my shoulders. You know the kind of picture that would send my mind into orbit with you. I would get on one knee and ask you to put your leg around my shoulder and those heels to dig into the side of my rib cage. Dam those white heeled shoes are fine . . . I bet when you walk it is a knock-out.
> Can you bring yourself to me for just a day[?] We can get a couple of those strawberry crunch ice creams on a stick and look into each other's eyes. [I] would softly rub one of your thighs as we sit knee to knee . . .
> You could take me places through letters that would be called Dottie's adventures. I would love to send you cards. And I would love to get to know

you as a person. I've been to the Statue of Liberty twice. My first school trip
in the second grade . . . was to a place called the Butterfly Farm.

BROOKE ASHLEY TOLD ME that 1997 was her "favorite year in porn." She kept mementos of her career, begun when she was "fresh eighteen," in a closet in her barely furnished Valley apartment—a stack of flattened video box covers and "slicks," glossy promotional mini posters. Brooke was Asian and Caucasian, and in photographs her face changed from shot to shot. She was always pretty, always cute, usually costumed in diminutive schoolgirl skirts and ankle socks, with her hair in pigtails. Some of her proudest achievements were making the covers of such XXX videos as *Gutter Mouths, Assy #5, Young and Anal #5* and *Whoriental*. One box cover superimposed a dialogue bubble next to Brooke's smiling face, so she appeared to be saying, "I'm such a filthy slut, I'm such a pig!"

In the spring of 1998, Brooke tested positive for HIV. She believed she had been infected by a male porn star named Marc Wallice during the production earlier that year of a film titled *World's Biggest Anal Gang Bang*. Brooke starred in it with fifty men.

Like other porn stars I knew, her biography might have been lifted from the more twisted girl copy in *Barely Legal*. As Brooke told it, she was born on an American air base in Korea, the offspring of a U.S. soldier and a Korean mother. She was raised in Kansas City and molested at the age of seven by "the old man down the hall." According to Brooke, the old man pretended he was an invalid and needed a walker, but he was actually very strong when he got her alone in his apartment. He had lured her with ice cream. Things went downhill from there. Her mother left. Her father, who Brooke says was an avid porn-video collector, became a born-again Christian. Brooke grew close to an uncle who groomed her for beauty pageants. She often bragged, "I was a runner-up in the Miss Teen Kansas City Beauty Pageant when I was sixteen." By the time she was eighteen, her uncle, who had functioned as her unofficial guardian, had been sent to federal prison on money-laundering charges. Brooke was working at Wal-Mart when she ran away to Florida, where she became an exotic dancer, and then to L.A., where she became a porn star.

The night I first visited her apartment, located in a sprawling stucco complex off Ventura Boulevard, Brooke hadn't yet seen her gang-bang video. I had come over to show her the advance review copy that I'd received at LFP.

Brooke greeted me at the door in jeans and a gray T-shirt. "Dude, that better not be a Bible," she said, laughing and pointing to a brown-leather appointment book I was carrying. "My dad sent me one when he found out I was sick. I threw it in the closet."

As she entered the kitchen to get me a drink, her cat, Chronic—named after her favorite bud—scampered under her feet and tripped her. Brooke fell to her knees, laughing and cursing, and discovered her pager in a gap beneath the dishwasher. "I lost that thing a week ago." She picked it up and walked into the living room, engrossed as she scrolled through all the calls she'd missed, forgetting about the drinks and the refrigerator door hanging open behind her.

Brooke's pratfalls—knocking over her bong, tripping on a phone cord—were frequent and usually followed by loud fits of laughter. She had a comedian's gift for rueful expressions that mocked her own ditziness, like Lucy Ricardo after an especially harebrained stunt. Just as quickly, she turned angry.

"Marc's been calling me at seven in the morning and leaving harassing messages." Brooke jabbed at the buttons on her answering machine. Marc Wallice's flat, emotionless voice came from the speaker: "Pick up the phone, Brooke. You bitch, you whore. Pick up the phone."

A few days earlier I had met Marc at his mother's house, where he had been living since blowing his last dollar on a freebasing binge after news broke of his own HIV-positive status. "I used to be a big, famous star," he told me. "Now, I'm a nobody." Since quitting his job bagging groceries at Trader Joe's when he was twenty-one, Marc had done little else but appear in porn videos. In the past nineteen years, he estimated, he'd had sex with two thousand women. "I've never dated," he said. "I've never had to be desirable. How do I just walk up to a girl and say hi?" Then he had played me phone messages from Brooke: "You fucker. You don't have any friends."

She had called around seven in the morning too. Both of them were up at that hour—Brooke taking her meds, Marc at the end of a bumpy coke ride. In happier times, they had been "fuck buddies" off the set and had binged on drugs together. Now, in their respective messages, each sounded scared and desperate, like someone who really needed to talk to an old friend.

"Dude, he is so guilty," Brooke said to me, gazing at the picture of herself on the cover of *World's Biggest Anal Gang Bang*.

She claimed she was unable to operate her VCR, and asked me to do it. It was a matter of pressing the On button and sliding the tape in. I sat next to her on the couch. "I can't watch this without smoking a bowl," she said. She loaded her bong, then forgot to light it as the video began.

On the screen, Brooke appeared in a dressing room having her makeup done. She wore a gold silk suit jacket and thong panties.

"Oh, God!" Brooke shouted. "Look how wrinkled my suit is!"

On the screen, the makeup girl asked her in a stagy voice, "Do you think you're going to be all right?"

"I'll be okay." Brooke giggled, making a wacky face.

Next to me on the couch, Brooke began to cry. "Oh, my God! This is so sad."

The scene shifted to a familiar one, a gang bang, featuring Brooke on a gloomily lit stage surrounded by men, barely visible through the forest of hairy legs.

"Everyone can see what's happening to me," Brooke said, still weeping. "I'm so humiliated."

A moment later, her tone changed from plaintive to angry. "I see it!" she said. "There's Marc's pale, white penis. It's shaped like a banana."

The penis in question penetrated Brooke's rear, without a condom. Marc's head ducked into the frame, confirming her suspicion—she could have ID'd his member in a police lineup. The camera pulled in for a close-up of the suspect ejaculate sliding down her bare skin.

Behind me, Brooke giggled. I turned. She was speaking into the phone, now sugary and playful. "Sweetie, will you bring me over some of that French Champagne in the bottle with the orange label?" Whining, "Please?"

When she hung up, Brooke explained that she had a cabdriver friend who did things for her. In addition to being a porn star, Brooke hustled men. Sometimes she did so professionally, as a call girl. She could do a wicked imitation of a local weatherman talking dirty to her, his distinctive voice breathless and excited. I believed her about the weatherman, because I had once met him on the set of a John Wayne Bobbitt porn shoot. He had told me he was there researching a potential news story, though I'd never seen his station run news stories reported by weathermen.

While her gang-bang video still played on the TV, Brooke ran into her bedroom. She ran out a few minutes later completely naked, holding a gold raw-silk suit on a hanger.

"This is what I wore in the video," she said. She wiggled into the skirt and turned in profile, smoothing it with her hands. "I used to hate my body when I was younger. Producers were always trying to talk me into getting implants." She pressed her hands to her breasts. "See how nice they are? I'm glad I'm still natural. I like my body now."

She stood, bare-chested, in front of the TV. "I don't believe in God. But I pray. I pray to goodness. I believe in something good. I'm not going to let this illness stop me. I'm going to dance, I'm going to have my own website. And dude, you know what?" She sounded determined, inspired. "I am going to make porn movies again. Fuck. I'm all about the word *fuck*."

She let the skirt fall to the carpet and sat naked on the couch. She picked up her bong. "Dude, I'm not saying I'm not scared. I've got HIV. How can I ever be a normal twenty-five-year-old girl again?"

WHENEVER HE WAS KICKING HEROIN, a friend in the business used to dream of Asians. A typical dream: He is living in an El Monte trailer park and has a twin sister who is Chinese. She is beautiful, and he must fight her to the death in an unusual form of combat involving shish-kebab skewers. Their left wrists are bound together with straps, and they begin stabbing each other.

Most of the relations I had with women before becoming a pornographer were along the lines of my coworker's dream life. A wife or girlfriend functioned as a narcotic, fixing whatever emotional or spiritual maladies I was suffering from, but we would inevitably end up psychically bound at the wrists and engaged in mortal combat.

The girlfriend I was living with when I was hired at LFP was a professional in a field far from pornography. She had no issues with my new job; her concerns were that I was controlling, emotionally distant and psychologically abusive. My concerns were that she had an explosive temper and had once carved "Pig Motherfucker" on my front door with a knife. In our sessions with a couples therapist in Century City, we quietly discussed the need to listen to each other and develop mutual respect.

After these morning sessions, I would drive to the Flynt building in Beverly Hills to review XXX videos. In the Erotic Entertainment section of *Hustler*, which I wrote for and edited, I probably never used the word "woman." Women dominated every description and image that ran in my section of the magazine, but I referred to them using a pornographic lexicon handed down through time and enshrined in the copyediting department. They were sluts, bitches, pixies, nymphs, cunts, twists, slatterns, tramps, ginches, chicks, gashes, honeys, babes, squacks, pies, hootchies, snatches, trollops, tarts, dolls, quims, skanks, trims, split-tails and holes. For legal reasons, the terms "whore" and "prostitute" could not be used as nouns in reviews, but "whore" was acceptable as an adjective—as in describing a performer as, for example, a "whore-face blonde."

I wrote reviews under the pseudonym "Mack Assarian." This helped reinforce the notion I maintained to my girlfriend, my therapist or anyone who asked that my life was separate from my job. The words I wrote in Flynt publications in no way reflected my own thoughts or feelings. Mack Assarian had the voice of an unrepentant misogynist, wise to the games played by manipulative bitches. But he was not me.

The day after my girlfriend dumped me, I reviewed a video titled *Piece of Ass*. As it played on the TV in my office—with the sound down and in fast-forward, standard review mode—I wrote: "Anyone who has had his life repeatedly wrecked by living, breathing cunts finds increasing solace in snatches that are safely contained in videocassette boxes. . . . If fuck bitches in real life were half as nasty as the cushiony degenerates in *Piece of Ass*, the defenseless male dupe would jump at the chance to have one wreck his life even quicker than the last cunt did."

In this review, Mack Assarian had expressed my own anger and self-pity. He had said what I had never been able to say in a $175-per-hour therapy session. The persona had merged with the person, and I had found truth in my own mean-spirited *Hustler* copy. This was not necessarily the sort of breakthrough that my therapist would have approved of, but I felt more at peace with the world than I ever had before. Murderers probably feel better, too, after committing a crime.

THE FIRST TIME I SAW Jasmin St. Claire at an industry function, it was on a yacht anchored near the Cheesecake Factory in Marina del Rey. Lights were strung in the rigging and twinkled on the water. Jasmin, whose dream of becoming an internationally recognized porn star was realized with the release of *The World's Biggest Gang Bang II*, stood outside on the upper deck. She wore open-toe sandals with straps that twined up her calves, and a vaguely Grecian gown that made her resemble the type of alluring alien woman bedded by Captain Kirk on *Star Trek*. I noticed her, turned, and a moment later felt cold hands around my neck. She had thrown down her drink, walked swiftly across the deck and was choking me.

"Asshole!" she said.

I pried her hands off my neck and twisted around to face her. "I should have thrown my drink at you," she said.

Weeks earlier, in an interview with *Hustler*, Jasmin had bragged of her business acumen. She had told me she was investing her porn proceeds in giant-gumball machines located on boardwalks in beach cities up and down the West Coast. She was furious not because I'd mocked her investment strategy in the published interview, but because I'd exposed her secret for getting rich.

"Everyone in the whole fucking world knows about my plans," she said.

Our small violent struggle broke the ice, and Jasmin and I became friends. She began dropping by the office to chat about her appearances on *Howard Stern* and new acquisitions to her Barbie doll collection, and to spread vicious rumors. She was upset when Kendra Jade, a rival porn star, grabbed international headlines for taping herself having sex with Jerry Springer. For several weeks, Jasmin tried to persuade me to write an exposé about Kendra having the clap (an allegation she never substantiated). But Jasmin easily switched gears from nasty gossipmongering to heartfelt revelations about her private life. She was seeing a man who had a drug problem. Several days a week, she took him to recovery meetings. Her eyes grew misty as she described holding hands with recovering drug addicts as they joined to say the Lord's Prayer at the end of a meeting.

Attractive, confident, sure of her career, possessed of an entertaining if sometimes cruel wit but revealing hints of an underlying compassionate nature, Jasmin sometimes struck me as the ideal girlfriend.

In the pages of *Hustler*, director Gregory Dark was often heralded as a genius, perhaps the only one in a field of triple-X hacks. This critical acclaim might have stemmed from the gratitude the magazine's staff felt toward him, since over the years he had employed several *Hustler* editors to write his screenplays. In 1998, *Psycho Sexuals*, which I'd written under the pseudonym "Louis Umbro," had been voted Best Video of the Year by the X-Rated Critics Organization (which I belonged to). Greg took a self-effacing view of his job as a triple-X director and my role as his writer, telling me, "Making porn videos isn't for entertainment. They're for whacking your wick. As long as we have the sex scenes, you can write a story about dogs barking in English rhyme."

If Satan had come to Earth in the guise of an amiable person, he would probably have looked like Greg Dark. In his late forties, he stood over six feet tall. He favored black jeans and white T-shirts, and clipped his wallet to his belt loop with a long silver chain with links in the shape of miniature human skulls. His thickly muscled arms—he wrestled and boxed five days a week at a gym in the Valley—were tattooed with a snake and a devil's head. His piercing blue-green eyes brought to mind an evil hypnotist in a cheesy horror film. A cigarette usually dangled from his lips, and his skin was the same color as the smoke curling from his mouth.

Greg was never happier than on the set of a porn shoot, and he was excited to get going on *Psycho Sexuals II* because he would be trying a second-hand Fisher-Price video camera he'd obtained after a six-month search in the classified ads. The camera was sold as a children's toy in the early eighties and recorded black-and-white images on looped cassettes. "It creates these really weird pixellations," Greg said. His emphasis on really weird effects in adult films had begun early in his career, with his New Wave Hookers series, when he'd shot underage Traci Lords in a film about women being enslaved by the voodoo powers of punk and rap music. His vision of weirdness had carried him to the top of the adult industry, and within two years of shooting *Psycho Sexuals II* it would take him to the top of the music-video industry, where he would apply his talents to directing a hit video for Britney Spears, the pop-music wunderkind equivalent of Traci Lords.

Psycho Sexuals II, which I'd also written, was filmed in a stucco Spanish knock-off in Las Virgenes canyon. The house was a 1970s masterpiece, with floor-to-ceiling windows and a poured-concrete spiral staircase twisting above a shag-carpeted conversation pit. A white-enamel fireplace dominated one side of the room, its blackened interior yawning open like an empty mouth. Greg's video monitor would be set up here. The refrigerator in the kitchen was decorated with drawings and God's eyes—Popsicle sticks formed into crosses and wrapped with multicolored yarn—and a note, in blocky, childish handwriting, that said, "Bring bathing suit, towel, happy faces and Betty Boop pillow to Grandma's." The house had been rented from a family who had vacated it for the day.

Out on the veranda, Shayla LaVeaux, the twenty-seven-year-old star of *Psycho Sexuals II*, lounged on a pool chair, smoking cigarettes and baking her skin. Like many dancers and porn stars, Shayla had the classic looks and proportions of a model, but she was short, perhaps only five-two. She had doll-blue eyes and thick ringlets of natural blond hair piled up and pinned atop her head. Her shapely legs, shaved pubic mound and pointed, implanted breasts were completely visible through her sheer nightie top, which afforded little more cover than a prayer.

Shayla's voice was gravelly and sweet, as if her vocal cords had been marinated in whiskey sours since puberty. Her laughter, for which she was well known in the industry, was a cackle that would be deafening in a crowded sports bar. Her body rippled from her stomach to her back and shoulders with well-developed muscles.

I asked her if she worked out.

"Are you kidding me?" She cackled and snorted, blowing plumes of smoke from her nostrils. "I got my body from dancing on the road for seven years. I do my workouts on the pole every night, honey."

Though Shayla was getting top billing and her image on the video-box cover, the scene being filmed this day would feature a relative newcomer, Shelbee Myne, doing anal with her husband, Pat.

Shelbee, in her early twenties, was a dirty-blond and pretty, but with an overly tanned face that made her mouth look hard. In a tube top and shorts, she looked like a girl at the beach. She stood on the veranda, dabbing suntan lotion on her husband's nose.

"You've got to be careful about getting a burn," Shelbee said.

Pat drooped his head like an obedient mutt. His hair was close-cropped and bleached white-blond. He wore shorts and boots like the guys on the film crew. Though he was just two years older than his wife, his nose already had gin blossoms, accentuated by a sunburn.

Shelbee and Pat had met when she worked at a paging company and he worked as a shipping clerk in a warehouse. She entered porn first. Her husband followed when he discovered that he had a talent for maintaining an erection. Of the couple, Shelbee was the star. Women were more in demand than men. Her pay for her anal scene in *Psycho Sexuals II* would be $1,500. His pay would be $100.

When the filming began, Greg sat with his back to the set and watched the action unfold on the video monitor. Shelbee and Shayla entered the conversation pit. They played roommates stalked by a peeping Tom, played by Pat, who was supposed to be outside in the bushes making obscene phone calls from a cell phone. According to my script, the girls were turned on by the stalker and decided to give him a show rather than call the police, as women probably would in real life.

Since Shayla was the older and more experienced porn star, she assumed the role of alpha female, gently dominating Shelbee while Greg issued commands. He obsessively controlled every move. For scenes that would take fifteen minutes in the final product, he made the performers work for five to eight hours.

"Shayla," Greg called. "Rotate counterclockwise. Make your legs symmetrical, cross your ankles. Shelbee, look up at Shayla. Move your thumb down."

After an hour of Greg's exhaustive directions—he claimed to block sex scenes based on his experience as a wrestler—the two performers' bodies were satiny with perspiration. Shayla's back muscles rippled and veins bulged on her neck as she held one convoluted pose, while Greg circled and peered through their limbs, looking for sweet spots to capture with his prized Fisher-Price camera.

When shooting paused, the performers giggled and chitchatted. "You're doing great, honey," Shayla repeated to Shelbee several times, giving the novice porn star encouragement like a big sister.

During a break, when Shelbee knelt on all fours, Shayla played with her by tapping out rhythms on her butt, saying *boop, boop, boop* with each beat. Shelbee laughed. Shayla traced her finger from Shelbee's neck to the small of her back. "You've got killer lines," she said. "Did you do gymnastics in high school?"

"No. Swim team."

Shelbee's husband was brought into the scene after two hours. His entry had to be reshot several times, since he had trouble following Greg's directions. "Come in to the left of the table and enter the pit on the right," Greg said.

Pat kept screwing it up until Greg said, "Come in by the window and go past the TV set." Pat did it perfectly.

"Is my face okay?" he asked.

"It's fine," Greg answered. Pat was in the frame only from his chin to his penis.

"Pat," Greg called, "jack off and . . ." He thought, then added, "Drool on yourself."

On a break, Pat sat staring out the window. His hard-on remained upright. Shayla sauntered past, looked down at his talent and said, "That's great, Pat."

He nodded and gazed at his hard-on as if it were an animal standing on its hind legs and staring back at him.

It is often said that the difference between a violent Hollywood movie and a hard-core sex film is that no one shoots real bullets or actually dies in the making of a Hollywood movie, but performers in a sex film really do fuck. Indeed, one of the most overpowering sensations on a triple-X set, especially after the performers have labored for hours under the hot lights, is the smell. But if sex is an intimate act, bordering on sacred, what I saw on porn shoots seemed no more real than eating a wax apple.

PORN STARS' CAREERS LAST about as long as votive candles. As the novelty of Jasmin St. Claire's gang bang faded, she came up with another publicity stunt. She was going to star in a movie called *Blow It Out Your Ass*. For several weeks she had been working with a "master magician" named Randall Richman, developing an act in which she would shoot four-foot flames from her anus.

The shock value of this stunt ensured that the Valley studio where it was being filmed was jammed with paparazzi from the adult press, as well as local radio personality Larry Wachs from KLSX's *Regular Guys* show. After two hours in makeup, Jasmin walked onto the stage and shed her robe. The photographers and writers sat amid the video and electrical cables on the concrete floor, crouching beneath the lights and a low-slung boom. A few in the press tried to engage Jasmin in banter, but she was focused, tuning everyone out as she entered her pre-performance zone.

She knelt on the carpeted stage. Her surgically scarred, conical breasts jutted forward as she leaned down and raised her posterior. Richman, the magician, a boyish twenty-eight-year-old, tinkered with his apparatus. He had handcrafted an anal plug with a brass nozzle and a small, clear plastic hose attached to a can of butane. The idea was that he would hide behind a wall and pipe the butane into the plug as the director filmed.

Both Richman and Jasmin were nervous. They had never performed the stunt before. Richman explained to me that the danger was that the plastic plug could superheat, melt down and possibly explode—though he assured me he had performed several practice runs in the garage of his apartment building without incident.

The room hushed as Richman delicately inserted the device and tested the control valve on his butane can. The sound of hissing gas filled the room.

I sat near the stage, closest to Jasmin. Kneeling on all fours, she turned to me. She was crying. "I'm scared," she said. "Will somebody hold my hand?" She slid her hand across the stage and waved her fingers.

This was our most intimate moment. Jasmin's vulnerability and fear had shown through her mask of supreme confidence.

I averted my eyes and fumbled with my notes. I had developed such an overwhelming crush on Jasmin St. Claire that I could not face her. I feared if our eyes met in this charged moment, my feelings would be evident to everyone in the room. Finally, a tech girl walked up and took Jasmin's hand.

My shirking the opportunity to offer emotional reassurance proved to be our last magical moment together. Jasmin ceased her morning phone calls and her lunchtime visits to the office. Things were never the same.

Her stunt came off successfully, beyond expectation. She achieved six-foot flames. Photos appeared in adult magazines around the world of Jasmin shooting fire from her ass as men held skewers and roasted marshmallows.

Two weeks later, however, a mysterious blaze destroyed Randall "Master Magician" Richman's apartment complex.

EACH WEEK, dozens of adult videos arrived at my office on the third floor of the Flynt building. Occasionally, other products arrived—dildos, butt plugs, artificial vaginas, bondage hardware—that their manufacturers hoped *Hustler* would review and promote. One day, a representative from a company arrived to deliver in person what she claimed was a revolutionary product: a rubberized female torso with a removable vaginal insert made of a patented substance that she guaranteed "feels like the real thing." The torso came with its own carrying case, lubricants and a cleaning brush for the vaginal cavity.

The rubber coating of the torso approximated the color of skin about as well as a Band-Aid. The vaginal insert did feel remarkably like human flesh, but touching it brought to mind feeling up a cadaver.

I never reviewed it. I gave it some thought, because someone had obviously gone to a lot of expense to develop and manufacture the product. I tried to see in it what they must have seen. But I couldn't get around the fact that to use the product as it was intended would entail copulating with something that resembled an armless, legless, headless body. It was a nightmarish prospect. Thankfully, my editor never asked me to write a review.

I placed the torso on top of my bookshelf, where it remained for about a year. During that time, my thoughts began to turn. What if this torso were the last woman on Earth? What if I were trapped on a desert island with it? Would I fill it with memories of women I've longed for and loved? Would I eventually develop a sexual relationship with it? Would I pour out my heart to her and feel that she understood me?

As I read more of the letters to *Barely Legal* models from men who led desert-island existences of their own, I concluded that under the right circumstances I could probably love the torso. Perhaps she could even become a better alternative to the real thing. Just as methadone mimics heroin without any of its intoxicating side effects, a pornographic substitute might simulate intimacy without any of its dangerous consequences, emotional pain, fear of loss.

GREG DARK'S PERSONA WAS BASED on several essential myths. His father had been an anthropologist who disappeared in Haiti. Or he was a criminal who disappeared in the state prison system, depending on which story Greg was telling. His mother had been a "party girl," a Las Vegas entertainer who had raised Greg with a series of common-law stepfathers. When he was a teenager, he and his mother moved to L.A., where he went to Fairfax High and developed a fascination for Charles Manson, whom he claims to have met once at a party on Sunset. Greg said he studied art at Stanford, moved to New York, became a conceptual artist, then wound up as a documentary filmmaker. In 1983 he codirected and produced *Fallen Angels*, an antiporn documentary that would nevertheless inspire him to enter the adult business.

But in all his myriad past experiences and encounters, Greg credited one man with teaching him the most important lesson of his life. He met his teacher in the early seventies on the tennis courts at Stanford. During certain hours of the week, the courts were open to the public. According to Greg, a man showed up one morning driving a garishly painted Cadillac. He wore a peacock-feather hat and an ankle-length fur coat, which he slipped off to reveal standard tennis whites. The man was a street pimp from Oakland. Greg and the pimp became friends on and off the court. In Greg's personal lore, the pimp taught him the essentials of the "whore con":

A. Men are powerless before the lure of female sexuality.
B. The whore lures men by promising unlimited sexual fulfillment.
C. As soon as she has lured a man and has begun to extract payment, the whore withholds as much sex as she can get away with.

D. The whore understands that the more she withholds, the
greater her value.

E. All women are whores.

After dropping out of therapy, I increasingly turned to Greg for personal guidance. According to him, the object of being a man was to outsmart the whore con. Outwardly, he seemed to be a master of the game. There were weeks when he bragged of bedding a new beautiful woman every night—dancers, porn girls and young, college-educated women working entry-level Hollywood jobs.

But the more time I spent with Greg, the more he seemed to be a woefully inept player. Inevitably, he developed infatuations with women who moved into his apartment and began treating him with the cold, disinterested contempt they thought he deserved.

For several months it was Treatie, a peep-show dancer more than twenty years Greg's junior. Greg would pick me up in his red Corvette, we would have dinner at the Daily Grill or Louise's Trattoria, then we would drive up and down Sunset and Hollywood discussing his problems with her, occasionally pulling over to chat with a streetwalker.

"Treatie and I have nothing in common," Greg lamented. "She doesn't even want to fuck anymore. You give the girl a joint and a goth comic book, and that's all she needs to be happy. She doesn't care about anything else, except my car. She hates my car. She says it's 'cheesy.' I tell her, 'Treatie, my choice of vehicle is severely limited. I'm a pornographer. I'm supposed to drive a cheesy car.'"

Then there was the heroin-addict prostitute he met on Hollywood Boulevard. Greg portrayed his first encounter with her as a conquest in which he had beaten the whore con. "She was on the street in a baby-doll T-shirt and velvet hip-huggers. I pulled over, and she gets in the car. She asks, 'Do you want to date me?' I say, 'Yeah, show me your pussy.' She says, 'That'll cost you sixty bucks.' I say, 'I ain't paying for it, sweetheart. Get out of the car.'" He laughed. "She pulled down her pants and showed me anyway. We went to a motel, and she fucked me for free."

The most appealing aspect of this relationship to Greg was that the girl was a hooker. "As long as she stays a prostitute," he reasoned, "there's not a big danger of getting committed." But one night, when we were supposed to be planning a five-day video shoot, Greg was unable to work. His mind was on his hooker girlfriend. "There are things about her I don't understand," he said. "She does these feminine tricks, like she cried when I left her the other night."

I suggested the possibility that her crying had not been a "trick" but an expression of authentic sadness.

"Maybe it's not a trick, but it looks like one," Greg answered. Then he added, worriedly, "The problem is, I have a feeling that if I angered her, I would never see her again. She told me she once packed up and left a guy while he was out playing with his dog."

Not long after his affair with the hooker ended, Greg fell in love with a giant blond bondage performer. The master of the whore con capitulated and married his new love. The extent of his violation of his former principles was made clear to me when he confessed that he actually intended to be monogamous.

Six months after the honeymoon, Greg called to report that marriage was as bad as everyone he knew had told him it was: "I'm depressed all the time, unless I'm working. I throw myself into my work, which is trivial and stupid."

He had concluded that there was no happiness to be found anywhere.

"Girls bring happiness for a while. People think happiness is like a Band-Aid that fixes everything. A Band-Aid just goes over a wound—it doesn't fix anything. You always have desire for other women, but you keep chasing them, and end up like Ouroboros, the snake eating its own tail."

THE BURAKUMIN ARE JAPAN's untouchable class. Racially and religiously identical to the Japanese, they are separated from broader society because of their labor. Burakumin are meat and leather handlers, and when Japan converted to Buddhism, with its vegetarian code, in the eighth century, these workers became outcasts. Their profession was considered to be dirty, and they were deemed "polluted people." Despite the fact that Japan shed its vegetarian strictures hundreds of years ago, their ostracism has been enforced to this day. Pornographers, creating a product that is widely consumed by society, face a similarly paradoxical ostracism.

On a personal level, when I dated women outside the industry, I had to overcome the perception that I was probably a creepy pervert because I worked at *Hustler*. Even if this could be overcome, women from the straight world labored under the misconception that I was surrounded in my job by beautiful, alluring babes offering free and easy sexual gratification. Those who believed this were buying into the illusion offered by porn, and it was not always easy to convince them that the hookers and porn stars I met in the course of my job were just as complicated and demanding as anyone else.

I attempted to get through all of this on a blind date with a twenty-six-year-old I'd been set up with by a mutual acquaintance. Her eyes were young and gray like a baby wolf's and scrutinized me closely as she asked the standard questions: *Have you ever dated a porn star? Does your job affect how you view women? Are you personally into porn?* I answered no to all of the questions, lying to varying degrees each time.

She suggested a second date at a small Italian restaurant near an S&M-and-magick shop in Silver Lake. This time she did most of the talking, discussing her ex-boyfriend, who was trying to be a rock star, her aspirations to quit her temp job and become a painter or a photographer or a designer—any creative field that would offer a measure of fame. She sounded like all the porn girls I knew who credited Madonna as the single biggest influence in their lives.

After dinner, my date invited me to her apartment. Her roommate sat in the kitchen painting her nails in preparation for a red-eye flight she was taking to New York later that night. She had dressed for the flight in four-inch heels and a tight skirt and baby tee. She wore her hair in long, white-blond braids, and with her thick white goth makeup resembled a depraved Pippi Longstocking. I'd been told she, too, aspired to be a rock star.

She stood when we entered, and pushed her breasts forward. "Is my bra lumpy?" she asked my date. Then she turned to me and asked, "How do I look?"

On the basis of my experience studying thousands of slides and photo sets of nude women her age in order to determine their suitability for use in *Hustler* and *Barely Legal*, I did a rapid thumbnail assessment. I pictured her with her clothes off. Her large breasts, combined with her slenderness, indicated that she'd probably had augmentation. She would not be suitable for a "natural" magazine such as *Barely Legal* if scars or saline-sack deformations were visible. Her face was pretty, but her eyes were too close together, and her butt was flat. She might have made the end of the first half of the book, where the so-so photo sets ran.

"Isn't my roommate beautiful?" my date asked as she led me to her bedroom.

When she shut the door, she informed me that she had a deep interest in kinky, perverted sex. "I think it's hot that you work at *Hustler*," she said, dropping onto her wrought-iron bed.

"I want to suck your cock," she said, making a slurping sound that caused her face to grimace. It was the sort of expression made by porn performers when simulating a "hot, nasty" sex scene.

I sat next to her. "Talk dirty to me," she whispered.

I was speechless.

She offered specific directions. "I like stories about my daddy being bad."

She reached into her skirt and began to masturbate. I gathered that my role was to stimulate the exercise by providing a pornographic narrative. I had spent the day writing girl copy about perverted stepfathers and nymphomaniac women driven to compulsively give oral sex. My mind reeled with all of the filthy words I had strung together that day for female body parts and sexual acts. But I couldn't speak them. I had writer's block.

Writhing on the bed next to me, she picked up the slack. She launched into a scenario about a birthday party in which she and her friends relentlessly teased her father until he could stand it no more and began molesting them. "Stick your cock in me, Daddy," she taunted him—or me.

The eroticism of the moment seemed no more authentic than the lifelike torso beckoning in my office.

When my date stopped twisting on the bed, I went to the door.

She leveled her young, gray eyes at me. "I can tell you have issues with women," she said.

A FEW MONTHS BEFORE I LEFT LFP, a thief broke into my car and stole a half-dozen XXX videos. They had been shipped to the office in a box with my name on it. The police caught the hapless criminal walking down the street with the box, and I was called to testify about the crime in a Beverly Hills courtroom. I waited in the hall with the cop who was handling the case. He was a detective a few months shy of retirement who, with his New York accent, knowing blue eyes and rumpled brown suit, seemed more like a sympathetic TV character actor than a real cop. He talked about his thirty-year marriage, his daughters, his involvement in a well-known case a decade earlier when he'd killed a murder suspect during a foot chase and shoot-out. The detective brought up porn videos and confessed that he liked them. His tastes, he said, were specific. He liked the directors who focused on the women's faces. "It's all bullshit," he said. "But sometimes you're looking at the girl in the video and she reveals herself. Maybe it's just a moment in her eyes, but it's human, it's genuine."

To me, what was real and unreal had ceased to be clear.

What was unreal was my final visit to a porn shoot. This was held at a luxury suite in a Las Vegas hotel filled with guests specially invited to watch a porn star named Montana Gunn have sex with a few fans. The party was to inaugurate her "Fuck the World" tour, a yearlong event in which she planned to repeat this evening's performance with two thousand fans in hotel rooms and on stages across North and South America and Europe.

What was real was Montana entering late, intoxicated and burned to a crisp from a marathon session in a hotel tanning booth. What was unreal was Montana fleeing the expectant crowd in tears, because, she later said, she realized nobody in the whole room cared about her as a person. That was probably real. What was unreal was Montana emerging from the bathroom after her crying jag and going on with her job, fucking strangers on the hotel suite's coffee table while partygoers cheered and the cameras rolled. What was also unreal was standing in the bathroom with Montana later that night while she splashed in the bathtub, giggling, pointing to the freckles on her chest, saying, "My mother always called these kisses from the sun."

I finally left the porn business not because I had any sort of moral awakening, but because I found a better job. Today, whenever I see a new issue of *Hustler* or *Barely Legal* at the liquor store, I always flip it open, and forget everything I know. The illusions are real.

Mötley Crüe arrives at a radio station in Cleveland to promote their new album, *Generation Swine*, to be released in a few days. The rock stars enter the studio toting their own carry-on luggage. They have come from Detroit, where they performed the night before. Drummer Tommy Lee wears black leather overalls, without a shirt. He flashes an amiable grin and a brightly inked torso that gives him the look of the tattooed man at the carnival. When Tommy fires up a cigarette in the no-smoking studio, three flunkies rush to bring an ashtray.

Nikki Sixx, the bassist, clunks the boom microphone with his commodious brown cowboy hat, as he sits. A chrome chain gleams on his neck; a padlock with a skull hangs as a pendant.

Vince Neil, the singer, wears black plastic boot-cut pants and a swirling orange velour shirt unbuttoned to reveal the tattooed pendant on his chest: a swollen heart with an inverted medieval sword through it and the name "Skylar," for his five-year-old daughter who died of cancer a year ago.

Mick Mars, the guitar player, takes a seat on the far end of the studio. Hunched over, dressed entirely in black, with long black hair flowing out beneath a black hat, Mars's outfit is a disappearing act.

The Crüe members are bombarded with questions. "Is heavy metal back to kick some ass?" asks the balding DJ with a sweaty smile and a rear end that overflows from his stool like a soggy hamburger bun.

"I'd love the chance to show up Pamela Lee," a blond DJ coos, scissoring her legs over Tommy's knee, as her denim mini-skirt rides up to reveal tanned flesh and thong panties.

"What's the deal with Mötley Brüe?" Fat Ass queries, referring to the soda being marketed in coffee shops that bears the Mötley Crüe name.

"It's kind of a triple Jolt cola that turns everything blue," says Tommy.

"I know," the blond giggles, "I had one, and I was pooping Smurfs for days."

"Is it true your record label was going to dump Mötley Crüe if you didn't bring Vince back?" Sweaty DJ cuts in, smirking at the ambush style of his question.

"This is Mike calling from Cleveland," a voice crackles over the speaker with a quavery, adolescent timbre that brings to mind pimples and a uniform spattered in deep-fryer grease. "I just wanted to say you guys rock!"

"Right on," Nikki cheerfully answers, turning sharply as the miniskirted blond DJ clamps her thighs onto his lap and strokes his legs with the toes of her white cowboy boots. "I'd love to hang out with you guys after the concert and party," the blond sighs, with a smile that accentuates the heavy lines around her eyes.

"Maybe you should tell them about the time you partied with Alex Van Halen," Sweaty DJ chortles, glancing at his colleague.

"I'm way into partying with bands," she says.

DURING THEIR FIFTEEN MINUTES ON AIR, a cluster of fans has already made it to the downtown offices of the radio station. They greet Mötley Crüe with outstretched hands holding Sharpies, asking them to sign CDs, photos and tits peeled out fresh from trashy lingerie bra cups.

Tour personnel attempt to push aside the fans and corral Mötley Crüe into a waiting van, because they are running late for their sound check at the Agora, where they are performing in a few hours. The band members stop anyway and satisfy the demand for autographs.

A woman fishes into her halter top and pulls out her breast for the band members to sign. Mick Mars is the last to sign, squeezing his signature alongside the three others on the pale white skin above the fan's nipple, hardening in the wind.

The owner of the breast, an amphetamine-thin brunette with a feathered biker-chick hairdo, solemnly thanks them and declares that she is heading straight to the tattoo parlor to have their signatures gone over in indelible skin ink.

AFTER THEY TUMBLE into the van taking them to the sound check at the Agora, Mötley Crüe's thoughts turn to their radio interview.

"What a slut!" blurts Tommy, recalling the antics of the blond DJ.

"Dude, all she wanted was some pipe," Nikki adds.

"If she'd do Alex [Van Halen]," Tommy considers, with a grim shake of his head, "she'd do anybody."

"And you know," Vince joins in, "it would be all over the radio the next day."

"Doing interviews is like combat," Nikki states. "Mötley Crüe doesn't want to be the spokesman for rock. We're not here to say that heavy metal is back to kick alternative music's ass. There's a lot of good music out there."

"Billy Corrigan [of Smashing Pumpkins] told me he used to play 'Shout at the Devil' and 'Live Wire' in his cover band," Tommy enthuses. "How cool is that?"

"Mötley Crüe is about having fun," Nikki explains. "You put on an R.E.M. record and you feel like 'Okay, I'm politically correct.' You put on a Mötley Crüe record and you feel like licking your girlfriend's pussy in the backseat of a car."

THEIR DRESSING ROOM at the Agora resembles all the others they have been in over the past week and a half, thanks to the efforts of their wardrobe woman, Karen, who brings leopard-print throw rugs to drape over the ratty backstage furniture, a black "Theater of Pain" flag (from the 1985 tour) and incense candles to every show. Karen is somewhere in her forties and has almost faded blue eyes and a tiny mouth that is usually shaped in a worried pucker. She is sprinkling talcum powder into Tommy's entire stage ward- robe, a pair of black rubber G-thong ball-hugger briefs the size of a wadded- up ball of rubber bands.

"Make sure you put the talc all over," tour manager Dave Callums re- minds her, as he walks in with a case of three hundred CDs to be signed by the band for a promotion at an area record store. "Tommy said he pulled off a bunch of hairs when he took his shorts off after Detroit."

"Managing a tour is easy," states Callums, "if you're good at putting socks on an octopus." A veteran tour manager whose thirty-year career began with Jerry and the Pacemakers and included Coolio last year, Callums has a clipped gray beard, a matching fringe of white around his bald dome and a sturdy, rounded physique that has earned him the nickname "Frosty" from three members of Mötley Crüe. Tommy is the lone dissenter on the Frosty the Snowman moniker, believing instead that "if we put him in one of Mick's hats, he'd be full-on Mr. French."

Mick Mars enters the room, walking with a stooped, crooked gait that suggests the physique of a Halloween skeleton. He picks up the pair of knee-high, six-inch-heel platform boots that Karen has laid out for him.

"Time to get tall," he mutters. When Mick's leather pants abut the leather seat cushion of the chair, they make a loud farting sound. "Excuse me," he deadpans.

This is the only conversation he will make for the next several hours.

"If they ever made a Mick Mars doll," Vince says, "you'd pull the string, and it wouldn't say anything."

THE CATERED FOOD provided for the band consists of little more than deli meats, tuna salad, bread and sodas. Wisely, they are all on the wagon after well-publicized troubles with booze and chemicals. Vince has a vehicular homicide under his belt. Nikki wins bragging rights for being draped under a sheet and pronounced dead after a 1988 heroin overdose. Tommy can cite a long list of alcoholic calamities that includes the singular achievement of once running himself over with his own car.

"I pulled over to pee after drinking tons of beers," Tommy relates. "I left my Corvette in neutral, and it ran over both my legs. And dude, my leather pants fucking exploded."

IN ADDITION TO BEING SOBER, all of them are currently attempting to live under the gentle tyranny of committed relationships with wives or long-term girlfriends.

An hour before showtime, Nikki is on his cell phone speaking to his wife, former *Playboy* model and *Baywatch* star Donna D'Errico, about a medical problem with one of their four children.

"My six-year-old is having dizzy spells and headaches," he says, flipping his phone off. "He's having a CAT scan next week, but you never know what can cause it. I just finished reading a book about all the problems drinking milk can cause." Nikki looks up portentously. He is the band's deep thinker. "Do you realize we are the only species on earth that drinks milk as adults?"

"Cats drink milk," Vince counters.

"You're right." Nikki laughs, with a huge grin that spreads out beneath the shadow cast by his cowboy hat. "Fuck that stupid book."

"When Pam was lactating," Tommy recalls, "I was wigging on the sweetness of her milk. A while ago Pam and I were in the kitchen with her mother. Her mom bent over in the refrigerator, and Pam started squirting me with it. Her mom saw us, and was like, 'Can't you guys wait!'"

"We freaked out Pam's doctor. We were screwing eleven days after Brandon was born."

"Donna told me she's coming in to New York tomorrow with her suitcase stuffed full of stuff she bought at Trashy Lingerie."

"Heidi's coming in tonight." Vince stretches back in a Barcalounger draped in leopard skin, smiling at the thought of seeing his girlfriend, *Playboy* model Heidi Mark. "I can't wait to crack her open."

"Donna told me I have to wait four hours before I bang her," Nikki states grimly, then brightens with a scheme. "Maybe if I can have Frosty deliver flowers to the hotel room when she arrives, I can get in sooner."

"What works with Heidi," Vince says, with the confidence of experience, "is beer. It works a lot quicker on her than flowers."

THE SOUND OF TWO THOUSAND FANS all chanting "Crüe, Crüe, Crüe!" outside in the auditorium rouses Mötley Crüe from reveries of reuniting with their women.

With twenty minutes to showtime, Mötley Crüe begins to dress, demonstrating about as much concern as a high school punk band gearing up for a performance in the neighbor's garage.

Nikki sprays his hair so it spikes up Sid Vicious style and dons a fishnet top, knee-length leather shorts and fishnet stockings. He wraps himself in a floor-length coat that looks to be made of bright orange, shag carpeting.

"Do I look like Pimp Daddy Orange?" he asks.

"You look like a cheap whore," Vince says.

"Cool!" Nikki enthuses, attaching orange space goggles to the brim of his cowboy hat.

Vince matches his shiny black patent-leather pants with a silver sequined top and saunters down to the stage with a "See you later." He will start the show suspended twenty feet above the stage, swinging atop a Gothic chandelier.

Mick, who put on his platform boots earlier, performs in the same clothes he wears offstage. His preparation consists of smoking a final Marlboro Light. The excitement of going onstage makes him grow talkative.

"Uh-oh," Mick warns, "Nikki hasn't greased a towel yet."

"We can tell how good the show is going to be," Tommy explains, as he clips a microphone transmitter to the back of his rubber thongs, "depending on how much dick cheese Nikki wipes out of his balls before we go on-stage."

Ignoring the gibes of his bandmates, Nikki hunts for a place to take a leak, before settling on a trash can.

Nearly buck naked, bone skinny and as brightly inked as the Sunday comics, Tommy resembles a strange white savage. He leans against the cracked brick wall of the dressing room and graffitis, "We're back, mother-fuckers!—Mötley Crüe." He throws the pen down, spits into the palms of his hands, smacks them together several times and runs down to the stage.

IT WAS FIVE YEARS AGO that Vince left Mötley Crüe to pursue his interests in golfing, fast cars and babes. Before his departure, things had not been going well in the band. Vince had seriously injured his arm, severing ten-dons and muscles, in a backstage mishap with a mustard bottle. A roadie had mistakenly placed the wrong brand of mustard next to the tray of back-stage deli meats always provided for the Crüe under contractual obligation. Outraged at finding the wrong brand of mustard—Gulden's, not French's, as specified in the band's contract riders—Vince threw the bottle at the wall. Being severely drunk at the time, Vince forgot to let go, resulting in the bottle exploding in his fist, sending shrapnel-like shards of glass into his hand and forearm. Because of his injuries, which required a series of surgeries, as well as Nikki's and Tommy's struggles with drugs, the band ceased performing a couple of years before Vince left. So it's been many years—nearly eight—since the band has performed for an audience.

Mötley Crüe is determined to prove their reunion is not merely a business decision to exploit fans with a greatest-hits, nostalgia act. To that end, they are performing all twelve songs from their new *Generation Swine* album, followed by a handful of crowd-pleasing standards at the close. This is a particularly ballsy or foolish move, since no one in the audience has heard their new album. It doesn't go on sale until midnight after their final show in New York.

The sellout crowd, chanting in Cleveland, represents a cross section of ages and white suburban life-forms. There are the cheesecake blonds with feathered bangs lacquered onto their heads with hair spray, wearing tight shorts with black lace fringe. There are pencil-thin kids in black Iron Maiden T-shirts who lean against walls, gazing openmouthed with blank, detention-period stares. There are burly guys with the classic heavy-metal short-in-front-long-in-back El Camino haircuts, who wear sleeveless jean jackets and look like pro wrestlers trying to dress like Hells Angels. There are die-hard punks, including a girl at the door with a metal-studded face who pulls down her lower lip to reveal a tattoo that says "Clevoscum." She's the kind of person about whom, if you looked at her even without reading her tattoo, you'd probably still think "scum."

Standing in the aisle closer to the stage is a guy in a tuxedo who got married a few hours ago. The bride he is now stuck with, presumably for life, hangs on his arm in a ruffled dress. Her eyes are rolled partially back in her head, apparently from excess drink. Vomit strings hang from her chin and trail the side of her dress.

The first riff of "Find Myself" triggers a mass Pavlovian response in the audience. As one, the crowd begins the headbangers' jerk—chopping their heads down like ax blades. Those on their feet begin body slamming. Even the aisles take on the feel and intimacy of a mosh pit.

Vince starts the chorus with the line "I'm a sick motherfucker!" and his voice, the quintessential heavy-metal screech that approximates the sound of a tomcat being neutered with a rusty can opener, quickly has the audience singing along.

Tommy described their first performance in L.A. nearly two weeks earlier as being like "scared deer trapped in headlights."

It was worse than that. Vince was supposed to enter the stage by dropping down from between the spokes of a chandelier suspended above it and shaped like a wagon wheel. But somehow he became trapped in the spokes. He sang all of "Find Myself" with his tiny legs kicking helplessly as the chandelier swung more violently, until a stagehand assisted him down.

By the time of the Cleveland show, they have tightened their set (and worked out Vince's entry via the chandelier) to the point where they carry the audience through the eleven brand-new songs, but it is only during the final renditions of "Shout at the Devil" and "Dr. Feelgood" that the girls riding atop the shoulders of their boyfriends demonstrate their gratitude by raising their baby T-shirts and unbuckling their halter tops to wiggle their naked pulchritude at the band.

Cleveland is now officially having a good time.

When Nikki stage-dives into the audience, he rides atop hundreds of clenching, grabbing fists. Stagehands engage in a furious tug-of-war before the audience finally lets him go.

IN THE DRESSING ROOM after the show, Nikki and Tommy lie with their backs on the floor, passing a mask back and forth that they use to suck pure oxygen from a tank.

Their grueling schedule calls for two more hours of post-concert promotions—a question-and-answer period from the stage, a meet-and-greet with fans, and an event in which they will give away a signed guitar for charity.

"I felt terrible a couple nights ago," Vince says. "The guy who won our guitar didn't have any hands. I tried giving him the guitar, and I just blurted out without thinking, 'Dude! You don't have any hands!'"

Nikki leaps from the floor, rejuvenated with his pure-oxygen blast. "Vince, did you see that chick in the front row motioning the whole time?"

"The one stroking her hand over her mouth like she wanted to suck my dick? This must be the horniest fucking city we've played."

"The power of rock never stops amazing me." Nikki shakes his head. "The little girl sitting there. She's fourteen years old watching the band, and she's getting achy down there, and she doesn't know why."

BY ONE IN THE MORNING they have signed their last autograph of the night. Mick and Vince go straight to the hotel to meet their girlfriends, who have flown in from Los Angeles. Tommy and Nikki climb into the crew van hoping to find a hot meal somewhere. The van driver informs Dave, the tour manager, that most restaurants are closed in downtown Cleveland at this time of night, but the driver's brother-in-law, who comes from Rome, runs one of the finest Italian restaurants in Little Italy. He's kept it open especially for Mötley Crüe and has laid out a sumptuous feast.

"Dude," Tommy cuts in, "let's just go to Taco Bell and get some burritos."

"Burritos," Nikki repeats. "I'll be sliding my burrito into Donna in a few hours when we get to New York."

"One of the things people don't expect about Mötley Crüe is that we are computer literate," Tommy lectures on the drive to Taco Bell. "We're having a cybercast of our concert in New York. I read all the e-mail that comes into our website."

"Dude, Donna just sent me this e-mail today," Nikki interrupts. "She used her digital camera to take a picture. She's on her knees, and her ass is right in front of the lens, and she's got both her hands on her cheeks pulling it wide open."

"Digital cameras rule!" Tommy shouts.

"I sent her this nasty picture back," Nikki continues, "where there's jizz going down my legs. Thank God I'm sober. Imagine if I e-mailed it to the wrong person."

The late-night Taco Bell in downtown Cleveland is a bulletproof-glass fortress protected by an armed guard who waves Mötley Crüe off when Tommy tries opening the door of the van to go inside the restaurant. The guard grunts a few syllables, directing the van to the drive-thru line.

Because of the garbled drive-thru speaker system and the poor grasp of English demonstrated by the Taco Bell employee on the other end, ordering the couple dozen different varieties of burrito for the Crüe and their crew turns into a twenty-minute ordeal.

Sensing hurt feelings on the other side of the squawk box, Tommy becomes convinced the Taco Bell employees are going to tamper with their order. He climbs over the driver's head in the front seat of the van to peer into the kitchen window of the Taco Bell. "I want to make sure nobody's busting a nut in my burrito," he informs his bandmates, watching intently.

When the food arrives, it is apparent that there is no spoiled-rock-star hierarchy in the van. Tommy hands out crew members' burritos and hot sauce packets before taking his own. The band members and crew members eat. The silence doesn't hold for long.

"Do you think Mick's piling it into his old lady right now?" Tommy says, pondering the sex life of the band's least talkative member, as he tears into his second or third burrito.

"He's probably riding her now, got his hat on backwards," Nikki says between munches. "I wonder if Mick gets all freaky. Gets out the duct tape, puts on Three Stooges movies, constructs some elaborate scenario."

"Wait till we see him in New York, after he's deloaded his balls," Tommy adds. "Maybe he'll start talking again."

"I'll be in New York with Donna in a few hours," Nikki says in an unusually tender tone, then adds, "I better wash out my ass."

AT SEVEN-THIRTY A.M. ON MONDAY, Mötley Crüe gathers in the lobby of the Rihga Royal Hotel in Manhattan in preparation for their appearance later in the morning on *The Howard Stern Show*.

The band members spent the previous day—their first time off in two weeks—holed up in their suites at the hotel. All of them except Tommy were with their women, and all of them except Tommy seem relaxed and well rested as they cut through the autograph seekers in front of the hotel, signing whatever is put in front of them, and climb into the van that will take them to the studio.

Nikki stares at the window as the van rides through the cavernous New York streets and reminisces with Vince about their first time in New York, more than fifteen years ago, when they did their first show here. "I wanted to stay in the where-Sid-killed-Nancy hotel," states Nikki.

"We stayed in a dump, whatever it was," Vince laughs. "You and me shared that room that had the giant cockroaches."

"I remember the first time we sold out at the Whiskey," Tommy calls from the front passenger seat. "I phoned my mom and dad and told them we'd made it. My mom was so proud."

Thoughts of his mother put Tommy in a pensive frame of mind. "My mom was a beautiful lady, Greek. She never learned English very well. My therapist told me the reason I am so into tattoos is I had a lot of pain when I was a kid because I couldn't use words to communicate with my mom. It made me feel frightened and alone. So I turned to pictures. I put them all over my body to communicate my pain to my mother. That's why I have 'MAYHEM' tattooed on my stomach."

"But that's a word tattoo, not a picture," a reporter points out.

"I know, dude," Tommy says, missing the point but tripping out anyway. "It's fucking heavy how the mind works."

Vince gazes at the passing buildings, reminiscing. "The first time I ever saw snow was on our first tour." He adds, "Remember that apartment we had in Hollywood when AC/DC and the Scorpions used to hang out with us all the time."

Tommy: "Why did they hang out with us?"

Vince: "They did our drugs."

Mick: "No, man, we did their drugs, and they did our girls."

Nikki: "In the old days for every album we sold, I think we ingested a different drug and tried to destroy ourselves and wreck the whole process.

"We tried to blow up, and every time we tried, we kept getting bigger. Every car we wrecked, every overdose just made us bigger. It was ridiculous. I was never in it for the success. I was in it for the crash and burn."

BY EIGHT A.M. the Crüe arrive at the CBS Radio studios high above Manhattan. Vince prepares his vocal cords for the live band performance they will do on-air by shutting himself into a soundproof room and screaming.

In the hallway outside the green room, Gary Dell'Abate argues with Dave, the tour manager, about the Mötley Crüe wives and girlfriends, who the record label promised would be on the show.

"I hate it when people at the record label lie," Nikki sighs.

A sound technician who's been setting up equipment for their live performance approaches Nikki and Tommy. "You guys are so much cooler to work with than Judas Priest."

"That's 'cause we don't have jizz on our breath," Tommy says.

"You guys will go on and do one song and an interview without the girls," a *Howard Stern* producer says to Nikki. "It's okay with our people, if it's okay with your people."

"Of course it's okay." Nikki laughs. "We are 'our people.'"

THE INTERVIEW WITH HOWARD STERN goes without a snag until Stern asks Nikki about the bet once held between Mötley Crüe members to see who could screw the most girls without taking a shower.

"I won after thirty days with seventeen girls," Nikki boasts. "I was getting a blow job . . ."

"You can't say that!" Stern shouts, breaking out of his damn-the-FCC persona.

"I can't say 'blow job'?" Nikki asks, amazed.

"No, man," Stern whines. "I've been fined over two million dollars for that. We've got to bleep it."

THAT EVENING'S SELLOUT SHOW at New York's Roseland is something of a triumphal return for Mötley Crüe. Their last gig here, when they were touring with another singer in place of Vince, had to be canceled for lack of interest.

During the sound check inside the Roseland, Vince taps the tail section of a rocket ship lying on the stage. Nikki uses it as a prop for his song "Rocketship."

"This is right out of *Spinal Tap*." Vince kicks it. "Hopefully, by the time we do our big tour in the fall, this will be in Nikki's backyard in L.A., and his kids will be playing on it. This is fucking lame."

IN THE DRESSING ROOM DOWNSTAIRS, Mick, who has spent the afternoon with his girlfriend, is uncharacteristically talkative.

He warms to his favorite subject, guns. He explains how he and his brother, a lieutenant in the California Highway Patrol, set up elaborate shooting courses in the desert and blow up human figures with melon heads.

Mick waxes sentimental about the tripod-mounted World War II antiaircraft gun that fired explosive rounds with an incredibly flat trajectory, and which he had to sell a few years back in order to "save my house during a divorce."

The arrival of Mick's girlfriend puts an end to the discussion of weapons. Robbie-Lauren Mantooth describes herself as a "blond Cherokee from Tennessee and Australia." A Guess jeans model, *Sports Illustrated* swimsuitissue model and an underwater photographer for *National Geographic*, Mantooth perches on Mick's knee, modeling an aquamarine halter top that clings to state-of-the-art breast implants (according to Mick Mars).

Mantooth speaks passionately about the plight of great white sharks, and her work lecturing in elementary schools to preserve them. "I show a film where I'm hugging a shark," she prattles, looking up with jumbo blue eyes, serene as the summer sky, and abruptly changes the subject. "Would you like to see the heart on my butt?"

Mantooth wiggles off Mick's lap and bends over in her lavender leather pants, to reveal a heart shape stitched into the leather that covers her heart-shaped butt cheeks.

"I wonder if Larry Flynt would ever let me take a picture with him that I could use in Christmas cards for my friends. I mean with my clothes on."

"Larry would probably ask if he could lick your pussy," Mick mumbles.

"Oh, well," Mantooth says in her cheerful, bell-tone voice, as she trots out of the room to fetch a diet soda.

In her absence the room still smells faintly of perfume. Mick breaks the silence. "Thank God I left Indiana. Where I grew up the only life was getting fat, driving a tractor, growing corn and raising hogs."

THE ROSELAND PERFORMANCE ENDS with Mötley Crüe slumped dejectedly in their dressing room, feeling that, despite the enthusiastically mindless slamming in the crowd, their performance was off.

Vince has the added problem that while stepping off the stage, his girlfriend, *Playboy* model Heidi Clark, ran up behind him to give him a hug, just as he flicked his head back, causing an impact that left her with a shiner.

Heidi sits behind him on the dressing room chair. "Vinnie, you really hurt my eye," Heidi says, wincing.

Across the room, Nikki strips out of his leather shorts and wraps himself in a towel. Heidi screams, "God damn it! I just saw Nikki's balls. I'm getting the hell out of here!"

Moments after Heidi runs out, the tour assistant knocks on the door and says Sebastian Bach, the lead singer of the now defunct glam heavy metal band Skid Row, is outside and would like to come in and say hello.

"How is he?" Tommy asks.

"He seems pretty sober," answers the tour assistant.

Bach zigzags in, waving his mane of shoulder-length hair from side to side. "You guys put on a wicked show! Nikki, I thought you were too rich to stage-dive, bro!"

"How've you been?" Tommy asks, slapping his palm.

"Great, man! Fucking great." Bach drops into a chair. "The truth is, terrible. My band kicked me out. I'm broke, and some Hells Angels dude just punched me in the nose." Bach gingerly touches his face with both hands. "It should be bleeding but it's not, for some reason."

MÖTLEY CRÜE ARRIVE at Tower Records at midnight. A crowd of nearly a thousand curls around the store waiting to buy their new *Generation Swine* CD.

The Crüe sit at a table raised on a platform inside and begin signing for their fans.

"Tommy, man. I'm an engineer, and I designed a drum kit for you," a wiry teenager says, approaching the table. He raises a camera and tries snapping a picture unsuccessfully.

"Dude, you've got to wind the camera." Tommy takes it from his hands and snaps the picture for him.

"Oh my friggin' God!" a group of chicks from Long Island cry out. They lean against the table, touching Crüe members' hands as they indicate where they want their pictures and CDs signed. "You guys are so rad!" a girl shouts, pulling her top down momentarily to expose herself.

"Thanks," Nikki mumbles, barely noticing the bare breasts inches from his nose. The twenty-hour workday is taking its toll. Hundreds of girls slide past the table, repeating the scene again and again.

Three hours into the signing, Nikki slumps back in his chair and falls asleep. The rear chair legs slide off the stand, and a couple of store employees catch his fall inches before his head cracks against the floor.

As they tilt his chair back up to the table, Nikki's eyes open. He resumes signing autographs and bantering with the fans.

"It takes a lot for Nikki to say uncle," Dave, the tour manager, groans. "We can't keep them away from their fans."

The last kid walks out of the store at four-thirty in the morning.

"WOW! I COULD USE A HAMBURGER!" Nikki jumps into the van, escaping the clutches of fans outside the Tower store who want more.

"That was cool," Vince says, in a red-eyed daze.

"Pass me some of those mushy fries," Mick mumbles in the back, as Tommy rips into a greasy McDonald's sack that somebody loaded into the van hours ago.

A publicist from their management company has joined them for the ride back to the hotel to strategize for the next day. "I wanted to feel you out about doing a CNN spot tomorrow at two."

"That sounds okay," Nikki mumbles, scarfing down a cold hamburger.

"It'll be a hip thing that a lot of kids are into. At the virtual laser-tag center."

"What's that?"

"You'll dress up in laser-tag suits and play the game."

"That doesn't sound very cool."

"So you guys aren't into it?"

"That sounds like something Bon Jovi might do."

"I'm very protective of Mötley Crüe," Mick says the next day on the way to David Letterman's show. "I dreamed of being in a successful band since I was kid. I don't want to ruin it by dressing up in space suits."

"We've been around for seventeen years," Nikki says. "We've survived the drugs, the alcohol . . ."

"Breaking up," Vince adds.

"The lawsuits," Nikki says. "We've been sued by people who claimed our music inspired them to commit suicide. We were sued by a guy who said Mick's guitar playing made him go deaf. We were sued by a guy who saw me set my pants on fire in a show, and went home and did it, so he nearly burned himself to death. We ought to change our name to Mötley Sue."

FOR THE TAPING of *Late Night with David Letterman*, a block of Fifty-third Street has been closed by the NYPD. A stage has been erected in the middle of the road.

Humid, cloudy weather has blown off by late afternoon to a blue sky. After the sound check ensures that windowpanes will rattle for a several-block area, the Crüe retreats to the cramped dressing rooms above the Ed Sullivan Theater.

Heidi Mark, wearing a leopard-print jacket, and Robbie-Lauren Mantooth, in a lime-green Chanel suit, wait in the dressing room. Heidi's shiner is barely visible, and her spirits have improved remarkably. "Did you see my new tattoo?" Heidi babbles contentedly, twisting her ankle to reveal the fairy dancing around a rose inked on her calf. "Roses are my favorite. See my shoes?" Heidi turns her black pumps up, to reveal a rose pattern on the heel.

Donna D'Errico bounces into the room, wearing a white-polka-dot slip. As she adjusts a strap on her top, a tanned, freakishly large breast tumbles out. She casually pulls the top down and puts her breast back into place, before extending her hand to a reporter and introducing herself.

She turns to Heidi and offers her a compliment. "You have stick legs. I'm jealous."

The Crüe women bond, comparing notes on such topics as silicone versus saline and anything else related to their shared interest in breast augmentation surgery.

"I've heard that something like seventy-five percent of all American women have them," Robbie states with complete certainty.

"All I know is"—Heidi laughs—"my first job was a disaster. I got stuck with a set of baseball tits."

When the live taping of the Letterman show pops onto the dressing room monitor, Heidi glances as Dave introduces the first guest, Daisy Fuentes.

"Daisy Fuentes was right next door to us," Heidi states, blond hackles rising. "She could have said hello to us."

"Look at those Farrah Fawcett boobs," one of the Crüe girlfriends observes, commenting on Fuentes's prominent nipples, visible on the monitor.

"Total doorknob nipples," another Crüe mate chips in.

BY SIX P.M., the height of Manhattan's rush hour, the studio audience, now crowded outside on the stage on Fifty-third Street, applauds as Letterman introduces Mötley Crüe.

In their agreement with CBS and the NYPD, Mötley Crüe has consented to cease performing at six-thirty.

At seven o'clock, Vince is still screaming out Crüe songs. Nikki has switched to his bass guitar that has a "Stop AIDS! Aim for the Chin" sticker on it.

Several of the show's producers are at the edge of the stage angrily gesturing for them to stop. A huge crowd is spilling out from Fifty-third Street, slowing traffic on Broadway. Vince and Nikki look down at the angry producers, exchange grins and promise the crowd one last song.

THEIR FINAL NIGHT IN NEW YORK, before flying on to Europe, is spent at a dinner the Crüe girls have organized at Madame Chen's, a Chinese restaurant downtown that features transvestite waiters. Throughout most of the dinner, Mick stares in stern, midwestern disapproval, shaking his head at the antics of the cross-dressed waiters. "Hideous. I don't get it."

Before their food arrives, Nikki leans forward to huddle with his bandmates across the table and share a sentiment that overcame him during their outdoor *Letterman* appearance. "Today, when we were up on that platform playing, I looked up at the clouds moving across the sky, and it felt like the platform we were on was moving. Like we were all moving together, gliding through the sky. Then I looked at you guys"—Nikki's eyes move from

Tommy to Vince to Mick—"and suddenly, it all felt good, so right that we were back playing our music together."

Their moment is interrupted by the approach of their waiter, an Asian transvestite in a slinky, low-cut dress. "Dude, check out the rack on our waiter," Tommy enthuses. "Maybe we can boost ticket sales on the big fall tour if we have Vince get a pair of tits."

"The only problem is, I'd get stuck backstage feeling myself up," Vince says.

"Tits are fucking awesome," Tommy says. "I mean I really fucking love them."

The rest of the band members agree. Tits rock.

The day before Thanksgiving 2004, Pat Dollard, a Hollywood agent who represented Steven Soderbergh, sent an e-mail to just about everyone he knew containing one word: "Later." Friends worried it was a suicide note. Dollard, forty-two, had spent nearly twenty years in the film business. On a good day he seemed little different from any other successful operator, a sort of hipper version of *Entourage*'s Ari Gold. But often in his turbulent career, bad days outnumbered the good. Once a rising star at William Morris, he was fired in the mid-nineties for chronic absenteeism brought on by drinking and drug abuse. He attended 12-step meetings and bounced back, playing a critical role in getting Soderbergh's *Traffic* made. Propaganda Films tapped him to head its management division, and in 2002 he produced *Auto Focus*, the Paul Schrader–directed biopic about the murder of *Hogan's Heroes* star Bob Crane—a film in which Dollard has a cameo in drag. Dollard cofounded Relativity, a firm that would assist the Marvel Entertainment Group in its half-billion-dollar production deal and went on to produce, after Dollard's exit, *Talladega Nights*. But by 2004, Dollard was bingeing again. His fourth wife left him, and his third wife was suing for sole custody of their daughter. News that his daughter would be spending Thanksgiving at the home of Robert Evans—for whom his ex-wife worked as a development executive—sent Dollard into a morbid depression. Late one night he phoned a friend and suggested that everyone might be better off if he were dead. Then he sent his good-bye e-mail.

But Dollard was not planning a suicide, at least not a quick one. Dressed in what he would later describe as his "scumbag hipster agent's uniform"—Prada boots, jeans and a black leather jacket—he boarded a plane for New York, then Kuwait City. From there he hopped a military transport to Baghdad and embedded with U.S. Marines in order to make a "pro-war documentary." Given the decades of substance abuse, the idea of the chain-smoking, middle-aged Hollywood agent accompanying Marines into battle was sort of like Keith Richards competing in an Ironman Triathlon. But Dollard thrived. "My first time in a combat zone, I felt like I had walked into some bizarre fucking ultra-expensive movie set," he would later say. "I had this vivid clarity, like when I used to take LSD. I felt joy. I felt like I had a message from God, or whoever, that this is exactly what I should be doing with my life. I belong in war. I am a warrior."

To those at home it seemed that Dollard had entered dangerous mental territory. Around the New Year in 2005, he e-mailed a photo of himself to friends. In it he is clutching a machine gun, surrounded by Marines. Dressed in combat gear, his hair in a Mohawk and the word "DIE" shaved into his chest hair, Dollard looks like the mascot of Camp Lord of the Flies.

"THE H'WOOD WARRIOR"

MIDSUMMER 2006. Dollard sits across from me at a hotel restaurant near the Los Angeles airport, tearing into a breakfast of waffles, bacon and black coffee while talking about his ambition to become a "conservative icon, the Michael Moore of the right." He is well on his way, thanks in no small part to a terrible incident that occurred last February in Iraq. While Dollard was filming U.S. troops in Ramadi, a Humvee he was riding in was struck by a bomb. Two Marines were killed, but Dollard—in keeping with a streak of freakishly good luck—was thrown clear from the fiery wreckage and emerged unharmed but for a two-inch cut on his right leg. The bombing was, appropriately enough, first reported in *Variety*. Dollard was soon invited on Tony Snow's radio show on Fox and spent as much time railing against Hollywood liberalism as he did talking about Iraq. Snow, weeks away from becoming White House press secretary, loved it. He called Dollard a "true believer" and invited him back for two more appearances. Dollard was soon hailed by conservative columnists in *U.S. News & World Report* and *The Washington Times*. The *New York Post* dubbed him the "H'wood Warrior." No small part of his appeal to the right is the fact that Dollard was once a "doctrinaire liberal" who could even boast of close ties to Robert Kennedy, Jr., but now speaks of his pro-war stance in the most militant terms: "This is a propaganda war, and if I can fight with a camera the same as a Marine with his rifle, I will."

Last May he launched a website (patdollard.com) and began airing a five-minute trailer of his as yet unfinished documentary, *Young Americans*. The response was overwhelming: one hundred thousand hits in the first week, hundreds of supportive e-mails, and unsolicited offers of money. "Dude, I'm becoming a national hero," Dollard tells me.

Compactly built, Dollard dresses in clothes—jeans, Wal-Mart work boots and an olive-drab T-shirt—that look like they've been slept in. His hair is close-cropped, but nevertheless manages to appear disheveled. He hasn't shaved in a few days. His teeth are cracked and stained, and, worst of all, from a health standpoint, his right eye is obscured by a milky blob: a cataract that developed in Iraq, which he has never treated. Also in need of attention is a wretched cough, which sounds like a snow shovel scraping on the sidewalk. If he were a homeless man, you'd probably wash your hands after giving him your change.

Beneath the unkempt appearance, Dollard projects unnerving vitality. Even with the cataract, his green eyes are alert and engaging. Words tumble from his mouth at a rapid clip, his voice a parched growl acquired from a lifetime of cigarettes and liquor. One moment he is laughing about the time he picked up hookers on the set of *Dragon: The Bruce Lee Story*, a film his second wife worked on as an assistant to producer Raffaella De Laurentiis— a moment later he is pounding the table, railing against Cindy Sheehan's antiwar protests. "Cindy Sheehan is pathologically self-centered. It's a tragedy she lost her son. Anyway, we all lose family members. So fuck Cindy Sheehan."

From hilarity to rage in less than two minutes. In layman's terms, Dollard is "intense." Some might use words like "manic" or "bipolar"—a condition Dollard's mother believes he might suffer from—but Dollard bristles at any suggestion he is clinically off balance. "True," he says, chewing a strip of bacon, "I was told to get a CAT scan"—after being blown up in Iraq—"but I feel fucking fine."

And true, Dollard was pretty much the same before he got blown up. He possesses a quality common among celebrities, children and the insane. You are compelled to watch him because you never know what he will do or say next. His third wife, Alicia Allain, sums up her ex-husband, saying, "He may be the biggest asshole I've met, but he's got twisted charisma."

Not everyone succumbs to it. When Dollard first posted the story of escaping death in Iraq, his younger sister, deeply opposed to the war, speculated that her older brother was just "too evil to die." (Dollard dismisses her as a "nutcase—even nuttier than I am.")

When it comes to practicing the Hollywood art of salesmanship, Dollard was among the best. Steven Soderbergh says, "Pat has a quality that's essential to selling movies: making people see things that can't be seen yet. I mean, if Pat says he saw a UFO, he will convince me it was there, even if I didn't see it."

Upon returning from his second trip to Iraq, last March, Dollard moved from Los Angeles to an undisclosed location out of state to complete his film. (He is so obsessed with secrecy he recently had the OnStar system yanked from his SUV, fearing it might be used by "enemies" to locate him.) He is in L.A. today at the invitation of Andrew Breitbart—longtime contributor to the Drudge Report and self-described "right-leaning Hollywood basher," but a freethinker who helped create the Huffington Post. Breitbart plans to introduce him to potential financial backers.

Dollard's film teaser is less like a documentary than agitprop. It opens on two young Marines hunched over their machine guns at a roadblock. It's the winter of 2005. Both are shivering from the cold, warily eyeing the civilian cars that at any moment they may be called upon to shoot. The Marines pass the time speculating about what kids their age might be doing back home. One of them turns to the camera, concluding, "They're over at home smoking blunts, fucking watching MTV, sitting on their fat ass. Well, fuck you."

A montage of violent clips slides past—an Arab fighter being shot to death by American soldiers; a Marine rifleman dancing and clutching his groin, then firing a machine gun into an Iraqi town; the minaret of a mosque being blown to pieces. The violence is intercut with iconic images from American pop culture—the smiling face of *Jackass* prince Johnny Knoxville, college kids dancing at an MTV beach party, antiwar rallies, the faces of archliberals Jane Fonda and Michael Moore. The soundtrack is provided by Boston hard-core punk band Blood for Blood. Their song "Ain't Like You (Wasted Youth II)," with its chorus of "Fuck you, I ain't like you," becomes the refrain of the troops as they blow away insurgents and give the finger to antiwar activists and kids at home enjoying the fruits of America's mindless civilian culture.

There is evidence of a possible war crime in the trailer: a Marine clutches the head of a dead Iraqi and raises it in front of the camera like a jack-o'-lantern. (This footage was given to Dollard by troops, and he claims not to know the provenance of the decapitated man, or why a Marine was playing with his severed head.) In Dollard's presentation, the act of desecration, accompanied by the faces of grinning Marines, is treated as a macabre joke.

By intercutting this with actual *Jackass* footage, the trailer seems to suggest that, for the young, wild and patriotic American, war in Iraq is sort of like the ultimate *Jackass*.

When I mention to Dollard that his severed-head scene might turn more Americans against the war, or even against the troops, he laughs. "The true savagery in this war is being committed by the American left on the minds of the young men and women serving over there by repeatedly telling them that their cause is lost." He adds, "My goal is to desensitize young people to violence. I want kids to watch my film and understand that brutality is the fucking appropriate response to a brutal enemy."

Dollard's target audience is the same as any rock band's: kids—the more disaffected the better. He aims to alter the course of pop culture. "What we've celebrated since at least the 1950s is the antihero," Dollard says. "Today, even though our country has been attacked, nothing has changed. If you are a young man in America right now, the coolest fucking thing you can aspire to be is like a gangsta rapper, or a pseudo bad guy. The message of my movie is simple: If you're a young person in America, the coolest, fucking most badass and most noble thing you can be today is a combat Marine. Period."

Breitbart believes Dollard is onto something important. "There needs to be a confrontation at the pop-culture level of the kids who are over there fighting versus the kids at home who are totally disconnected, immersed in this mindless Abercrombie & Fitch/MTV culture." Breitbart adds, "There needs to be a revolution, and Dollard is the man who can kick it off. I don't care if older conservatives are offended by Pat Dollard. I was not looking for someone pristine. He brings to our cause this whole spirit of, like, the Merry Pranksters Two."

Perhaps it's no surprise that Ann Coulter adores his work. Like Breitbart, she recognizes his ability to reach young people in ways that other conservatives don't. She says of his Web postings, "What's great about them is that they have the panache of a professional MTV video with a very un-MTV message." In an e-mail she sent to Dollard after an initial viewing of his trailer, she simply gushed, "wow! wow! that certainly is attention-grabbing!

I like it—especially the 'fuck you' melange with michael moore and [former Democratic Party chairman] terry mccaulliffe [*sic*]. I like it!"

The reaction to Dollard from soldiers and their family members has been even more enthusiastic. One Marine officer he encountered in Ramadi expressed his admiration in a terse note: "Thank God and Chesty Puller for people like you, Pat Dollard, who truly get us. Semper Fi."

As for those Americans who believe in the conspiracy of a liberal-controlled media, Dollard tells them that their worst fears are true, that the entertainment industry is run by a form of reverse McCarthyism. "If you're conservative in Hollywood today, you're not necessarily getting blacklisted, but you essentially are blacklisted. You are reviled and treated like shit." That a former Hollywood big shot would descend from the heights and admit to the people that he was once part of the liberal cabal electrifies them. The father of a Marine Dollard met while filming in Ramadi wrote him, "[My son] told me that you were one of those very rare media types that didn't suck and had nuts equal to that of any Marine infantry rifleman. [Your film] will be mighty powerful ordnance deployed against the bed-wetting peace-niks on the left."

Most important from Dollard's standpoint, he is reaching his target audience, the MySpace crowd. Typical of the many e-mails he receives is this: "Hey Pat im a 17 year old high school student. I lived most of my life as a liberal and over the last year realized I was only a product of the leftist school system and the media. The clips I've seen of 'Young Americans' are an inspiration and it's time someone tells the truth. Thanks for putting your life on the line for the better of the country."

When you consider that just eighteen months earlier Dollard was a confessed whore-loving, alcoholic, coked-out Hollywood agent, his transformation into the great hope of conservative America is nothing short of astonishing. "It's fucking crazy, dude," he admits as he stands at the entrance of his hotel, smoking and watching planes take off from LAX. "I was afraid conservatives wouldn't have me, but they're fucking all over me."

He brings up George Clooney and Steve Gaghan, both of whom he knew through his work with Soderbergh. In Dollard's view, the two of them represent everything wrong and shallow about Hollywood liberalism. Dollard claims that he was having lunch with Gaghan—who wrote *Traffic*—a few years ago when Gaghan was struck by his inspiration to make *Syriana*. "He literally held up the bottle of olive oil on the table and said, 'Oh my God! It's all about the oil.'"

(Though Gaghan remembers the lunch, his version of events differs from Dollard's. And by that point, Gaghan says, he was already a few years into his research for *Syriana*, which was based on Robert Baer's 2002 book *See No Evil*.)

Nothing irks Dollard more than the praise Clooney received for making *Syriana* and *Good Night, and Good Luck*. "Clooney actually goes around letting people say he was 'brave' for making those movies. Everybody in Hollywood is obsessed with wanting to be perceived as tough. Is it brave making films that serve the agenda of every liberal in Hollywood, when real heroes are spilling their blood in Iraq?" Dollard sputters. "Clooney is a pompous jackass."

Another plane takes off from LAX. Lighting another post-breakfast cigarette, Dollard turns to me and laughs. "Dude, I spent twenty years being a pimp for the stars—now I'm becoming a political star."

THE YOUNG TURK

BILLY BOB THORNTON, at one point a client of Dollard's, once told a mutual friend, "Pat Dollard is the only person I know in Hollywood who's crazier than me." When Dollard was a teenager his goal in life was to become a "stoned artist." Inspired by his hero, Jim Morrison, Dollard dreamed of spreading a "metaphysical message throughout the world."

He grew up, the second eldest of five children, in a "Puerto Rican–Irish welfare family." When Dollard was three his mother, Eva, packed up the kids and fled from their alcoholic, Irish-American father in New Jersey, moving to Paramount, California, a smog-bound blue-collar city on the southern fringes of the Los Angeles basin, where Eva took a job as a night-shift switchboard operator.

Dollard's father stalked the family to California. Living on skid row, the elder Dollard would show up at his ex-wife's house and terrorize the kids. As Dollard remembers it, his dad would inevitably end up leaping onto the cinder-block wall in the backyard to punch and threaten imaginary enemies. "My dad thought we were being attacked by pirates, and the police would come," he says. "But it wasn't my mom who called them. My dad would call the police to help him fight the pirates."

His mother again moved the family, but Dollard's father found them. Dollard was in first grade, a scholarship student at a Catholic elementary school, when his dad took a job parking cars nearby. During recess his father would approach the chain-link fence by the playground and call Pat's name.

According to Eva Dollard, she warned her son, "No matter what he asks, you don't answer any questions." Dollard remembers standing with friends on the playground when his dad, dressed in shabby clothes and an orange reflector vest, approached. "I told the other kids I didn't know him—he was a crazy drunk."

That was the last time Dollard saw his father. He died within a year, at age forty-five, of cirrhosis of the liver. "I was chewed up by guilt for treating him like that," Dollard says. "I stopped believing in God, and felt guiltier because my mom was this big Catholic. I seriously believed I must be some kind of psychopath."

In addition to her faith, Eva possessed a commitment to liberalism that was once almost a birthright of working-class Catholics. "My mother had this belief in, like, the nobility of being poor and the eternal fight for social justice," he says.

No one was more touched by Eva's faith than her eldest child, Ann, eight years older than Pat. Ann's involvement in activism would, strangely enough, put her on a fairy-tale ascent into the highest reaches of the American social strata. In 1976, a year after graduating from high school, Ann took a job as an extra in Hal Ashby's *Coming Home*, which was being filmed at a nearby hospital. During a break, Ann chatted up one of the film's stars, Jane Fonda. The conversation resulted in Ann's taking a job with Fonda's husband Tom Hayden's Campaign for Economic Democracy, then with César Chávez's United Farm Workers of America. Her work inevitably took her deeper into Hollywood's activist-entertainment circles. By the early eighties, Ann had found her professional niche as a junior agent at Leading Artists Agency. Her activism continued, particularly in the nuclear-freeze movement, which led to an intimate friendship with Robert Kennedy, Jr., who says, "Ann was one of my closest friends. She was extremely smart and extremely forceful and was absolutely committed to progressive issues, a vision of social justice for America."

In the Dollard family, no one was closer to Pat than Ann. Kennedy recalls, "Ann would bring Pat to whatever she was doing. Pat idolized her, and she adored him." Through his middle-school years, Dollard followed his older sister to marches and fund-raisers and spent weekends canvassing door-to-door for her.

But he was also beginning to follow in his father's footsteps. Dollard had become a blackout drinker by age fifteen. Nevertheless, with the help of his parish priest, he won a scholarship to a Jesuit prep school. The priests nicknamed him "Nemesis." He was the smart-ass who debated them about religion based on his extensive readings of South American–born writer Carlos Castaneda, and the kid who, when asked to do a book report on Colombia, brought in a live pot plant as a visual aid. Dollard claims he was nearly thrown out after being implicated in a plot to put LSD in the priests' drinking water. By his junior year, Dollard had discovered L.A.'s punk scene, which only accelerated his drinking. "I remember being in honors algebra, drunk out of my mind every fucking day."

Yet Dollard believed fate held something grand in store for him. Some nights he would take a girlfriend drunken-driving in the hills above Los Angeles, and when she would scream, "Slow down! You're going to kill us!" he would say, "Maybe you'll die. But not me. I can't die. I have a destiny." At seventeen, believing he was onto that destiny, he dropped out of high school to become a rock star. "I didn't play an instrument, and I couldn't sing," he says, "but I thought I could make it on ego and mouth."

He formed a band but admits, "I was too loaded to ever get up onstage." His most memorable performance would be at another band's show: the time he cracked his skull stage-diving at a Black Flag concert, then stayed in the mosh pit slamming for hours, despite later requiring twelve stitches. "I remember coming out covered in blood and everyone telling me how cool I looked," says Dollard. "That was as far as my career went in music." Married briefly at twenty-one, Dollard became a telemarketer, spending the next few years in various boiler rooms, selling pens, printer ink, and charity vouchers for the Long Beach Police Department. "It was dismal," he says. "But I learned how to close."

When Dollard was twenty-two, Ann performed a career intervention, hiring him to answer her phone at Leading Artists. He lasted two years before she fired him. But destiny, which he still believed in, had other plans. He would get his break, but only through enduring the greatest tragedy of his life. Two days after Ann fired him, she was killed in a freak horse-riding accident. Dollard was offered her job and her client list, which included a then unknown Steven Soderbergh, about a year away from releasing his breakthrough, *Sex, Lies, and Videotape.*

Dollard was twenty-five when Soderbergh shot to fame, and quickly proved himself in his own right. In the early nineties he moved to William Morris, where he worked with Mike Simpson, today a senior vice president of the agency, whose best-known clients are Tim Burton, Quentin Tarantino, Wes Craven and Trey Parker and Matt Stone. "Pat was outspoken, very articulate, and knew how to operate in the world," Simpson says. "He became an important soldier in our army."

His biggest contribution was to help establish the agency's independent-film division, which, Simpson says, "was extremely important to our success in the nineties." In addition to Soderbergh, Dollard represented Billy Bob Thornton and his writing partner Tom Epperson; Mike Werb, who wrote *The Mask* and *Face/Off;* Don Mancini (writer of the Child's Play movie series); director Alan Rudolph; writer Fina Torres and actor Malcolm-Jamal Warner.

To Dollard, the sudden success felt as if "someone handed me a basket of power." One of his favorite movies as a teenager had been Stanley Kubrick's *Barry Lyndon*, based on the Thackeray novel about a fatherless Irish rogue who fakes his way into the aristocracy. For Dollard, becoming an agent fulfilled this fantasy. "It was like being a fucking duke or count in Europe back in the day," he says.

Dollard did what many other twentysomethings in his shoes would have done: he became a swine of the first order. He wore Armani suits, drove whatever car was "tasty" at the time—from a Miata to a Porsche, to a Range Rover—and "plowed through more pussy than I thought was imaginable."

Outwardly, Dollard was the consummate Hollywood player. A former client says, "Pat seemed like the archetypical agent. He was hyperslick in that hyperglib, dismissive, hipper-than-thou, bullshit-Hollywood way. He was your basic Young Turk prick."

Simpson saw something different in him. "The main thing I always liked about Pat from day one is that I felt like he had a soul. There was something else going on besides just who his clients were, what the deal was, that kind of agent veneer."

Dollard was earning a reputation for intense but passing infatuations, such as the time in the early nineties when he converted to Judaism and took the name Schlomo Bin Avrihim. ("The rabbis who held my *beth din*," says Dollard, referring to the council that determines a candidate's suitability for conversion, "told me afterwards that they wished all converts could reach my spiritual level.") The conversion didn't last. Dollard's second wife, for whom he'd become a Jew, divorced him not long after his romp with hookers on the set of *Dragon: The Bruce Lee Story*.

While visiting his wife on the *Dragon* set, Dollard found the time to chat up one of the hairdressers, Alicia Allain, who would become his third wife, in 1994. Alicia, nineteen, had come to Los Angeles from Louisiana with ambitions of becoming a producer, but was still relegated to the hair-and-makeup department.

The Dollard whom Alicia met "always wore these very tasteful Italian suits and was so gifted I believed he was going to end up running a studio." Alicia was open-minded in a way that should have made theirs the ideal Hollywood marriage. When I ask her if she was aware that her future husband was having sex with hookers at the same time he was wooing her on the set of *Dragon*, she corrects me. "No, Pat didn't have sex with those girls," she says. "They just gave him some blow jobs."

But as tolerant as Alicia was, Dollard's increasing drug use plunged her into despair. While he controlled it at the office, after hours he typically functioned in a chemically induced haze. She says, "Those guys at William Morris loved Pat. They saw him as this happy-go-lucky dude. They didn't see Pat locking himself in his bedroom at our apartment, him high as a kite, and me and his mother finally having the police and firemen get him because we're afraid he's killing himself in there. I saw he hated himself for what he was doing. After these runs Pat would just be balled up on the floor crying."

Dollard estimates that he wound up in emergency rooms half a dozen times for overdoses.

By 1995, at age thirty, Dollard was barely functioning. Mike Simpson tried to intervene. He says, "I talked to him, kind of like up against the wall, and said, 'What are you doing, man? You're gonna kill yourself.'"

According to Simpson, Dollard simply laughed and said, "You're right."

That year, he was fired from William Morris. Pat and Alicia moved back to her hometown, near Baton Rouge, where initially she supported them by working at a hair salon. "We lived on clipping coupons for pizzas," Dollard recalls. He began attending AA meetings and took a job at a Baton Rouge commercial-production house, and in 1996, Alicia gave birth to their daughter. He and Alicia produced two independent films, *Notes from Underground* and *Lush*, a portrait of a man suffering from alcoholic blackouts who is accused of murder. Neither film put Dollard back on the map. Nor was Soderbergh, who remained a client, doing especially well. After he failed to connect with audiences with films like *The Underneath* and *Schizopolis*, Soderbergh's relations with major studios had chilled. "For a while there," says Dollard, "the most successful film I was involved with was a Louisiana State Lottery commercial I worked on."

Everything changed in 1998, when Soderbergh's *Out of Sight* was released to critical acclaim. Dollard's career came roaring back to life. In short order he set up lucrative deals for Soderbergh to make *The Limey*, *Full Frontal* and *Erin Brockovich*. But *Traffic* was Dollard's biggest coup. Dollard is credited by Soderbergh and others with getting the film made after it fell apart during preproduction. When *Traffic* won four Academy Awards, including Soderbergh's first as a director, Dollard was a made man in Hollywood.

Propaganda Films hired Dollard to be president of its management division. Then at its peak as a commercial- and feature-production company, Propaganda's stable included some of the hottest directors in town, including David Fincher, Michael Bay and Spike Jonze. Dollard moved into a home in Bel Air. He and Alicia had separated in 1999, but continued to work together as a producing team.

With *Traffic* having moved the national debate over the war on drugs to the forefront, Dollard spoke candidly to the press about his own struggles with addiction, telling one reporter that his practices as an agent were now "consistent with AA principles."

Despite preaching about sobriety, Dollard began using again. Initially, he attempted to hide it. "I would take drug vacations," he explains. "I'd check into a hotel on Sunset and just binge for a few days." Soon his addictions spilled into his work life. According to Dollard, in 2001, after starting at Propaganda, he initiated monthly drug-and-hooker parties, which he called "the Hotel Club."

Dollard claims that the Hotel Club became part of his executive plan at Propaganda. "I'm not saying we expensed any of this," Dollard says. "Once a month, a select group of executives at the company would have non-wedding-connected bachelor parties with drugs and hookers we'd book at all the different trendy hotels—the Avalon, the Four Seasons, the Argyle. We would invite potential clients and get them loaded and get them laid. I was participating in the fucking Roman orgy."

Propaganda soon went belly-up—industry-watchers blame a post-9/11 recession in commercial production, not Dollard—but he landed on his feet, taking a senior position at Catch-23, the management firm that represented Renée Zellweger, among others. In 2004 he and manager Ryan Kavanaugh cofounded Relativity Management, with up to $150 million in financing and ambitious plans to produce films as well as manage talent. "My career had never been better," Dollard says. "My personal life was this ongoing disaster."

In 2000 he had married for the fourth time. He and his wife moved into a Hollywood Hills mansion previously inhabited by Kirstie Alley. It was owned by Alley's former boyfriend *Melrose Place* actor James Wilder, who lived next door. After Dollard reverted to old habits and began locking himself in the master bedroom to binge in privacy, his new wife enlisted Wilder's help breaking in—by climbing across a walkway that connected the two homes—in order to check on her husband. She says, "Poor James went from Kirstie Alley to Pat and me."

At a dinner party at Stockard Channing's house, Dollard's third wife, Alicia, heard alarming stories about her ex-husband. She says, "Pat was seen running naked down the street waving a sword." (Dollard disputes key details of the account, saying, "I was wearing my boxers and I never left my balcony.")

What's not in dispute is that police were called to Dollard's house in the spring of 2004, handcuffed him and took him to the psych unit at Cedars-Sinai for observation. Around this time he began his political conversion. Somewhere between the Roman orgy and the mental ward he became a staunch supporter of George W. Bush.

To show his support for the war in Iraq, he acquired vanity plates for his Hummer that spelled "US WINS." He told friends, "President Bush is the Che Guevara of our time. He's already liberated two countries from tyranny. Those kids walking around in T-shirts with Che on them in a red beret, someday they'll be wearing shirts with Bush's face on them in a cowboy hat."

Paul Schrader, who became close to him during the making of *Auto*

Focus, says, "Pat is a passionista, just like Jimmy Toback or John Milius. These are guys who have never allowed logic or, actually, their own thought process to interfere with the progress of an interesting argument. The danger with Pat comes when he moves into that territory where everything gets blurred, and he becomes the object of his own imagination."

Soon, Dollard was telling people that it was his intention to "personally fight Al Qaeda." As he told me, "If I could, I'd kill jihadis with my bare hands. That's really the goal."

KIDNAPPED

MY FIRST ENCOUNTER WITH DOLLARD takes place in the spring of 2004. We are introduced by a mutual friend who believes Dollard might be interested in representing the film rights of a book I wrote about Marines in Iraq. "He's a little crazy," my friend warns, "but he's Steven Soderbergh's agent. This guy makes movies."

We meet in the offices of Relativity, on the fourth floor of a reassuringly Modernist concrete-and-glass building on Beverly Drive. The reception area is a jumble of cardboard boxes and partially assembled desk components, with phone lines snaking through the mess. It looks like the company is just moving in, rapidly expanding or folding. (As it would turn out, it was doing all three at once.) It's populated by attractive, young, female assistants who seem to be doing nothing when Dollard—still in his Prada-boots-jeans-and-silk-T-shirt phase—strides in, shakes my hand and tells me he'll be right back. He has to go to the bathroom. I can wait in his office down the hall.

Dollard returns twenty minutes later. We sit on black leather chairs around a chrome-and-glass coffee table. He smokes, ashing in a paper cup, and rambles about killing jihadis and his dream of making a pro-war film.

Despite his ease in discussing his travails with drugs, he lowers his voice when discussing his incipient Republicanism. "Dude," he says, "when I have meetings with George Clooney, I'm afraid to drive my Hummer on the lot. I'm afraid if I come out as a Republican it will jeopardize my business relations. How fucked is that, dude? I live in fear of George Clooney."

At the end of our meeting Dollard offers to become my manager. "Seriously, dude, I could get something set up for you like that," he says, clapping his hands to indicate how fast he is going to make a deal.

But Dollard never becomes my manager. In the coming weeks, he breaks several appointments. One day he phones. Rapid, shallow breaths come across the line. "Dude, I am so, so, so fucking sorry for not calling you." No explanation is required, but Dollard offers one anyway. "I was fucking kidnapped."

Dollard claims that members of an AA meeting abducted him after promising his wife to get him sober. Instead, they held him prisoner at a hotel in Palm Springs while plying him with call girls and coke. Meanwhile, they used his credit cards to charter a yacht and a plane for business deals they were conducting. The story is incredible, but Dollard's fourth wife later confirms its essential truth, adding, "I'm sure those AA people started with good intentions, but Pat twisted their intervention around until they thought the right thing to do was buying coke and hiring prostitutes for him."

On Election Day 2004, I receive an urgent phone call from Dollard. I must come to his office immediately. When I show up, two agents from Relativity are on the couch. Dollard paces, making introductions at a rapid clip.

His eyes are glassy. He speaks with those shallow breaths I'd heard when he phoned after the "kidnapping." I get the feeling he may be seriously messed up. The two agents slink from the room.

Dollard reveals why he asked me over. *New York Times* reporter Sharon Waxman, a friend of mine, has completed a book on directors of the nineties, *Rebels on the Back Lot*, for which she interviewed him. He wants to know if he is quoted in it. I tell him Waxman mentioned to me that he is.

Dollard summons an assistant. "I want you to take a letter for me," he tells her. "Send it to all my clients. Tell them I might be quoted in Sharon

Waxman's book. I don't recall what I told her. I was on drugs and I retract my quotes."

"HOLLYWOOD YUPPIE FAGGOT"

THREE WEEKS LATER Dollard leaves for Iraq. He persuaded a former client—a director who had previously won accolades at Sundance for a small, gritty film—to accompany him. The director says that when he first glimpsed Dollard on their way to the airport, "he looked like he was detoxing. He didn't have any proper gear. I knew this would be a disaster."

As it turned out, disaster befell Dollard's partner. Shortly after their arrival, he was severely injured in a Humvee accident and had to be medevaced home. Dollard decided to push ahead on his own. The military embedded him with Marines at a forward operating base about twenty-five miles south of Baghdad in an area troops christened "the Triangle of Death." About two hundred Marines occupied the camp, a dusty crater surrounded by concrete blast barriers and razor wire, which insurgents showered with mortars every other day or so.

Dollard wandered the camp befriending anyone who would talk to him. Sergeant Brandon Welsh, then twenty-two, recalls their first encounter. "He came up and said, 'I'm Pat Dollard from Hollywood.' He talked fast, was all uppity and shit. We thought he was a cokehead."

The troops nicknamed him "Hollywood Yuppie Faggot." Welsh's section leader, Sergeant John Callan, says, "Pat came up with these stories about partying with movie stars and rock stars and models, and the Marines just ate it up."

Dollard pulled the ultimate trump card. Using his sat phone, he called Lucy Walsh, daughter of former Eagles guitarist Joe Walsh. Lucy, a client of Dollard's, had toured as a keyboardist for Ashlee Simpson. Dollard managed to catch her when she was visiting with Simpson. Callan says, "Pat put this kid from West Virginia on the line with Ashlee Simpson. I was told she was like, 'Well, thanks for going out there and getting your dumb ass blown up. I gotta go.'"

As far as the troops were concerned, Dollard was now in. Says Callan, "For the younger guys he became, like, their leader. Nobody from the command ever told us he was attached to us. He just kind of went out for a ride with us one time, then said, 'I'm gonna get my stuff,' and he moved in."

From a First Amendment standpoint, it's to be applauded that commanders never sought to supervise the activities of their embedded reporter from Hollywood. But to Callan, Dollard was a constant headache. "I'm the guy that has to talk to these guys' mothers if one of them gets killed. With Pat around, it was hard to get people to do their jobs."

Dollard claims he was sober when he arrived in Iraq, but he soon fell off the wagon. As one Marine describes it, "One afternoon, on patrol, we bought beer from a hajji." Later, back at the base, he says, "We all got buzzed, and Pat was like, 'Let's get Mohawks.'"

After Dollard shaved the word "DIE" in his chest hair, the night was immortalized in the photo he e-mailed back to friends in Hollywood. By then, Dollard was wearing Marine fatigues. Another reporter at the camp recalls, "I was there when the commander, a lieutenant colonel, saw this clown running around in cammies with a Mohawk. The colonel called over the platoon sergeant of the unit he was with and asked, 'Is that your fucking reporter?'"

Welsh and the others were ordered to shave off their Mohawks. Shortly after the incident, the platoon Welsh and Callan belonged to was ordered to Al-Musayyib, a town of an estimated ten thousand on the Euphrates where a few days earlier insurgents had destroyed one of two main bridges with a truck bomb. Their platoon was sent in to hold the remaining bridge. Dollard accompanied them—fewer than two dozen troops in three light armored vehicles—as they rolled into the center of Al-Musayyib. At sunset, a muezzin sang calls to prayer from loudspeakers on a nearby mosque, and the Marines were ordered on foot patrols through the narrow streets surrounding their position. Dollard joined them.

Unfortunately, the patrol Dollard accompanied encountered an Iraqi selling whiskey. Dollard purchased several bottles and drank himself into a blackout. Callan says, "He was wandering around singing and spewing stupid shit. It was the middle of the night, and he was turning on the light to his camera to film us, putting a spotlight on us in the middle of our security patrols."

Sergeant Brandon Wong, another Marine in the unit, who was then twenty-two, says, "When Pat first showed up in Iraq he was all, like, he's an alcoholic and can't drink.

"We saw what he meant that night. He was fucking trashed. Pat ran up to a mosque and ripped the fucking sign off it"—a cloth banner with hand-painted Arabic on it. Later that night, Wong says, "a patrol of Humvees was driving by and I look and there's Pat just standing in the middle of the fucking road trying to wave them through, like he's directing traffic."

The Marines returned from their patrol before dawn and were allotted a couple of hours to sleep. Dollard continued babbling and singing—a sort of shanty that went, as Callan recalls, "'Three bottles of whiskey and a couple of hajji sodas and just got shitty.'"

The antics pushed Wong to the breaking point. "I could not fucking sleep because of his ass," he says. "I flipped out on him." Wong, who later became friends with Dollard, regrets what happened next. "I pulled my gun on him. I put it to his head and told him he'd better shut the fuck up or I would pull the trigger." Wong adds, "It's fucked up to say now, but I really didn't care if he lived or died."

Other Marines talked Wong out of shooting Dollard. Callan wasn't told about Wong's threat on Dollard's life until the next day. He recalls, "When I heard about it, I said, 'You should have just shot him.'"

The following morning Dollard returned to the main base with another unit, while Callan's platoon remained in Al-Musayyib. At about noon, a mob gathered in front of the mosque whose banner Dollard had stolen as the imam delivered an angry denunciation of the American occupiers. Soon, the Marines came under fire from gunmen around the mosque. "Our whole platoon opened up on that side of the city," says a Marine. "We could never prove Pat is the one who caused it, but that's what we thought started it."

No Marines were injured in the engagement. Among some, affection for Dollard actually grew. "It wouldn't make sense to anyone who wasn't there," says Welsh, "but Pat brought this civilian craziness to our lives. He made being in Iraq fun."

Among troops, Dollard's next stunt gave him almost mythic status as a wild man. For several weeks an urban legend circulated on the base that a derelict former palace beyond their perimeter was a whorehouse. Marines talked of seeing attractive young women, dressed in provocative clothes and makeup, coming and going from it. But given the abductions and beheadings meted out to unaccompanied Westerners, no one dared leave their fortified perimeter to investigate—until Dollard informed them that he was going out alone to search for the alleged whorehouse.

According to Wong, he and other young Marines decided to help. "We gave him a pistol and a grenade and showed him how to work the shit. We told him, 'If you start shooting, we'll come running after you,' but, you know, we weren't allowed to leave the patrol base."

As Marines watched from the base, Dollard walked alone into the city. He says all he found in the shattered palace was a family living in the rubble. Walking to the rear of the building, he found a hole blasted through the back wall, which offered a view into the city, where something caught his eye. "It was like this blue sign. I don't remember if there was a crescent on it or not," Dollard says, "but something about it said 'pharmacy' to me."

He set off into the city toward the blue sign. His instincts proved correct. The shop with the sign was a pharmacy, where Dollard lived out a drug addict's dream. Armed, dressed in American military attire, he entered the shop to take anything he wanted. "The man at the counter just looked at me," Dollard says. "I showed my weapons and pointed at the stuff on the shelves. The man started speaking in Arabic, but I heard the word 'analgesics.' I knew that was the shit I wanted."

Dollard left with several bottles of liquid Valium and other substances he wasn't quite sure of. "I never pointed my gun at the guy," he explains. "But it was robbery at gunpoint by implication."

Dollard at one point claimed that his dealer in L.A. sent him an unsolicited care package of coke through military mail. Later, he retracts this story and denies robbing a pharmacy of Valium. But several Marines I interview confirm that Dollard shared liquid Valium and other substances with men in the unit, and say he told them they were legally acquired in Iraq. Two Marines claim to have done rails of coke provided by Dollard on top of their armored vehicle after their tour of duty on the way back to Kuwait. "The shit we got into with Pat was crazy," says one.

Dollard himself contradicts one of his retractions later while showing me raw footage he shot. "You can tell we're all on Valium," he says, "because everyone is heavy-tongued when we talk."

Hours of tape Dollard has shown me reveal an embedded reporter verging out of control. In one sequence, filmed at a checkpoint where Marines are stopping civilian cars, Dollard cuts in front of the Marines to accost the occupants. A Marine shouts at the driver, "You got any bombs, dickface? Any booms? Any women?"

Dollard backs away, laughing, then shouts to nearby Marines, "Will you fucking kill something while I am here?"

Dollard argues that his reckless behavior was calculated to get the Marines to loosen up in front of his camera. Leaving aside whatever damage he did to the combat effectiveness of the unit by distributing drugs, as well as the harm he did to American-Iraqi relations by vandalizing a mosque and robbing a drugstore while dressed as a U.S. soldier, his footage from Iraq stands as a peculiar and often compelling record of war.

Most documentaries emerging from Iraq, no matter how scrupulously their makers strive to be neutral, have the feel of an adult presence, an intermediary at the controls. In Dollard's work, there is no filter. It's not the work of a grown-up. There's no authority interpreting how the young troops ought to feel about their experiences. It's the kind of film a nineteen- or twenty-year-old Marine would make to show his buddies. It captures the raw experience of a combat zone about as well as anything I have seen— short of actually going to a combat zone. No small part of the loyalty Dollard engenders among young Marines stems from what they see as the honesty of his work. "No one else out there I know of," says Wong, "has gone as far as Pat to show people what our lives are like."

There are some Marines Dollard never won over. "His presence endangered lives," says Callan. "I have no doubt that he's insane."

ESCAPE AND EVASION

DOLLARD RETURNED TO L.A. in March 2005 to find that his business and personal affairs had imploded. Relativity was in the process of ousting him. An ex–business partner in an unrelated venture was seeking a $700,000 judgment against him. His fourth wife, Megan, had filed for divorce. Even worse, the three most influential women in his life—Megan, Alicia and his mother—had sided together, like a freak alignment of stars, in a legal action to deny him custody of his daughter. His Porsche and Range Rover were repossessed. Megan sold their furniture to pay bills. Dollard still had his Hummer, but a thief stole his "US WINS" vanity plates.

Dollard dealt with everything by going on a massive binge, living alone in the empty Hollywood Hills home. The four-story house was built into the side of a cliff, with panoramic views, an open steel-cage elevator running through its center, and walls adorned with his collections (not yet sold off) of African art, swords and battle helmets. Soon he was living like a bum. The electricity was turned off. He slept on a mattress on the floor of a bathroom.

In mid-April, when an agent colleague showed up at his house to check on him, she found the front door open. The place was filled with trash. It smelled. As she entered the kitchen, Dollard stumbled in, so filthy she initially thought he was a homeless man. Dollard lunged and threatened, "I'm going to fucking kill you."

She fled and called the LAPD, who showed up in force. "They had shotguns out," she says. "I was terrified they were going to kill him."

Dollard left peacefully, but given his proximity to neighbors like Bill Condon, Russell Crowe's agent Bill Freeman, and James Wilder, his arrest was a bizarre industry event. "Everyone came out to see what was going on, and there was Pat being taken away in handcuffs," says Dollard's colleague. "It was one of the most traumatic experiences of my life."

No criminal charges were filed. Police deposited him at the Los Angeles County/USC Medical Center for psychiatric evaluation. Dollard describes the place as a "ghetto psych ward full of true nut jobs and power-mad nurses." They tied him down and shot him full of Ativan. He was held for three days and released.

Dollard returned to his home and picked up where he'd left off. Two of the Marines he'd befriended in Iraq, Welsh and Wong, flew out to L.A. to visit. Dollard was still wearing his hospital bracelet, doing lines and down-ing jug vodka when his visitors showed up.

"He was obliterated," says Welsh. "At first, we thought it was normal because that's what everybody does when they come back from Iraq. But then one day we're driving his truck down the freeway, and he's so fucking yea-yoed out he's like speaking in tongues in the backseat. Then he tries climbing out the window. We ended up beating the shit out of him just to hold him down."

As the Marines left, Dollard promised them he'd taper down. Shortly thereafter, someone—Dollard still doesn't know who—again called the cops. This time Dollard, on foot, led police on a pursuit through the hills. Even his landlord, James Wilder, became involved, grabbing a stick and thrashing the bushes in an attempt to corner Dollard. But Dollard evaded capture. He crawled into a hole and hid out Saddam-style through the night. "In my ability to run and find cover, my experience in Iraq really paid off," Dollard would later tell me. "It's what the Marines call 'E and E,' escape and evasion."

By May, Dollard was ready to call it quits. He voluntarily entered Impact House, a live-in, highly regimented rehab in Pasadena.

ALWAYS THE TRUTH

IN EARLY JUNE 2005, I see Dollard after his departure from Impact House. Friends have helped him move into an apartment on Sunset Boulevard, where he is staging a comeback. Outside his window the dome of the ArcLight Cinemas appears to be melting in a liquid sunset. Inside, the air-conditioning blasts. It's on because Dollard actually abhors cigarettes: the smell, the taste, the ruinous effects on the lungs—everything about cigarettes, except, of course, smoking them. He paces beneath the ceiling vents, chain-smoking and discussing his newfound sobriety. "I had this realization about my drug use," he tells me. "Until my last binge, I held on to the idea that I could just drop out for a day or two and do drugs. I would have this James Bond fantasy where I'm in, like, the Mondrian [hotel], drinking martinis and shit with beautiful women, then having, like, great coked-out sex." He laughs. "But I always seem to end up, like, homeless within a matter of hours."

Dollard has acquired his new, post-agent look: crew cut, Marine Corps fatigues, the haggard, unshaven face. The cataract is just starting to appear over his right eye. He looks wrecked, but Dollard insists he has never felt better, saying, "I wasted twenty years of my life on the narcotic of being a Hollywood agent. Iraq gave me a shot at redemption, but I didn't realize it, dude, until it was almost too late."

Dollard is full of new morality. "Ultimately, you realize that the purpose of life isn't just to take from it whatever you can get," he says, bending over the stove to light another cigarette on the gas flame. "You can't spend your life as a sexual libertine and end up being at peace." He walks up to me and points to my chest. "We were not just born to be sexual pirates."

I ask if he is involved in outpatient therapy or going to AA meetings. "I've just been through a war," he says. "How can I sit around listening to a bunch of grown men whine about their fucked-up childhoods? I'm part of something bigger than myself—the war, the conservative cause. I can't get loaded anymore."

Dollard shares a profound discovery he's recently made. "I'm a warrior, dude. I am of the class of people whose role has been genetically determined to be protectors. My role is to fight the battle against Islamic fundamentalist fascism."

There are people in Dollard's life who believe he's gone completely out of his mind. His mother believes that at a minimum he may be bipolar. His third wife, Alicia, offers a blunter assessment: "I think he brain-damaged himself in one of those last drug runs."

Exhibit A in her argument that he has gone mad is Dollard's recent announcement that he is terminating his relationship with Soderbergh. "Pat owned ten percent of Steven Soderbergh, and he goes and fires him," Alicia says. "How crazy is that?"

Dollard tells me, "I'm a director now. A director can't represent a director."

His future lies in 243 hourlong videocassettes piled on the floor in the corner. There is no furniture, just wall-to-wall white carpet and a sleeping bag. Dollard can't afford a computer yet on which to edit his tapes. What keeps him motivated is a tattered Iraqi flag tacked to the wall, signed by Marines and inscribed, "Always the truth." I later ask Captain Brian Iglesias, who signed the flag, about the inscription. He answers, "'Always the truth,' because the truth is what Pat Dollard champions."

Most people in Dollard's life have written him off. Yet for an industry where relationships are reputed to be calculated solely on the basis of self-interest, loyalists remain, from Soderbergh—who helped pay for Dollard's stay at rehab—to William Morris's Mike Simpson. (After my visit, Simpson will give Dollard an editing system.) Before moving into his apartment, Dollard couch-surfed at the Bel Air home of Erik Hyman, an entertainment lawyer and the partner of photographer Herb Ritts until his death, in 2002. Explaining his surprising bond with Dollard, Hyman says, "Our friendship transcends whatever nuttiness he's involved in at the moment. After Herb died, Pat showed up for me. He wouldn't let me be alone. He is an extremely caring friend."

Dollard argues that those most critical of his career abandonment are either his ex-wives and mother, who depend on him financially, or those whose "empty lives making crap films" he now rejects. "People expect me to regret going to Iraq, because I lost everything," he says. "What's really going on here is I left the whorehouse. The people who stayed behind are the ones saying I'm a psychopath. Why? Because I rejected being a self-centered, moneygrubbing pig, which is what you are supposed to be in this town if you want to be considered sane."

Dollard's mother believes that her son is a near genius "at taking any information and transferring it into self-serving data." A case in point is his argument that his recent trips to area mental wards prove his mental health is solid. "Psychiatrists checked me out. If I were truly pathological, they never would have released me," he says, accidentally banging his cigarette against the side of his face. Sparks fly from his smoldering whiskers. "I have often asked myself the question 'Am I a psychopath?' But it just doesn't add up. I am one of the sanest people I know."

Dollard sucks mightily on his mangled cigarette. The aroma of burned hair lingers. "The only exception is, if you fill me with drugs and alcohol, I do become insane. I concede that point."

I ask him whether there is any difference in his thought process when he's sober or on drugs. Dollard laughs. "None. When I'm on drugs, the same garbage comes out of my mouth, only it's amplified."

THE PITCH

LATE AUGUST 2005. Pat Dollard is bombing down Sunset Boulevard at the wheel of his new, gray Hummer, on his way to a meeting at William Morris. He handles the massive vehicle with about as much caution as the average eleven-year-old at the wheel of a carnival bumper car. "I love the Hummer," he says, weaving through the lanes. "It's like driving your fucking living room from your Barcalounger."

Sober for nearly 120 days now, Dollard's comeback is well under way. He has created a ninety-minute rough cut of his documentary, now titled *Young Americans*. Both Soderbergh and Simpson viewed it in his apartment and, as they say in Hollywood, "went crazy." Soderbergh has offered to help arrange distribution. Simpson has scheduled a screening at William Morris this morning at eleven, with the idea that the agency that once fired Dollard will take him on as a client.

A couple of weeks ago, Dollard received an unexpected cash windfall. Hence, the new Hummer, including a new set of "US WINS" plates. His military fatigues—what he now refers to as his "Travis Bickle uniform"—are neatly pressed. His hair is slicked flat on his head, and he is clean-shaven.

Three days a week he's been training in krav maga, Israeli martial arts. "I have to get my body up to the level my mind is at," he says. "When I was in Iraq, I learned all this will-to-power shit. I could kill now."

The exception to his new, squared-away life is his failure to obtain treatment for the cataract clotting his right eye—a result of Dollard's fear of doctors and hospitals. Driving partially blind has become a sort of experiment. Cutting recklessly through traffic, Dollard laughs. "I'm just a puppet in the hands of God, dude," he says, repeating a saying he picked up at an AA meeting.

Nowhere is God's grace more evident than in Dollard's resurrection in Hollywood. People who long ago wrote him off have begun to pop out of the woodwork. In the past few days, even one of the most powerful men in town, ICM's chairman, Jeff Berg, has been asking him for a chance to see *Young Americans*.

"Berg's a sensitive matter," Dollard says, sounding oddly calculating—more like an agent than I am accustomed to hearing. "I can't blow him off, but I have an obligation to show it to Mike Simpson first."

"How do you know Berg?" I ask.

"Business," Dollard says. "We crawled through the slime together." (Dollard later explains that Berg once provided him with helpful advice on a deal.)

Outside William Morris, Dollard is seized by a fit of self-objectivity. He admits to qualms about involving an old, loyal friend like Simpson in his current scheme. "People who get involved with me tend to end up feeling that they've been put through the wringer at some point," he says. "Oh, well. What the fuck."

Inside the lobby, receptionists do double takes as he approaches their desk and announces himself. God only knows what they make of him. He's too old to be a recent vet, but his digital camouflage trousers, with their futuristic abstract pattern, have only recently become standard issue. Perhaps they think he's a homeless man from the future.

An assistant escorts us to a screening room on the fourth floor. Mike Simpson, over six feet tall, lanky and fair-haired, approaches in the hall, grinning. In his early fifties and dressed in his regulation William Morris blue suit, Simpson looks more like a small-town banker than an industry player. He is originally from Texas, and his voice retains a rural twang. Patting Dollard's shoulder, Simpson seems slightly in awe of him, like the strait-laced kid in high school who secretly yearns to be accepted by the delinquents.

To help evaluate the potential of Dollard's film, Simpson has invited fellow agent John Ferriter to the screening. Simpson believes the agency ought to sell *Young Americans* as a hybrid documentary/reality-TV series, for which Dollard's rough cut would be a pilot.

When I ask Simpson if he's at all worried about representing Dollard, whose drug lunacies are a known quantity, he replies, "What we look at is the success of films like *Fahrenheit 9/11* and the ability to go into that territory with Pat's very different point of view. As far as his personal issues, this is the entertainment business. It's not banking."

John Ferriter enters the room, dressed in a baggy black suit like the hit men from *Pulp Fiction*—a look that has never gone out of style among some agents. In his early thirties, Ferriter has earned a reputation as one of Hollywood's top reality-TV agents. As they make introductions, Ferriter drops his business card (Senior Vice President, Worldwide Head of Non-Scripted Television) on the table, then flips it like a blackjack dealer. Dollard appears momentarily unsure of himself. He tries shaking Ferriter's hand, but fails to connect on the first pass.

"How are you?" Ferriter asks.

"Fine, good," Dollard says, sitting down.

"You just got back from Iraq?"

"A few months ago."

"Are you OK?" Ferriter leans closer to Dollard.

"Fucking fine." Dollard fidgets.

"I mean, how are you doing?" Ferriter radiates deep concern.

"Dude, I didn't fucking come here for fucking psychotherapy," Dollard says.

(Dollard later tells me, "It's important to show your agent he's just the fucking cleaning lady. Ferriter obviously has good agent training. He didn't even act insulted when I insulted him.")

Simpson, watching from the back, laughs quietly.

Dollard feeds his DVD into the player by the TV at the head of the conference table. Ferriter sits about four feet from the TV screen, shaking his foot, tugging at his cuffs, running his hand through his longish black hair. When the "Blood for Blood" song begins to blast, Ferriter seems to relax, bopping his head to the rhythm. At about the twenty-minute mark, he stands and hits the stop button.

"Great, great," Ferriter says. "I totally get it."

"Is that all you want to see?" Dollard asks.

"This is going to be like *The Aristocrats*," Ferriter says. "Every college kid in America is going to want to see this. It's like Tom Green, Jackass in a war zone. And it's real."

Ferriter asks Dollard the most important question. "Can we get Steven [Soderbergh] to come in the room with us?"

"Yeah," Dollard says.

Ferriter and Simpson discuss possible buyers, then a price. "What do you think?" Ferriter asks. "Eight to ten million?"

"Sounds about right to me," Simpson says.

Ferriter tells Dollard to shorten the rough cut at future screenings. "This is like a drug. You've got to give them just a little bit, so they want more."

A few minutes later, as we emerge into the brightness of the street, Dollard seems amazed Ferriter went for it. "He didn't even watch it. The guy was twitching the whole time." Dollard is incredulous. "He bought it on a vibe and the fact I can bring Steven Soderbergh into the room with me."

Dollard turns to the William Morris sign on the building. "This is the place that fired me. Now I'm the fucking getting-my-ass-licked client. How cool is that?"

IN THE ROOM WITH SODERBERGH

LATER THAT AFTERNOON, Dollard has an appointment with Soderbergh on the Paramount lot to deliver a copy of *Young Americans*. Soderbergh is then flying to Italy, where he plans to hand-deliver the film to entrepreneur and HDNet founder Mark Cuban at the Venice Film Festival.

Bouncing through traffic on his way to the meeting, Dollard is on a high, dreaming of the millions he stands to make, which has made him forgetful of the lecture on sexual continence he delivered weeks earlier. "Once I get some production money, this is my M.O.," Dollard says. "Hire a hot, twenty-one-year-old assistant, get her to do all my shit—paying bills, laundry—then I start banging her. Serious, dude. I had one in the nineties I literally trained to lick my ass. She was so good I even took her on a fancy vacation abroad once. Two weeks. But all we did was stay in the hotel room so she could lick my ass."

Soderbergh's office is off Gower, where he is in preproduction for *The Good German*. Soderbergh enters the reception area wearing jeans and heavy black shoes that look as if they have paint spattered on them. He greets Dollard with a quiet hello. Like Simpson, Soderbergh is genuinely enthusiastic about Dollard's project. He believes *Young Americans* transcends Dollard's political message and is simply "riveting." He tells me, "I knew Pat was going to come back with something pure. I believe in Pat's sense of what's compelling."

Soderbergh works from a drab office fairly typical of those on studio back lots. He and Dollard sit opposite each other on threadbare lounge chairs. Soderbergh has often spoken of his need for anonymity in order to function as an artist—"So I can eavesdrop, sit in an airport behind somebody and listen to their conversation, spy on people and hear stuff in undiluted form." The drive for self-effacement seems to guide his social interaction as well.

Soderbergh's presence in the room is like this: he arranges his body on the chair, then somehow astrally projects himself into a corner of the ceiling to watch himself interacting with his guests. To a guest, being seated across from Soderbergh is like sitting in front of a two-way mirror. You know someone is there, but you can't quite make him out, just shadows and indecipherable movements. A throat clears. A chair scrapes. Dollard fidgets nervously, as if he's straining to rein in his normal impulses to do and say the wrong things. He appears paralyzed.

Soderbergh breaks the ice: "Did you bring the DVD?" His voice is as lively as a prerecorded message.

It turns out Dollard had a change of heart. He doesn't want Mark Cuban to have it. He wants Cuban to see it, but he doesn't trust him to possess it. "It's like laying my dick out," Dollard tells Soderbergh. "This guy could be in a hotel and might lose it."

Soderbergh reveals the faintest annoyance: "Pat, we should move fast on this."

"I'll fly to New York or something, and show it to him there," Dollard says.

Soderbergh shakes his head.

"We'll work something out." Dollard grins, as if oddly satisfied to have put a spanner in the works. I am seated between Dollard and Soderbergh, what would be the therapist's position if they were a couple in need of help, which they in fact are. I ask Soderbergh if he was surprised when he found out Dollard had gone to Iraq.

"No," Soderbergh says, "I've known him a long time. When you get a call from Pat you never know what to expect. It could be 'I just got married,' 'I'm making a new film,' 'I'm in Mexico getting an operation.' Pat is sort of an adrenaline junkie."

Dollard leans around me to bicker with Soderbergh. "I have no history of being the adrenaline junkie, an adventurer, blood-fucking-thirsty, or anything like that," he says.

"I'm saying you were looking for a change in your life," Soderbergh says.

"I didn't change intentionally by going to Iraq," Dollard argues. "It wasn't so much this noble thing where I was trying to change myself."

Soderbergh measures his words carefully. "I think you had created a circumstance last fall in which, if there was ever a time when going to Iraq would seem like an appealing thing, that was the time."

"It's really easy to say that," Dollard says, "but I was not going to go to Iraq and risk my life just to not deal with some hassles. It's almost insulting to, like, fucking say that."

Soderbergh sticks to his point. "Do you think if you'd been totally happy and things were great, would you still have gone to Iraq?"

"There was no fucking way I was running away." Dollard gives a feeble wave of his hand, running out of steam. "That's my argument and whatever."

Soderbergh turns to me, now animated. "When you look at Pat's narrative, which I think for Pat is probably really exciting, for a lot of the supporting people it can be crazy."

It's an odd reversal that he, the star director, would cast himself in the supporting role with his agent. I ask Soderbergh about his friendship with Dollard, and he says, "The formative years of our relationship were strange because we were really young"—Soderbergh twenty-three and Dollard twenty-two when they first met. "We had nothing in common with people in Hollywood," Soderbergh says, "no interest in the high school aspects of the social life in Hollywood."

Dollard says, "We'd just sit around fucking talking about chicks."

"Yeah, we would," Soderbergh says, laughing. "We'd swap stories about fucking chicks." Soderbergh corrects himself. "I don't mean fucking chicks. I mean . . ."

"Steven, we would talk about fucking chicks," Dollard insists.

Soderbergh leans closer to me. "I was just so close to Pat's family. And of course because of the horrible event that happened, it stepped up the relationship with Pat several levels. It made us much closer."

Dollard twists in his chair. The subject of his sister's death makes him uncomfortable. He says, "Let's talk about whatever, dude."

Soderbergh ignores Dollard. He says, "There are certain people who have an integrity, whether you can articulate it or not." He pauses. "I guess I fall back to the word 'soul' for lack of a better term. It's just a feeling. You meet them and you have an instantaneous reaction to them. It's certainly the reaction I had when I met Ann."

ANN

IT WAS PAT DOLLARD'S great fortune and misfortune to have Ann as his sister. She was so good, when people talk about her, you wonder if canonization would do her justice. Robert Kennedy, Jr., says, "She was beautiful and she was charming and you couldn't meet her without loving her." Larry Jackson, the president of Northern Arts Entertainment and former executive VP of acquisitions and coproductions at Miramax, says, "There was something magical about Ann. She had such a rosy expectation of what the world could become."

No small part of Ann's expectations were poured into her little brother. Their mother, Eva, says, "Ann was probably more of a mother figure to Pat than I was." Both Ann and Eva believed Pat would be the first in the family to attend college. After he dashed those hopes by dropping out of high school, Ann continued to try to guide him until finally hiring him as her assistant at Leading Artists.

Initially, Dollard cleaned up his act. Other agents nicknamed him "Beaver Cleaver." Ann began grooming him to become an agent, but Dollard began screwing off on the job. On the last workday before the Fourth of July weekend in 1988, Ann fired him. Dollard claims he had already decided he didn't want to be an agent and was relieved.

Two days later, Ann went horseback riding with friends and fell while crossing a field. Though it was a relatively minor fall, Ann wasn't wearing a helmet and her brain stem was crushed. She lingered for two days in the hospital before being removed from life support. Scott Kramer, a producer and close friend, arrived at the hospital about the same time as Dollard. "Pat literally couldn't bear to see her," Kramer recalls. "He began hitting his head on the wall to the point where we had to grab him and hold him down and take him out of the hospital."

Dollard says, "I was blown apart by the horror. I'll never forget trying to see Ann's face and looking down at these two massive purple lumps of flesh sticking out like eggs where her eyes were supposed to be. For years after, if I saw a hospital I would start crying."

Her death was no less mourned in Hollywood. Ann's memorial service, held at the Wilshire Ebell Theatre, became an industry event, drawing more than seven hundred people. Julia Phillips described the gathering in her 1991 book *You'll Never Eat Lunch in This Town Again* as "all of young Hollywood looking stricken." Stephen Stills sang, and eulogies were delivered by filmmaker Lionel Chetwynd and Robert Kennedy, Jr., who later held a private ceremony with Ann's mother, Eva, at his home in Mount Kisco, New York, where they spread her ashes.

Among Ann's clients, Steven Soderbergh was one of the closest to her. When they met, Soderbergh was twenty-two and had just finished directing his Grammy-nominated documentary about the band Yes, but a couple years later he was drifting, uncertain of his next move. Their meeting wasn't so much a typical agent-client encounter as the start of an intense creative collaboration. Ann encouraged Soderbergh to continue work on his own scripts. Scott Kramer says, "Ann believed in Steven in such a way that it filled him." Production on *Sex, Lies, and Videotape* was about to begin when she died.

Soderbergh was devastated. "The idea of replacing Ann was something I couldn't contemplate," he says. He and a few of Ann's other clients decided to ask Pat to fill her shoes, which, Soderbergh explains, "felt like a way to process and transcend the awful thing that had happened." He approached Dollard and told him, "I want you to be my agent. If you won't be my agent, I just won't have an agent, because I can't."

"My family was ripped apart by Ann's death," says Dollard. "I felt like I had to take her job, to hold it together." At the time of her death, Ann hadn't yet come into her own as an agent. Had she lived another year, it would have been a different story.

In addition to Soderbergh, clients on her list such as screenwriters Michael Blake (*Dances with Wolves*) and Scott Frank (*Out of Sight, The Interpreter*) became major successes shortly after her death.

Inheriting most of Ann's list, Dollard had assumed his sister's life (much as the protagonist of his favorite film, Barry Lyndon, had risen by assuming the life of a deceased nobleman), and though he loved the trappings of success and power that came with it, he says it filled him with self-loathing. "I had this idea that I was going to be a subversive inside the system and do great things," he says. "But when they said, 'OK, you're Steven Soderbergh's agent'—and suddenly Steven becomes the biggest filmmaker in the world in terms of the hype—all my greed and power lust and alcoholism kicked in." He adds, "It's like I went to hell when I became an agent, and I've been trying to fight my way out ever since."

THE DARK ARTS

A DAY AFTER HIS MEETING at William Morris, Dollard sits across from me at Kabuki, a restaurant near his apartment, eating a celebratory meal of ribs and flan, while unloading on his former profession. All the clichés are true, he tells me: Agents are "assholes, these morons who have an entirely superior attitude. They believe that they are better than everybody else because they think they've pulled off this scam where they're doing the coolest thing in the world."

Though Dollard is loud and obnoxious in most matters, when it comes to discussing the dark Hollywood arts he practiced as an agent, he looks over his shoulders, as if expecting a squad of agent hit men to show up in their black suits, armed with bland smiles and Uzis. Leaning forward, he claims that, as much as he embraced every possible excess during his rise to the top, the life appalled him. "There was just so much fucking money and whores and power that people actually got bored with it," he says. "An agent I worked with—I guess he was bored out of his fucking mind—he trained his fucking Chihuahua to lick his balls and would have people come into his office to watch."

He continues: "There was another guy I worked with"—Dollard names a prominent manager—"who was such a pathological liar they did a whole intervention, like a 12-step thing on him to get him to stop lying, hired fucking psychiatrists and brought, like, his mother and wife in to confront him in his office."

What troubles Dollard the most about his past as an agent were the business practices. "A lot of what we did was just your basic nasty, lying, backstabbing stuff that's part of the normal business world," he says. "But some of what we did, it's like *The Firm*, like overbilling." He explains that during the heyday of the speculative-script market, in the nineties, a form of overbilling commonly perpetrated against clients was cutting side deals with producers for secret commissions. He says, "You're talking about, like, white-collar crime here—virtually—about some of this stuff."

He adds, "I was taught when I was a kid that you're supposed to grow up and contribute to society and be a good person. No kid thinks, When I grow up, I want to fuck other people." He laughs. "I always used to tell myself it's all going to be worth it because eventually I'm going to make good films."

THE DELIVERY DUDE

A FEW DAYS LATER Dollard phones with good news. One of the Marines from *Young Americans* is visiting him. Sergeant Brandon Welsh greets me at the door of Dollard's apartment. Dressed in jeans and a knit surf shirt, Welsh is compactly built and fair-haired, with a gravity to him that seems at odds with his boyish smile.

Dollard saunters in, looking unusually relaxed. His apartment has been transformed. There's an Oriental rug, velvet couches, African art on the walls and a six-foot-tall Buddha statue by the entry—all purchased out of hock with his recent cash windfall. Dollard drops onto a velvet chaise.

"Doesn't he look good?" Welsh asks. He obviously cares a great deal for Dollard. Welsh is also an ardent supporter of Dollard's film on the grounds that "he's the only one in the media telling my story."

For Welsh the war is a deeply personal matter. Friends of his died in Iraq. Welsh nearly died. And he believes the fatal patrols undertaken by his unit helped stabilize the area and will in the long run improve the lives of Iraqis. Still, terrible things, which trouble him today, did happen. He tells me of one instance when his unit came under fire and, in the confusion that followed, Marines may have ended up killing innocent civilians. Welsh shakes his head. "It was so fucked up."

"Welsh, you're a killer, and that's a good thing," Dollard says, walking up behind him and gesturing toward him like he is an exhibit in a science project. "Earlier today Welsh was having anxiety about killing and I had to tell him, 'Look, dude, appropriate killing is one of the most sacred and noble and greatest things to go on in the world. The world cannot survive without killing. Good killing is required to hold society together and to protect it. This involves nobility and sacrifice. It's about subsuming the self to the whole.' Welsh volunteered to kill on behalf of our society. That is a good, noble thing."

I point out that Welsh's anxiety was about killing innocent people.

"Chaotic and terrible and tragic things are just part and parcel of the natural laws of war," Dollard says, pacing. "War is its own state of being. It's like another planet, Planet War. And the people who live on Planet Peace read about the terrible things that happen on Planet War—friendly fire, innocents killed—and are shocked. They naturally say we need to punish these boys"—Dollard points to Welsh—"because they're not playing by the rules of civilization. The point is these are two worlds, each with their own set of natural laws. And they just don't get it. Everything that's happening in Iraq is completely in line with the rules-of-war state."

Welsh runs his hands through his hair, worn out by Dollard's frenetic arguing. "I'm fucking hungry," Welsh says. "You said we were going to get takeout."

"We can't call on my phone," Dollard says. "You've got to make the fucking call on your fucking phone."

Dollard explains the problem: His favorite delivery place is a nearby Brazilian restaurant, but a couple of nights ago he had a run-in with the delivery dude. Dollard ordered a meal, and the delivery dude showed up more than an hour late. Dollard demanded the delivery dude give him his chocolate cake for free, but he refused. Dollard sent him packing. He fears the restaurant won't deliver to his address. The plan is for Welsh to have the food delivered to the security guard in the lobby.

But Welsh runs into an unforeseen glitch. The woman taking our order doesn't understand English very well. He tells her we are at the building on the corner of Sunset and Vine, but she doesn't understand. Welsh holds the phone up. We hear the heavily accented voice of the woman on the other end. "Vane?" she asks. "Where is Vane Street?"

Dollard grabs the phone and shouts, "Vine, you dumb bitch!" He throws the phone across the room. Welsh collapses, laughing. Dollard broods. "There are all these people in this town I've been waiting to get back at. It's going to start now."

Dollard suggests the three of us go to the restaurant, hide out in the parking lot until closing time, and fuck up the delivery dude. "This whole war started with him," Dollard says. "Fucking delivery dude was two hours late and wouldn't comp me with a four-dollar slice of chocolate cake on a fifty-dollar order."

Welsh punches his fist into the palm of his hand. "I'm down."

Dollard rushes to the front door, then hesitates. "The thing is, this restaurant has gotten me through so many binges."

They decide not to fuck up the delivery dude, and instead we go to the 101 Coffee Shop. Welsh leaves the next day.

AMERICAN JIHADI

IN MID-SEPTEMBER, Dollard screens *Young Americans* for Bob Greenblatt, the president of entertainment for Showtime. Afterward, Dollard leaves a message for me: "Hey. Dude. They fucking loved it, man. I was fucking shocked. They watched the whole thing. First thing out of Greenblatt's mouth: 'These Marines are movie stars!'"

Hours later Dollard evidently begins to crash from his emotional high. He leaves a string of messages with nothing but dead air before he finally says, *"Dude, I'm just . . . I'm so fucking lonely."*

The next day I visit. He greets me at the door drinking root beer and ice cream from an enormous bowl. "You want a root-beer float?" he asks, nodding toward a quart of Häagen-Dazs vanilla melting on the counter. Dollard admits last night was a little rough. After the fantastic news from Showtime, he learned of a setback in his custody battle for his daughter. Dollard is particularly incensed that his ex-wife Alicia has been taking their daughter to Robert Evans's house. Dollard fumes, "Alicia tells me that Bob bought a fucking bicycle for her." (Evans recalls Alicia bringing her daughter to his home a few times, but laughs at the suggestion he bought her a bicycle.)

He stayed up all night writing letters to a therapist and a lawyer involved in his custody battle. Dollard insists I read some of these communications. He says, "You will uncover the fact that I am not a paranoid schizophrenic about all of these people. But I am right. They are all psychopaths."

I have scarcely digested one of these letters when Dollard leads me into the editing room to reveal his next inspiration. The editing system is set up against the back wall of the bedroom. Along the opposite wall is a child's bed, with an ornate iron frame and a ruffled cover, which was his daughter's in his old home and is set up for a visit from her that never happens. I sit on the bed as Dollard plays jihadi videos: YouTube-quality clips made by insurgents to showcase attacks on Americans, beheadings and other violent doings. Designed to recruit young men into the insurgency, many are set to jihadi hip-hop. Watching them, Dollard becomes outraged (even as I am struck by how similar they are to his own film). "This is the Islamofascist death machine at work," he says. "This is the breath of Darth Vader."

Dollard has long conceived of his film as a work of guerrilla cinema, a sort of American version of a jihad video to galvanize the domestic audience. But recently the videos have inspired him further. Dollard wants to launch an anti-jihadi action cell in the West. He explains, "This will be an educational, activism and political organization dedicated to waging final war on modern jihadism. There will be a manifesto, guides for maintaining political pressure in favor of the overthrow of the Syrian and Iranian governments. Aggressive militarism in support of these goals will generally be encouraged, dependent on current conditions within the target nations and regimes."

He tells me that he has already registered the domain name, jihadikiller .com, then shows me a note to his business manager, Evan Bell (whose other clients include Steven Soderbergh and Bill O'Reilly), telling him to incorporate a business named Jihadi Killer, Inc.

(Dollard forwards me the e-mail from Bell responding to his request: "Pat you sure you want this name? I fear extra, extra scrutiny towards the LLC & everybody & everything associated with it. Pat, we are in uncertain times. Really don't think a name like that would have any kind of positive (except shock value) impact. I do think it is a mistake.")

I leave at about ten as a delivery guy shows up from a corner store with cigarettes and more root beer and vanilla ice cream. "You sure you don't want a root-beer float?" Dollard asks, grabbing his bowl from the sink.

THE BUDDY SYSTEM

A FEW DAYS LATER, Dollard calls, sounding rattled, to tell me that the night before "the Devil was back." Driving alone in Hollywood, he was seized by a powerful urge to get loaded. Though he resisted, he says that since then he's "just felt literally sick."

Dollard assures me he's taken steps to maintain his sobriety. He's having a young man he met in rehab move in with him. "I'm doing it just like the Marines," he says. "I'm going on the buddy system."

Dollard describes his new roommate as a "metrosexual gangbanger." Josiah Hernandez is twenty-two and slight of stature, about five-two, but with eyes so large his face looks like that of an anime character. His dark hair is fragrantly pomaded. He dresses like any kid in a low-rent Hollywood club—black Skechers, a dark striped shirt and pressed jeans worn so low his plaid boxers fluff out like feathers. When I meet him at Dollard's place, Josiah shakes my hand, grinning. His smile is so big it makes his eyes squint.

Before he and Dollard met at Impact House, in May, Josiah had recently finished serving three and a half years in prison for armed robbery. "Josiah has a long history of occasionally going crazy and stabbing people," Dollard explains, eyeing the young man with a look of paternal pride.

Josiah had been folding Dollard's laundry on the coffee table when he let me in. In addition to serving as Dollard's sobriety helpmate, he works around the house as a sort of manservant (while also working as a busboy at Hamburger Hamlet). Josiah fetches me a drink, then resumes sorting Dollard's socks. He tells me about his past.

"I used to be a stickup kid, eh?" He finishes his sentences with an "eh?" the way Canadians do, but in L.A. it's part of the *cholo* slang. "Fifteen years old, eh? Fucking tweaked out on meth, eh? My homey and me would just rob people on the street."

Josiah was an industrious petty criminal, but also an unlucky one. He was in and out of various youth facilities until the age of eighteen, when the state of California sent him to prison. After his release, seven months earlier, he began smoking meth again, fell in with his old homeys, and was arrested and charged with possession of stolen checks. He is out now on bail, pending trial. If convicted, he could face another four years in prison.

Josiah claims he is a changed man since going to rehab and meeting Dollard. "I fucking take responsibility for my actions," he says. "They want to throw me back in prison, so be it, eh? But if I stay out, I've got a new life now. I'm fucking clean, eh? I work for Pat fucking Dollard. I'm a movie assistant."

Dollard gazes affectionately at Josiah. "For the first time in probably six, eight years, Josiah's clean and sober. He's working for me and flourishing at Hamburger Hamlet. He's leading a really good, squared-away life. I trust Josiah completely."

There's no more compelling evidence of his trust than the large sums of cash piled on the coffee table where Josiah is sorting laundry. Owing to Dollard's pronounced fear of banks, he prefers to keep his money in liquid form. One-hundred-dollar bills are bundled in ten-thousand-dollar bricks, which Josiah delicately brushes aside as he stacks the socks.

Josiah says when he met Dollard—whom the staff nicknamed "Saddam Manson" because of his crazed appearance and wild talk of Iraq—he "had no idea Pat was a rich Hollywood agent."

Dollard checked himself out of Impact ahead of Josiah. The day Josiah left, Dollard picked him up and drove him to his father's house. "I told Josiah's father I was adopting him," Dollard says. "He turned Josiah over to me." Though Dollard's claim has no legal standing whatsoever, Josiah enthusiastically nods.

Dollard himself had no money or place to go. He and Josiah spent a weekend sleeping at Dollard's mother's house, then split up. But the two have kept tabs on each other ever since. In the wake of Dollard's recent scare over using drugs, both feel it's prudent to live together.

For Josiah, the move comes at a convenient time. As he explains it, owing to his incredible good looks, charm and sexual prowess, he has been experiencing female trouble. Until a couple of days ago he had been living with a girlfriend. But, according to Josiah, she had recently grown unreasonable.

"Dumb bitch didn't want me seeing other bitches," Josiah says. Their contretemps grew to a head. The other morning Josiah awakened to find himself being held prisoner. "Bitch took all my clothes, told me I couldn't leave," Josiah says. "I don't hit bitches. But I said, 'You don't give me my clothes, I'm gonna kick the shit out of you, bitch.'"

"Tell him about the bitch you fucked up in seventh grade," Dollard says, egging him on.

"It only happened one time," Josiah says. "In elementary school there was this bitch, she was so big she used to fuck up the dudes."

Although he was the smallest boy in his grade, Josiah stood up to the giant bully girl, telling her he wasn't afraid. "Bam!" Josiah says. "Bitch hit me in the face. Tore off my shark-tooth necklace."

Josiah reenacts the fight, throwing kicks and punches to demonstrate how he felled her. "I got that big bitch down and whaled on her, eh?" Josiah straddles an imaginary human on the floor and pummels. "Boom, boom, boom," he says. "Bitch was all lumped up and drooling."

Warmed up by the fight tale, Josiah dances across the room, recounting his years of being the littlest guy in youth camps, county jail, and then prison, but who was always ready to throw chingasos with the big vatos. He drops onto a couch, seemingly exhausted. "I been fighting my whole life."

Josiah points to Dollard. "But thanks to this dick, for the first time I got a reason to stay clean." Josiah's mouth wobbles. He chokes back tears, thumping his chest to regain composure. "This motherfucker's been there for me."

Dollard turns to me. "We're friends against all probability. When we met at Impact, we were a gangbanger and a Hollywood agent. It was funny because Josiah came from this hard prison culture and yet he became my vassal. Everyone thought he was my bitch."

"I wasn't his bitch, eh?" Josiah clarifies.

"Josiah," Dollard explains, "in the sense that I was your friend and protector, you were my bitch."

"I wasn't your fucking bitch." Josiah's face darkens.

"Josiah, you are my lieutenant. I am the general." Dollard gestures to the apartment. "Someday, you will inherit everything."

Josiah continues to brood. Dollard shoots me a frustrated look, then hits upon something guaranteed to lift Josiah from his funk. "Josiah," Dollard says. "Tell Evan about the helicopter."

Josiah snaps to, laughing. "When I was tweaked out staying at motels, and I knew some bitch was on her way over, I'd take my clothes off," he recounts. "When she comes to the door, I open it swinging my dick like a helicopter."

ON FIRE WITH SOBRIETY

SEPTEMBER 19, 2005. I accompany Dollard to a screening of his film for a small company seeking content for outlets like Spike TV. Dollard meets the head of the firm's film division—a tall, wiry, cerebral-seeming man whom Dollard nicknames "Spock"—in a spacious Beverly Hills suite. A few minutes into the screening, things start to go badly when Spock leaps from his couch to turn down the obscenity-laden soundtrack. "They can hear this outside," he says.

Dollard immediately jumps from his seat and twists the volume up. To my astonishment, the two go back and forth like this until Spock finally has enough. He hits the pause button and stands blocking the equipment from any more interference from Dollard. "This is great," Spock says through a tight grin, "but I'm having trouble getting my head around it."

"This is cinéma vérité," Dollard says, standing up, beginning to rant. I time Dollard on my watch. He talks for twelve straight minutes. The cords on his neck pop out. Spit flies. By the end of the tirade he paces, talking about whores in Iraq, robbing pharmacies, liberals, Valium. He finally sputters to a stop.

Spock breaks the silence. "I don't even know how we could market this."

"I don't want you to market it," Dollard yells. "I don't want an audience talked into watching this by marketing tricks. Fuck that."

Spock shakes Dollard's hand. "The thing is, I totally respect you as an artist."

Careening down Wilshire Boulevard minutes later, Dollard grouses, "He turned my shit off. You do not tell the artist to turn his shit off early." Then his face brightens with inspiration. "Let's take ten grand, go to Las Vegas, get a bunch of hookers and blow, and have fun for a few days."

"What makes you think you'd be able to stop?" I ask.

"What we'll do is hire a couple of big niggers to shut us down at the end of five days and put us in suitcases and bring us home."

Dollard catches me writing down the word "nigger" in my notes.

"I can say that word," he says. "I'm half Puerto Rican, and if I'm Puerto Rican, then I'm a nigger. End of story."

He also insists for the record that he has no desire to actually get high, that he is merely joking. "The fact is Josiah and I are on fire with sobriety."

MEGAN

IT SEEMS THE GODS do favor Pat Dollard. Mike Simpson informs him that the HBO executives who saw the film in L.A. have recommended it to the head of the documentary division in New York, Sheila Nevins, arguably the single most influential person in America in the realm of documentary. The plan is for Dollard to fly to New York for a screening.

After sharing this news with me, Dollard says, "I called Megan"—his fourth wife, who left him a year ago. "I told her I'm going to be getting eight million bucks. I told her I'd pay her ten grand if she'd come over here and suck my dick."

"Calling me up and saying disgusting things like that to me is Pat's idea of a joke," Megan tells me when we meet a few days later. She is twenty-five, tall and blond, and speaks in a silky Louisiana accent. We sit outdoors at a restaurant near Dollard's apartment. He has invited her over to watch his film. She has agreed to go only because she needs to pick up papers related to their divorce.

When I sit down, Megan is reading a cheap romance novel. "One of my vices," says Megan, who has been known to often carry one in her purse. But her worst vice, she allows, is still caring about her soon-to-be ex-husband.

From the moment Megan met Dollard it was as if his almost supernaturally good luck was working on her, only in reverse. She was twenty-one, about to graduate from college in Baton Rouge, when early one evening she burned down her apartment trying to heat potpourri on the stove—something she'd read about in a magazine article. After the firemen left, Megan walked to the bar where she worked part-time as a waitress to commiserate with some coworkers, who plied her with free drinks. Soon she was plastered. Then her girlfriend pointed out that there was a celebrity in the bar, Billy Bob Thornton, who was in town filming.

Megan's friend dared her to say hello. At that moment Billy Bob happened to be sharing a cigarette with his former agent, Pat Dollard, who was in town visiting his ex-wife Alicia. Megan approached Billy Bob and said, "I'm Megan. Want to drink some martinis with me?"

Billy Bob declined the invitation. He was due to pick up Angelina Jolie at the airport and excused himself. Megan was alone with Dollard. She admits that by this point "I was too drunk to know anything." (Dollard claims, "Megan was so drunk she thought I was Billy Bob.") All Megan knows is that when she woke up the next day she was smitten. A couple months later, they flew to Las Vegas, where Soderbergh had just wrapped the location shooting for *Ocean's Eleven* at the Bellagio, where Dollard was comped a suite. According to Megan, "Our second night there Pat was like, 'Hey, you want to marry me?' and I was like, 'Yeah,' and we got married at the Little White Wedding Chapel."

A few days later she moved into Dollard's Bel Air home. "My first week in L.A.," Megan says, "I met Brad Pitt and George Clooney. Pat introduced us on the *Ocean's Eleven* set, and Brad gave me this knowing look and said, 'I've heard a lot about you.' And I was like, Holy shit, Brad Pitt has heard about me? Then I went to Cannes with Pat, and I hung out with Julia Roberts. I would call my friends back home every night and I'd be like, 'Guess who I just met tonight.'"

Megan tamps out her cigarette. "It was very surreal, for sure." She adds, "I grew up with very little, and Pat offered me this total fantasy of staying at home, not working, and raising children."

The fantasy quickly bumped into the realities of his addictions. Initially, Megan was prepared to help. She encouraged him to attend AA meetings and opened their home to informal gatherings of recovering addicts. It didn't work. Once, she says, she saw "a vagrant walking around" outside the house who turned out to be "Pat's drug dealer leaving coke underneath the rocks."

The relationship went terminal soon after Dollard began "sponsoring"— serving as a 12-step adviser to—a young, recovering female crack addict he'd met at an AA meeting. "Pat told me it would help him stay sober if he was helping another addict," Megan explains. Dollard got his "sponsee" a job and moved her into their house. Megan moved out and later discovered e-mails Dollard had written his "sponsee" in which he suggested that both their lives would be better off if she killed Megan. (Dollard says, "Anyone who knows me knows I was only joking.") As the controversy played out, Dollard made his first trip to Iraq.

Megan now works as a waitress at a swanky Sunset hotel. As a result of her three years of marriage to Dollard, she is left with tens of thousands of dollars in debts. "Pat told me when we first got married that it would help build my credit if we put everything in my name," Megan says as we enter his building. "As awful as this sounds," she confesses, "sometimes I wish he was dead."

Dollard greets us at the door. He is neatly shaved. The living room is pristine. Josiah kneels in front of a TV Dollard purchased for him, playing Hitman 2, a game he likes because "it teaches you how to become a professional killer."

"Is this your new little slave?" Megan says, nodding toward Josiah. She says to me, "Pat always manages to get a little slave. Like I was."

Dollard laughs indulgently and corrals her into the editing room for her viewing of *Young Americans*. Megan sits on the bed and watches the first few minutes with a stony expression. Then she starts to sob.

"Jesus, they're so young," she says of the Marines on screen. "They're like the boys I went to school with."

"I told you this was good," Dollard says.

"Have you talked to your mother?" Megan asks. "You need to call her."

"How's that fucking bitch?" Dollard says.

"You don't talk about your mother that way."

"Watch me—I just did. I just did."

"Your mother is the most wonderful woman that I've ever met," Megan says. "I want to punch you in the face right now."

She sits up and inadvertently knocks over an ashtray concealed under the blanket on the bed. She leaps up, brushing ashes from her jeans. "This brings back memories," she says, growing angry. "This is definitely why I left you."

"You left because you're a quitter," Dollard says.

"I left because you are an alcoholic and you won't get help," Megan says.

"You didn't stick around like Bill Wilson's wife," Dollard says, referring to the wife of the AA cofounder. "If Bill Wilson's wife hadn't stuck by his side when he was drinking, there would be no AA."

"My husband was hiring hookers on my credit card—to buy coke [for him]," Megan says to me.

She walks to the door. Dollard hurries after her and hands her the papers he promised her. She kisses him on the cheek and leaves.

Dollard stares at the door. "This really hurts," he says. "Am I over her? Maybe not. But the question with having a woman is, to what extent do I want to continue to engage with civilization?"

"Jesus Christ, Pat," Josiah says, still playing Hitman 2. "You said she was hot, eh? But she's really fucking hot."

THE JESUS ROOM

DOLLARD'S SCREENING WITH SHEILA NEVINS, in New York, is scheduled for mid-October. During the two weeks before his scheduled departure, his behavior becomes increasingly bizarre. He phones early one morning and says, "I need your help."

I ask him what's going on.

"I'm taking steps," he says, "but they ain't the twelve steps." He won't explain any further, because he feels it's unsafe to talk on the phone. A couple hours later he shows up at my apartment. There is a massive safe in the back of his Hummer. All his money is in there, he tells me. He plans to hide it. To that end, he needs to leave his cell phone at my house so no one will track him while he's on his mission. Several days later he phones from a new telephone number and leaves a message: "Driving on Washington Boulevard I clutch the receipt for my new forty-five-caliber Glock and the feeling that I will be very disappointed if I die before I kill jihadis with this gun."

It turns out that in the state of California people who have been taken into custody as a danger to themselves and others and held for psychiatric evaluation—as Dollard has been—are potentially ineligible to purchase firearms for the next five years. Days later, he calls: "Yo, call me as soon as you get this, please. I need to know if you have a clean record in California, and if you could purchase guns. I will pay you."

I decline the offer.

Dollard is eager for me to accompany him to New York and witness what he expects will be his triumphant screening for HBO. The day we are to fly out, a girl named Sunshine (I've changed her name) phones and introduces herself as one of Pat Dollard's assistants. She is calling to arrange the final details of our flight. An hour later Dollard phones to say his new assistant will be flying to New York with us. "Oh, yeah," he adds. "Sunshine will be smoking meth."

The two never show up for the flight.

Josiah phones the next morning from New York. He has taken it upon himself to rescue Dollard's appointment with Nevins by hand-delivering the screener DVD. He took the red-eye to New York—his first time on an airplane and his first trip outside California. When he checked into the Times Square Quality Hotel moments before phoning me, something happened that totally tripped him out. The hotel put him in Room 316. "Can you fucking believe it?" Josiah shouts. "I'm in three-sixteen, the Jesus room. That's who I am. My middle name is Jesus."

I tell Josiah I don't get the relationship between the number 316 and Jesus.

"'God so loved the world that he gave his only begotten son,'" Josiah says, quoting the Scriptures. "John 3:16."

"Have you guys been smoking meth?" I ask.

"Yeah, I ain't going to lie," Josiah answers. "Pat's fucked up. He's fucking psychotic, fucking psycho, fucking, a fucking weirdo. We all are, you know?"

Dollard phones minutes after Josiah hangs up. Unlike Josiah, Dollard sounds supremely relaxed, groggy, maybe a little drunk. He informs me that he was unable to fly to New York because he has fallen in love with Sunshine. "She has a golden heart," he tells me.

There is a complication. Sunshine is Josiah's girlfriend, one who, at times, meant a great deal to him. "This is rough for Josiah," Dollard says. "She came here to see him and . . ." He whispers, "What happened between us had to happen. She's the one."

I ask him why he skipped his meeting in New York, and he cuts me off. "Dude, I can't talk right now. I'm having my dick sucked."

NO REDEMPTION

AUTO FOCUS, the film that Dollard produced and Paul Schrader directed, is about *Hogan's Heroes* star Bob Crane's self-destruction through his addiction to sex as well as the murky homoeroticism of his relationship with a hanger-on who films Crane's exploits with women and ultimately beats him to death with a camera tripod. The film did not do well at the box office, but Schrader remains pleased with his collaboration with Dollard. "He wasn't scared about doing stuff that may offend people," Schrader tells me. "I knew that if we did something warped, he would get it." Despite its lackluster reception, Schrader believes the film stands as a pure story, unencumbered by hack studio convention, which he attributes in part to Dollard's influence. "Pat was attracted to the idea that we just weren't going to redeem or glorify our main character. That this was the story of the life of an extremist, what happens if you release the reins on a normal powerful passion and let the horse run. Will you achieve some kind of balance, or will it break you apart?"

Unlike the fictionalization of Bob Crane's life in *Auto Focus*, Dollard since I have known him has been obsessed with redemption. This was the whole point of going to Iraq. While I'm not totally surprised that he has apparently gone out on a bender, I hadn't expected he would so casually skip the all-important meeting with Nevins. As a practical matter it also seems potentially dangerous to be having sex with the girlfriend of a violent felon.

Josiah phones after delivering the film to Nevins's apartment. "There I was, eh, in this rich bitch's apartment," Josiah says. "These broads were fucking all into me, saying how handsome I am. They thought me and Pat were gay. I was all 'Wait, I know I'm fucking fine, eh? But that doesn't mean I have to be gay and shit.'" Josiah states for the record, "Gay is not my position."

I ask Josiah what's going on with Dollard and his girlfriend. "He's fucking fucking her," he says. Josiah admits this was initially hard for him to take. He and Sunshine have known each other for several years. "Then I got busted and went to prison and she wrote me, giving me hope, 'cause she was the only broad there for me," Josiah says.

He confides, "I don't even know why she still talks to me after all of the bad shit I did to her." He explains, "You know what it's like, eh? You're with your homeys, and she starts talking to me, and I say, 'Hey, check this out, bitch, you shut the fuck up. When I'm talking you just sit there and shut the fuck up.'" Once he arranged for Sunshine and her family to be away from her home so his "homeys could jack her, take all the shit from her house." He observes, "I treat bitches like shit, and the more you treat them like shit the more they love you, eh? It fucking works, I don't know why."

But when Sunshine, who hadn't seen Josiah in months, showed up at Dollard's apartment several days ago, she turned the tables. She refused to have sex with him and, as Josiah saw it, was trying to make him jealous by flirting with Dollard. "It hurt, eh, 'cause I fucking love that girl."

About this time, Josiah says, he and Dollard, then Sunshine, began smoking meth. Soon, Dollard advised Josiah on the best way to handle the situation with Sunshine. Josiah says, "Pat told me she was trying to play a game on me." Dollard gave Josiah a pep talk to remind him who he is: "I'm the pimp. I'm the one that plays the games. She thinks she's playing me? I'll use her to my fucking advantage. So I pimped her out." Josiah laughs. "Last night he gave me five grand. She got fucked, and I got paid."

When I later speak with Dollard, he laughs off the notion that he talked Josiah into pimping his girlfriend to him. "The fact is," Dollard says, "Josiah can't stop watching her fuck me." Dollard informs me that Josiah filmed him as he had sex with his girlfriend.

I point out to Dollard that he has now entered the realm of *Auto Focus*. He says, "The difference is, in *Auto Focus* the girls Bob Crane was fucking were just girls, but Josiah's filming me fucking the love of his life." Dollard laughs. "People get killed over this."

THREE DAYS

MIKE SIMPSON PHONES ME in the midst of this to ask how my story on Dollard is going. I don't want to divulge anything that will screw up Dollard's prospects at William Morris. Moreover, there's something so strangely decent about Mike Simpson, so at odds with Dollard's portrayals of agents as whoremongering, borderline white-collar criminals, I'm at a loss to say anything. I tell him Pat is certainly an interesting subject. "We're hearing such good things about his project at Showtime and now HBO," Simpson says, sounding pleased. "Pat is really coming into his own as a filmmaker."

On an unseasonably hot October afternoon Dollard invites me to his apartment to show me something. Josiah greets me outside the door. He asks if I've come alone. Dollard is afraid I might have brought his mother. Ever since the first time his family had the police take him to the psych ward, he's grown wary. (As he once told me, "They figured out they could pick up the phone, and, boom, I'm in a mental hospital. It fucking sucks, dude.") I assure Josiah I've come alone.

The apartment is a rat's nest. One couch is overturned. Cigarette butts are burned into the carpet. Tear-gas grenades—part of an arms cache Dollard hoped to acquire to launch his anti-jihadi network—are scattered on the floor. The bathroom looks like someone skinned a deer in it: everything is covered in tufts of hair and blood from Dollard's effort to cut off the beard that grew during the past couple of weeks.

Dollard enters in shorts and sandals, drinking vodka and cranberry juice from a plastic cup. "I'm tapering down," he says. "This is medicine."

Gesturing to the wrecked apartment, Dollard attempts a joke. "I go on a drug binge for ten days, and when I come out of it I find out my agents have done less work than I have."

Dollard boasts he has just completed a new film that he plans to send to Sheila Nevins. "This is the woman who is the grande dame of interesting, weird documentaries. Part of what I am trying to sell them is that I am a madman—this, quote, insane genius."

"It's called *Three Days*," says Josiah, kneeling at the coffee table and playing with a large hunting knife.

Dollard says, "I want to send *Three Days* to Sheila as an explanation as to why I missed my meeting with her." He adds that *Three Days* may be one of the greatest films ever made, whose meaning is, well . . . I just have to watch it.

I sit on the tiny bed in the editing room. Josiah is next to me, his hunting knife now sheathed. Dollard hunches by the monitor and starts the film.

The face of a girl with long black hair fills the screen. Sunshine. Though she is of legal age, she speaks in a child's voice, plaintive and quavering, as Dollard, still off screen, barks at her, "What's your job on the team?"

She giggles. "To sexually satisfy you and clean the house."

Dollard enters the frame, totally nude, a decrepit satyr. A montage ensues of him performing various sex acts with her, intercut with close-ups of the girl smoking a glass pipe. There is unintended comedy: while Dollard is having sex with her on the couch, it catches fire, and the two fail to notice until flames engulf their feet. There is intended comedy: Dollard performs anal sex with her while simultaneously talking on the phone with an agent at William Morris.

In the film, Josiah, who serves as cameraman, does not have sex with Sunshine. He later explained that he enjoyed watching it and pleasuring himself. His most significant on-screen presence is to lean close to Sunshine and offer encouragements: "What's his name? Say 'Pat.' You're fucking a rich man with accomplishments, not a fucking loser."

In the room with me, Dollard and Josiah howl and tap knuckles. I stand up.

Dollard shoots me an annoyed glance. "You have to pay attention," he says. "You're going to miss that this is not really a porn film."

The film fades to black. Jim Morrison comes across the loudspeakers singing "The End." Dollard narrates in the background about immortality, death and the horrors he witnessed in Iraq. It cuts to Dollard readying to make his money shot on Sunshine.

In *Auto Focus*, when Bob Crane and his sidekick watch their homemade porn together, they masturbate. Fortunately, Dollard takes a different route. He turns to Josiah, speaking excitedly. "You love this girl, Josiah. But you know what? You wandered off into a room by yourself to fucking jerk off to a tape of her fucking somebody else. That's who we are. That's who people are! They're scumbags!"

"This is so fucked up," Josiah shouts, "but I like it."

"Exactly, dude!" Dollard claps his hands, like a teacher whose pupil is about to achieve satori. "That's what I told you! That's the whole point to everything around here, with this whole thing, all of it, beyond! It's what everything in my life is about. It's about finding all those truths and those fucking experiences that other people just don't get."

Josiah seems paralyzed, staring at the screen, his huge eyes unblinking. "This is so fucked up," he repeats.

"That's what we do here," Dollard says, pounding the editing table. "We take everything to its furthest limits. We go out. We go get in cars. We fucking kill people. We kill terrorists."

I'm guessing that Dollard has veered into the realm of his jihadi-killer fantasies, or that he is in some sort of meth psychosis. The final moments of the film play. Dollard stares at the decrepit-satyr version of himself on-screen executing the money shot. When it's over, he turns to me. "So what do you think?"

All I can think of is Ben Stiller's line in *Meet the Parents* after Robert De Niro asks Stiller for his reaction to the awful poem he reads about his deceased mother. "Wow," I say. "Your film contains a lot of information." I urge Dollard not to send it to HBO.

"Our taste may be too cutting-edge, too extreme," he admits. Despite these reservations, Dollard stands. "We need to film Sunshine more." He tells Josiah to phone her and ask her to come back over. It turns out Sunshine has a responsible day job. Josiah reaches her, but she refuses to come over. Dollard takes the phone and pleads, "We'll make right on the mistake from when you were here the last time. I promise."

He hangs up and drops onto the partially burned couch in the living room. "Josiah," he says, "we need to reconcile ourselves to the fact that she may not be coming back."

THE GEOGRAPHIC CURE

DOLLARD DOES NOT GET a deal for *Young Americans*. Nor does he send Nevins a copy of *Three Days*. He drops out of sight for nearly a month. About a week before Thanksgiving he resurfaces in a phone message: "Where you been, dude? I'm having the D.T.'s—it's awesome. Give me a call. Bye."

We speak. "I feel like suicide, or going into a hospital," he tells me. Dollard says he nearly died recently while smoking meth. "I couldn't move. It was like my body had turned to ice." He mourns wrecking the prospects of his film, then adds, "I failed Josiah in all of this." A few days ago Josiah totaled the Humvee, and Dollard kicked him out. (Dollard subsequently found an attorney and helped pay nearly $5,000 to defend Josiah in his outstanding case, but in March 2006, he was convicted of receiving stolen property and sent back to prison with a four-year sentence.) "Do you think you could help get me to a hospital or something?" Dollard asks.

I call Impact House, and they agree to take Dollard back. I don't reach him again until after midnight. I am about to deliver the good news when Dollard cuts me off. "I need a favor," Dollard says. He informs me that he e-mailed a Marine Corps public-affairs officer who offered him an embed spot if he could get to Kuwait in the next seventy-two hours. The only problem is that Dollard's credit card is maxed out and he can't buy tickets. He wants to know if he can use my credit card to buy the tickets. "What am I going to do in a rehab?" Dollard asks. "I'm going to feel like shit no matter where I am. I'd rather be lying in a hole in Iraq than in a bed somewhere in L.A."

Brian Michael Jenkins, a counterterrorism analyst with Rand, has argued, like other experts in his field, that a primary lure of jihad in radical Islam is the notion that war offers "purification." I am beginning to think that it's much the same for Dollard in his indomitable drive to purge himself of his afflictions.

I give him my credit-card number. In recovery-speak, people might say I'm "enabling" the "untreated alcoholic" by helping him run away from his troubles with a "geographic cure." I know this because I have had my own struggles with drugs and alcohol. It's probably why I like Dollard, feel a kinship with him in his madness. Unlike him, I haven't had bad experiences with people in 12-step meetings. But from what I have seen, you just can't force it on someone. The way I look at it, if the untreated alcoholic wants to take his geographic cure by going to Iraq, that's his business.

The night before Thanksgiving a taxi delivers him to my apartment. Dollard wants to say good-bye. He gets out of the cab lugging his camera equipment, a few changes of underwear, and a jacket, all packed in several shopping bags. I give him an old suitcase. Stuffing his possessions into it, Dollard laughs, watching how badly his hands shake. He is totally blind in his right eye from his cataract, and the contact lens in his left eye—which he hasn't removed for more than six months—is filthy. He nearly tumbles down the steps when he walks out my door. The apartment below mine belongs to a devout Mormon woman, who every year puts up a large fir tree in her window facing the courtyard. The tree is up, but not yet decorated. My neighbor opens her door as Dollard clatters past. "Hey, it's fucking Christmas," he tells her. "Put some shit on your tree."

I yell after him, "It's Thanksgiving, Pat, not Christmas."

"Fuck it, dude. Whatever."

THE THIRD ACT

THE MARINE CORPS SENDS Dollard to Ramadi. After the relatively calm national elections on December 15, 2005, a new wave of insurgent attacks erupts in Ramadi, making it one of the most dangerous cities in Iraq for U.S. troops. The media largely ignore the city. Dollard becomes one of the few Western journalists to continuously cover the battle for the city throughout the winter and early spring of 2006.

Dollard is the first reporter on the scene on January 5, 2006, when insurgents bomb a recruitment center for Iraqi police. An estimated forty men are killed and eighty wounded. Lieutenant Aaron Awtry, a Marine platoon commander who arrived with Dollard at the blast site, says, "We were the first ones at the scene, where a formation of Iraqis had been blown apart. Body parts were everywhere. Pat was really struggling with what we were seeing. We both were, but Pat was doing his job filming. On that day, he became part of our platoon like any other Marine."

This time in Iraq, Dollard does not engage in the antics that had so entertained and enraged troops on his first tour. In the course of nearly five months, Dollard films Marines on well over two hundred combat patrols. Says Lieutenant Awtry, "Nobody covered the war like he did."

While in Iraq, Dollard sends me an e-mail, revisiting his Hollywood past:

"I was like a junkie who never kicked because someone kept throwing me a bag of heroin every Friday. Who loves you, baby? If you're an agent, you really don't want to know the answer. . . . You ever watch terrified 55-year-old men begging for praise every week in a staff meeting . . . ? It's not pretty. Any Hollywood agent or executive who criticizes my career doesn't understand how much of a geek they sound like. 'He wasn't really one of us.' No shit, Maynard, I didn't want to be a geek like you. Go back to your cappuccino, auto-fellatio, and faux tough-guy posturing. It took me forever to escape, and that's arguably pathetic, but I have the whole third act of my life left, and there's an old Hollywood maxim: The first two acts of a movie can suck, but if the third act rocks, everyone leaves the theater saying, 'Damn, that was a great movie.'"

All of Dollard's efforts seem geared toward that third act. When he survives the February 18 bombing that killed two Marines, Dollard continues to join patrols, surviving yet another vehicle bombing on March 9. At the ceremony troops hold in Iraq for their brother Marines killed there, Dollard is given a place of respect.

HOMECOMING

IN LATE MARCH, Dollard flies home with the Marines. An ex-girlfriend of Dollard's drives to the base at Twentynine Palms, California, to join military families at the welcoming ceremony. Dollard had phoned her asking if she would take him back to L.A., promising that he had cleaned up his act. "The parents of the boy Pat was with when he died met him and were hugging him and it was so powerful," she says. "Then we went out to a restaurant and Pat started drinking and told me he wasn't coming back to L.A., and he disappeared."

In April he calls me from an undisclosed location. Dollard says he is not doing well, and insists he must tell me about the February 18 bombing that killed Second Lieutenant Almar L. Fitzgerald, twenty-three, and Corporal Matthew D. Conley, twenty-one. Dollard says he was in the lead Humvee of a patrol going through Ramadi when a bomb hit the Humvee behind his. The patrol stopped. Nobody could see what was going on, because it was the middle of the night and the city, with no electricity, was pitch-black. Adding to the confusion, the Marines' radios stopped working. Lieutenant Fitzgerald, the officer seated next to Dollard, ordered Conley, the radioman, to exit the vehicle and see what was going on with the Humvee behind them that had just been hit. As Conley stepped out, insurgents detonated a second bomb buried in the asphalt, underneath their Humvee. Conley was blown to pieces. Dollard's armored door flew open, and he was thrown from the Humvee. A four-inch piece of shrapnel had penetrated his calf muscle, and he was covered in diesel fuel, but he was otherwise OK. As insurgents began to rake the area with machine-gun fire, he crawled back to the crumpled, smoking Humvee and climbed inside for cover.

I ask him what happened to Fitzgerald. "He was next to me," Dollard says, "pushed forward in a prone position, dying." Over the phone he emits a series of sharp noises. He's sobbing. He hangs up, then phones back about half an hour later. "This is why I've got to stop doing drugs and finish this project," he says, sounding desperate. "It's their film."

He turns to two former Marines to help him complete his project. Sergeant Brandon Welsh, honorably discharged in early 2006, and another young vet offer Dollard a place to stay at a town house they rent in a Sun Belt metropolis. (Dollard requests that the city not be named.) By early May, Welsh helps Dollard create the website that draws the attention of Andrew Breitbart and his invitation to return to Los Angeles for a series of meetings with operatives on the right.

THE EVIL GENIUS

OUR BREAKFAST AT THE LAX HOTEL is the first time I have seen Dollard since his return from Iraq. A couple of days later I accompany him to an invitation-only pool party on the roof of the downtown Standard hotel. Breitbart has introduced Dollard to Morgan Warstler, a thirty-something entrepreneur who dabbles as a conservative operative. Warstler has promised to be Dollard's "evil genius."

We meet Warstler, an impish redhead (with an uncanny resemblance to Danny Bonaduce), by the pool. Dressed in jeans and a green baseball cap, he invites Dollard to sit on some plastic cube chairs by the dance floor. While sipping a rum-and-Coke, Warstler lists his credentials: "I was a national-champion debater. I made the president of the Yale debate team cry. I called him a dildo in front of five hundred people."

"Mad props to you," Dollard says, drinking a black coffee.

"I deal in ideas," Warstler continues. "People are hosts to ideas, like viruses. When two people meet, ideas jump out of their heads, looking for new hosts. What I'm after is for my idea to jump out of my head and crush the ideas in someone else's head."

Warstler lays out a series of schemes for Dollard to spread his conservative, pro-war views, using viral-marketing techniques. "There is a whole vast, untapped market of Americans who don't know shit about geopolitical bullshit, but who want this war to succeed," Warstler says. "Those people need arguments. So if they're in a bar somewhere arguing with somebody, they can just hold up their cell phone, play the latest installment from you, and be like, 'End of argument.'"

Dollard warms to the plan. "I'm like this gonzo character, but I fucking support the whole conservative agenda."

Warstler takes a long, reflective pull from his drink. He tells Dollard that he personally digs "the whole Hunter S. Thompson direction you've been going in." He says, "I loved the guy. I once spent a night drinking with him, but once he killed himself, that brand died."

BLOWING SMOKE

A FEW DAYS LATER, Breitbart arranges Dollard's introduction to Ann Coulter. They meet after she tapes an appearance on *The Tonight Show*, rendezvousing at the Acapulco, across from the NBC studios in Burbank. When I enter, Coulter is standing on the patio surrounded by about thirty fans, leading them in a chorus of "God Bless America." Coulter wears a black dress stretched tightly over her thin, angular, almost starved-looking frame.

Dollard hovers by the entrance, dressed in a Morrison Hotel T-shirt, waiting for their dinner, which will take place at a nearby steak house. When Coulter finally walks out, Breitbart hustles Dollard over for the introduction.

Dollard attempts to ditch his cigarette. "No, no," Coulter tells him. "Blow smoke in my face." She leans her oblong, Brazil-nut-shaped face toward Dollard's lips, and he exhales through his yellow, cracked teeth. Coulter, who later explains she recently quit smoking and is still jonesing for tobacco, shuts her eyes and coos, "Thank you."

A few days after their dinner Coulter e-mails me her impression of Dollard: "The main thing I'd say about Dollard is that when you first meet him, he looks like a bad-ass degenerate and then the moment he starts talking, you realize he's highly intelligent, interesting and funny. . . . I would trust anything he says implicitly."

Through Breitbart's tireless networking, Dollard travels to New York in July to meet with a magazine editor, who offers him a job as a war correspondent. In an e-mail to Dollard, the editor reveals the mixture of awe and obsequiousness Dollard increasingly receives from the swelling ranks of new acolytes:

"So . . . I shit my pants just thinking about all the shit you've been through Your shit is so raw and real. . . . The knives must be out for you. . . . Hollywood eats its young so my God they must be sending some liberal fucking hit squad out after you. . . . I want to know everything about your project and I want to promote it in a good way with your voice and diary. . . . I'm sure you think [the magazine] is frivolous shit that is part of the problem but we are read by the soldiers. We are the dick that is to be sucked by the vapid, MTV bullshit, I know all that but imagine if your shit ran on MTV. . . . You can trust me, I'm one of the good guys. . . ."

While in New York, Dollard also appears on *Hannity & Colmes*. Introduced by Colmes as a former talent agent who left "Tinseltown behind to see what the Iraqis themselves think of the liberal antiwar movement," Dollard plays a clip of an Iraqi translator who calls Michael Moore a "little bitch" and crushes a DVD purported to be *Fahrenheit 9/11* (but appears to be *I, Robot*). Dollard rambles about "an incredibly strong [anti-Republican] bias in Hollywood that denies people work." Hannity adds, "The truth isn't being told, is it? The left is undermining [the soldiers'] effort and stabbing them in the back."

After viewing her ex-husband on the show, Megan Dollard tells me, "It's really scary that a person who is completely crazy can go on TV and have that influence." Having seen him come unglued so many times in front of me, I hadn't anticipated how effective he would be on TV. Isn't somebody going to notice he's insane? I had wondered while watching him trade sound bites with Hannity. But of course he would fit in. In the pro-wrestling world of opinion TV, Dollard is a natural.

In my conversations with Breitbart, he, like other conservatives, harps on the "nihilism of the left." He brings up anti–Vietnam War protesters, like yippies, who attacked the Establishment "by spitting on people. They debased people and institutions and values with anger and disrespect."

Despite his outrage, Breitbart advocates a right-wing version of the Merry Pranksters led by people like Coulter and Dollard. Perhaps America has experienced a circular movement in its social history. The freaks are now on the right. Dollard takes this even further. With his drug-fueled excursions into combat zones, his lust for booze and hookers and porn, and, above all, his madness for life, he is an authentic antiestablishment figure and is certainly in the running to be the first true gonzo journalist to emerge from this war. And yet he supports the Republican Party platform, George Bush and the Pledge of Allegiance.

Four days after Dollard's *Hannity & Colmes* appearance, I receive a call from a security guard at the W Times Square hotel, where Dollard is staying. The guard tells me NYPD officers are on their way to possibly arrest Dollard. Throughout the call, I hear a drunk slurring in the background. It's Dollard. The guard tells me that earlier that morning a woman from room service had brought him cigarettes and found the room trashed, covered in what she thought was blood. (Dollard would later claim it was coffee.) Dollard allegedly told the woman from room service, "I killed someone." Welsh, who accompanied Dollard to New York, tells me that after his appearance on *Hannity & Colmes* a magazine editor "trying to kiss Pat's ass and believing all his Hunter S. Thompson bullshit" gave him "a bunch of coke, and Pat got all retarded as usual." Welsh left him a few days ago.

When the cops show up at the W, instead of arresting him, they have an ambulance take him to St. Vincent's hospital for observation. He is released hours later and flies back home.

Welsh informs me that he and an ex-Marine buddy plan to tie Dollard up and use a Taser gun if he acts out. Dollard sobers up for a few weeks. But in early September, Welsh moves out after an incident in which Dollard shoots a hole through the ceiling of his bedroom while playing with a .45. "The motherfucker's out of his mind," Welsh tells me. "I'm just fucking tired of being a twenty-three-year-old babysitting a forty-two-year-old."

Two weeks after Welsh's departure, Dollard contacts me. He has finished cutting his second version of *Young Americans* (without any pornographic scenes). According to Dollard, since the new version of his film includes footage of the two bombings he survived and graphic footage of Marines in close-quarters firefights, "William Morris thinks it's going to be fucking big. Fucking liberals are going to buy this. That's the thing about all the dark-side stuff I've done, which I didn't truly understand until now: it's appealing to everybody. I guess that's why in the bottom of their hearts most people fucking love war."

EPILOGUE

DOLLARD AND I MEET for dinner at a Santa Monica steak house a couple of nights before Christmas. He claims that on September 11 he underwent an experience—part spiritual, part patriotic—in which he was struck sober, and has been clean ever since. He certainly looks better than I expected. A few weeks earlier he had cataract surgery, and for the first time in more than a year his gaze is clear. Over Caesar salads and steaks, Dollard tells me it's important that people in the public realize he doesn't "advocate drugs or the drug lifestyle. I don't think taking drugs is cool. I suffer from the disease of alcoholism like millions of other people." Unable to stomach the "whiny assclowns" at AA meetings, Dollard remains in solo combat with his personal demons.

In the battle against Islamofascism he is gaining new allies. He says that Frank J. Gaffney, Jr., an assistant secretary of defense during the Reagan administration and charter member of the Project for the New American Century, has begun discussions with him about helping to distribute *Young Americans*. (Gaffney's Center for Security Policy has produced TV ads and promoted documentaries aimed at stiffening the American public's resolve to carry on the war in Iraq.) Dollard is also in direct negotiations with Fox News VP Ken LaCorte to provide clips to the network. "I'm becoming a member of the Fox family," he tells me.

In mid-January, Andrew Breitbart hosts a conservative coming-out party for Dollard to celebrate his upcoming Fox deal. (According to Dollard, Fox News head Roger Ailes was "stoked" about bringing him into the Fox fold after viewing his website.) About thirty people gather at Breitbart's hillside home in Brentwood to view Dollard's clips. When I enter, Ann Coulter stands by a bowl of guacamole, eating tortilla chips and venting about the lack of spine shown by her own partisans. "I meet so many conservative men afraid to say they still support the war," she says. "Conservatives are pussies. That should be the title of my next book." The large man behind her in a double-breasted, white linen suit is Richard Miniter, author of *Losing Bin Laden* (plot spoiler: It's Clinton's fault). Miniter, chewing an unlit cigar, huddles in conversation with a bald guy in a baseball cap, discussing battle plans to promote more "pro-war content" in the movies. The guy in the baseball cap is part of a small contingent of movie-industry people on hand, a writer and a couple of producers who represent the new face of butch Hollywood. While maintaining the same careers they had before 9/11, at parties like this they now talk forcefully of the need to confront the Islamo-fascist threat. I find Dollard—who flew in from his undisclosed location—in the living room wrestling with loudspeakers and computer cables in preparation for his screening. When he sees me, Dollard throws his arm around my shoulder and asks, "Dude, how's your fucking mother?"

Having recently learned of an illness in my family, Dollard has bombarded me with phone calls and e-mails inquiring about my well-being, providing me with leads on experimental medical clinics offering nontraditional cures. Dollard, when he is not off in a war, on an anti-liberal rant, or locked away on a binge, becomes an obsessively and at times intrusively caring friend. Tonight, he scolds me for not being at the hospital with my mother, and offers "anything, anything I can do to help. Just ask, dude." After I decline, Dollard switches gears, asking if I have read his latest e-mail. In it he writes that liberal enclaves in Manhattan and Los Angeles "basically need to be exterminated in order for the planet to move ahead into peace." In Dollard's view, the liberal media based on both coasts are "literally allied with the Islamic Fascist Imperialists out of a short-sighted grab for domestic political power. You are seeing the age of treason in America."

Breitbart, who expresses his views in less genocidal terms, says simply, "Liberals have a vested interest in defeat since a loss in Iraq will put their favorite politicians back in power." With unruly blond hair and a tattered button-down shirt, Breitbart resembles an overgrown prep school stoner. He nods toward Dollard. "There's nobody else like him on the conservative side. This is the birth of a new voice. It's like a star is born. Pat's story with all of its glorious imperfection needs to be told. What I want is for Pat to be known by every kid on the street and them to go, 'That guy is gnarly.'"

The screening—a series of interviews Pat conducted with Marines complaining about the liberal bias of the media—concludes with polite applause.

Back in the kitchen, Ann Coulter resumes her assault on the guacamole and chips. A Marine whom Dollard invited to the viewing stands in a loud yet somehow tasteful plaid sport coat, describing to Coulter the increasingly sophisticated tactics employed by insurgents in Iraq. The Marine explains that insurgent groups now operate civil affairs groups that go into villages and instruct the locals on how to fool the Americans. "Like they tell Iraqis to just smile when we come to their houses and say, 'We love America,' even if they support the insurgency," the Marine says.

"You're kidding," Coulter says. "And we just can't kill all those villagers?"

The Marine shoots her a quizzical look.

"No wonder we're losing the war."

A male guest approaches, slips Coulter his number and delivers what must be the ultimate pick-up line at a conservative party. "I'm having dinner tomorrow night with Richard Perle. Would you like to join us?"

I find Dollard on the balcony conferring with a producer. The producer tells him he could help him walk into a major studio and get a deal. Dollard listens attentively. The producer says, "My problem is the title. *Young Americans*—I don't like it."

One thing you can't criticize is Dollard's title. He believes it is not only one of the best things he's ever come up with but that it's been plagiarized at the highest levels. He believes that last summer President Bush himself checked out his website, saw the trailer, and began slipping the phrase "young Americans" into speeches as a not-so-subtle nod to his film. Dollard turns from the producer and pulls the last cigarette from a pack of Marlboro Lights. "Fuck, I'm out."

The producer slinks back into the living room. Dollard lights his last cigarette and looks up at the twinkling lights on the hills. I point out that he is now essentially back at a Hollywood party.

"It's like I never left," he says.

I remind him of his e-mail arguing that Los Angeles needs to be wiped off the face of the planet.

"After I get my deal." Dollard shrugs. "Fuck that. I just want to get back to Ramadi this spring. I'm supposed to die there."

He turns to me. "Dude, drive down to a gas station and buy me some cigarettes."

ACKNOWLEDGMENTS

I would like to make grateful acknowledgment to: the publishers who gave me the opportunity to work, Larry Flynt, Sue Horton, Jann Wenner and Graydon Carter. Without the madness of Dana Brown at *Vanity Fair*, Pat Dollard's War would never have been chronicled. Ari Emanuel, Richard Abate, Greg Hodes, Tom Wellington, Jason Spitz and Susan Solomon are warriors all. Kate Lee, Robert Lazar and Josh Hornstock have earned undying recognition for their dedication to the grand struggle. Alex Kohner, Amy Chai, Eric Blank and Dan Prinz deserve that special circle of perdition for good-hearted attorneys whose wise counsel I intend to follow someday. Some of the teachers who helped with this project are Martha Brown, Clyde Henry, Peter Scott, Robert Hawkes, Bruce Carr, Everett Weedin, Jr., James Day and Ben Kohl. Special thanks to Ivan Held, Peternelle Van Arsdale, Marilyn Ducksworth, Kate Stark and the shock troops at Putnam: Rachel Holtzman, Allison "Anti-Echo" Hargraves and Anna "Quick Query" Jardine. The entire work owes a unique debt to Zari, head of the Monkey Enterprise and the pride at Mar Vista.

PUBLICATION CREDITS

ILLUSTRATION GUIDE

Frontispiece. Copyright Evan Wright. Fan outside a Mötley Crüe concert, 1998.

Page viii. Copyright Evan Wright. Lay minister in Topeka, Kansas, interviewed and photographed by the author for a book on social life in America.

Page 17. Copyright Evan Wright. Specialist Armando Ramos and Private First Class Andrew Wiser, U.S. Army, in Afghanistan, 2002.

Page 35. Copyright Robert Yager. Jim Greco, 2001. (Originally published in *Rolling Stone*, July 19, 2001.)

Page 48. Copyright Evan Wright. Club Paradise, Los Angeles, 1999.

Page 69. Copyright Mark Seliger. Wingnut in Los Angeles, 2000. (Originally published in *Rolling Stone*, March 30, 2000.)

Page 106. Copyrighted photo courtesy Evan Wright. Neo-Nazi women at Aryan Nation compound in Idaho, 1996.

Page 119. Copyright Evan Wright. Sean Southland and his children, 2002.

Page 160. Copyright Evan Wright. Slum Dog, 1998.

Page 181. Copyright Rob Howard. Tito Ortiz, 2001.

Page 198. Copyright Evan Wright. Adult entertainer hawking wares at the Las Vegas Consumer Electronics Show, 1998.

Page 224. Copyright Evan Wright. Jasmin St. Claire at home, 2004.

Page 251. Copyright Evan Wright. Smiley Pants, 1998.

Page 271. Copyright Evan Wright. Pat Dollard, 2006.

I wish to thank Robert Yager, Mark Seliger and Rob Howard for the insights their work provided in our shared subjects and for their generosity in helping with this book.